Democratic Transition and Human Rights

Democratic Transition and Human Rights

Perspectives on U.S. Foreign Policy

Sara Steinmetz

STATE UNIVERSITY
OF NEW YORK PRESS

Published by
State University of New York Press, Albany

For information, address the State University of New York Press,
State University Plaza, Albany, NY 12246

Production by Bernadine Dawes
Marketing by Nancy Farrell

Library of Congress Cataloging-in-Publication Data

Steinmetz, Sara. date
    Democratic transition and human rights : perspectives on U.S. foreign
policy / Sara Steinmetz.
        p.   cm.
    Includes bibliographical references and index.
    ISBN 0-7914-1433-7 (hard : acid-free paper). — ISBN
0-7914-1434-5 (pbk. : acid-free paper)
    1. Civil rights. 2. Human rights. 3. Democracy. 4. United
States—Foreign Relations.   I. Title.
    JC571.S789   1992
323—dc20   92-22424
                                                                     CIP

1   2   3   4   5   6   7   8   9   10

To my Father,
A. Josef Mordechai Steinmetz

and

To the memory of my Mother,
Dori Josevicz Steinmetz
For the words she never wrote
And the chapters she never finished

CONTENTS

Acknowledgments / ix
Introduction / 1

1. Human Rights in the Realpolitik Debate / 3
    The National Interest / 3
    The Neoconservative Proposal / 5
    The Neorealist Proposal / 9
    Which Human Rights? / 14
    Human Rights as a Policy Choice / 16
    U.S. Human Rights Foreign Policy:
        A Realpolitik Alternative / 18

2. Approaching the Human Rights Problem / 21
    Comparing Foreign Policy Decisions / 21
    Foreign Policy Instruments / 25

3. Iran: High Stakes for U.S. Interests—
   Low Priority for Democracy / 36
    Iran Under the Shah / 36
    Iran Unravels and Revolution Erupts: 1977 to 1979 / 41
    Iran's Revolution and the Failure of Moderate Politics / 43
    The U.S. Presence in Prerevolutionary Iran / 47
    The U.S. National Interest and Human Rights in
        Prerevolutionary Iran / 57
    The Coming of the Revolution: U.S. Support of the Shah / 60
    The United States and Postrevolutionary Iran / 62
    The United States in Iran: Problems and Policies / 65
    The Lessons of Neoconservatism Examined / 70
    The Neorealist Perspective Reviewed / 73

4. Nicaragua: Useful Policies Rendered Impotent / 78
    Nicaragua under the Somozas / 78
    Revolution in Nicaragua / 82
    Nicaragua after Somoza / 92

vii

United States-Nicaraguan Relations before the Revolution / 97
After the Revolution: United States–Nicaraguan Relations / 118
The United States in Nicaragua: Policy and Problems / 125
Nicaragua and the U.S. National Interest / 130
The Lessons of Neoconservatism Examined / 133
The Neorealist Perspective Reviewed / 135

5. The Philippines: U.S. Foreign Policy—An Inadvertent Success / 140
   The U.S. Presence in the Philippines / 140
   Ferdinand Marcos (1965–1986): From Weak Democracy to Dictatorship / 144
   United States–Philippine Relations During the Marcos Years / 153
   Marcos and U.S. Interests / 157
   Washington Ignores a Deteriorating Philippines / 164
   Protecting U.S. Interests: The Role of Diplomacy / 167
   U.S. Policy and the Postrevolutionary Philippines / 176
   Realpolitik in the Philippines / 178
   U.S. Policy in the Philippines: An Inadvertent Success / 181
   The Lessons of Neoconservatism Examined / 182
   The Neorealist Perspective Reviewed / 184

6. Summary and Conclusion / 187
   Instruments of Foreign Policy to Support Human Rights / 187
   U.S. Human Rights Policy Abroad: The Cases Summarized / 192
   Realpolitik Reassessed / 199
   Targeting the Moderates: An Alternative Realpolitik Human Rights Foreign Policy / 203
   Alternative Approaches to the Study of Democratic Transition and Human Rights / 205
   Protecting Human Rights Abroad: Moral Pursuit in the Interest of Realpolitik / 209

Tables
   Iran 3–1: U.S. Military Assistance and Sales 1967–1980 / 51
   Iran 3–2: U.S. Economic Assistance 1967–1981 / 54–55
   Nicaragua 4–1: U.S. Economic Assistance 1967–1980 / 102–103
   Nicaragua 4–2: U.S. Military Assistance and Sales 1967–1980 / 104
   Philippines 5–1: U.S. Military Assistance and Sales 1967–1986 / 155
   Philippines 5–2: U.S. Economic Assistance 1967–1985 / 158–59

Notes / 213

Selected Bibliography / 257

Index / 279

ACKNOWLEDGMENTS

In writing this book, I benefitted from the support, wisdom and generous allocations of time shared with me by many. Farhad Kazemi served as mentor, adviser, and *deus ex machina* throughout. I am greatly indebted to him for his guidance, his unfailing encouragement, and for all he has done to make the writing and completion of this book possible. I am also especially grateful to Miroslav Nincic for his insights, his advice, and for his continuous support throughout the course of this project.

Discussions with Kenneth Rodman and Ben Mor, at critical junctures in this writing, were invaluable. Youssef Cohen, Gary King, George Lister, and Martin Weinstein gave me useful suggestions for which I am most thankful. The support of James Crown, David Denoon, Kevin Featherstone, Elizabeth Rosenthal King, Pierre Najlis, and Martin Schain were also much appreciated. Clay Morgan of SUNY Press oversaw the process of publication, from its beginning, with good humor, patience, and diplomacy. My thanks, too, to Bernadine Dawes for her efforts in moving this book to production.

This book was written at the New York University Department of Politics. My thanks are due to its faculty and staff for the encouragement and assistance they always willingly gave. Marilyn La Porte, Administrative Assistant of the Department of Politics, gave me her tireless support and the benefits of her wisdom. I deeply appreciate all she has done. Lisa Baum, former Graduate Administrative Aide, helped me with a myriad of kindnesses.

The author is grateful to the following publishers for permission to reprint extracts from the following publications:

America Press: excerpts from *America*, no. 16 (16 November 1986), "Interview with Miguel d'Escoto Brockman, Foreign Minister of Nicaragua," by Thomas H. Stahel, S. J. Copyright (c) 1986. All Rights Reserved. Reprinted by permission of America Press, Inc., 106 West 56th Street, New York, New York 10019.

Greenwood Publishing Group: excerpts from *Dilemmas of Economic Coercion: Sanctions in World Politics*, edited by Miroslav Nincic and Peter Wallensteen. Copyright (c) 1983 by Praeger Publishers and published in 1983 by Praeger Publishers/CBS Educational and Professional Publishing, Division of CBS, Inc. Reprinted by permission of Greenwood Publishing Group, Westport, CT.

Greenwood Publishing Group: excerpts from *International Handbook of Human Rights*, edited by Jack Donnely and Rhoda E. Howard. Copyright (c) 1987 by Jack Donnelly and Rhoda E. Howard.

Greenwood Publishing Group: excerpts from *The United States and Iran: A Documentary History*, edited by Yonah Alexander and Alan Nanes. Copyright (c) 1980 by University Publications of America, Inc.

Macmillan Publishing Company: excerpts from *Central America: Anatomy of Conflict*, edited by Robert S. Leiken. Copyright (c) 1984 by Pergamon Press.

Pathfinder Press: excerpts from *Sandinistas Speak*, edited by Tomas Borge, Carlos Fonseca, Daniel Ortega, Humberto Ortega, and Jaime Wheelock. Copyright (c) 1982 by Pathfinder Press. Reprinted by permission.

Princeton University Press: excerpts *Condemned to Repetition: The United States in Nicaragua*, by Robert Pastor. Copyright (c) 1987 by Robert A. Pastor. Reprinted by permission of Princeton University Press.

South End Press: excerpts from *The Philippines Reader: A History of Colonialism, Necolonialism, Dictatorship, and Resistance*, edited by Daniel B. Schirmer and Stephen Rosskamm Shalom. Copyright (c) 1987 by Daniel B. Schirmer and Stephen Rosskamm Shalom.

Washington Institute Press: excerpts from *Rebuilding a Nation: Philippine Challenges and American Policy*, edited by Carl H. Lande. Copyright (c) 1987.

Yale University Press: excerpts from *The Eagle and the Lion*, by James A. Bill. Copyright (c) 1988 by James A. Bill.

INTRODUCTION

During the post–World War II period, it was often noted that the democratic rights and aspirations of peoples abroad were subverted by a U.S. crusade against communism and by Washington's mission to protect democracy at home. In a comparative analysis of U.S. foreign policy, this book examines American priorities in relation to democratic transition and human rights in authoritarian states that have been perceived to protect U.S. interests. It focuses on Washington's responses to economic grievances and social/political disintegration in countries tied to the United States by aid, trade, or security commitments; it also examines the U.S. role in supporting or discouraging democratic alternatives to authoritarian governments. The cases studied are: Iran under Shah Mohammad Reza Pahlavi (1941–1979), Nicaragua under the Somozas (1936–1979), and the Philippines under Ferdinand Marcos (1965–1986)

Within this context, the impact and consequences of foreign policy prescriptions of two schools of realpolitik are compared. These perspectives are represented by two ideal types: "neo-conservatives," who demand support of pro-U.S. authoritarian rulers as a means of preventing leftist, anti-American revolutions, and "neorealists," who seek dissociation from such regimes in the expectation that revolutions will occur, and that the United States will at least not have antagonized the winning side. Proponents of the two schools disagree both in their understanding of what U.S. interests are, and as to how they should be achieved.

Although neoconservative foreign policy guidelines, in particular, are framed by Cold War perspectives, the analysis is fundamentally relevant to U.S. foreign policy in the new world order. America's post–Cold War economic, political, and strategic interests abroad are focused on continued access to resources, trade, and investment opportunities; on alliance obligations; and on the pursuit of restrictions on missile technology, nuclear, chemical, and biological weapons. Threats to these interests may derive from ethnic or nationalist rivalries, or from ideological or religious movements; they may come from a resurgence of support for communist

1

or authoritarian government that may develop in reaction to economic discontent and unresponsive political institutions in newly democratizing states. Such potential threats will likely continue to force Washington to make fundamental choices between support for democratic processes that may exacerbate political tensions, and support of authoritarian regimes that are expected to impose order, a *sine qua non* for the preservation of U.S. interests.

The collapse of communism may have substantially reduced the likelihood that the United States will find common ground with authoritarian rulers, as it had in the past. Nonetheless, Washington's post-Cold War inclinations regarding support of democracy abroad remain questionable. A reluctance to focus on democracy when other interests intervene, was made eminently clear, for example, by initial U.S. relations with the republics of the former Soviet Union. Despite the diplomatic recognition extended to the former Soviet republics, Washington refrained from establishing embassies unless commitments were made on human rights, arms control, and free markets. These demands, however, were soon relegated to secondary status. The pragmatism which prompted this foreign policy revision was explained by a senior U.S. official, who pointed to the administration's concerns that, ''They [the republics] are up for grabs, and we need to make sure they look north and west and not south and east. ''[1]

What follows is neither a theoretical study nor an examination of the bureaucratic processes of U.S. foreign policy-making; it is a test of foreign policy prescriptions based on relevant arguments made by policymakers and scholars. The study focuses on states that figured prominently in U.S. foreign policy calculations. By necessity, therefore, the analysis narrows to cases where foreign policy decisions were weighed with great deliberation, and where the cause of democracy abroad was more likely to be sacrificed to ostensibly more critical U.S. national interests. Where important national interests are not at stake, foreign policy decision making is more flexible; support for human rights and democracy, even where this may lead to deteriorating bilateral relations, is more likely. As the debate about U.S. foreign policy priorities and commitments in the post-Cold War period continues, it is this author's hope that this book will contribute to further discussion about options Washington might pursue when national interests are in apparent conflict with democratic transitions and the support of human rights abroad.

1   Human Rights in the Realpolitik Debate

The United States was founded on principles of human rights and political liberty. It is often argued, however, that to safeguard these rights and the national interest that protects them, pragmatism must prevail over principle, and morality abandoned in the name of self-preservation. This book studies the possibilities and consequences of such policy prescriptions; its purpose is to determine if and how human rights policies, or their neglect, have led to realpolitik successes for the United States. Are American interests best served when the United States pursues realpolitik pragmatism devoid of ethical considerations? Does the preservation of human rights at home require its disregard abroad? Should the United States, in its own interest, ignore human rights and support conservative, pro-American "authoritarian"[1] rulers even where popular discontent is evident? Or should the nation cut itself loose from what may later become a political albatross and attempt to encourage internal reform via sanctions and/or inducements? Is the national interest ensured when we support pro-U.S. dictators? Is it undermined when we attempt to ameliorate repressive conditions?

The National Interest

Support and expansion of human rights abroad has been an element of U.S. foreign policy since the founding of the nation. Human rights gained prominence as a central foreign policy consideration, however, during the Carter administration. Since then, a debate about the role of human rights in American foreign policy has arisen not only between moralist philosophers and advocates of realpolitik, but also among the proponents of realpolitik themselves.

Adherents of realpolitik assume states to be central actors in an anarchic and "essentially competitive" environment.[2] Rationality, rather than

3

the individual preferences of decision-makers or an assumed universal morality, guides foreign policy decisions.[3] Such decisions are calculated in "terms of interest defined as power,"[4] where power is used as an end in itself, or as a means of achieving other national interest goals.[5] A successful policy of realpolitik would, therefore, be one that serves to preserve and strengthen the state.[6]

Elements that constitute the U.S. national interest may vary with different epochs and individual states. The United States, for example, may depend on resources from a particular region; it may desire basing rights in some countries, listening posts in others; it may find markets of little interest in some areas, or seek to expand trade and investment where lucrative possibilities appear to exist. National interest in terms of political or ideological orientations became a predominant factor in U.S. foreign policy during the Cold War. If a government was communist, pro-Soviet Union, or pro-China, a loss of U.S. influence was to be expected, and the future of U.S. interests was assumed to be jeopardized. In all its variations, however, the central focus of the national interest is on preserving or enhancing the physical security, economic prosperity, and strategic interests (in terms of defense and resources) of the United States; it is aimed at maintaining or enhancing the nation's power and position.

Realpolitik and Human Rights Foreign Policy

The roots of realpolitik can be traced to Thucydides in the fifth century B.C. His writings emphasized key elements of realist thought, including the importance of structure in the international system, the "circumscribed place of morality in foreign policy," the notion that a benign human nature cannot be assumed, and the centrality of power both in defining the national interest and in determining interstate relations.[7] These defining concepts of realpolitik were further expounded upon by others, including Niccolo Machiavelli (early sixteenth century), Thomas Hobbes (seventeenth century), G. W. F. Hegel (early nineteenth century), Max Weber, Reinhold Niebuhr, and E. H. Carr in the early twentieth century, Hans Morgenthau, Henry Kissinger, John Herz, and George Kennan in the latter half of the century.

Two approaches to the conduct of U.S. human rights foreign policy, which became prominent particularly since the Carter administration, are derived from the literature of classical realpolitik. On one side of the debate are the neoconservatives, who have included in their numbers Jeane Kirkpatrick, Ernest Lefever, Robert W. Tucker, Joshua Muravchik, and Samuel P. Huntington. This school has advocated a view of the U.S. national interest framed by traditional Cold War perspectives; its central interest has been the maintenance and enhancement of U.S. power and strategic security and, historically, the limitation of Soviet influence. Proponents have considered the preservation of pro-American governments to be in the best interest of the United States, and the defense of friendly right-wing regimes to be a necessary foreign policy strategy. Consequently, neoconservatism has vehemently criticized, as politically naive, consideration of human rights in the making and implementation of foreign policy; it has condemned as self-defeating interventions in support of domestic reform within right-wing authoritarian regimes.

A different view of the national interest has been argued by the neorealists,[8] among them Richard Feinberg, Alan Tonelson, Tom Farer, William LeoGrande, Walter Lafeber, and Walter Laqueur. The goals of realpolitik for this group are also centered on the preservation and pursuit of the U.S. national interest; the means of its preservation and the meaning of the "interest" itself, however, differ considerably from those of the neoconservatives. From the neorealist perspective, the U.S. national interest, as it relates to the Third World, must rely on pragmatism rather than ideology. Until the collapse of the communist bloc, proponents argued that historical developments in the Third World required that the ideological absolutes associated with the Cold War be discarded. International relations and the U.S. interest would be better served by concentrating on particular economic and/or security concerns.

Events in the developing world, neorealists argue, have belied neoconservative expectations that U.S. power would effectively preserve unpopular authoritarian regimes and, thereby, U.S. interests. An evolutionary view of the political process is, therefore, required: the overthrow of dictatorships and the rise of new elites ought to be expected. The long-term U.S. national interest, as a result, is tied to U.S. relations with these new elites. "Dissociation" from repressive governments via diplomatic, economic, or military sanctions is urged as a means of demonstrating disapproval of repressive governments and of fostering cordial relations with future leaders.[9]

The Neoconservative Proposal

The neoconservative proposal asserts that the short- and long-term interests of the nation are best served when pro-American right-wing regimes are protected by the United States. The argument rests on assumptions that American power can influence the course of history and that, in the absence of democratic states, American economic, political, and security interests are best preserved in the Third World by pro-American right-wing authoritarian regimes. The view is tempered by a realization that the United States has a limited capacity to influence domestic developments abroad. Ernest Lefever and Robert W. Tucker warn that the United States ought not attempt to alter the domestic practices, institutions, or ideologies of other nations; instead, it should concern itself only with their foreign policy behaviors and orientations.[10] As a consequence, the United States must remain loyal to its ideological friends despite evidence of human rights abuse and/or popular discontent.

Further underlying the neoconservative view is the assumption that military, economic, and diplomatic pressures for reform will increase domestic instability and the likelihood of revolution in target states. This argument also extends to assumptions that left-wing or communist governments will ascend to power when right-wing regimes are overthrown, and that left-wing regimes will not serve the interest of the United States.

Representing the neoconservative perspective, Jeane Kirkpatrick argued strenuously against incorporating human rights considerations in the making of foreign policy. She condemned U.S. abandonment of the Shah of Iran and Somoza of Nicaragua in their final hours, and complained that a lack of consistent support for these leaders ultimately led to the rise of regimes that were more repressive and less inclined to support U.S. interests. Carter-administration policies in these cases, she asserted, created anxiety and distrust among leaders who had become dependent upon their alliance with the United States.[11]

Protecting the national interest and ensuring "the survival of liberal democracies in the world," Kirkpatrick and other neoconservatives have argued, requires that the viability of right-wing authoritarian regimes be safeguarded. Carter's subversion of this policy was guided by "a quasi-Marxist theory of historical development," which was based on a belief that "history was on the side of our opponents," and that "U.S. power was, at best, irrelevant."[12] It was, therefore, a policy inimical to the most central requirements of the national interest.

Incorporation of human rights considerations in foreign policy calculations has been denigrated by Ernest Lefever as both arrogant in conception and inconsistent in application. Such a process, he has noted, unfairly focuses on right-wing "authoritarian" regimes, when it is more often "totalitarian" states that flagrantly violate human rights and are the most threatening to U.S. interests.[13] A similar view was expressed by Henry Kissinger, who warned in 1977 that U.S. administrations ought to "maintain the moral distinction between aggressive totalitarianism and other governments which, with all their imperfections, are trying to resist foreign pressures or subversions, and which thereby help the balance of power in behalf of all peoples."[14]

Samuel P. Huntington has attempted to show that the principles of democracy that define the United States, impel its advocacy of democracy abroad. The correlation between U.S. democracy and democracy abroad, Huntington explains, becomes evident when one observes that "when American intervention ended, democracy ended." As a result, such "unsavory characters" as Somoza of Nicaragua were able to ascend to power. In Asia, he writes, "when President Marcos instituted his martial law regime in 1972, America's influence in Southeast Asia was clearly on the wane, and the United States held few effective levers with which to affect the course of Philippine politics." In South Korea, the United States began to lose its influence by the late 1950s as U.S. economic assistance declined. The "increasing authoritarian direction" taken by Korea's politics was thus not to be associated with dependence on the United States.[15]

A Critique of Neoconservatism

A concern with a threat from the Left, inherent in the neoconservative debate, seems inconsistent with the school's stated interest in responding to the democratic impulses evident in the developing world. Thus, Kirkpatrick seems to have contradicted herself when she argued that "although there is no instance of revolutionary 'socialist' or communist societies being democratized," right-wing autocracies ought to be supported because, given the right economic, social, and political conditions, these regimes could evolve into democracies.[16] How could such conditions have been encouraged and fostered if, from the neoconservative perspective, intervention in support of domestic reform was to have been avoided? Although written before the collapse of communism, the caveat, read in a post-Cold War world, seems even less justified; while many communist states have attempted to democratize, many authoritarian regimes have continued in attempts to maintain their power. Huntington's attempt to link American intervention with democracy abroad is also questionable. As the following chapters show, U.S. involvement in Nicaragua and the Philippines remained extensive as the Somozas of Nicaragua held power and as Marcos of the Philippines imposed martial law.

Apparent contradictions between policy prescriptions and historical evidence suggest that the neoconservative foreign policy program may be lacking in critical perspective. Scenarios which had been generated by neoconservative Cold War perceptions, for example, have not particularly reflected reality. The fall of right-wing dictatorships has not, automatically, led to the rise of "revolutionary autocracies" (left-wing or communist regimes): Spain, Portugal, and the Philippines serve as examples. Conversely, the demise of communism in the Soviet Union and Eastern Europe, and the transition from leftist government to moderate pro-Western regime in Nicaragua, indicate that left-wing and communist societies are as amenable to the process of democratization as are right-wing authoritarian regimes. Furthermore, while it often appears that governments that have arisen from the debris of fallen pro-American authoritarian regimes are hostile to the United States, neoconservatives fail to ask why this is so. Did past American policy in any way contribute to this hostility? Could negative perceptions of the United States have been ameliorated with earlier and more comprehensive implementation of a human rights policy? In recommending that Americans intervene on behalf of endangered friends, the neoconservative school ignores its own caveats about the limits of American power. Could the United States keep an unpopular regime in power? For how long and at what cost? Indeed, the logic that the United States can manipulate the course of history is also, in some measure, contradicted by events of past decades. The United States extended its support, despite widespread discontent, to dictatorial regimes in Ethiopia, Greece, Spain, Portugal, Iran, the Philippines, Haiti, and Nicaragua. These dictatorships nevertheless fell, often leaving in their wake prevalent sentiments of anti-Americanism. In fact, as many of these cases indicate, U.S. support of right-wing authoritarian regimes has not been able to ensure democracy and human rights abroad.

The arrogance attributed by neoconservatives to those who support human rights policies in opposition to authoritarian dictatorships, may be equally directed to the neoconservatives themselves, who would presume to prop up dictatorships despite public outcry from discontented populations. Neoconservative complaints about the inconsistencies of U.S. policies which, they say, single out right-wing regimes while neglecting the abuses of left-wing governments, are also unfounded. That a policy is rendered inconsistent by international conditions, that it is not universally applied, does not require that it be voided. The prospect that the international political system may deny the United States the power to influence the behavior of some nations should not prevent this country from acting when and where leverage can be exerted. Certainly, in relation to human rights, the claim that totalitarian regimes are more repressive than those which are authoritarian is a moot point. Human rights abuse is equally repugnant whether it comes from the Left or the Right.

For the neoconservative proposal to be shown to be correct, a number of conditions would have to be met: American interest would have to be well-served by right-wing regimes; the United States would have to prove itself able to preserve authoritarian rulers (or their ideological successors) in the long term, despite widespread popular discontent; and, the long-term economic and/or strategic interests of the United States would have to be protected and/or enhanced where such policy is pursued. The foreign policy prescriptions of the neoconservative school will have lost some credibility if, despite U.S. support, American military, strategic, or economic interests are threatened, an unpopular right-wing authoritarian regime falls, and/or an anti-American regime assumes power.

The Neorealist Proposal

Neorealists share the neoconservative assumption that the United States can influence conditions abroad; however, they perceive U.S. capacity to shape history as more limited. The dichotomies represented by the neoconservative world view are replaced by a more complex vision of world affairs. Tempered by events of past decades, neorealism assumes that disaffection will eventually lead to revolution and that it is in the U.S. interest to pursue a human rights policy that would create a favorable opinion of the United States among opposition leaders. These pro-American perceptions, it is hoped, would either clear the way for close links between postrevolutionary governments and the West, or, at the least, prevent resentment and hostility from impelling new regimes into an opposing camp. The imposition of sanctions on regimes violating human rights is advocated by the neorealists as politically useful in the long term and, perhaps, even efficacious in the short term. Opposition groups would perceive such measures as supportive and thus adopt a positive view of the United States; the target regimes would likely try to retain friendly relations with the United States because of an assumed ideological bias and/or aid dependence.

The thesis proffered by the neorealists contends that if the United States encourages improvements in human rights—particularly by dissociating itself from rulers via diplomatic pressure, economic, and/or military sanctions—then the U.S. national interest will be protected in the short term and the long term. This proposal is based on a number of assumptions:

    1. The United States can have a limited influence on events abroad. It cannot, however, control the course of history in which change is inevitable.

    2. Right-wing rulers are too dependent ideologically or materially on the United States to abandon their relationship with Washington;

sanctions can, therefore, be imposed without significantly damaging U.S. relations with such regimes.

3. The issue of human rights is important to opposition groups in these states.

4. U.S. policy affects perceptions held by opposition groups about the United States.

5. Perceptions determine the kind of foreign policy an elite will follow.

6. Pursuit of economic opportunity and strategic security should take precedence over ideological proclivities in determining the U.S. national interest.

7. A non-aligned foreign policy in the Third World is, therefore, adequate for the preservation of the U.S. national interest.

As a consequence of the above assumptions, neorealists argue that the stronger the diplomatic, military, and/or economic relationship between the United States and a dictator, the greater the identification between the two governments as perceived by others. Such identification would create great resentment toward the United States and, therefore, increase the likelihood that U.S. interests will be endangered once a new regime is in place. A corollary to this position is that the greater the level of political, economic, and military dissociation, the greater the pro-American sentiment among the new elite.

Neoconservative criticism directed at the Carter administration's human rights policy, argued that the policy surrendered to a fatalist perspective of history antithetical to U.S. interests. Indeed, such a perspective serves as the underpinning for the human rights rationale proffered by neorealists. The neorealist view accepts that repression and injustice will ultimately lead to rebellion, regardless of external manipulation, and that it is in the U.S. interest to work with this almost inevitable process rather than against it.

In a speech about Iran, the Carter administration's deputy secretary of state, Warren Christopher, succinctly stated the case for the irrelevance of intervention:

> The Iranian experience should encourage a sense of realism in our dealings with developing countries. For their internal politics are shaped almost wholly by internal forces, and very little by external pressures. A wise nation, however powerful, understands the peril it invites in confronting the will of another people. Outside powers have an effect, if any, only at the margins.[17]

Richard Feinberg and Alan Tonelson criticize continued U.S. support of dictators who, although friendly to the United States, have obviously lost the support of their people. Support of such regimes only prolongs an inevitable sequence of repression, protest, and revolution, and links the United States to a doomed regime. Authoritarian rulers may come to rely on foreign assistance as the pillar of their power, rendering the pursuit of even a modicum of popular support irrelevant. Feinberg notes that loyalty inappropriately directed on the basis of ideological bias often leads U.S. intelligence agencies and policymakers to lose perspective on events and to misperceive conditions until it is too late—until moderate forces that could have been courted become radicalized and the possibility of exerting influence is lost.[18] Sandra Vogelgesang, a human rights officer in the Carter State Department, has charged, for example, that the United States ignored economic and political realities in Africa during the 1960s and 1970s, thereby opening opportunities for Soviet and Cuban intervention.[19]

Ironically, Robert W. Tucker, a representative of the neoconservative school, points to this very logic in his argument for limited U.S. intervention:

> Preoccupied with the need to maintain the status quo and finding communism in every challenge to the status quo, we are driven to equate revolutionary violence with communism. Even where this equation is valid, the question remains in each case whether a communist regime would pose a threat to American interests. In the great majority of cases, however, the equation is not valid, at least initially. Yet it may and already has increasingly become so through American insistence. By equating revolutionary violence with communism, by a policy of indiscriminate opposition to violent change in the status quo, we assume the unenviable role of counterrevolutionary power per se and either allow communist movements to seize the banner of nationalism or force noncommunist revolutionaries into a communist stance.[20]

Neorealists further argue that the ideological bias evident in the neoconservative perspective leads to a policy that ignores the possibility that American economic and military interests may be preserved, or even enhanced, under less-than-perfect conditions—that is, where governments are nonaligned and not particularly inclined to embrace an exclusive association with any ideological camp. Nonalignment allows governments to focus on their own national interests. Third World economic and trade concerns are likely to lead to increased dialogue with the West—conditions which, for the most part, are favorable for the preservation of U.S. interests.[21] As a consequence, neorealists have encouraged a view of the U.S. national interest that accepts and, indeed, promotes the pursuit of nonalignment in the developing world.

Neoconservative warnings that depict Third World revolutionary regimes as strategic and economic threats to the United States are also questioned. Tom Farer, for example, claims that technological developments have reduced the need for foreign military bases, especially for the United States. Furthermore, even the states that by neoconservative logic were expected to serve Soviet interests during the Cold War, proved less than tractable.[22] Basing rights were not extended to the Soviet Union by its allies in Angola and Mozambique, while former allies, such as Egypt and Ethiopia, reversed their pro-Soviet orientations.

In the economic sphere, leftist-oriented regimes did not prove overwhelmingly loyal to the Soviet camp either. The economic strength of the United States and the West served as a magnet to developing nations that needed the technological know-how, markets, and investments that only the West could provide. Indeed, Farer notes that it has not always been easy to determine the nature of economic relationships from the political character of domestic systems. The Kuwaitis, for example, have endeavored to displace foreign ownership, while the radical Libyans have generally preferred to maintain Western companies and concessionaires. In Angola, Cuban troops helped protect American oil facilities in Cabinda,[23] while a Marxist government in Mozambique endeavored to improve relations with the United States and South Africa.

Perceptions held by neoconservatives, that American allies protect American strategic and security interests, are also in some measure contradicted by reality. U.S. allies have often proven less than cooperative in allowing basing rights or docking privileges for nuclear vessels. Until the Iraq crisis of 1990, only Oman, in the Persian Gulf, allowed American bases on its soil;[24] basing rights in countries allied to the United States have been, or may be, denied. Fred Ikle, undersecretary of defense during the Reagan administration, lamented in 1988 that "what's certainly disappointing is the unwillingness of several allies in both Europe and the Pacific to share the risks of common defense with us. They want to deny bases for certain contingencies or reduce the number of bases, but what they have to realize is that, if they want to enjoy the benefits, they have to share the risks."[25]

Examples where American allies did not support American economic and political interests exist as well. In 1990, the Kingdom of Jordan not only resisted the imposition of sanctions against Iraq demanded by the United States and the United Nations, but also supplied Iraq with U.S. technology and intelligence information. Iran under the Shah was a leader of OPEC's (the Organization of Petroleum Exporting Countries) price hawks in the 1970s. Saudi Arabia has not been consistent in preventing climbing oil prices; it refused to lend its support to the Camp David process; and, in the 1960s, it supported the Royalist camp in North Yemen against the U.S.-backed Republican forces. Brazil was among the first nations to confer diplomatic recognition on Angola's MPLA (People's Movement for the Liberation of Angola) government; and members of the OAS (Organization of American States), friendly to the United States, refused to support a U.S. plan to prevent a Sandinista victory in Nicaragua. During the 1973 Middle East war, and when American forces attempted a rescue mission in Iran in 1980, American allies in Europe refused landing rights to the United States.

A Critique of Neorealism

As is the case for neoconservatism, questions about the neorealist argument remain unanswered. Although neorealist admonitions ostensibly ring true when recent history is taken into account, processes of political change and the international relationships that have developed as a result, may have little to do with the specific policies of outside powers. Events abroad may have depended more on historical influences, ideology, or national character than on U.S. policy.

Even if the United States were to attempt to influence or coerce improvements in human rights conditions, as suggested by the neorealists, success would not necessarily be guaranteed. A policy that punishes authoritarian regimes might prove of minimal consequence. Brazil, Argentina, Uruguay, and Guatemala, for example, retracted requests for military assistance when, during the Carter administration, human rights considerations were incorporated into aid decisions. Efforts to ameliorate problems of civil/political repression might succeed, but only for a limited period of time and without affecting political institutions that would change long-term conditions. Indeed, where reform is instituted, the United States may find that it has defeated its own interests. Opening channels of participation, even partially, may open the floodgates of opposition and protest that could lead to unintended effects—including revolution. The protection right-wing authoritarian regimes are presumed to provide to U.S. interests, may thus be swept away and exchanged for revolution and uncertainty. In cases where U.S. policy is inadequate, or where quiet diplomacy serves as the primary strategy, pro-American sentiments will not necessarily be fostered or reinforced. Furthermore, because increased participation and freedom of speech and assembly may lead to open declarations of discontent, and possibly revolution, genuine reform will probably be resisted by the dictator as an act of self-preservation. No matter what the ideological affinities of a ruler, no matter the economic or military interests shared with the United States, leverage likely will prove of little utility when survival is at stake. The

success of a U.S. human rights policy may thus be limited by the availability of alternative partners to the target regime, or even a ruler's determination to "go it alone."

In addition, whatever its actual impact on the amelioration of abuses,
a human rights policy may have little impact one way or the other on the
long-term preservation of U.S. ties and interests. If aid and technology
from the industrialized West are desired, any resentments toward the
United States will be shelved for the sake of more pragmatic objectives.
The fact that governments that have been adversaries—such as Vietnam,
China, Eastern Europe, the former republics of the Soviet Union, and even
Iran—now pursue economic ties with the United States, indicates the
plausibility of such an assumption.[26] If a revolutionary leadership em-
braces an anti-Western ideology, no role the United States may have
played will affect its foreign policy orientation—at least in the initial
stages.

A U.S. human rights policy, therefore, might be desirable on moral
grounds, but might be practically and politically irrelevant. The efficacy
of the neorealist formula could only be confirmed under certain conditions: if the United States imposed sanctions while the targeted right-wing
dictator continued to maintain relations with Washington; if U.S. interests
continued to be protected; and, if once a revolution occurred, the new elite
continued cordial relations with the United States—even if it adopted
a nonaligned policy. (U.S. interests, in this case, would not necessarily
be delineated in the same terms as they had been under the right-wing
regime.)

Which Human Rights?

The term *human rights* has evolved into a widely inclusive phrase gaining
its definition from documents ranging from the U.S. Bill of Rights to the
U.N. Convention on the Elimination of All Forms of Discrimination
Against Women. It includes freedom from torture, arbitrary arrest, and
imprisonment; the right to privacy, to freedom of thought, speech, assembly, religion, press, movement, and to participation in government; the
right to food, property, nationality, social security, and leisure; and the
right to receive equal pay for equal work, participate in the cultural life of
the community, and have equal rights in marriage.[27]

In a 1977 address at the University of Georgia School of Law, Secretary of State Cyrus Vance outlined the Carter administration's human
rights policy. The rights the administration sought to encourage included:

[The] right to be free from governmental violations of the integrity of the person. Such violations include torture; cruel, inhuman or degrading treatment or punishment; and arbitrary arrest or imprisonment; . . . denial of fair public trial and invasion of the home;

[The] right to the fulfillment of such vital needs as food, shelter, health care, and education;

[The] right to enjoy civil and political liberties: freedom of thought, of religion, of assembly; freedom of speech; freedom of the press; freedom of movement both within and outside one's country; freedom to take part in government.[28]

Conceding to Third World demands, the "Vienna Declaration and Program of Action," adopted by the 1993 U.N. World Conference on Human Rights, proclaimed the "right to [economic] development to be universal" and "inalienable." "Democracy, development and respect for human rights and fundamental freedoms," the document stated, "are interdependent and mutually reinforcing." Nonetheless, Third World dictators, and those who would support them, often argue that civil and political liberties are secondary to economic development. But this is a view challenged by many. Nepal's former prime minister, B. P. Koirala, complained that "economic development starts from politics . . . it is insulting the dignity of people of the poor nations to present the issue as a choice between poverty and democracy."[29] Raymond Gastil of Freedom House testified before Congress that,

All peoples may not have the organization, knowledge, or experience to achieve or maintain fully democratic systems today, but is demeaning to imagine that they are so engrossed in materialism that they do not desire basic equality and dignity represented by institutional human rights. . . . It should also be remembered that many poor people want political rights because they see them as the only way to guarantee their material wants. Democratic countries . . . are less likely to divert money away from meeting fundamental needs.[30]

Sandra Vogelgesang points to the fundamental problems created by the inextricable relationship between economic development and human rights—problems that have beset most developing nations:

Deprivation of freedom often indicates that the political system is not working well for either the rulers or the ruled. For example, peasant leaders in Central America have, for the most part, resorted to terrorism only when avenues to peaceful reform, such as the opportunity to vote in honest national elections seem closed. . . . Pursuit of full human rights can thus amount to a frontal assault by the disenfranchised majority against entrenched elites. To stop underlying deprivation of economic opportunity may require ending political oppression.[31]

Vogelgesang contended that the economic progress achieved by authoritarian regimes in Burma, Pakistan, Bangladesh, and Afghanistan did not prove superior to that of more democratic nations, such as India and Sri Lanka.[32] Indeed, the 1991 United Nations Development Programme's *Human Development Report* indicated that "most of the world's poorest countries, including China, Zaire, Bangladesh, Tanzania, Liberia, and Kenya have little freedom." Political freedom, it noted, seems to unleash creative energies that "lead to ever higher levels of income and human progress."[33] Reflecting a similar perspective, opposition members in Kenya complained in a November 1991 open letter that "the current trends in our country show the limits of reforming economic policy in a deformed political environment."[34]

While economic development is critical, this book focuses on the freedoms of human dignity and on the political and social liberties described in the Vance speech. It examines situations where discontent is evident and reform is demanded.[35] Economic rights are rights of a different category; they represent positive obligations of a state rather than the requirement to abstain from particular behaviors. While rights related to economic development may require that political freedoms be observed, they also demand financial wherewithal rarely available to developing nations. Where underdevelopment is a direct consequence of political conditions, affected groups will become politicized; respect for human dignity and political freedom will therefore be central to any struggle for human rights.

Human Rights as a Policy Choice

In his book, *United States Foreign Policy: Choices and Tradeoffs*, Miroslav Nincic notes that "the business" of U.S. foreign policy involves "confronting dilemmas which often have no optimal solution . . . it is in essence a matter of making appropriate compromises and establishing workable tradeoffs."[36] The policy choices are not a question of "human rights or no human rights," explains Lars Schoultz, "instead it is human rights versus national security, versus friendly relations with existing regimes, versus economic benefits to the domestic economy, versus humanitarian aid to impoverished people."[37] Most of the choices, however, are directly or indirectly related to the national interest.

In the post–World War II era, the issue of human rights appeared tangentially on Washington's agenda as part of the Truman Doctrine and containment policy. The United States vowed to support the continued independence of "free peoples" throughout the world. Although the nations it initially proposed to support, Greece and Turkey, were not democratic states in 1947, the promise of support meant that they would be given the opportunity to move toward democracy.[38] The human rights issue was also in evidence during the 1960s, when the Alliance for Progress attempted to encourage economic development as a means of inhibiting the expansion of communism in Latin America.

Human rights waned significantly as a policy determinant during the Nixon administration. In 1971, President Nixon expressed a quintessentially neoconservative perspective on the issue:

> The United States has a strong interest in maintaining cooperation with our neighbors regardless of their domestic viewpoint. . . . We hope that governments will evolve toward constitutional procedures but it is not our mission to try to provide, except by example, the answers to such questions to other sovereign nations. We deal with governments as they are.[39]

Henry Kissinger explained in 1975 that, "if the infringement of human rights is not so offensive that we cannot live with it, we will seek to work out what we can with the country involved in order to increase our influence. If the infringement was so offensive that we cannot live with it, we will avoid dealing with the offending country."[40]

By the mid-1970s, Congress had begun to focus on human rights and to establish laws requiring that U.S. policy take into account the human rights situations of aid recipients. The Ford administration made an effort to conform to Congressional concerns, noting that it would set a limit on the "extent to which governments engaged in the systemic repression of their citizens' human rights could be 'congenial partners' with the United States."[41]

President Carter paid rhetorical allegiance to the human rights issue, raising it to public prominence. His administration's policy was fundamentally in alignment with the neorealist perspective in seeking to dissociate the United States from dictators as a means of protecting U.S. interests. The new policy "had both a moral and a national security premise," wrote Robert Pastor, a member of Carter's National Security Council staff.

> By supporting a dictator, the United States would lose the support of his nation and especially of its youth, which would identify the United

States as part of its national problem. . . . There were risks in withdraw-
ing support from dictators, but the administration believed that the prospect of violent revolutions would be greater in the long run if
possibilities for change were precluded.[42]

Indeed, Carter recalls in his memoirs that when he "met with the leader
of a government which had been accused of wronging its own people, the
subject of human rights was near the top of my agenda."[43] Nonetheless,
even under Carter, interests other than human rights took precedence in
the making of U.S. foreign policy. Secretary of State Vance testified in
1977 that U.S. policy would be determined on a country-by-country basis.
"In each case," he said, "we must balance a political concern for human
rights against economic and security goals."[44]

A neoconservative human rights perspective again dominated U.S.
policy during the Reagan administration. In a 1984 speech, Secretary of
State George Shultz declared,

Human rights policy cannot mean simply dissociating or distancing ourselves from regimes whose practices we find deficient. Too much of
what passes for human rights policy has taken the form of shunning
those we find do not live up to internationally accepted standards. But
this to me is a "cop-out"; it seems more concerned with making us feel
better than with having an impact on the situation we deplore. It is really
a form of isolationism.[45]

The issue of human rights abroad has frequently been relegated to a
secondary place on the foreign policy agenda; it has proven useful insofar
as it has complemented pursuit of the national interest or, at least, did not
interfere with it. This book will consider the efficacy of such an orientation to human rights in the cases it examines.

U.S. Human Rights Foreign Policy: A Realpolitik Alternative

As disciples of realpolitik, the neoconservative and neorealist schools define their arguments in terms of the state as primary actor. Nonetheless,
they represent widely disparate ideological and analytical views: neither
their assumptions, nor their prescriptions, nor their perspectives on outcomes agree. The cases in the following chapters test whether and when
either perspective applies. In none of the cases are the prescriptions of either school adhered to strictly. The cases, nonetheless, give some indication that the hypotheses of neither school are particularly accurate in
predicting events.

Failure by either school to establish the complete accuracy of its predictions indicates a need for proponents of realpolitik to reconsider their calculations about how the national interest might be achieved. Instead of relying only on the *state as actor* level of analysis, realpolitik strategies might incorporate the perspectives of the *complex interdependence* approach. This approach, for example, emphasizes the centrality of nongovernmental actors in influencing events in the international system. A foreign policy framework that would encompass both the realpolitik and the complex interdependence approaches would thus define the national interest more broadly by focusing on both state and nongovernmental actors.[46]

Within such a framework, the United States could follow a consistent policy of support for moderate opposition groups within target countries. By doing so, it could establish countervailing power bases through which reform could be encouraged. In addition, if organized and trained, these groups could assume the responsibilities of government in case of the overthrow of the previous regime. A history of U.S. support for the moderates, as well as American assistance and the ideological inclinations of the moderates, would make it possible for cordial relations to be maintained.

The very parameters of the national interest as defined by the realpolitik and complex interdependence perspectives, also argues for linking the two approaches. The national interest in terms of realpolitik focuses primarily on issues of national security and power. Complex interdependence, on the other hand, argues that military power is not necessarily the central determinant affecting international relations, and that power may not always be defined in terms of military capability. Economic and ecological issue areas also play critical roles in defining the forces that shape international politics.[47]

The salience of the complex interdependence assumptions for U.S. foreign policy calculations is underlined by the cases in this book. U.S. military power was not imposed in any of the three cases because its utility was deemed questionable. Military intervention would have meant nationwide bloodshed in the target states and might well have incited national, if not regional and international, resentment. These were outcomes the United States proved either unwilling or incapable of accepting.

Realpolitik calculations that include the role of nonstate actors and reassess the primacy of military power in interstate relations may thus prove useful. The assumptions underlying such an integrated approach would be derived from the neorealist school and the complex interdependence approach. These are:

1. Change is inevitable.

2. U.S. influence abroad is limited.

3. Nongovernmental actors are important in affecting international politics.

4. Differing systemic conditions may require that state interests be defined differently.

5. Power is not always defined in terms of military capacity.

The assumptions and prescriptions of the neoconservative and neorealist schools are tested in the following chapters to determine whether and where they have been successful, and if the alternative model for U.S. human rights policy might have better served U.S. interests. Chapter 2 delineates the specific questions addressed in all the cases and discusses the foreign policy instruments Washington had, or might have used in pursuing U.S. interests abroad.

2   Approaching the Human Rights Problem

Comparing Foreign Policy Decisions

This book compares three cases to examine the relationship between U.S. human rights policy and the preservation of U.S. interests. These include: Iran under Shah Mohammad Reza Pahlavi (1941–1979), Nicaragua under the Somozas (1936–1979), and the Philippines under Ferdinand Marcos (1965–1986). The examples may explain why close relations with the United States are maintained or severed when new elites come to power, and whether the lack of a human rights policy (or its degree of implementation, if any) has any effect on the attitude of post-revolutionary elites toward the United States.

Comparing the Cases

Differences exist among the cases in terms of region, religion, and, most important, the U.S. administrations under whose watch they fell. Their similarities, however, make the cases appropriate samples for a comparative analysis. Certain identifiable conditions are common to all the cases: sharp disparities existed between rural and urban populations and between a relatively rich few and the predominant poor; religion played a prominent role—the Catholic Church in the Philippines and Nicaragua, and the Islamic ulama in Iran; civil and political rights were abused in each case, although a facade of representative government existed (i.e., political parties, elections, legislative bodies); in each case, disaffection grew with economic decline, opposition to the regime became salient, and a large moderate opposition developed. The United States had had extensive involvement in each of the countries—in the Philippines and Nicaragua since the 19th century, and in Iran during the latter half of the twentieth century. American interests were perceived to be integrally dependent on the stability of each regime, and a strong identification had developed between the U.S. government and the ruler in each country. Although human rights were abused, the issue never became a central theme in bilateral relations in any of the cases; the United States supported each of the dictators almost to the end of his rule. Despite the similarities, however, new elites in these nations demonstrated dissimilar foreign policy orientations. The Islamic Republic of Iran and Nicaragua under the Sandinistas transformed relations with the United States from alliance to opposition; the Philippines has retained friendly relations.

In order to determine why the foreign policy orientations of the post-revolutionary elite differed with respect to the United States, the following issues are addressed in each case:

1. *Domestic conditions,* including the human rights situation, that might contribute to revolution.

2. *The composition and ideological orientation of opposition movements in each country.* Neorealists assume human rights issues to be central in impelling revolution and in creating positive or negative perceptions about the United States. It is, therefore, important to consider what domestic conditions led to rebellion in the three cases, what the complaints of the opposition were, and what perceptions were held about the United States.

3. *U.S. policy in relation to human rights and to revolutions that attempt to overthrow pro-American right-wing dictatorships.* American belief systems or ideologies that may have influenced U.S. decision-makers become apparent in each case. The focus of the study, however, is not these belief systems or their role in determining U.S. foreign policy behavior, but the policies themselves—their impact on human rights and democratic development abroad, and their effects on U.S. interests.

4. *Factors, other than the above, which might affect perceptions about the United States.*

The following questions are posed in each case:

1. What was the nature of civil and political rights under each regime?

2. What, if any, manifestations of discontent were present? What were the ideological and class orientations of the opposition groups? What were the causes of their disaffection and how did they make their opposition known? What was the strength of the opposition in terms of members and sympathizers among the general public?

3. To what extent were U.S. policymakers aware of problems and the existence of opposition in each case?

4. What was U.S. policy in relation to human rights and the target regime in each case? What policy instruments did the United States utilize in implementing its human rights foreign policy objectives and what was the extent of their use? Were economic and/or military inducements or sanctions used? Was diplomatic support given or public condemnation issued?

5. What was the U.S. role during the revolutionary crisis in each country? Did it intervene in the process, and, if so, how and on behalf of which interest or group in the target state?

6. What were the ideological foreign policy orientations of the postrevolutionary regimes? Were they pro- or anti-American, pro- or anti-Soviet, or nonaligned?

7. What was the U.S. policy in relation to the postrevolutionary governments? Was diplomatic recognition immediately given? Were public pronouncements sympathetic or antagonistic toward the new regimes? Was economic or military aid extended? Were sanctions imposed?

8. What was the history of U.S. involvement in each case?

9. Could U.S. policy have been more effective in achieving its national interest goals in each case?

U.S. policy abroad may be affected by regional and international obligations or constraints. For policies defined by neoconservative guidelines, constraints might also include the degree of diplomatic, economic, and military support Washington is able to extend to the old regime, and the length of time the United States is willing or able to extend such support. For the neorealists the constraints include:

1. *the economic strength of the target nation* and its consequent ability to withstand economic pressure;

2. *the kind of military relationship a country has with the United States*—its dependence on the United States as protector; its dependence on aid programs for arms procurement; and its financial ability to buy military equipment elsewhere;

3. *the nature of the opposition*—including the weight of its composition in terms of pro-Western or anti-Western elements, and the degree of popular support it gains;

4. *the nature of U.S. relations with the particular country*—more specifically, U.S. history and policy toward the particular regime in relation to its human rights record; the kinds of strategies, if any, that

were implemented (e.g., inducements, diplomatic pressure, economic or military sanctions); the point at which the strategies were applied (i.e. were continuous efforts made to effect reform, or did the United States act only when confronted with a *fait accompli?*); the kind and degree of support given to opposition groups.

The role played by Congress, particularly in the budget-approval process, may also influence the making and execution of foreign policy. Where sharp divisions occur between administration and congressional opinion, dual messages may be sent to other nations and the impact of U.S. foreign policy diluted. Such differences were likely to occur in the area of U.S. human rights policy particularly after 1973–1974, when Congress began a concerted effort to impose aid restrictions on governments abusing human rights.

As was noted earlier in this chapter, some conditions remain relatively constant across the cases. These include political and civil rights abuse, economic disparities, urban and rural poverty, increasing nationalist sentiment, and growing manifestations of popular opposition. Varying across the cases are such factors as the strength, motivation, and ideology of opposition groups; the history of U.S. involvement in each country; the degree of dependence of the target state on the United States; and, the degree of mutual vulnerability between the two states in terms of economic, security, and political dependence. The final status of the U.S. national interest in the target states differs in each case and is defined in terms of the outcomes produced by U.S. human rights foreign policy. Thus, the foreign policy orientations and conduct of the postrevolutionary elite, as they related to the United States, determined how U.S. interests fared in each case.

Despite the similarities in factors that impelled the revolutions in the three cases, the Philippine revolution—unlike those in Nicaragua and Iran—ultimately proved *not* to be a revolution in fact. Neither the institutions, the elite, nor the socioeconomic structures that had previously defined Philippine society underwent any change. Both government and military under the post-Marcos Aquino regime were largely composed of, and run by, the same elite who had participated in the previous government. Following the revolution, habeas corpus was reinstated, decrees permitting indefinite detention without trial were repealed, and political participation was more widely encouraged; nonetheless, abuses still continued. Political intolerance—particularly against the Philippine Left— still existed, and human rights abuse continued to be perpetrated by government-supported paramilitary groups. Under Fidel Ramos, President

Aquino's successor, reconciliation efforts with the Philippine communist movement were intensified.

Definitions

In examining the cases, political disaffection is measured by the incidence of public demonstrations, public statements by the opposition, election boycotts, military and/or guerrilla activity. Indicators of human rights abuse include suspension of habeas corpus, torture, extrajudicial killings, restrictions on a free press, and restrictions on political participation (e.g., voting intimidation, parties/candidates limited by government, rigged elections). The moderate opposition is defined in terms of pro-Western orientations and a professed adherence to representative political systems. Economic discontent is evaluated in terms of relative national economic health, degree of disparity in income distribution and in income per capita, and rate and amount of unemployment (urban and rural). Dissatisfaction with economic conditions is assumed to exist if public pronouncements are made and protests are held across socioeconomic sectors.

Foreign Policy Instruments

The strategy and tactics of American foreign policy may range from persuasion to compellence; from the use of diplomacy or economic inducements, to the imposition of economic or military sanctions. The instruments of foreign policy may be used individually or in conjunction with each other.

Diplomacy

Diplomatic measures are often preferable as an initial step in enforcing a human rights policy: they allow for greater flexibility and room for escalation, and are the least costly of foreign policy instruments. Diplomacy is employed as a noncoercive measure and centers on processes of communication, persuasion, and negotiation.[1]

Instruments of diplomacy vary from the very subtle to the most obvious, from unpublicized discussion to public condemnation. Closed-door discussions between leaders and/or government representatives allow for a process of persuasion and negotiation, and for a sober exchange of views without the pandering to public domestic or international opinion which often accompanies international negotiation. A strategy of quiet, or private diplomacy may preserve a political atmosphere conducive to continued friendly bilateral relations; it also leaves room for increasing pressure in the form of public denunciation. Quiet diplomacy, however, is often criticized as too soft a measure, one which creates little pressure for change.[2] By its nature, such a strategy will likely leave opposition groups unaware of the external support they have garnered. Perceptions of isolation may serve to discourage opposition activity and thus serve the purposes of the incumbent regime.

Where private diplomacy is ineffective, or where the United States does not maintain diplomatic relations, public diplomacy may be pursued. Such avenues include public addresses or policy statements by the president or administration representatives—tactics that may serve to distance the United States from the offending regime rather than change its internal policies.[3] Other measures of public diplomacy include meetings with dissidents, and reductions—or increases—in educational, cultural, and scientific exchange. While the seriousness of U.S. intent is more dramatically demonstrated through public than private diplomacy, such actions may aggravate already difficult situations. Target regimes, determined to prove their sovereignty despite American pressures, may persist in or increase oppression; irritation with policy pronouncements may endanger U.S. nationals and threaten U.S. military and/or economic interests.

The subtleties of diplomacy may create contradictions of their own. The emphasis on human rights, for example, was quite clear during the Carter administration. Nonetheless, during his 1978 visit to Brazil, President Carter met with a human rights leader as well as with officials of the military government. While in attendance at signing ceremonies for the Panama Canal Treaty, the president met with Augusto Pinochet of Chile and Jorge Rafael Videla of Argentina. Such meetings seemed to signal a precedence in which hemispheric security was elevated above human rights, regardless of the rhetoric.[4]

In addition to diplomatic activity associated directly with government-to-government relations, the United States can use tactics of "informal penetration" to gain access to policymakers and influential members of society in another country. Such access is used to "influence the policies or stability" of a target country and is achieved by giving advice or financial support to political parties, labor unions, and other organizations or individuals.[5] Informal penetration of this sort may be pursued via the Central Intelligence Agency, Agency for International Development, U.S. Information Agency (International Visitors Program), National Endowment for Democracy, the AFL-CIO (George Meany Institute), and the American Institute for Free Labor Development.

Where diplomacy proves ineffective, more costly measures may be deemed necessary to effect policy changes abroad. To demonstrate U.S. determination, economic and/or military sanctions may be imposed.

Economic and Military Sanctions

The effectiveness of economic and/or military sanctions, such as refusal to extend aid or permit the import or export of goods or weapons, is dependent upon the vulnerability of the target state and the availability of alternative sources for aid and/or trade. Once sanctions are imposed, leverage decreases and trade or aid may be sought elsewhere. In 1977, for example, the linkage of U.S. aid to human rights conditions led Argentina, Uruguay, Brazil, Guatemala, and El Salvador to reject assistance.[6] Bilateral relations, particularly with Argentina and Chile, deteriorated. Furthermore, although sanctions are intended to influence events abroad, the initiating state, or its allies, may be adversely affected as well.[7] In the cases of Iran and the Philippines, the reverse impact of a sanctions policy would have meant economic and strategic losses for the United States.

A successful sanctions policy may also depend upon domestic reaction in the target state; punitive measures imposed by an initiating government may in fact serve to rally domestic support for a regime that would otherwise suffer public disfavor.[8] Following U.S. human rights–related aid cuts to Brazil in 1977, for example, members of Brazil's opposition party, who had previously criticized human rights violations in their country, denounced the United States. The secretary-general of the Brazilian Democratic Movement offered President Geisel the party's support, in what he viewed as a "moment when the sovereignty of the country is at stake." He vowed that his party would "carry out opposition to the government, not to the nation."[9]

Economic Sanctions. Economic sanctions may be imposed as a means of inflicting "pain" to achieve desired objectives in target states.[10] Such strategies may include embargoes, boycotts, tariff increases, quotas, withdrawal or non-conferral of most-favored-nation (MFN) status, denial of licenses, the freezing of assets, or suspension of aid. Trade relations may also be manipulated through intermediary institutions such as the Export-Import (Ex-Im) Bank, which finances and insures transactions of U.S. exporters, and OPIC (Overseas Private Investment Corporation), which guarantees U.S. private investments in the developing world.

Trade sanctions, and more specifically import restrictions, are among the most effective forms of nonmilitary sanctions. They have, however, often been avoided. A vocal business lobby, for example, ensured that the Carter administration would not employ sanctions that might affect U.S. commercial interests.[11] In testimony submitted to Congress in 1979, Warren Christopher explained that

> as a general rule, we have sought to implement the human rights policy without interfering with private commercial operations abroad. The primary means for implementing that policy is private diplomacy. Further, we start from a very strong presumption in favor of free trade and against interference. Free and open commercial activities abroad are critical to our economic well being.[12]

There has also been an unwillingness to place limits on U.S. Export-Import Bank activity. Warren Christopher testified in 1979,

> Ex-Im credits are designed primarily to benefit the United States by helping American exporters compete with businessmen of other important trading countries, most of which have similar programs. We have therefore recommended the use of these credits as a human rights policy instrument only in exceptional cases, involving the most extreme human rights violations, and where the use of other policy instruments has failed to produce improvements.[13]

In line with such philosophy, only 4 of 169 countries had Ex-Im credits limited, delayed, or denied in 1978: South Africa, Argentina, Chile, and Uruguay. Indeed, although a 1977 amendment to the Ex-Im Bank Act required that human rights be considered in loan decisions, Congress lifted these restraints by 1978. OPIC, too, although subject to Congressional requirements that it take into account human rights conditions before approving guarantees, only vetoed insurance for El Salvador during the Carter era.

Even where bilateral aid is decreased or halted, private business activity and multinational assistance often continues to flow; the threat or use of economic sanctions may therefore be rendered impotent. Lars Schoultz has noted that during the Carter administration, "for every dime halted by the U.S. government, a dollar was sent to repressive governments by U.S. corporations."[14] Thus, while Argentina rejected $15 million in U.S. military aid in 1977, American private investment rose from $1.5 billion to $2.4 billion; private bank claims went from $2.6 billion to $6.9 billion. Multilateral aid receipts from 1977 to 1980 ranged from $387.7 million to $495.4 million. In the period from 1977 to 1978, U.S. assistance to Guatemala fell from $21.3 million to $10.6 million; multilateral aid, however, climbed from $84.3 million to $108.7 million.[15] Before Chile rejected $27.5 million in aid in 1977 (which the administration, in any case, decided to withhold because of human rights violations), it received assurances for ten times that amount from private American banks.[16]

Such contradictory measures were supported by the U.S. government. In responding to a question about linkage between commercial bank lending and U.S. human rights policy, particularly as it related to Brazil, President Carter replied, "It would be inconceivable to me that any act of Congress would try to restrict the lending of money by American private banks to Brazil under any circumstances. This would violate the principles of our own free enterprise system. And if such an act was passed by Congress, I would not approve it."[17]

While economic sanctions carry greater costs and indicate a more intense concern than the use of diplomatic measures alone, they have not proven to be wholly reliable as policy strategies. Numerous studies have questioned the effectiveness of economic sanctions in altering government behavior. In the Rhodesian case, for example, Harry Strack observed that "there seems to be a consensus among scholars that sanctions are not only an ineffective means to secure policy objectives, but may well be dysfunctional or counterproductive, producing results opposite to those desired by the initiators of sanctions." A study by Gunnar Adler-Karlsson of Western economic warfare between 1947 and 1967 concluded, "The burden of proof is clearly on those who claim that an embargo policy is an efficient instrument of foreign policy. Experience seems to indicate the contrary." In an analysis of 126 cases where aid was suspended, James Blessing found, "In general . . . it can be argued that the suspension of aid does not appear to have been a very effective means of inducing change in recipient behavior."[18]

Despite inconclusive evidence of their effectiveness in altering policy or effecting leadership changes, it could be argued that economic sanctions ought not be dismissed as useful political tools. Sanctions may be effective in deterring "future misbehavior rather than [modifying] present behavior. . . . Also the example of punishment may discourage other countries from engaging in the same kind of activities. If deterrence is indeed their chief intent, the record of economic sanctions may be more favorable."[19]

Economic inducements to encourage change may be offered as well. Such measures, however, are not frequently used. Inducements may come in the form of favorable tariff agreements, grants of MFN status, tariff reductions, subsidies for exports or imports, license approvals, provision of aid, and investment guarantees. Foreign aid, the most common of economic levers, includes the Food for Peace (PL-480) Program and Agency for International Development (AID) assistance. AID programs extend technical assistance for development projects, capital assistance, and commodity assistance for financing imports.

Economic levers, however, may prove unpredictable even where aid is directed to humanitarian purposes. Funds may be transferred by target states for use by the military or police. In the Philippines, for example, more than nine million dollars in Food for Peace (PL-480) funds were diverted to military uses in the late 1960s.[20] Indeed, even when foreign aid funds are not directly transferred to unapproved projects, assistance given for one purpose may free government budgets in recipient states for uses antithetical to human rights. In cases where aid is withheld, however, national resources may be funneled into inappropriate projects or used by the military; such a strategy would siphon off funds from useful public programs that could serve the poor.

Although drawbacks related to the use of sanctions are apparent, policymakers often rely on this strategy to demonstrate at least a symbolic dissociation from a target regime. To reinforce the effect of such measures, U.S. policymakers may turn to multilateral institutions or expand sanctions to include cuts in military assistance.

Multilateral Efforts. Pursuit of strategies in multilateral institutions is necessary where the United States has no direct bilateral leverage, or where the success of bilateral economic sanctions may be undermined by other nations in the international community. On the political level, institutions such as the United Nations and Organization of American States provide an opportunity for the United States to demonstrate its convictions with public statements and votes. In the United Nations, where the United States was often outvoted by Third World majorities in the past, this country's votes were often only symbolic. It is largely as a consequence of this perceived impotence that neither the Nixon, Ford, nor Carter administrations made serious use of the United Nations. Despite the continued presence of the nonaligned bloc, however, the end of the Cold War has created new opportunities for the United States in the United Nations and has led to an increased interest in its use.

Effective multilateral efforts in the economic sphere may be pursued via international and regional lending institutions. These include the International Monetary Fund, International Bank for Reconstruction and Development, International Development Association, International Finance Corporation, Inter-American Development Bank, African Development Bank, and Asian Development Bank. The United States funnels a large proportion of its aid dollars through such international financial institutions. Its participation in multilateral development banks (MDBs) is, by law, directed to "advance the cause of human rights" and to "oppose any loan, any extension of financial assistance, or any technical assistance to any country" that is recognized internationally to be violating human rights, "unless such assistance is directed specifically to programs which serve the basic human needs of the citizens of the country."[21]

Except in the Fund for Special Operations of the Inter-American Development Bank, where the United States holds sufficient shares to veto any project, the United States has been unable to block projects in MDBs unless joined by other governments. American opposition to loans in particular cases, however, has "been responsible for loans being delayed or indefinitely deferred."[22]

To effect internal changes abroad, several governments may choose to vote together; such united fronts may serve to deflect allegations of arrogance against any particular state. Multilateral economic efforts are vital if bilateral economic sanctions have been applied to force reform. The use of multilateral lending institutions to promote human rights abroad has, however, been the subject of criticism by those who maintain that noneconomic agendas are antithetical to the purposes of these institutions and ought not enter the decision-making process.[23] Yet multilateral lending institutions may themselves play a catalytic role in increasing oppression. As repressive regimes become financially solvent with MDB assistance, foreign private capital is attracted. In order to stimulate further investment, governments may try to create greater stability at the price of repression and ever-widening gaps between rich and poor. Furthermore, as is the case with bilateral aid, funds may be transferred to military rather than economic uses. For example, South Africa's 1976–1977 military budget rose by $464 million after the nation was granted an IMF loan for that exact amount.[24]

Multilateral sanctions provide an opportunity to establish clear signals of dissatisfaction which will be recognized by both repressive regimes and the forces that oppose them. It publicly dissociates the United States and other nations from those who would violate human rights. As in the case of diplomacy and economic sanctions, the actual effect of such dissociation on the course of developments remains to be tested.

Security Assistance. The form of foreign assistance perceived to be most directly tied to support of repression is that of security assistance. While economic aid can be variously interpreted as aid in support of a regime or assistance directed to improving the lives of its population, it is difficult for military aid to take on such disparate attributes.[25]

Security assistance is justified on several grounds. It may be used as a means of demonstrating commitment to friends;[26] containing communism; forestalling unfavorable regional military imbalances; maintaining favorable relations; influencing governments; establishing transit, economic, or basing rights; or developing relations with future leaders who may come from the military ranks. Military sales may serve security purposes and contribute to the development of infrastructure necessary for economic and social progress.

U.S. military and security assistance is extended through various programs. Both U.S. government transactions and commercial sales are designed to further U.S. policy goals;[27] all grants and sales are subject to the control and approval of the secretary of state. Military assistance and commercial programs include:

1. *Military Assistance Program* provides grants for combat equipment and other material.

2. *International Military Education and Training Program (IMET)* offers training, mainly in U.S. military schools and facilities. IMET is run as a grant/concessional aid program and has been the target of criticism for its internal security training.

3. *Foreign Military Sales* are processed through government channels and include equipment for internal security purposes. Credit financing is available from the U.S. government for the purchase of U.S. military equipment and services, as well as for payment for technicians and training. Financing is extended through direct loans or guarantees to lending institutions. Countries may also buy equipment through the Department of Defense (DoD) procurement process, paying for direct costs and administrative fees. Commercial sales valued over one hundred thousand dollars must also go through a DoD approval process. The program has been used to supply the Iranian Gendarmerie under Shah Mohammad Reza Pahlavi, the Philippine Constabulary under Ferdinand Marcos, the Saudi Arabian National Guard, and other paramilitary organizations charged with internal security responsibilities.[28]

4. *Commercial Sales Program* permits the direct sale of firearms, tear gas, and other munitions to foreign police and security agencies. An export license must be obtained from the Department of State, Office of Munitions Control. Transactions conducted with Nicaragua between September 1976 and May 1979, for example, included 500 gas grenades and projectiles; 6,054 rifles, carbines, and submachine guns, 447 pistols and revolvers; and 7,312 rounds of ammunition (given in thousands). During the same time period, Iran received 12,334 gas grenades and projectiles, 3,060 pistols and revolvers, and 10 rounds of ammunition (given in thousands).[29]

5. *Excess Defense Articles* provides obsolete or unneeded U.S. military equipment.

Even where military assistance is obviously associated with repression, past administrations have found justification for its continuation. The State Department under the Nixon and Ford administrations suggested that human rights abuse may be "symptomatic of a basic insecurity on the part of the government." By contributing to economic stability or security from outside attack, military assistance might "serve to improve local attitudes toward protection of human rights."[30] Henry Kissinger warned that the withdrawal of security assistance "harms our other objectives while holding little promise for effecting desirable changes. . . . Moreover, such withdrawal, or even the threat of withdrawal, depreciates the strength of the mutual defense relationship which we share with our allies and offers encouragement to potential enemies."[31] For the Carter administration, it was not "local attitudes" that justified military aid to violators of human rights, but access to bases and raw materials, particularly in the Middle East and East Asia.[32]

Reductions in security assistance for use by domestic security forces and the military were criticized as antithetical to the purposes of human rights in the January 1984 *Report of the President's National Bipartisan Commission on Central America,* which was chaired by Henry Kissinger. The report complained that

> the blanket legal prohibition against the provision of training and aid to police organizations has the paradoxical effect, in certain cases, of inhibiting our effort to improve human rights performance. For example, while it is now understood in the Salvadoran armed forces that human rights violations endanger the flow of U.S. assistance, in the police organizations there is no training to professionalize and humanize operations.

Thus, the report suggests, the United States ought to "settle on a level of aid related to the operational requirements for a humane anti-guerrilla strategy."[33]

The efficacy of military grants and sales in promoting the U.S. national interest remains a matter of contention among many analysts. In addition to establishing an identity between the United States and repressive regimes (thereby damaging possible future relations with new elites), such assistance may jeopardize other security and economic interests. American-supplied arms can ultimately be used against the United States or its allies; its weapons technology can fall into hands of adversaries, compromising any military edge the United States may have. The presence of U.S. technicians and instructors, who often accompany military hardware, reinforces U.S. identification with authoritarian governments; in periods of instability, these personnel may be held hostage in political struggles within host countries. Excessive arms purchases may divert resources that could be used for economic and social development, thereby further undermining regime stability.

Political leverage, the assumed payoff for arms assistance, is also not guaranteed. The U.S. military relationship with the Greek military regime failed to avert action that precipitated the 1974 Cyprus crisis; U.S. ties to Turkey did not prevent that nation from using American arms to invade Cyprus, nor did receipt of U.S. military aid restrain Jordan from assisting Iraq during the 1991 Persian Gulf War. Arms sales in the Middle East have not in the past expanded U.S. basing privileges. Furthermore, the enormous revenues required for the purchase of weapons may be extracted from Americans themselves. In the case of Iran, for example, one observer noted, "It was perfectly obvious" that the Shah "needed higher revenues from oil exports to pay for the expensive arms purchased from the West in the first place."[34]

The argument that military embargoes only lead to opportunities for other nations and an economic loss for our own is disputed by some U.S. officials. Deputy Assistant Secretary of State for Inter-American Affairs William G. Bowdler noted in 1978, "The number of times we failed to supply arms and someone else came in to supply them is fairly limited." Assertions that carried weight in some circles prior to the demise of the Soviet Union, that communist states would take up the slack in the arms market, did not prove entirely persuasive either. In 1978, General Howard Fish of the Defense Security Assistance Agency stated that countries whose arms requests have been turned down "are reluctant to go into the embrace of the Soviet bear. They do not want the kinds of equipment and supply relationship that they can get with some of their suppliers. So the result is that they cut back considerably."[35]

Furthermore, it has been argued that arms sales cover only about four to five percent of total U.S. exports; its significance to the U.S. economy is not, therefore, what is generally touted.[36] Should U.S. arms sales be reduced, economic losses might be offset by sales of equipment and services required for economic development.

While the grant or sale of arms may not lead to human rights reform, its restriction on the grounds of human rights may create negative repercussions. American arms were denied to Argentina and Ethiopia during the Carter administration, as was economic assistance to Uruguay. In response, Argentina refused any military credits the administration had retained in the budget, and Ethiopia expelled U.S. personnel. Uruguay announced that it had not asked to be included in any future programs of military assistance. Argentina, Brazil, El Salvador, Guatemala, and Uruguay rejected all types of assistance, complaining that U.S. concern about human rights was a violation of their sovereignty.

Even where the supply of military equipment is cut, it is difficult to gauge the direct impact of military aid restrictions; arms are delivered over a period of several years and delivery is generally not terminated. The punitive effects of a cutoff may therefore become evident (if at all) only after several years. Despite a cut in military aid to Nicaragua in 1977, for example, military deliveries did not decline substantially until 1979 (see Table 4-2). In the case of Chile, where restrictions on arms transfers were imposed in 1974, $100 million in military assistance was already in the pipeline. Had Congress not intervened to halt the flow, arms deliveries would have continued until 1979.[37]

Military relations between nations make very evident both a symbolic and pragmatic association between governments. When arms are provided to authoritarian regimes, they may have a direct impact on human rights by providing training and weapons easily transferable to use in repression. Consequently, a policy of military assistance would most directly influence public perceptions abroad and would most likely serve to identify the United States with a repressive government.

The questions posed in this chapter about U.S. policy toward revolution and toward allied authoritarian rulers serve as guideposts in the analysis of U.S. foreign policy in pre-revolutionary Iran, Nicaragua, and the Philippines. The answers to these questions, and an examination of the options Washington either pursued, or might have pursued, in protecting U.S. interests in each case, form the framework from which the success or failure of either realpolitik school will be judged.

3   Iran: High Stakes for U.S. Interests—
Low Priority for Democracy

American foreign policy in Iran, particularly since 1941, sought to protect U.S. strategic, military, and economic interests by supporting the pro-American regime of Shah Mohammad Reza Pahlavi. Although civil and political rights were to a large extent not honored, the issue of human rights did not assume great significance in U.S.-Iran relations. The vehement anti-Americanism that dominated the revolutionary and postrevolutionary periods in Iran derived from the decades in which such U.S. policy was pursued; it ultimately led to the dissolution of the U.S.-Iran alliance and to the destruction of the U.S. national interest in Iran.

Iran Under the Shah

Iran was ruled by the Qajar dynasty from 1796 to 1921. In 1921, the commander of the Persian Cossack Division, Reza Khan, led his forces in overthrowing the monarch. Reza Khan became prime minister and, in 1925, had himself crowned as the new Persian monarch, Reza Shah Pahlavi. His son, Mohammad Reza Pahlavi, assumed power in 1941.

Iran's politics in the twentieth century were defined by the institution of the monarchy and by a national legislature that sought to increase its power and reduce the system to one of constitutional monarchy, as defined by Iran's 1906 constitution. In 1951, National Front leader, Mohammed Mossadeq, became prime minister. The National Front—a coalition of religious and secular groups from the upper, middle, and lower-middle classes—objected to Iran's subservience to foreign interests and to concessions being considered, by the Shah, for foreign oil companies.[1] Pro-Mossadeq forces in Iran's National Assembly, the Majlis, rendered the monarch's position increasingly tenuous; in an ensuing collision between the Shah and nationalist groups, the king was temporarily forced to leave Iran. In 1953, Great Britain and the United States, calculating their interests to be with the Shah rather than with the nationalist forces, joined to overthrow the Mossadeq government and to restore the monarch to his thrown.

Repression Under the Shah

Martial law was imposed in 1953 after the Shah's return from brief exile; it remained in effect until 1957 when the Shah—with the assistance of the United States, Israel, and France—established SAVAK, the internal security agency charged with controlling antiregime activity inside and outside of Iran. SAVAK became so pervasive that, in 1971, a SAVAK official confirmed that its informers included "workers, farmers, students, professors, teachers, guild members, political parties, and other associations." In 1974, *Newsweek* claimed SAVAK's informants to number three million.[2] During the Nixon administration, and with its knowledge, SAVAK began to monitor students and dissidents in the United States— a practice that continued even in the Carter years.[3]

The Pahlavi reign was characterized by repression and occasional periods of liberalization. On the whole, however, the regime became virtually sacrosanct; freedom of expression was denied and opposition was stifled. A 1978 State Department document reported that Iranian law "prohibited the advocacy of communism and violence, as well as attacks on the monarch or the basic tenets of the political system. The interpretations given at any particular time by the authorities as to what constitutes violations of these prohibitions . . . in some instances limited freedom of speech, press and assembly."[4] Sermons were monitored by government agents. The two main dailies, *Kayhan* and *Etela'at*, were placed under state control and obliged to follow monthly censorship guidelines. Book publishers were pressured into strict self-censorship under threat that distribution rights might be denied after printing. In 1975, 95 percent of all publications were closed down with a decree specifying that only publications with circulations of 3,000 or more could continue distribution.[5]

Little in the way of democratic government actually existed. Trade unions were run by SAVAK, and many guilds and worker syndicates were organized and supervised by the Ministry of Labor. Strikes were illegal. Elections for the Majlis were often rigged; all candidates were subject to approval by SAVAK, and the limits of criticism were well defined. The prime minister was an appointee of the Shah, and popular cabinet ministers were removed.[6] A formal two-party system, established by the Shah in 1957, was replaced in 1975 by the Rastakhiz (National Resurgence) Party. Iranians were pressed to join and were warned by the Shah that:

> A person who does not enter the new political party . . . will have only two choices. He is either an individual who belongs to an illegal organization, or is related to the outlawed Tudeh Party, or in other words is a traitor. Such an individual belongs in an Iranian prison, or if he desires he can leave the country tomorrow, without even paying exit fees . . . because he is not an Iranian, he has no nation, and his activities are illegal and punishable according to the law.[7]

Civil liberties were frequently denied, and cases of political arrest and torture were reported throughout the Shah's reign.[8] By 1974, Martin Ennals, secretary-general of Amnesty International, stated, "No country in the world has a worse record than Iran" on human rights.[9] The organization estimated that by the mid-1970s, Iran held anywhere from twenty-five thousand to one hundred thousand political prisoners.[10] In 1977, the State Department reported that state security prisoners numbered approximately twenty-two hundred.[11]

Torture was also practiced. A 1976 study by the International Commission of Jurists reported that there was "abundant evidence showing the systematic use of impermissible methods of psychological and physical torture of political suspects during interrogation."[12] Indeed, by the mid-1960s, no less an authority than the Shah himself admitted to the existence of torture in Iran, commenting, "I am not bloodthirsty. I am working for my country and the coming generations. I can't waste my time on a few young idiots. I don't believe the tortures attributed to SAVAK are as common as people say, but I can't run everything. . . . My people have every kind of freedom, except the freedom to betray."[13] When questioned about the existence of torture in 1974, Prime Minister Amir Abbos Hoveida responded, "Perhaps. But that is not our business. This is police business. I have nothing to do with these activities. . . ."[14]

Socioeconomic Conditions in Prerevolutionary Iran

While limited opportunities to engage in the political system engendered discontent among Iran's intellectuals and within its middle class throughout much of the Shah's reign, the Shah's economic policies antagonized a wide range of other groups and classes. Although oil production put Iran's economy into full gear in the 1970s, the poor gained little from the prosperity. Economic reforms, which began in the early 1960s as part of the "White Revolution," did not significantly change the distribution of wealth.[15]

In 1975, one percent of all landowners, approximately twenty-five thousand persons, owned more than twenty percent of the land. In contrast, more than sixty-five percent of landowners held only fifteen percent of the land.[16] The agrarian labor force, which stood at 54 percent of the total work force in 1960, had fallen to 41 percent in 1977;[17] the unemployment rate for agricultural laborers had reached 13.9 percent in 1971. Land reform promised by the Shah's White Revolution failed because of relative government neglect.[18] By the 1970s, the flow of people from the countryside to the city had reached 100,000 per year.[19] In 1975, 41 percent of Iran's population lived in the country's four largest cities; in contrast, in 1960, only 26 percent of its people lived in Tehran, the nation's largest city.[20] In the urban areas, in 1973–1974, "the highest 10 percent of the households accounted for 37.9 percent of total expenditure; the lowest 10 percent accounted for only 1.1 percent."[21] Migrants in Tehran lived in "dilapidated housing" and were threatened by government policies that sought to eradicate squatter settlements. A "credit squeeze" in 1976 led to reductions in construction jobs upon which many of Tehran's laborers relied.[22]

Early Opposition to the Shah

Following the Mossadeq incident (1951–1953), opposition parties in Iran were suppressed. By the mid-1950s, the communist Tudeh Party (established in 1941) functioned almost entirely from outside the country. The National Front, established in 1949, and composed mainly of members of the middle class, also suffered repression. It was able to survive, however, by convening discreet, unpublicized meetings.[23]

The opposition Freedom Movement, a constituent wing of the National Front, was formed in the early 1960s and included in its leadership former National Front members Mehdi Bazargan and Ayatollah Taleghani. Like the National Front, the Freedom Movement had ties to professionals and white-collar employees. Following the repression of the early 1960s, leaders of the Freedom Movement were imprisoned and the organization outlawed. Members kept their networks viable, however, through religious events and meetings.[24]

Iran's moderate opposition found support within most of the nation's socioeconomic strata. Many Iranians resented or had suffered from the Shah's political constraints, or from the ambitious economic policies he instituted as part of the White Revolution of the early 1960s. Those who thus found common cause with the moderate opposition included the traditional elite, the middle class, the urban poor, professionals, intellectuals, and politicians. The old aristocracy perceived the economic reforms as an attack on its power base. Some clergy opposed land reform because they were landlords; many also opposed the monarch's intentions to confiscate lands belonging to mosques and religious institutions.[25] Clerical opposition was further fanned by the process of Westernization the Shah sought to impose, and which was viewed to be potential catalyst for social and religious disintegration. In time, government reform and modernization campaigns threatened to destroy the central role of the bazaar in Iran's economy. The bazaaris believed that their economic base would be preempted by the spread of department stores, supermarkets, large banks, and Western control of the Iranian economy; they responded by joining the ranks of the disgruntled.

Two left-of-center guerrilla movements, the Mujhadeen Khalq and the Fedayeen Khalq, were established in the early 1960s. Violent incidents attributed to these groups occurred throughout the 1970s.

Domestic Reform and Manifestations of Dissent:
1960 to 1963 and 1976 to 1979

Reform, particularly economic reform, was encouraged by the Kennedy administration during the early 1960s as a means of stemming communist influence. The Shah complied by relaxing restrictions on free speech and by instituting economic reforms through the White Revolution. Channels that had been opened by reform made it possible for Iranians to engage in public protest against the Shah's social, economic, and political policies. Between January 1960 and January 1963, Iran was shaken by unrest, experiencing a dozen serious incidents, including violent demonstrations in Tehran University in 1961 and 1962. The protests expanded beyond what the Shah could tolerate and were ultimately repressed. When Lyndon Johnson followed Kennedy to the presidency, he ceased to pressure the Shah to implement reform.

In mid-1976, months before President Carter took the oath of office, the Shah again began a process of political liberalization. The reforms came in anticipation of the Carter inauguration and the concerns he was known to have about human rights. The process, however, was also begun as a means of preserving the stability of the throne for the Shah's son (the Shah had been ill with cancer for years), and to silence international condemnation of abuses with which the regime had been charged.[26]

The liberalization included the pardon of several political prisoners, a relaxation of censorship, and the formation of "various study groups and commissions" to which Iranians could submit complaints and grievances. In 1977, the Shah permitted civil trials for political opponents and allowed conditions in Iran to be scrutinized by "three major international human rights groups."[27]

The 1976 liberalizations provided the Iranian public with an opportunity to demonstrate its continued opposition to the Shah's policies. In 1977, former National Front politicians—Karim Sanjabi, Shapur Bakhtiar, and Dariush Forouhar—submitted a letter to the Shah asking for a return of constitutional freedoms. Other open letters followed, including those from members of a writers guild, 54 judges, and 144 lawyers. The creation of the Iran Committee of the Defense of Freedoms and the Rights of Man was announced by thirty opposition figures. The bazaaris formed the Society of Merchants, Traders, and Craftsmen to protest government intervention in the commercial sector and to condemn the single-party system.[28] In Tehran and the provinces, thousands of students demonstrated in support of liberalization during October and November 1977. At the end of 1977, the third National Front was formed.

Iran Unravels and Revolution Erupts: 1977 to 1979

In late 1977, one of Ayatollah Khomeini's sons died in an event attributed to the government of Iran. Muslim clergy attending a mourning ceremony in December issued both religious and political demands, including the return of Khomeini to Iran, the release of political prisoners, and freedom of expression, press, and assembly. In January 1978, an article attacking Khomeini for his opposition to land reform and women's suffrage sent protesting clerical students into the streets of the city of Qum.[29] The protestors were attacked by troops and some were killed. Forty-day cycles of mourning, protest, and more deaths began throughout Iran. As the cycles continued, people from various sectors joined in protest. Demands began to escalate and moved from calls for social, economic, and political reform to demands for the ouster of the Shah. Iran's revolution and the demise of the Pahlavi dynasty began with these protests.

In an effort to defuse the growing antigovernment demonstrations, the Shah appointed Jafar Sharif-Emami as prime minister in August 1978. Sharif-Emami announced that his most important task would be to establish communication with opposition groups. He contacted religious leaders and the liberal opposition, and made efforts to assuage the growing opposition: the Rastakhiz party was dissolved; freedom of the press was reinstated; the right of all political parties, except the communist party, to organize was assured; and the Islamic calendar was reintroduced. The prime minister also announced that appropriate conditions for free elections would be established, taxes for lower-income classes would be reduced, government employees would be given more equitable salaries, inappropriate laws would be abolished, and government programs would be reconciled with national and religious traditions.[30]

The reforms were perceived as spurious, but served to convince the "revolutionaries that the Shah had stopped fighting back."[31] The demonstrations and protests that the Shah had hoped to preempt continued, leading to the imposition of martial law in twelve cities and to the deaths of many more protestors.

At the end of October 1978, the Shah attempted to save the deteriorating political situation by establishing a coalition government that would be led by a widely acceptable " 'neutral' figure." The hoped-for rapprochement, however, came too late. National Front leaders whom the Shah had hoped to attract had by then gone to Paris to make a deal with the central opposition figure in the rising revolution, Ayatollah Khomeini. Their intention to preserve a constitutional monarchy within the framework of the 1906 constitution was unacceptable to Khomeini, who insisted on the monarch's abdication. Lacking "both an effective popular organization and the kind of 'troops' that Khomeini could put into the streets," the leaders of the National Front acceded to Khomeini's demands and joined with him in forming a unified opposition.[32]

With the conciliation option lost, the Shah appointed a law-and-order military government in early November. In an address to the nation the next day, he said, "I swear to prevent the repetition of past errors. . . . I am with you in the struggle to secure fundamental freedoms."[33]

Promises of further reform came too late. Except for a short lull, demonstrations and the associated deaths continued. Increasing numbers of Iran's population joined the protests. Industrial workers went on strike for economic reasons; by December, as the death toll mounted and the emotions of the revolution intensified, a political dimension was incorporated. Strikers demanded the release of political prisoners, the lifting of martial law, expulsion of foreigners, dissolution of SAVAK, and punishment of corrupt officials. Bazaaris, who found their livelihoods threatened by the Shah's policies, joined in the movement, as did the urban poor who had been suffering from declining economic conditions.[34]

By December, the Shah decided "that he would not and could not rule a country in which he had to stand in the flowing blood of his people. In short, he understood that he could not militarily occupy his own country."[35] On December 29 he tried, again, to form a civilian government, nominating National Front member Shahpour Bakhtiar as prime minister. The compromise, however, would not satisfy the opposition, and Bakhtiar was disavowed by his colleagues.[36]

The upheaval and evident inability to maintain order without massive bloodshed persuaded the Shah to go into exile on January 16, 1979. Although he left behind Prime Minister Bakhtiar, resignations began to plague the government as the revolution intensified. By February 4, approximately forty members of the Majlis had resigned and another forty had fled or were in hiding. Segments of the army had refused to shoot at protestors; the military, which had suffered desertions since the autumn of 1978, succumbed to desertions on the order of five hundred to one thousand per day after the Shah's departure. By early February, desertions had reached fifteen hundred per day.[37]

Ayatollah Khomeini returned on February 1, 1979, and on February 5 created a dual government by appointing as prime minister, Mehdi Bazargan, a member of the moderate Freedom Movement. The military continued to dissolve under religious pressures and as a consequence of the demoralization created by government indecision. The military command structure, which the Shah had designed to ensure his own survival, began to fragment. As such, the institution that was expected to protect the monarchy and its interests "lost its will." On February 11, 1979, the military issued a Declaration of Neutrality, which, in effect, undercut any support the Shah's last appointed prime minister may have had.[38]

Iran's Revolution and the Failure of Moderate Politics

As Iran's revolution progressed, the clergy, rather than the moderate opposition, took control of events. Lack of organization within the secular camp forced the moderates onto the sidelines. Devastated by repression throughout the Shah's rule, moderate political forces proved unable and unprepared to lead the rebellion. In contrast to the secular opposition, the religious establishment "had the organization and leadership required to draw the disenfranchised elements into taking action against the regime."[41]

Religious institutions had permeated "most levels of the social order, especially the lower classes," which maintained a "strong affinity" to the "traditional belief, values, and practices of Shi'i Islam."[42] It was the clergy, too, who could couch the disaffection of the masses in Islamic expression when public condemnation was banned. The bazaaris joined the clergy with whom they maintained close associations via financial, cultural, and family ties: bazaaris contributed to clergy-run religious, educational, and charitable institutions, and the clergy maintained a viable network for national communication via its mosques and holy shrines.

This link led to a particularly effective opposition force in an Iran devoid of open political contest. Lacking an independent alternative, the moderate opposition also allied itself with the clergy in the interest of overthrowing the Shah, thereby repeating "a pattern reminiscent of . . . century-old clerical-liberal alliances."[43]

During the initial stages of the revolution and, indeed, even to its very end, the outcome that would finally develop—a conservative Islamic government—was not anticipated by most of the revolution's leaders. Although it was the clerical students who began the protests, most clergy remained nonpolitical even by the early half of 1978. Religious and secular opposition figures sought implementation of the constitution rather than the creation of an Islamic Republic. "When asked in May 1978 about the need for an Islamic Republic, [the moderate] Ayatollah Shariatmadari replied that such a society was their long-term goal; but that for the time being, the strict observance of the constitution would give people all that was necessary."[44] In August 1978, when Sharif-Emami was appointed prime minister, "Khomeini categorically rejected his government while Shariatmadari gave the new prime minister three months to prove that his government could meet the criteria of a just Islamic government." In the religious center of Mashad clerics followed a similar line, issuing a statement in which reforms, not abolition of the monarchy, were demanded.[45] Westernized liberals supported the protest demonstrations during the summer of 1978, believing that they "would start the regime on a path of true liberalization from which it could not turn back. . . . The possibilities that street demonstrations might culminate in the Shah's overturn and a regime headed by Khomeini . . . was scarcely discussed at this time by the new middle class."[46]

Even when the clergy took lead of the revolution, and when calls for constitutional monarchy were transformed into demands for the removal of the king, it was assumed that a relatively moderate coalition would take on leadership once a new government was established. Hedayat Matin-Daftari, grandson of Mossadeq and leader of the Democratic National Front, stated in a 1983 interview, "As I remember it, right up to the day when Khomeini arrived in Iran and introduced Bazargan as his prime minister, no one had seriously thought that a religious government would result."[47]

The Fall of the Moderates in Post-Revolution Iran

The central figure in the Iranian drama, and the ultimate arbiter of the revolution's design, Ayatollah Ruhollah Khomeini, demonstrated a vehement anti-Americanism in his foreign policy pronouncements. The Mossadeq experience of 1951–1953 had left its mark; Khomeini and others were determined not to allow a repeat of the CIA coup that ousted Mossadeq.[39]

The anti-Americanism espoused by Khomeini ranged from antagonism toward U.S.–Israel relations and U.S. support of the Shah, to criticism of a pervasive U.S. influence on Iranian society and of Washington's proclaimed commitment to human rights. During the Shah's reign, Khomeini protested the agrarian reform and the Westernization policies of the White Revolution; in 1964, he denounced the U.S.–Iran Status of Forces Agreement. In February 1978, Khomeini complained that the United States

> imposed the Shah upon us. . . . During the period he has ruled, this creature transformed Iran into an official colony of the U.S. What crimes he has committed in service to his masters.
>
> How many American officers there are in Iran now, and what huge salaries they receive! That is our problem—everything in our treasury has to be emptied into the pockets of America.[40]

Despite his anti-American rhetoric, Khomeini appointed a leader of the moderate Freedom Movement, Mehdi Bazargan, as prime minister in the new revolutionary government. Bazargan's Freedom Movement had been in close contact with U.S. officials in the latter months of 1978, seeking a resolution to the turmoil that had spread throughout the country. As prime minister, Bazargan was "willing to maintain normal diplomatic relations with the United States as long as the United States honored Iran's independence and autonomy."[48] Bazargan's government included as its foreign minister, Ibrahim Yazdi, an American-educated member of the Freedom Movement. The first cabinet was primarily composed of moderates.

The first Revolutionary Council, whose task it was to oversee the work of the government, was composed of five clerics, two bazaaris, two generals, and eight intellectuals and political activists—most of whom were members of the Freedom Movement. The clergy did not predominate within the government's formal structures, but controlled nongovernmental organizations such as the Komitehs (independent Islamic political/military committees) and the armed Revolutionary Guard.[49]

The policies and hopes of the moderates were subverted, however, by Khomeini's intrusions, and within nine months members of the provisional government began to resign in protest. On November 5, 1979, after two previous attempts to resign, and one day after the U.S. Embassy in Tehran was seized by radical students, Prime Minister Bazargan submitted a resignation that was accepted by Khomeini.[50]

Bazargan's replacement was a relative moderate, Abol Hassan Bani Sadr. Bani Sadr was elected as the first president of the Islamic Republic in January 1980; after the outbreak of the Iran–Iraq war in September 1980, he was also appointed commander-in-chief of the armed forces.

The political environment of postrevolution Iran was permeated with tensions "between the lower and lower middle-class religious forces and the Western-educated moderates of the middle and upper middle classes." These antagonisms were exacerbated following the November 1979 U.S. Embassy takeover. Public support, extended to the extremists who controlled the embassy, made evident the mass support the radicals could garner. The rising prominence of the radicals, and complaints about Bani Sadr, convinced Khomeini to extend his backing to the ulama and the conservatives in the tug of war between moderates and religious radicals. Bani Sadr was dismissed as commander-in-chief of the armed forces; in the summer of 1981 he was ousted from the presidency.[51]

With Bani Sadr's dismissal, the first stage of Iran's revolution ended; it also marked the end of the influence of secular moderates in the policies of the Islamic Republic.

Although all political organizations, including the National Front, were outlawed following Bani Sadr's ouster,[52] Ayatollah Khomeini seemed willing to compromise with most opposition groups during the early years of the Islamic Republic. Moderate forces, however, began to disintegrate by virtue of their own errors. Disorganization, which was problematic even during the revolution, accelerated their demise following the revolution's success.

Opposition groups could no longer rely on the mosques to mobilize constituents as they had during the course of the revolution. The various opposition groups were also apparently unable to unite in a common front. Mehdi Bazargan, a member of the Freedom Movement and the first prime minister of postrevolutionary Iran, commented on the lack of unity, organization, and foresight in an October 1979 interview:

> Something unforeseen and unforeseeable happened after the revolution. What happened was that the clergy supplanted us and succeeded in taking over the country. . . . If, instead of being distracted, we had behaved like a party, then this mess wouldn't have occurred. . . . In that respect, all the political parties . . . went to sleep after the revolution. . . . Yes, it was the lack of initiative by the laity that permitted the takeover by the clergy.[53]

Washington's support of the moderates only hastened their defeat. The moderates seemed willing to allow a return of the U.S. presence in Iran, and the United States continued its prerevolutionary contacts with Freedom Movement members, including Bazargan and other moderates in his government. "Many Iranian revolutionaries watched this mutual embrace sullenly and with a growing concern. They believed that the violent revolution against the Shah" had "also been carried out to destroy American influence in the political affairs of their country."[54] A U.S. official in Iran reflected the problem in a September 1979 cable to Washington. "Too many Americans [he wrote] have been too visible too long in too many aspects of life in Iran." Another U.S. diplomat told an interviewer, "We should have gone back with six men and a dog."[55]

Antagonisms toward the U.S. presence in Iran and its continuing links to Iranian leaders were exacerbated when on November 1, 1979, days after the Shah was admitted into the United States for treatment of his cancer, National Security Adviser Zbigniew Brzezinski met in Algiers with Mehdi Bazargan, Ibrahim Yazdi, and Defense Minister Mustafa Chamran. Three days later, on November 4, alientated radicals assaulted the U.S. Embassy in Tehran and took its diplomats hostage. Documents found in the embassy showed that the U.S. government, including the CIA, had been in contact before and after the revolution with several leaders of the Islamic Republic, including Prime Minister Bazargan, Foreign Minister Yazdi, and Deputy Prime Minister Amir Entezam. The CIA had also contacted Bani Sadr (under a business-related cover) while he was still in Paris with Khomeini. Discovery of these associations further eroded the credibility of the moderates.[56]

The U.S. Presence in Prerevolutionary Iran

The United States had minimal ties in Iran before World War II, although agreements, such as the Treaty of Friendship and Commerce (1856) and a Treaty Regulating Commercial Relations between the United States and Persia (1928), had been signed. Washington was perceived as a mediating influence in relation to British–Soviet rivalry in Iran, and as a disinterested party in Iran's domestic affairs. When Iran needed assistance in reorganizing its finances, it looked to the United States, which dispatched the Shuster (1911) and the Millspaugh Missions (1922–27 and 1944).

The high regard in which the United States was held was delineated in a 1924 letter written by Hussein Alai, a minister of the Persian government, to the U.S. secretary of state: "The Persian Government and people," he wrote, "have always recognized the altruism and impartiality which distinguish the American Government and people. They particularly appreciate the concern of the United States for fair play, for the respect of the independence of the smaller nations and for the maintenance of the economic open door."[57]

Iran's reliance on the United States began to expand beyond pro forma treaties and requests for financial advisers. By 1942, Iran had requested agricultural, health, transportation, and security experts. A political adviser in the U.S. Department of State noted that "the obvious fact is that we shall soon be in the position of actually 'running' Iran through an impressive body of American advisers eagerly sought by the Iranian government." Undersecretary of State Sumner Welles wrote to President Roosevelt in October 1942 that U.S. advisers will "be able to assist in the rehabilitation of the country, which would seem to be a fundamental requisite for the ultimate conversion of Iran into an active and willing partner on our side."[58]

Beginning with World War II, the U.S. role in Iran increased dramatically. Britain, the Soviet Union, and eventually the United States, entered into closer relations with Iran in an effort to mitigate a dominant German influence. At the same time, thirty thousand U.S. troops were stationed in Iran to assist in the supply of the Soviet Union through Iran's adjoining borders. In 1943, the United States entered into a Treaty of Reciprocal Relations with Iran; it also signed the Tehran Declaration, in which Washington pledged to uphold Iran's independence and integrity. In the aftermath of the war, when the Soviet Union refused to evacuate Azerbaijan (in northwestern Iran), and indeed sought to support a separatist government there, Iran's ambassador to Washington suggested that Iran "would welcome and appreciate American intervention at this critical juncture."[59] The United States protested the violation to the Soviet Union and supported Iran's position on the issue in the United Nations.

The 1951 election of a nationalist prime minister, Mohammed Mossadeq, brought further U.S. involvement. Mossadeq permitted the communist Tudeh party to operate openly, proposed the nationalization of Iran's oil industry, and campaigned for the dismantling of the monarchy. His agenda pleased neither Britain nor the United States. To ensure that their interests would be protected, Great Britain and the United States jointly intervened in a 1953 coup to oust the prime minister and reinstate the Shah.

The U.S. role in the 1953 coup, nationalist Shapur Bakhtiar later asserted, led Washington to forfeit "the goodwill [of the nationalists] and the collaboration which we offered in the face of the Russians."[60] A downward slide in the U.S. image in Iran continued thereafter. In 1954, American oil companies bought a 40 percent share in Iran's oil industry.[61] A Status of Forces Agreement, signed in 1964, conferred diplomatic immunity on American military personnel and their dependents in Iran. Capitulatory rights granted to U.S. citizens created widespread outrage and impelled Ayatollah Khomeini to complain, "Our dignity has been trampled underfoot. . . . They have reduced the Iranian people to a level lower than that of an American dog.''[62] It was a lament that would force Khomeini into exile.

The U.S. National Interest in Iran

By 1943, Iran's position in the calculus of U.S. interests had already begun to take on significance both in terms of the international environment, and in relation to the Middle East oil supply. Secretary of State Cordell Hull wrote:

> From a more directly selfish point of view, it is to our interest that no great power be established on the Persian Gulf opposite the important American petroleum development in Saudi Arabia.
>
> Therefore, the United States should adopt a policy of positive action in Iran. . . . We should take the lead wherever possible, in remedying internal difficulties, working as much as possible through American administrators freely employed by the Iranian government.[63]

After World War II, Iran was placed in a central position in U.S. strategic thinking. Assessments focused on Cold War dichotomies and the growing Western dependence on Iran's petroleum resources. A 1948 State Department analysis explained:

> Security of Iran is substantially as important to U.S. as is security Greece and Turkey. . . . Basic consideration re Soviet threat to Iranian security . . . still generally valid. . . . U.S. military assistance should continue be aimed at internal security, not national defense, of Iran. . . . Power relations Iran and USSR cannot be altered appreciably by provision U.S. military supplies.[64]

In 1950, the CIA warned of the dire consequences of Soviet domination of Iran:

> *a.* The extension of the Soviet frontiers to Iraq and Pakistan would facilitate penetration of the Near East and the Indian subcontinent.
>
> *b.* The USSR would also be in a more favorable position for extending its control over these areas in the event of global war.
>
> *c.* The USSR would have access to Iran's great oil resources.
>
> *d.* The United States would be denied an important potential base of operations against the USSR. Conversely, the USSR would obtain buffer territory between its vital Baku oil fields and the bases from which Baku might be attacked.[65]

There were more dangers to be considered in 1958, when Iraq's monarchy was overthrown. The new military rulers of Iraq withdrew from the Baghdad Pact (Central Treaty Organization—CENTO) and looked to the Soviet Union for military supplies.[66] The threat of advancing communism prompted President Eisenhower to sign a 1959 agreement with Iran pledging U.S. assistance in case of a Soviet (or Soviet-inspired) attack.[67]

Regional and international politics continued to place Iran in the center of U.S. policy calculations throughout the 1960s and 1970s: the Shah supported U.S. policy in Vietnam; his regime "stood as a strong regional antidote to the radicalism of President Nasser of Egypt"; Iran was an increasingly important trading partner with the United States and was becoming a major arms purchaser; and, the Shah was willing to support the state of Israel as well as ship oil to both Israel and Western Europe.[68] (By 1979, Iran supplied 6 percent of U.S. annual petroleum imports. It supplied approximately 16 percent of Western Europe's imports, as well as 24 percent of Japan's, and 70 percent of Israel's petroleum needs.)[69] Of central importance, too, was the access Iran was able to provide to information about Soviet intercontinental ballistic missile (ICBM) testing and capacity, and about radio conversations conducted by Soviet military aircraft, tanks, and field units.[70]

The Shah tried to reinforce Iran's importance to the United States by preying on U.S. fears of communist expansion. In the early 1970s, he warned of a " 'Soviet-inspired pincer movement' against Iran through Iraq and India." The warning was given credence when a Soviet-Indian Treaty of Friendship and Cooperation was announced in 1971, and when a similar accord was signed with Iraq in 1972.[71] Iran's value to the United States increased again when Great Britain's withdrawal from the Persian Gulf in 1971 created a vacuum that the Americans were not prepared to fill. Instead, Nixon's "twin pillar" policy looked to Iran and Saudi Arabia to maintain security in the Gulf. The United States would help provide the arms necessary for the region's defense, while seeking to disengage from direct military involvement.[72] Under such conditions, Henry Kissinger explained, the United States would

> especially value those friends who are prepared to make their own efforts for their economic advance and who are prepared to make a significant contribution to their own defense. . . .
>   . . . The stability of Iran, the commitment of Iran to its [Middle East] security, is a major factor for global peace and a major factor in the stability of the Middle East.
>   . . . Not out of sentimentality . . . but out of a calculation of our own national and global interests . . . there has developed a parallelism

Table 3–1
U.S. Military Assistance and Sales to Iran, 1967–1980
(in millions of U.S. dollars)

Fiscal Year International	U.S. Government		Commercial Sales Deliveries[c]	Number of Students in Military Education and Training Program
	Military Aid Approved[a]	Military Deliveries[b]		
1967	$197.6	$ 80.1	$ 2.0	408
1968	122.1	99.0	5.1	318
1969	128.2	143.5	1.1	765
1970	2.6	144.1	9.8	504
1971	2.1	85.4	28.3	354
1972	13.6	221.9	42.4	186
1973	0.4	247.9	19.5	0
1974	>.05*	648.7	35.3	0
1975	0.0	986.1	49.4	0
1976	0.0	1891.1	107.9	0
1977	0.0	2416.3	138.4	0
1978	0.0	1891.7	132.7	0
1979	0.0	1958.9	109.8	0
1980	0.0	0.0	7.0	0

[a]Includes Foreign Military Sales grants/credits, MAP, IMET, and EDA.

[b]Includes Foreign Military Sales for cash or credit, MAP, IMET, and EDA.

[c]Munitions purchased directly from U.S. manufacturers and requiring a U.S. export license.

*Less than $50,000.

Sources: *Foreign Military Sales, Foreign Military Construction Sales, and Military Assistance Facts:* December 1976; December 1978; December 1979; December 1980; September 1981; September 1982; 30 September 1983; 30 September 1984; 30 September 1985; 30 September 1986; 30 September 1987. (Washington, D.C.: Data Management Division, Comptroller, Defense Security Assistance Agency.)

of views on many key problems that has made our cooperation a matter that is in the profound national interest of both countries.[73]

As a consequence of the policy, arms sales to Iran increased and its military requests were generally approved without question. (Table 3-1 details U.S. military assistance to Iran from 1967 to 1980.)

U.S.-Iran Military Relations. In addition to the thirty thousand noncombat troops stationed in Iran during World War II, a U.S. military mission was set up in 1942 to train Iran's police force, the Gendarmerie.[74] The purpose of the mission, Acting Secretary of State Stettinius reported in 1944, was to "strengthen" Iran "so that it can maintain internal security and avoid the dissensions and weaknesses which breed interference and aggression. A cornerstone of this policy should be the building up of Iran's security forces."[75]

Secretary of State Byrnes supported the continued presence of the military mission noting, in 1945, that

> by increasing the ability of the Iranian Government to maintain order and security, it is hoped to remove any pretext for British or Soviet intervention in Iran's internal affairs and, accordingly, to remove such future threat to Allied solidarity and international security. The stabilization of Iran, moreover, will serve to lay a sound foundation for the development of American commercial, petroleum, and aviation interests in the Middle East.[76]

U.S. military missions were dispatched to train Iran's police and military forces until the fall of the Shah. The missions not only trained Iran's armed forces, but also sent officers and noncommissioned officers to the United States for specialized training, and helped "regulate the logistics problems of the armed forces."[77] The last U.S. head of mission, prior to the revolution, also served as an adviser to the Iranian General Staff.

The increasing importance of Iran in U.S. strategic thinking, and the perceived centrality of the Shah in supporting U.S. interests, were reflected in the military relationship established between the two governments. Between 1946 and 1968, Iran received $1.2 billion in military credits and grants.[78] By 1969, however, Iran was considered financially capable of purchasing arms and therefore became ineligible for the military grants program.[79] The Nixon Doctrine, enunciated in 1969, and its corollary "twin pillars" policy worked to give the Shah a virtual carte blanche in arms purchases. In 1971, military deliveries were valued at $85.4 million. Weapons orders increased as the price of oil and the Shah's ambitions grew. The value of deliveries went up from $221.9 million in fiscal year 1972 to $2.4 billion in fiscal year 1977 (see Table 3-1). A July 1976 Congressional staff report noted:

> Iran is the largest single purchaser of U.S. military equipment. Iran wants to buy its most sophisticated arms and defense equipment from the United States for political as well as economic reasons; it prefers to contract through the DoD [Department of Defense] on government-to-government basis. . . . Arms sales are, therefore, an important component of U.S.–Iranian foreign relations.

Because the United States has a major interest in the military security of Iran, most Iranian arms request have been favorably received.

In May 1972, President Nixon and then National Security Advisor Kissinger agreed for the first time to sell Iran virtually any conventional weapons it wanted.[80]

Washington believed the Shah's purchases to have a number of advantages: they helped to maintain the stability of the monarchy, ensure regional stability, and preserve the Cold War balance. Arms sales also contributed significantly to the U.S. balance of payments and to the flow of funds for military research and development.[81] These sales, however, exacerbated anti-American sentiments in Iran. Military equipment was being sent to an army seen as repressive and to an internal security organization identified with abuse. Iranians also viewed arms purchases as a drain on much-needed development programs. By 1978, Iran was spending $169 per capita on defense, but only $80 per capita on education and $23 per capita on health.[82]

U.S.-Iran Economic Relations. Throughout the Shah's reign, Iran absorbed ever-greater volumes of American aid, goods, and investments. Economic assistance between 1946 and 1967 totaled $758 million.[83] The aid, however, was met with criticism within Iran: the funding coincided with increasing political oppression; its existence was viewed as a factor contributing to burgeoning corruption in the bureaucracy; and, its bias toward military and security projects, rather than the social and economic needs of the poor, was condemned as unhelpful. American aid was also viewed as a tool through which the United States could gain control over policy-making in Iran: aid concessions were granted, for example, after the 1953 overthrow of Mossadeq; after the 1954 oil consortium agreement; in 1955, after Iran joined the Baghdad Pact; in 1958, when Iran gave its support to CENTO; and, in 1964, after the signing of the Status of Forces Agreement.[84]

By November 1967, economic aid was terminated: Iran was no longer considered a less-developed country and became eligible, therefore, for Export-Import Bank funding (see Table 3–2). American trade and investment increased as oil profits poured huge sums of money into Iranian coffers. U.S. business interests were involved in all sectors of the nation's economy. The U.S. oil industry had been in Iran since 1954, when U.S. companies acquired a 40 percent interest in Iran's oil industry. By 1975, a five-year American-Iranian economic accord committed Iran to expenditures of $15 billion on American goods and services, exclusive of oil and military trade. The five-year expenditure target was revised upward to $26

Table 3–2
U.S. Economic Assistance to Iran, 1967–1981 (in millions of U.S. dollars)

Fiscal Year	Total Economic Commitments[a]	Direct Economic Assistance AID		Other Economic Assistance		Multilateral Development Banks	
		Funds Committed	Funds Delivered	Ex-Im Bank Loans[b]	Other U.S. Loans/Grants[c]	Loans Approved[d]	Absentions[e]
1967	$4.8	$0.9	$ 8.3	$102.3	$ 0.0		
1968	2.3	0.1	4.9	26.7	13.0		
1969	1.4	0.0	4.5	6.5	0.0		
1970	1.4	0.0	1.8	41.7	3.0		
1971	1.2	0.0	1.4	177.9	25.7		
1972	2.4	0.0	1.1	104.9	38.3		
1973	1.3	0.0	0.6	237.7	44.2	$ 0.0	
1974	1.4	0.0	0.04	270.0	20.6	265.0	
1975	1.7	0.0	0.08	5.3	0.0	52.5	$ 0.0
1976f	1.1	0.0	0.01	40.0	0.0	0.0	0.0
1977	0.0	0.0	0.06	0.0	0.0	0.0	0.0
1978	0.0	0.0	0.0	17.9	0.0	0.0	0.0
1979	0.1	0.0	0.0	0.0	0.0	0.0	0.0
1980	0.0	0.0	0.01	0.0	0.0	0.0	0.0
1981	0.0	0.0	-0.01	0.0	0.0	0.0	0.0

[a]Includes AID grants and loans and AID Economic Support Funds (ESF); PL-480 Titles I and II (Sales and Grants); International Narcotics Control. ESF is given for security purposes. In the Philippines, ESF expenditures were committed as follows (in millions of U.S. dollars): FY1973—$49.3; 1974—$0.5; 1975—$0.3; 1980—$20.0; 1981—$30.0; 1982—$50.0; 1983—$50.0; 1984—$50.0; 1985—$140.0; 1986—$300.3; ESF for Nicaragua: FY1979—$80.0; 1980—$1.1.

[b]Does not include export credit insurance and guarantees.

[c]Short-term credit granted by U.S. Department of Agriculture under the Commodity Credit Corporation Charter Act; OPIC direct loans and private trade agreements; PL-480 (I) private-sales agreements financed by the act.

[d]World Bank Group—International Bank for Reconstruction and Development, International Development Association, and International Finance Corporation; Asian Development Bank; Inter-American Development Bank; African Development Bank.

[e]U.S. vetoes or abstentions on human rights grounds. U.S. votes recorded as of 1975. U.S. abstentions/vetoes related to human rights, against any country, began in FY 1977.

[f]1976 numbers include additional fifth transitional quarter 1976–1977, covering the period July 1, 1976, to September 30, 1976.

Sources: *Development Issues: U.S. Actions Affecting the Development of Low-Income Countries: Annual Report of the Chairman of the Development Coordination Committee Transmitted to the Congress.* (1979–1983.)

International Finance: The National Advisory Council on International Monetary and Financial Policies Annual Report to the President and the Congress. (Washington, D.C.: U.S. Government Printing Office, n.d.). (1979–1985.)

U.S. Agency for International Development, Office of Planning and Budget, Bureau for Program and Policy Coordination, *U.S. Overseas Loans and Grants and Assistance from International Organizations.* (1976–1987.)

U.S. Department of Commerce, Bureau of Economic Analysis, Balance of Payments Division, Government Grants and Capital Branch, unpublished data, letter dated 7 November 1990.

Notes: Figures are rounded off to the nearest $100,000, except for total amounts less than that.

billion in 1976.[85] During the Carter administration, Iran's exports to the United States reached approximately $3.6 billion.

American Personnel in Iran. The extensive military and economic relationship between the United States and Iran was accompanied by an increasing presence of American personnel—a presence that contributed to growing anti-Americanism. In 1963, ten thousand Americans worked in the country.[86] Henry Kissinger reported that the numbers had increased from 15,000 or 16,000 in 1972, to 24,000 by 1976. These numbers, Kissinger suggested, could rise to 50,000 or 60,000, or higher, by 1980.[87]

A 1976 Congressional staff report warned:

> The presence of large growing number of Americans in Iran had already given rise to socio-economic problems. . . . They could become worse should there be a major change in U.S.–Iranian relations. . . . Anti-Americanism could become a serious problem . . . if there were to be a change in government in Iran."[88]

As the gaps between the rich and poor, secular and religious, and urban and rural grew wider, it was perhaps inevitable that resentment of the United States—the government that most supported the regime that allowed these disparities to develop—would increase. Furthermore, the social and economic problems attributable to the presence of American personnel were many. These included economic dislocation, shortages, inflation, overcrowding, and the introduction of Western lifestyles that clashed with the tradition of the bazaar, the indigent masses, and the clerics.

Amin Saikal reported that complaints were frequently heard in Tehran that "While many working-age Iranians (about 30 percent) were either unemployed or could not find work matching their qualifications, thousands of foreigners were brought in at high wages to do the jobs for which Iranians could have been trained locally and employed at much lower wages."[89] Nikki Keddie portrayed the negative impact of the U.S. presence:

> American military suppliers like Grumman, Lockheed, and Westinghouse took over key positions in the economy. Many potentially productive Iranians, including a high percentage of the technically trained, were increasingly concentrated in the armed forces and in building projects for army and naval bases and for facilities to transport and house military equipment. New housing starts, and particularly the use of cement, were

at times outlawed or rendered impossible because of the heavy demands on cement and other building materials for sheltering military equipment. Thus, the growing housing shortage and rise in home prices was tied to military spending, and foreigners and foreign contractors' willingness to pay high rents added to the problem.[90]

The U.S. National Interest and Human Rights in Prerevolutionary Iran

The preeminence of U.S. strategic and economic interests in Iran forced any American concerns about human rights in that country to the sidelines. U.S. administrations made certain to show public allegiance to the Shah via economic and military agreements, statements of support, and high-level visits, that included trips by President Eisenhower, Vice President Nixon, Vice President Johnson, and President Carter. The Shah, too, made numerous visits to Washington.

During a December 1959 visit to Tehran, President Eisenhower commented, "We see eye to eye when it comes to the fundamentals which govern the relations between men and between nations."[91] When demonstrations against reforms erupted in 1963, President Kennedy wrote to the Shah that he shared "the regret you must feel over the loss of life connected with the recent unfortunate attempts to block your reform programs." Kennedy told the Shah that he was confident that "such manifestations will gradually disappear as your people realize the importance of the measure you are taking to extend social justice and equal opportunity for all Iranians."[92]

President Johnson praised the Shah during the monarch's 1967 visit to Washington:

> Iran is a different country now from the one that we saw in 1962. The difference has sprung from Your Majesty's dedicated inspirational and progressive leadership.
>
> I see another difference, another lesson that your leadership provides for all who prize real progress. Because you are winning progress without violence and without any bloodshed.[93]

Indeed, the U.S. government seemed intent upon ignoring both the problems in Iran and any possible alternatives to the Shah's rule. A 1973 National Security Council document reported:

> The monarchy, which provides the stability not yet available through popular institutions or long popular experience in political affairs, is in

fact the sole element in the country that can at present give continuity to
public policy. The Shah, therefore, remains a linchpin for the safeguarding of our basic security interests in Iran.

. . . The United States is strongly identified with the regime and
the reform program [White Revolution]. Any major failure by the Shah
would inevitably adversely affect U.S. interests.

. . . At present we do not feel that the devotion of roughly 25% of
total budgetary expenditures (developmental plus ordinary) to the military establishment (including the Gendarmerie . . .) is incompatible
with overall U.S. national security interests. . . . The military forces are
now playing a key role in maintaining in power a progressive and pro-
Western monarch over the next few years.[94]

To protect its interests, Washington was willing to encourage the Shah
in imposing nondemocratic rule and in stifling the development of an independent, moderate opposition. The report went on to make the following recommendations for U.S. policy:

[Maintain] the Shah in a position of ultimate control over Iran's foreign
policies; and [maintain] internal political stability [to prevent] the coming to power of neutralist elements, by . . .

improving the counter-insurgency capacity of the military and of rural and urban police forces;

discouraging governmental impulses toward unduly harsh and repressive measures against non-communist opposition elements;

encouraging the detaching of moderate conservative and liberal opposition elements and the enlistment of their loyalties and energies in the
Shah's program of social reform and emancipation.[95]

Even after 1974 Congressional stipulations required that human rights
be factored into policy decisions, administration reports on human rights
in Iran sought to protect the relationship by presenting repressive conditions in as innocuous a manner as possible. A December 1976 State Department document described Iran's political system:

The present governmental system is a constitutional monarchy headed by
the Shah and a two-chamber parliament. Until March 1975, Iran had a
multi-party system. This was replaced by a new broad-based single
party, the Resurgence Party of the People of Iran. Elections for both the
Majlis and the Senate were held in June 1975 and were recognized as
among the most honest in Iran's history. However, these democratic institutions have limited powers; the Shah makes all important decisions.[96]

The subject of human rights continued to be lost in the foreign policy
agenda. In 1976, Alfred Atherton, assistant secretary of state for Near
Eastern and South Asian affairs, testified that the U.S. administration had

not made official representation to Iran on the condition of human rights in that country for two reasons. First, we believe that the administration of Iranian judicial and penal systems is above all a matter of internal Iranian responsibility and that one sovereign country should not interfere lightly in another's domestic affairs.

. . . In reaching our judgment, we have also taken into account the remarkable progress which has been made in Iran in many areas of human rights as well as the unique and extraordinarily difficult problems of terrorism and other manifestations of social disruption. If Iran's internal practices in matters relating to human rights were a growing affront to international standards, we would of course reconsider our judgment. The trend appears to us, however, to be in the opposite direction.[97]

A December 1976 State Department report, however, contradicted the Atherton testimony. It noted:

Over the past two years U.S. Government officials have discussed privately with Iranian officials our views about human rights in general and the human rights situation in Iran specifically. These contacts have been guided by our belief that handling this subject privately would be most effective in the Iranian context. To do otherwise would certainly become widely known and would put the matter of human rights in confrontational and self-defeating terms. We have made clear in private conversations our views and laws.[98]

U.S. diplomacy may indeed have been so quiet that the assistant secretary of state had not even heard about it.

Even under the Carter administration, which had come to office proclaiming human rights as a central foreign policy concern, protecting the U.S.–Iran relationship superseded all other considerations. In a May 1977 meeting in Tehran, Secretary of State Cyrus Vance informed the Shah of Washington's decision to pursue the sale of 160 F-16 jets to Iran. He also assured the monarch of President Carter's intentions to get Congressional approval for the Airborne Warning and Control Systems the Shah had requested. (Seven AWACs were later approved, down from the ten requested by the Shah.) Vance also made clear the administration's interest in the issue of human rights and commended the Shah for his liberalization efforts. During the Shah's November 1977 visit to Washington, the subject of human rights did not appear as a significant issue on the discussion agenda.[99]

Prior to his visit to Iran in December 1977, President Carter received a letter, signed by leading Iranian political and intellectual figures, condemning the oppression and brutality of the Shah. The letter warned that failure to take note of the protest would lead to punishment of the signatories. Notwithstanding his stated convictions about human rights, and despite the warning from the signatories, the president chose to ignore the letter. Indeed, although Carter's December 1977 visit to Iran was preceded by a year of protest, the president extolled the Shah and called Iran an "island of stability." This was a message that many thought gave the Shah confidence to crack down on rising dissent and that led to the violent repression of the 1978 Qum protest.[100]

The Coming of the Revolution: U.S. Support of the Shah

Despite evidence of growing problems and domestic opposition in Iran throughout 1977 and 1978, U.S. perceptions and U.S. policy were colored by Washington's dependence on the Shah. President Carter continued to extend his support and the administration continued to supply the monarch's with military equipment. In July 1978, $600 million in military equipment, including 31 Phantom airplanes, was approved; on September 6, the sale of tear-gas canisters, small-arms ammunition, and a variety of other riot-control equipment was authorized.[101] Following the September 1978 "Black Friday" massacre in Tehran, the White House announced that President Carter had called the Shah to reiterate his personal support for the monarch and to wish him the best in "resolving these problems and his efforts to introduce reform."[102] The statement led Iranians to assume that just as the initial liberalization was in large measure an outcome of Carter's human rights agenda, the Shah's oppressive tactics were a result of U.S. consent.[103] A suggested meeting with Ibrahim Yazdi, Khomeini's representative in the United States, was rejected in September because of the administration's concern in showing unswerving support for the king.[104] During a visit by Crown Prince Reza at the end of October 1978, Carter announced, "Our friendship and alliance with Iran is one of the important bases on which our entire foreign policy depends. We wish the Shah our best and hope the present disturbances can soon be resolved. We are thankful for this move toward democracy and we know that it is opposed by some who do not like democratic principles."[105]

In early November 1978, the U.S. ambassador to Iran, William Sullivan, was instructed to assure the Shah that he had American support "without reservation," and that the administration would support any "decisive action" he might take.[106] At a November 3 news conference, Secretary of State Vance reiterated the administration's support for the Shah's reforms and his efforts to restore order.[107] National Security Adviser Zbigniew Brzezinski, called the king the same day to assure him of U.S. support for any government he might form.[108] The sale of tear gas was approved in November 1978,[109] and in early December, Brzezinski called Iran's ambassador to the United States to reassure him of U.S. support for the Shah. Several days later, and then again in mid-December, the president made public statements in support of the monarch.[110] Even as late as December 27, 1978, with the monarch on the verge of departure, Washington announced its hopes that the Shah would continue to "play an important role" in forming a new government of "national reconciliation."[111]

By December 29, the administration seemed to have conceded, at least privately, that the Shah might not be able to withstand the national assault. The king was told that he had U.S. support, but that it was essential to terminate the continuing uncertainty. Ambassador Sullivan informed the monarch that the United States would support any of three alternatives: restoration of order with a moderate civilian government, a "firm military government," or a "regency council" that would supervise a military government.[112]

The Shah rejected a military option, fearing that it would lead to greater "bloodshed". A regency council, the monarch noted, would act only in the king's "absence or incapacitation"; should he choose this alternative, the Shah pointed out, he would be expected to leave the country. Although Sullivan had not received detailed instructions about the regency council option from Washington, the ambassador assured the king that should he leave, he would be welcome in the United States.[113]

While behind-the-scenes discussions went on, public support of the Shah, by the administration, continued. A presidential memo, issued on January 3, 1979, supported the Shah's effort to form a civilian government under Bakhtiar, and his plan for a regency council.[114] On January 11, Secretary of State Vance announced that the Shah "has said that he plans to leave Iran on vacation. . . . The Shah remains the constitutional head of state, and we continue to work with him in that capacity."[115]

While the Carter administration was publicly proclaiming its support of the Shah, it also indicated that the United States would not interfere in the internal affairs of Iran.[116] In October and December 1978, and even on January 17, 1979, after the Shah's departure from Iran, President Carter repeated remarks regarding U.S. noninterference. During a December 7, 1978, interview, for example, the president commented, "This [situation in Iran] is something in the hands of the people of Iran. We never had any intention and don't have any intention of trying to intervene in the internal political affairs of Iran. We primarily want an absence of violence and bloodshed, and stability. We personally prefer that the Shah maintain a major role in the government, but that is a decision for the Iranian people to make."[117]

Despite protestations of noninterference, the United States was very much involved in the closing acts of the Iranian drama. General Robert

Huyser, deputy commander of U.S. forces in Europe, was sent to Iran on January 4, 1979, to orchestrate a satisfactory dénouement to the crisis. Huyser's mission had several goals: to assure senior Iranian military officers of the "continuity of American logistical support," to "urge them to maintain the integrity of their forces at the difficult time of the Shah's departure," to "shift allegiance from the Shah to the civilian government of Bakhtiar," to "prepare the Iranian military to suppress massive civilian disorder and . . . ensure that the armed forces could take over and operate the oil fields if workers' strikes persisted."[118] By mid-January, Huyser advised the Iranian chief of staff to meet with Khomeini's representatives, including Dr. Beheshti and Mehdi Bazargan. Such a meeting, he insisted, would be useful in clarifying opposition views and in ensuring that lines of communication remained open.[119]

In addition to the interventions of the Huyser mission, the British Broadcasting Corporation and the foreign media reported on January 21, 1979, that the United States was pursuing efforts to keep Khomeini out of Iran. Mehdi Bazargan also stated that in late January 1979, the U.S. ambassador was involved in talks regarding a referendum on changing the structure of the regime from monarchy to republic.[120]

The United States and Postrevolutionary Iran

Virtually throughout the Shah's reign, U.S. policy ignored opposition leaders and organizations. By isolating itself, the United States not only failed to foster a viable moderate opposition, but also alienated itself from Iran's clerics, the ultimate power brokers in the Iranian revolution. Even as the revolution took on nationwide dimensions in September 1978, the administration refused to meet with Ibrahim Yazdi, Ayatollah Khomeini's representative in the United States.

By December 1978, however, the U.S. Embassy in Tehran had contacted senior clerics, the National Front, and the Freedom Movement about a post-Shah coalition. Ambassador Sullivan's request to the State Department that a U.S. representative meet with Khomeini in Paris to confirm the outlines of the plan, were, however, vetoed.[121] Instead, on January 10, 1979—only a week before the Shah's departure—Washington decided to ask the French to intermediate with Khomeini to request that he give the Bakhtiar government an opportunity to reestablish order.[122] Unable to persuade the French to act on its behalf, Washington authorized a U.S. Embassy official in Paris to meet with Khomeini's representative, Ibrahim Yazdi.[123]

The two men met several times between January 15 (a day before the Shah went into exile) and January 27. The United States attempted to convince Khomeini not to undermine Bakhtiar and that he should instead encourage contacts that had begun between representatives of the military and religious forces in Tehran. Yazdi, on the other hand, expressed vehement criticism of the Bakhtiar government and urged the United States to stop giving it its backing.[124]

Once Khomeini's assumption of power became a *fait accompli* in Iran, the United States did make an effort to reconcile itself to the Khomeini-led regime. Offers were made to sell Iran oil products, wheat, rice, and spare parts for military equipment.[125] U.S. Ambassador Sullivan was, for the first time, instructed to call on the new prime minister, Mehdi Bazargan. Sullivan assured the prime minister, "and through him Khomeini, that the United States accepted the revolution and did not intend to intervene in Iran's internal affairs." He acknowledged that the United States was willing to continue selling arms to the new government, but protested the executions and violations of human rights that had occurred.[126] On February 27, 1979, President Carter claimed that "the Khomeini government has made it clear ever since it came into power, through our direct negotiations with Prime Minister Bazargan and our ambassador and through their emissaries who have even today talked to Secretary Vance, that they desire a close working and friendly relationship with the United States."[127]

In April and May 1979, the U.S. chargé d'affaires in Iran, Charles Naas, began discussions about the first proposed meeting between U.S. government officials and Ayatollah Khomeini. The proposal was approved by Washington and by Prime Minister Bazargan. A U.S. Senate resolution condemning revolution-related executions, however, was passed in May. The ill-feeling it produced in Iran destroyed hopes for the meeting with Khomeini and led Iran to withdraw its approval of Walter Cutler, the newly designated U.S. ambassador. Washington refused to accept the decision on the ambassador and announced that it would continue diplomatic relations on the level of chargé d'affaires.[128]

Although immediately after the revolution Iran's new government cancelled military contracts signed by the Shah, plans to launch an anti-Kurd offensive prompted renewed interest in obtaining weapons. The issue of arms sales was discussed with U.S. representatives in the course of several meetings between July and October 20, 1979. By August 1979, the United States had agreed to resume limited supply of spare parts and was discussing possibilities for new contracts in the amount of $5 or $6 million.[129] Throughout the meetings, Iranian officials complained about

U.S. unwillingness to fully accept the Iranian revolution. In early October, for example, Foreign Minister Ibrahim Yazdi insisted that the United States take "concrete steps" towards showing such acceptance. While Secretary of State Vance protested that public pronouncements by the administration demonstrated such recognition, Yazdi demanded that the United States honor military contracts signed by the Shah, and that it return Iranian "criminals" who found shelter in the United States after the revolution.[130] As a consequence of the November 1979 U.S. embassy takeover, tensions between the United States and Iran mounted and meetings between officials of the two countries were permanently stalled.

U.S. reaction following the takeover came in the form of sanctions, which did not serve to improve relations. Iranian assets in the United States were blocked and the Iranian government taken to the World Court. The United States demanded that the United Nations impose sanctions, and U.S.–Iran transactions were limited. The failed U.S. rescue mission in April 1980 intensified Iranian suspicions about a U.S. conspiracy against Iran. Iran's 1982 successes in the Iran–Iraq war led to fears in Washington that a victorious Iran would threaten Saudi Arabia. In reaction, U.S. policy tilted toward Iraq. Iraq was deleted from a State Department list identifying governments involved in international terrorism and, in late 1983, played host to a high-level delegation from the United States. Commodity credits worth approximately $2 billion were also granted to Baghdad, and intelligence, provided by U.S. AWACS, was delivered to Iraq's military beginning in 1984. In November 1984, U.S.–Iraq diplomatic relations were restored.[131]

U.S. actions vis-à-vis Iran contributed to deteriorating relations. By neglecting its options, however, Washington further decreased the likelihood that U.S.–Iranian relations would improve. Throughout the early postrevolutionary period, policymakers persisted in repeating errors made in the past. Thus, after the revolution, the United States focused its attention on the same moderates with whom it had had contacts before the revolution. As of September 1979, eight months after the Shah's fall, direct contact with Khomeini had not been established; the United States thereby assured its continued isolation from the central players in the new Iran.

Bruce Laingen, the chargé d'affaires in Tehran, cabled Washington in August 1979 that the United States needed to demonstrate its support for the new government. "Even the moderate Iranian government" he wrote, found "in the virtual absence on our part of any public statements" of support for the revolution "a reflection of less than full endorsement."[132] Assistant Secretary of State Harold Saunders warned in a September 1979 memorandum:

We have had no direct contact with the man who remains the strongest political leader in Iran. His hostility towards us is unlikely to abate significantly, although there have been fewer venomous statements against us recently. Clearly, a first meeting could be a bruising affair.

A meeting with Khomeini will signal our definite acceptance of the revolution and could ease somewhat his suspicions of us. . . .

. . . The symbolism of a call on Khomeini would not attach to visits to other religious leaders, but they will not see us until we have seen him. We badly need contacts with Taleghani, Shariatmadari, and other moderate clerics. We want to reassure them of our acceptance of the revolution, as their influence may rise in the months ahead.[133]

The policies pursued and the possibilities neglected by the United States in relation to postrevolutionary Iran were not the sole determinants of the manner in which U.S.–Iranian relations would proceed. Certainly the intense distrust and hostility toward the United States exhibited by Ayatollah Khomeini and the Iranian radicals could not be easily ameliorated. Nonetheless, a different U.S. policy before the fall of the Shah might have prevented the situation from deteriorating to a point where only revolution would be acceptable; actions the United States could have taken, but did not pursue, after the formation of the Islamic Republic might have eased suspicions and antagonisms.

The United States in Iran: Problems and Policies

In terms of human life, the cost to Iran of fourteen months of revolution was ten to twelve thousand dead and forty-five thousand to fifty thousand wounded.[134] For the United States, the revolution meant the estrangement of a political ally and the loss of an economic, military, and strategic asset.

As would be the case in Nicaragua and the Philippines, the United States was caught unprepared for revolution in Iran. Having personified the U.S. national interest in the monarch, Washington neglected to objectively analyze conditions in Iran and seek alternative strategies to serve its interests. Although likely avoidable, Iran's revolution became virtually inevitable as repression was relaxed in an atmosphere charged with widespread social, economic, and political discontent. Once caught up in the revolution, the policies pursued by the Carter administration lagged behind events: the United States found itself unable to shape the course of developments in a country it had virtually helped form in the three decades past.

Following the Shah's departure from Iran, President Carter noted, "The revolution in Iran is a product of deep social, political, religious, and economic factors growing out of the history of Iran itself. Those who argue that the United States should or could intervene directly to thwart these events are wrong about the realities of Iran."[135] Days earlier the president remarked, "Even if we had been able to anticipate events that were going to take place in Iran or other countries, obviously our ability to determine those events is very limited. The Shah, his advisers, great military capabilities, police, and others, couldn't completely prevent rioting and disturbances in Iran."[136] He later added, "we cannot freeze the status quo in a country when it's very friendly to us."[137]

Carter's analysis may not have completely represented the dimensions of the problem in terms of the role the United States had played, or might have played, in developments in Iran. Although it did not, indeed could not, freeze the status quo, Washington had since the 1950s made every effort to keep the Shah in power. In this case, as would also be the case in Nicaragua, a foreign policy founded on one particular political figure proved a critical error for the United States.

Implementation of genuine political reform up until 1977 might well have preempted the events of 1978–1979, and could have saved the United States from the precarious position in which it found itself after the revolution.[138] An exclusive concern with the Shah, however, made it all but certain that a human rights policy for Iran would be virtually nonexistent. Thus, even during those periods when liberalization was encouraged by the United States (i.e., the early 1960s and late 1970s), pressure for reform was not consistently applied and liberalization not consistently supported. Although the Kennedy administration encouraged reform in the early 1960s, once public opposition to the Shah erupted, both Kennedy and Johnson fully supported attempts to quell public manifestations of discontent. The liberalization of 1976 (triggered only in part by Carter's forthcoming inauguration), conceded only limited reforms. When nationwide protest followed, threatening the Shah's position, the Carter administration condoned, indeed encouraged, the monarch's use of all necessary measures to suppress the emerging rebellion.[139]

Concern for the U.S. national interest, which prompted an evident lack of enthusiasm for reform, was also manifested in Washington's behavior toward the opposition in Iran. Throughout the Shah's reign, opportunities existed for the United States to support the development of a moderate secular and religious opposition, without significantly jeopardizing American interests. The opposition in Iran had, since the early 1960s, directed its demands toward enforcing a constitutional monarchy based on the 1906 constitution. Indeed, moderate forces involved in the 1978–1979 revolution sought such a political solution until as late as November 1978; destruction of the monarchy was neither an initial demand nor an inevitable outcome of the situation. Furthermore, a cutoff of relations with the

United States was not envisioned. Members of the moderate opposition met often with U.S. representatives during the latter months of 1978 to consider means of resolving Iran's growing unrest. During the first months following the revolution, when moderates held senior government posts, U.S.–Iran relations remained relatively cordial: American officials, including those from the CIA, met with high-level government officials; talks aimed at renewing the U.S.–Iran arms relationship were begun; and, a resurgence in the American presence was tolerated. By supporting the Shah's attempts to co-opt or suppress his opposition, however, Washington helped create a political vacuum that would ultimately be filled by political elements who would pursue policies antithetical to U.S. interests.

Ignoring the Warnings in Washington—Towing the Line in Tehran

Evidence that Iran might erupt had not been in short supply throughout the decades. The preeminence of the U.S. national interest, however, blinded policymakers to problems in Iran and to the role the United States was playing in their exacerbation. Washington ignored political repression and civil rights abuse, and discounted warnings of growing resentment against the American presence in Iran; it did not even heed the advice of State Department analysts who urged that moderate opponents to the Shah be sought out and supported. The U.S. State Department reported in February 1961:

> The elections were largely rigged, and diverse opposition political forces have not been able to force their cancellation, despite several minor riots in Tehran and a few disturbances in other parts of the nation. The possibility . . . of a combination of circumstances in the future leading a combination of opposition political elements and disaffected members of the security forces toward an attempt to overthrow the regime cannot be discounted, and will probably increase over the long run if present political trends continue.
>
> . . . There is a growing tendency, particularly among the younger and more radical elements, to identify the United States with the Shah and with the security forces and to hold the United States responsible for the Shah's misdeeds and mistakes. . . .
>
> . . . [Economic] progress has . . . taken place without participation in the government by the main opposition groups . . . The force and power of the urban semi-Westernized elements continue to grow at the expense of other elements of society. Unless and until the Shah can come to terms with them and bring them, or part of them, into the process of policy making, he faces a remorseless and slowly increasing pressure, which will become sharper and more dangerous to the West as moderate leadership elements are displaced by the radicals.

. . . Two other factors of the internal political situation often mentioned as important are corruption and the suppression of civil liberties. . . .

We should, of course, continue to be on the alert for the rise of competent and creative alternative leadership, in or out of the military, which might allow a reconsideration of our alternative.[140]

In March 1961, the State Department warned,

There is no discernible competent leadership in the urban middle class at present. Should its incompetent leadership of today be catapulted into power, it is likely that . . . confused demagoguery would ensue. . . .

. . . Elements of U.S. policy which are presently open and which would serve to protect U.S. interests against the danger represented by the rise of the urban middle class in Iran are as follows:

. . . Inducing the Shah to turn his political talents and his attention . . . to the broad task of winning the confidence of the urban middle class by providing them with a sense of participation [in] and identification with, his regime. . . .

. . . Watching political developments carefully with a view to the identification and analysis of effective and responsible alternative political leaders who might, as a last resort, be available to replace the Shah should he fall completely as a political leader.[141]

Warnings of impending trouble came later too. A 1975 National Intelligence Estimate reviewed the status of several opposition groups in Iran and "warned of serious internal opposition."[142] As late as November 9, 1978, a month before the Shah's fall, U.S. Ambassador Sullivan notified Washington that the Shah's authority "had shrunk considerably, to the point where his support among the general population had become almost invisible."[143]

As would be the case in Nicaragua and the Philippines, a misguided U.S. foreign policy was in some measure formed by optimistic but imprecise embassy and intelligence reports that outweighed all warnings and supported the views Washington insisted upon holding. Pressures to write such slanted analyses led an Iran-based diplomat to complain in 1969, "Reporting officers are under pressure from their superiors (and more subtle pressure from Washington) to make their reports conform to the post's previous reporting, and to the views of senior officials. The result is to encourage adherence to the 'conventional wisdom' or the 'establishment' point of view."[144] Thus, for example, at the end of October 1978, even as the Shah's regime was collapsing, Ambassador Sullivan informed Washington that "our destiny is to work with the Shah."[145] Even in

January 1979, when the Shah's departure was imminent and Iran's military was suffering defections, General Huyser continued to transmit assurances that Iran's military forces maintained their coherence and strength.[146]

U.S. embassy personnel in Iran, as well as in Nicaragua and the Philippines, also often couched their assessments in terms acceptable to the ruler and his elite. In Iran, concern that any associations with the opposition would offend the monarch led U.S. embassy personnel to refrain from making necessary contacts.[147] A 1976 State Department report indicated, "The embassy . . . has difficulty in developing information about dissidence . . . because of Iranian sensitivities and the Government of Iran's disapproval of foreign contacts with these groups."[148] On January 17, 1979, after the Shah left Iran, Harold Saunders, assistant secretary of state for Near Eastern and South Asian affairs, testified,

> As is often the case with governments where authority is highly centralized and where important economic and strategic interests are at stake, our ability to maintain contact with all elements of the society and press effectively and consistently for constructive change has been limited.[149]

U.S. intelligence agencies also contributed to the distortion of the analyses by being lax in gathering information.[150] They concentrated on monitoring Soviet activity and focused rather narrowly on leftist movements such as the Fedayeen Khalq and the Mujhadeen Khalq. SAVAK, and the biased intelligence it provided, served as a central information source for the CIA.[151] The CIA could thus assert in August 1977 that the Shah "will be an active participant in Iran's life well into the 1980s," and that "no radical change in Iran's political behavior in the near future" is expected.[152] Even as Iran was in the midst of revolt in August 1978, the CIA reported that "Iran is not in a revolutionary or even 'prerevolutionary' situation." The Defense Intelligence Agency concluded in late September 1978 that the "Shah is expected to remain actively in power over the next ten years."[153]

Having made little effort to seek information about the opposition prior to the Shah's fall, U.S. policy-making was hampered by a lack of information after the revolution. On July 20, 1979, State Department desk officer Henry Precht complained to the U.S. chargé d'affaires in Tehran, Bruce Laingen, that: "We simply do not have the bios, inventory of political groups or current picture of daily life as it evolves at various levels in Iran. Ignorance here of Iran's events is massive. The U.S. press does not do a good job but in the absence of embassy reporting, we have to rely on inexperienced newsmen."[154]

In summary, the United States might have pursued a more constructive foreign policy—one which would have addressed both the issues of human rights and the U.S. interest in Iran—if it had supported institutional political reform and the development of a moderate political opposition. Washington had an opportunity to extricate itself from impending disaster by mediating a compromise between the Shah and the moderate opposition even as late as mid-1978. Failure to protect the long-term U.S. national interest in Iran seems, therefore, more a product of self-willed ignorance than the inevitable outcome of historical evolution.

The Lessons of Neoconservatism Examined

Contrary to neoconservative complaints, American policy in Iran adhered closely to the prescriptions proffered by this school. Even under a Carter administration inclined toward a neorealist perspective, the policies pursued between 1977 and 1979 were, in execution, almost paradigmatic examples of neoconservative strategy. Despite initial signals regarding U.S. concerns about human rights, the Carter administration supported the Shah in public statements, as well as in military and economic relations. Even when Iran was in the midst of revolution, Washington continued to pronounce its faith in the Shah and to approve shipments of security and military supplies. General Huyser was sent to Iran to assure its military of U.S. support and to obtain its allegiance to the Shah and his appointed prime minister. Washington even conveyed messages to Ayatollah Khomeini, asking that he give the Bakhtiar government a chance to resolve the crisis and requesting that Khomeini not return to Iran.

Revolution nonetheless swept Iran: the American-supported Shah was dethroned, and the Iranian military, which the United States had spent decades developing and training, collapsed. U.S. support of Iran's military forces was intended as a safeguard; its mission was to preserve the Shah and thereby ensure that the U.S. interest in Iran was protected. When the time for action came, however, the grand designs of U.S. policy dissolved with the collapsing Iranian military. Appeals to the religious sentiments of soldiers led to desertions and refusals to shoot. Furthermore, "the fragmented military command structure that the Shah had developed over the years for his own self defense" made it improbable that a coherent effort to confront the revolution would be mounted.[155]

Other than dispatching the U.S. military to protect the Shah's regime and prop up his armed forces, Washington was left with few options. George Ball, who had been asked by the administration to carry out an independent study, wrote:

The reason the Shah did not stand and fight was that his whole country was solidly against him and his army was beginning to disintegrate under pressure of competing loyalties. . . . It is fatuous to think that we could have kept a hated absolute monarch in power by encouraging the progressive use of military force. This was, after all, an internal revolt. What would Mr. Kissinger have done? Sent the Sixth Fleet steaming up the Gulf?[156]

National Security Council staff member Gary Sick noted that intervention by the U.S. military, the only option that seemed to remain, would indeed have spelled disaster for the United States. He wrote,

Underlying all considerations of a military takeover was the question of U.S. direct intervention. Once the United States committed itself to a military solution, there was no turning back. The Shah and the generals would expect full U.S. support if things went wrong . . . or if it turned into a civil war. It was a no-win situation. . . . Even if the military succeeded in restoring control, the United States would have mortgaged any future relationship with Iran by associating itself with what almost certainly would have been extensive bloodletting and a direct confrontation with Islam. . . . [157]

Despite its determination to save the Shah, U.S. policy would prove impotent when, at the last moment, it tried to resolve problems that had festered for decades. Warren Christopher later analyzed the situation, and warned:

The Iranian experience should encourage a sense of realism in our dealings with developing countries. For their internal politics are shaped almost wholly by internal forces, and very little by external pressures. A wise nation, however powerful, understands the peril it invites in confronting the will of another people. Outside powers have an effect, if any, only at the margins.[158]

Washington's ability to shape events was constrained not only by internal conditions in Iran, but also by regional and international dynamics. The Soviet Union issued a warning to the United States on November 19, 1978, that, "It must be clear that any interference, especially military interference in the affairs of Iran—a state which directly borders on the Soviet Union—would be regarded as a matter affecting security interests. . . . The events taking place in that country constitute purely internal affairs, and the questions involved in them should be decided by the Iranians themselves."[159]

Secretary of State Vance responded the next day. His statement conceded the Soviet interest in Iran, and explained,

> The United States will continue to support the Shah in his efforts to restore domestic tranquility . . . the United States does not intend to interfere in the affairs of any other country. Reports to the contrary are totally without foundation. We note the Soviet Union has said it will not interfere in the affairs of Iran and will respect its territorial integrity, sovereignty, and independence.[160]

The constraints imposed by domestic conditions in Iran, and the demands of regional and international politics, thus render questionable the neoconservative assumption that American power can manipulate historical processes.

The neoconservative proposition that human rights abroad are protected by the international pursuit of U.S. interests also seems rather spurious in this case. U.S. policies had centered on preserving the stability of the Shah, thereby ensuring U.S. interests. The Shah's security forces were trained and armed in order to maintain stability of the regime, but were often used to commit acts of repression. Few attempts to encourage democracy were made, and where they were, the focus on liberalization was based on interests other than human rights. Reforms in Iran during the early 1960s were supported by the United States not directly because of human rights concerns, but because it was believed that reform would inhibit the spread of pro-communist sympathies. As soon as liberalization was seen to be a threat to the Shah's throne, both in the early 1960s and from 1977 to 1979, the United States came to the defense of the Shah and his repressive responses.

Neoconservative warnings that pressure for reform would lead to unknown consequences, including revolution and leftist takeovers, present a mixed picture. In the 1960s and late 1970s, reform in Iran led to nationwide outbursts of discontent. In the 1960s, however, these protests focused on economic grievances and on policies that attempted to Westernize Iranian society—not on the overthrow of the Shah. Even among those who protested political conditions, demands were centered not on eliminating the monarchy, but on opening channels for political participation within the framework of the 1906 constitution. The repression that followed destroyed the possibilities for change at a time when reform, rather than revolution, represented an acceptable solution to the majority of Iran's population.

Demands made following the liberalization of mid-1976 initially centered on religious issues, economic grievances, and political reform related to the 1906 constitution. The Shah's October 1978 attempt to placate the protestors by forming a coalition government with moderates came too late. Revolution was thus not inevitable: it erupted not directly as a result of liberalization, but because reform was delayed until frustration and demands had intensified to a point where concessions no longer represented a sufficient condition for conciliation. Zbigniew Brzezinski confirmed this perception in his memoirs. "In my view," he wrote, "a policy of conciliation and concessions might have worked, had it been adopted two or three years earlier, before the crisis reached a politically acute stage."[161]

Dire warnings that revolution will lead to a leftist, likely communist, regime were in this case unfounded. Islamic Iran's foreign policy orientation, although anti-American, was also anticommunist. While the United States lost much as a result of the revolution, the Soviet Union did not claim a new partner. Indeed, the American-supported Shah had himself attempted to manipulate the United States by raising the specter of an Iranian-Soviet friendship. In 1962, the Shah prohibited basing rights for foreign missiles in Iran, and in the years that followed seemed to cultivate warm relations with the Eastern bloc. The Shah visited the Soviet Union in 1965 and 1968; in 1966, he made trips to Romania, Yugoslavia, Bulgaria, Hungary, and Poland. Leaders of all these countries, except Hungary, came to Iran in 1966, as did Soviet Premier Aleksei Kosygin in 1968.[162]

In sum, the neoconservative thesis that protection of right-wing, pro-American, authoritarian regimes would assure short-term and long-term U.S. interests is only partly established. While the Shah remained in power, the U.S. national interest was, indeed, well served in Iran. The very policies that guaranteed those interests, however, led to their long-term destruction. The assumptions and prescriptions of the neoconservative school, therefore, as applied to the case of Iran, appear not to constitute a constructive foreign policy agenda for the United States.

The Neorealist Perspective Reviewed

The neorealist formula proposes that liberalization of right-wing regimes be encouraged and relations with opposition groups be cultivated through a policy of U.S. dissociation from authoritarian rulers. A number of problems arise from this prescription, as the case of Iran has suggested and the cases of Nicaragua and the Philippines will confirm.

The central premise of the neorealist prescription focuses on the issue of human rights as an impelling force in revolution. As it relates to Iran, the assumption has only partial validity. Scholars have variously explained the causes of Iran's revolution as an outcome of a disintegrating social system, a result of a disjunction between economic growth and limited political participation, or as a reaction to the frustrations engendered by unfulfilled economic expectations.[163] The issue of human rights, particularly in the form of political participation, was undeniably a theme in Iran's revolution; the initial impetus for rebellion, however, derived from social and economic grievances. A State Department evaluation reported that between 1976 and 1978,

> Most prominent among the causes of dissatisfaction were popular resentment of what was seen as widespread corruption, harsh repression, some ineptitude in high places, disregard for the deep religious feelings of the population, imbalances between revenues and expenses, shortcomings in planning and carrying out ambitious projects, rising unemployment in the cities as the construction boom began to subside, insufficient job opportunities for ever-larger numbers of graduating students, inequitable distribution of the benefits of development, sacrifice of civilian programs for military procurement, and a high rate of inflation that outstripped wage increases and frustrated expectations for a steadily rising standard of living. These grievances and the absence of political outlets for affecting government policy led moderate secular opposition leaders to make common cause with significant elements of the Muslim clergy.[164]

The secondary position of human rights on the opposition's agenda perhaps becomes more evident when viewed in terms of the failure of neorealist logic as applied to the policy of dissociation. This strategy is perceived by neorealists as a cornerstone of U.S. human rights policy; it is intended to ingratiate the United States in the eyes of opposition leaders who, neorealists assume, are focused on human rights issues. By dissociating itself from a dictator, Washington is expected to shape a positive image of the United States among opposition groups.

Contrary to the neorealist prescription, the United States did not make an effort to encourage reform in Iran or to separate itself from the embattled Shah. Indeed, it continued to give him public and private support, and urged that he defuse the rebellion with actions that might be considered contrary to the precepts of human rights. Iran's moderates were disappointed with this policy. Shapur Bakhtiar, for example, noted that the opposition had "derived hope from his [Carter's] electoral campaign when he said he would have problems with dictatorial regimes like South Korea. When he talked of human rights, we were with him. Unfortunately Carter could not make decisions."[165] An opposition leader told a reporter in July 1978, "the average Iranian cannot forget the fact that the dictatorship responsible for most—if not all—of his miseries was put on the throne by the United States in 1953''[166] Nonetheless, despite their disappointment with U.S. human rights policy, moderates consulted with U.S. government officials in the months before the Shah's fall about resolving Iran's turmoil. When they initially ran the postrevolutionary government, the moderates proved amenable to continuing friendly U.S.–Iran relations. Indeed, even the condemnations of the anti-American Ayatollah Khomeini focused primarily on the detrimental effects of U.S. influence on Iranian society, rather than on Washington's links to the human rights abuses of the Shah.

Neorealist guidelines also neglect the circumstances under which liberalization will occur. Without the existence of viable moderate parties and organizations that could take advantage of political reform, endorsement of liberalization may prove self-defeating to U.S. interests. The case of Iran amply demonstrates this dilemma. Washington made no objections to the suppression or co-optation of moderate opposition elements. When revolution came, therefore, groups that might have preserved a part of the old order (by reintroducing a constitutional monarchy), and which would have been most inclined to help preserve U.S. interests, proved unprepared to play a leading role in the new environment.

The impact of nonaligned foreign policy orientations on U.S. interests is also a focus of neorealist analysis. Nonalignment, for this school, is generally viewed as an acceptable outcome. In the case of postrevolutionary Iran, the foreign policy goals of the new elite proved less a case of maintaining neutral or friendly equidistance between the superpowers than of pursuing policies of hostility toward both. Nonetheless, the strident anti-American rhetoric of Ayatollah Khomeini and his supporters seemed to become somewhat tempered as the reality of a successful revolution neared. On January 1, 1979, Khomeini remarked, "It would be a mistake for the American government to fear the Shah's departure." A week later he explained, "If the United States behaves correctly, does not interfere in our affairs and withdraws the advisors who were intervening in our country, we will respect it in return."[167] On January 27, Khomeini warned that if the United States supported Prime Minister Shapur Bakhtiar, or if the army tried to stop the Ayatollah from returning, "it would be harmful to American interests in Iran." Khomeini gave assurances, however, that if he did not encounter opposition, he would "quiet things down." "Concerns about his attitude toward relations with the United States," he assured, "would be resolved when we saw the provisional government . . . name[d] to guide Iran to an Islamic republic."[168] Clark Clifford, who maintained contacts with National Front politicians associated with Khomeini, indicated that Khomeini intended to "set up a government drawn from moderate secular politicians with Islamic clergy remaining in the background as the guiding political and spiritual force of the revolution."[169]

A more moderate foreign policy thus might have guided postrevolutionary Iran. Indeed, although two and one-half years after the revolution, radical elements and a vehement anti-Americanism prevailed, Khomeini's first two choices for the leadership of the new government were Prime Minister Mehdi Bazargan and President Abolhasan Bani Sadr—both considered moderate nationalists. Many members of the first cabinet and provisional council represented moderate views, and Iran maintained friendly relations with the United States until the takeover of the American embassy in November 1979.

Even after radical religious elements had come to dominate the government, Iran was not averse to pursuing associations with the United States when pragmatic considerations demanded. Thus, for example, in the interest of acquiring needed arms and spare parts for its war with Iraq, Iran showed itself amenable to U.S. overtures that began in 1985. In 1991, after more than a decade of hostility toward the United States, Iran's efforts to revitalize its economy led to prospects for friendlier relations between the two states. Iran's foreign minister Velayati proposed in May 1991 that "from a global perspective, a new order is gradually superseding in which economic considerations overshadow political priorities." President Rafsanjani noted that "the concluding years of the twentieth century are marked by world events that have replaced the previous bipolar system by a new order. . . . If this order is to persist, cooperation should replace confrontation."[170] Indeed, by 1991, Iran imported $527 million in American goods; "nearly a nine-fold increase" over the two years previous.[171] In September 1991, Mohammed Javad Larijavi, a senior adviser to Iran's president, suggested that once the hostages were released in Lebanon, and Iranian assets frozen by the United States released, agreements could be negotiated on a number of "converging interests." Reestablishing normal ties with the United States, he said, was "theoretically not impossible."[172]

Anti-Americanism was not the exclusive domain of Iran's revolutionary leaders. The Shah, too, had fostered anti-U.S. sentiment in the mid-1960s and late 1970s as a means of deflecting criticism from himself. He encouraged condemnation of U.S. involvement in Vietnam and criticism of American colonialism.[173] In May 1976, a State Department report warned, "In recent months the Shah has permitted unusually severe criticisms of the United States in Iranian media. He has lent his own name to sweeping charges against the United States, raising public questions about the bases of the alliance and U.S. reliability."[174]

It becomes evident, that as is the case with the neoconservatives, neo-realist prescriptions for a human rights policy are not completely confirmed by the case of Iran. Reforms that do not sufficiently address popular demands may lead to unexpected and unwanted outcomes. Human rights concerns were not the central impetus for revolution, and dissociation was not as important a policy tool as the neorealists would claim. Washington did not dissociate itself from the Shah and, indeed, publicly exhibited its support for his regime. Nonetheless, the disappointed moderates did not break their associations with the United States once they assumed power in the new government.

The case of Iran seems to dispute the premises and prescriptions of both the neoconservative and neorealist schools. The United States was unable to influence the course of events while forces of revolution prevailed, and it could not have preserved its own interest by supporting reforms in late 1978.

4   Nicaragua: Useful Policies
Rendered Impotent

Of the three cases in this study, it is in the case of Anastasio Somoza Debayle's Nicaragua that U.S. foreign policy most closely conformed to the neorealist formula for maintaining and pursuing the national interest. Washington made its most concerted efforts to influence human rights and political reform, particularly during the Carter years, by extending and withholding economic and military assistance, by encouraging and participating in OAS-mediated negotiations between Somoza and opposition forces, and by pursuing subsequent compromise solutions until the final days of the Somoza regime. When the revolutionary junta took power, American diplomatic recognition and economic assistance was immediately extended. Ironically, however, it is in Nicaragua that a Marxist-oriented, anti-American regime ultimately assumed the responsibilities of government.

Nicaragua under the Somozas

Political and Civil Rights

Nicaragua under the Somozas was a country oppressed by repression and economic disparity. Human rights were trampled, and the political opposition either quashed or co-opted.

Rigged elections put Anastasio Somoza Garcia into the presidency in 1936; his sons, Luis and Anastasio Somoza Debayle, followed him into that post.[1] Except for short interludes, during which unrest forced the brothers to give up title to the presidency, the Somoza political dynasty remained intact.[2] During these interludes, too, however, the Somozas retained power by controlling the National Guard and by placing puppets in the presidency.

Politics in Nicaragua was directed to suit the aspirations of the So-moza family. If the constitution prevented the Somozas from running for the presidency, the constitution was revised. Revisions of convenience were instituted in 1945 and 1950 under Anastasio Somoza Garcia, and in 1971 and 1974 under his son Anastasio Somoza Debayle. Membership in the Somoza-controlled Nationalist Liberal Party (PLN) was compulsory for government workers and employees of Somoza-owned enterprises.[3] The party, along with the Nicaraguan Congress and judiciary, served as the personal tools of the dictators.[4]

Somoza Garcia's regime was corrupt and not much concerned with poverty or political and civil rights. The presidency of his son, Luis So-moza, coincided with the U.S. Alliance for Progress program of the early 1960s. The possibilities engendered by the program, and Luis Somoza's personal style, contributed to the development of projects in public hous-ing, education, social security, and agrarian reform. Luis Somoza encour-aged political participation, at least within his party, and in 1959 amended the constitution to prevent family members from running for the presi-dency in 1963.[5] From the time Luis Somoza's presidential term legally concluded in 1963, until his death in 1967, "he ruled through puppet pres-idents Rene Schick Gutierrez and Lorenzo Guerrero." In 1967, Luis's younger brother, Anastasio Somoza Debayle, had himself "elected" as president in fraudulent elections.[6] He effectively remained the power in Nicaragua until 1979.

Civil liberties were restricted in varying degrees throughout the So-moza regime, with restrictions at their most severe during periods of mar-tial law. States of siege were imposed in Nicaragua during World War II; in 1960, following violent protests against the regime of Luis Somoza; in 1972, after a devastating earthquake hit Managua; in 1974, after an FSLN (Frente Sandinista de Liberacion Nacional) commando raid; and again in 1978, after the Sandinistas attacked the National Palace and civil uprisings erupted in several cities. In Managua, in 1948, for example, it was re-ported that "every street corner was under observation and the movements of all important people were charted. Telephone calls were monitored, pri-vate mail was opened . . . the local press was under strict censorship," and "men disappeared from the streets."[7]

During states of siege, freedom of the press was suspended com-pletely. At other times, the liberties extended to the fourth estate varied in relation to the political climate. Although information critical of the re-gime was reported when martial law was not in force, journalists and other media employees were periodically subjected to police searches, arbitrary arrest, imprisonment, and beatings. Any rights enjoyed by the press came as a result of U.S. involvement in Nicaragua and the Somozas' willingness to pay "lip service" to civil liberties such as freedom of the press.[8]

The rights of workers were also abused. "The right to strike, while formally enshrined in law, was so severely restricted that most . . . strikes that took place in the 1960s and 1970s were declared illegal. Collective bargaining was made all but impossible" and employers were permitted "to fire, without explanation, any two leaders of the striking union."[9] Lower- and middle-class union leaders and members were subject to detention, torture, or disappearance, particularly from 1974 through 1978.[10]

Nicaragua's National Guard served as the Somozas' instrument for repression and spying. It was a corrupt institution: promotions and assignments depended on loyalty to the director rather than on competence, and key positions were filled by members of the Somoza family. The Guard maintained wide-ranging responsibilities which created opportunities for extortion, bribery, and kickbacks. It operated and controlled all police functions, the national radio, the telegraph network, postal and immigration services, the railway system, customs and tax collection, and the National Health Service; it controlled gambling, prostitution, and smuggling.[11]

In the countryside, Guardsmen stole peasant lands through force and fraud.[12] In the 1960s and 1970s, as the FSLN found support among peasants in the countryside, the Guard attempted to destroy that support by directing reprisals against campesinos. Property and belongings were confiscated without compensation, and rural populations were relocated in an effort to disperse guerrilla supporters.

So corrupt and unprofessional had the National Guard become, that when Managua was hit by a devastating earthquake in December 1972, most Guard members abandoned their posts to look after their families. Some Guard officers deserted during the initial emergency period; when international relief aid supplies were delivered, Guardsmen stole the material and sold it for personal profit. Following a December 1974 FSLN attack, the Guard was given a free hand in dealing with the opposition. Repression and violence escalated as anti-Somoza protest and insurrection increased.[13] The corruption that permeated the Guard, and the many years it served as the Somozas' agent of repression, rendered it among the least popular of Nicaragua's institutions.

Economic Conditions

In 1947, a visitor to Nicaragua reported that "the Nicaraguan people were so poor and ill-fed that, to keep them in place, all it took were some two thousand guardsmen armed with sharp bayonets."[14]

As an export-oriented economy based primarily on agricultural crops, particularly cotton and coffee, Nicaragua was subject to cyclical economic crises as world market prices rose and fell. During the 1960s and part of the 1970s, however, Nicaragua experienced economic growth: it participated in the Central American Common Market and the Alliance for Progress, and had negotiated ever-larger loans from the World Bank and the Inter-American Bank. Industrial production increased, and the average annual economic growth rate stood at 7.2 percent between 1960 and 1970. From 1970 to 1978, Nicaragua's annual growth rate was 5.8 percent, "among the fastest in the world." Employment opportunities were expanded primarily within the bureaucracy, and the growing economy provided the privileged with more opportunities for enrichment. A new middle class had emerged; by 1978, the average annual income had increased fourfold to $840. The middle class, which had benefited from this expansion, remained relatively quiescent during much of the Somoza reign.[15]

National prosperity, however, had little impact on the impoverished majority. Despite improved economic indicators, disparities remained between the rich and the poor, the rural and urban, and between the Somoza family and the rest of Nicaragua. Nicaragua's population had doubled within twenty years, reaching 2.2 million by the mid-1970s; half of the nation's population lived on annual incomes of between $200 and $300. Capital-intensive production had increased the GNP (gross national product), but did not create more jobs. In rural areas, where 60 percent of Nicaragua's population lived, peasants suffered economic dislocation as a result of expanded cotton and coffee production. By the 1970s, 3.4 percent of all farmland was owned by 50 percent of Nicaragua's farmers; in contrast, 1.4 percent of the country's wealthiest farmers held 41.2 percent of the rural land. The agricultural labor force fell from 62 percent of the total work force in 1960, to 44 percent in 1977.[16] Agricultural unemployment stood at 16 percent in 1977 and at 32 percent in 1979. Average annual income per capita for the rural population in the mid-1970s was under $35.[17]

The earthquake of December 1972 altered economic conditions and created discontent among Nicaragua's elite, its middle class, and its laborers. Inflation rose rapidly, real wages declined, unemployment increased, and economic cycles of growth and decline became more frequent. Nicaragua's population was forced to contribute to the reconstruction effort by working longer hours (increased from forty-eight to sixty hours per week), and public employees were required to contribute one month's salary per year. Demands for higher wages and protests against austerity measures were met with indifference. By 1975, the unemployment rate for the industrial/manufacturing sector stood at 9.7 percent. The salaried middle sector and university students who had expected to be absorbed into the job market felt the effects of the declining economy.[18]

Further exacerbating the discontent was the vast degree of corruption in which the Somoza regime was involved. Somoza interests ran monopolies and illegal business operations; they demanded bribes in exchange for licenses, contracts, and concessions, and took cuts from international development loans and contracts. Anastasio Somoza Debayle and his associates misappropriated earthquake relief funds while the rest of the population was asked to pay new emergency taxes. The United States, for example, provided Nicaragua with $32 million for earthquake relief; Nicaragua's treasury recorded American assistance at only $16.2 million. Somoza funneled foreign aid through his companies and bought properties in areas where he planned reconstruction. By the time the Sandinistas came to power, the Somozas owned 20 percent of Nicaragua's arable land and 154 commercial and industrial businesses.[19]

Growing political instability and violence led to a 43 percent drop in investments in 1978 and a consequent 5 percent fall in GNP. Economic losses that year were estimated at more than $60 million and inflation grew to 18 percent.[20] To finance its counterinsurgency efforts, the regime borrowed funds from private banks and international agencies, raising Nicaragua's foreign debt to $1.15 billion. External public debt as a percentage of GNP grew from 20.7 percent in 1970 to 40.3 percent in 1977. Nicaragua defaulted on a $23 million interest payment due in December 1978; in March 1979, the Nicaraguan Central Bank failed to pay $65 million in interest payments to international private banks.[21]

Revolution in Nicaragua

Nicaragua in Opposition

Political manipulation and fraudulent elections led to numerous election boycotts and political protests in 1936, 1944, 1946, 1954, 1956, 1960, 1963, 1967, 1974, and from 1978 to 1979.[22] Opposition under the Somozas was met with violence and repression. Following the assassination of Somoza Garcia in 1956, more than three thousand regime opponents were imprisoned and tortured. Antigovernment demonstrations by students and citizens in 1944 and 1960 were suppressed with gunfire and imprisonment. In 1967, sixty thousand Nicaraguans, who had gathered to protest the Somoza administration and to oppose a presidential election campaign, were fired upon by the National Guard. The organizers of a 1974 anti-election campaign were accused of "inciting to abstain" and denied their civil liberties for six months.[23]

In addition to the numerous antigovernment protests held through the years, several unsuccessful coup attempts were made against the Somoza regimes in 1947, 1954, 1959, 1960, and 1967.[24] The venality demonstrated by Anastasio Somoza Debayle after the 1972 earthquake, and the economic hardships associated with it, intensified economic and political disaffection among most of Nicaragua's population, including its elite. Nicaragua was hit by a number of strikes in 1973 and 1974. Labor conflicts and student opposition flared. Agricultural workers, discontented with falling wages and declining employment, participated in land seizures, strikes, and the formation of a union for rural workers.[25]

The business sector resented the corruption and Somoza's hold on the construction and banking industries; its criticism intensified and its political demands escalated as economic conditions deteriorated. In 1974, the danger of revolution persuaded two major business organizations, the Superior Council of Private Enterprise (COSEP) and the Nicaraguan Development Institute (INDE), to organize a meeting of private-sector interests; participants demanded "greater honesty in government" and more social reforms for the "great dispossessed majorities."[26]

"By 1974 it was obvious that Somoza's regime had become unpopular throughout Nicaraguan society."[27] Anastasio Somoza Debayle was accused of corruption by leaders of the business sector. A patently fraudulent September presidential election was boycotted by opposition leaders who, together with the Catholic Church, refused to attend Somoza's inauguration. In the same year, Nicaragua's business sector formed the Democratic Liberation Union (Union Democratica de Liberacion, or UDEL) under the leadership of Pedro Joaquin Chamorro and Ramiro Sacasa Guerrero. The organization hoped to encourage reform instead of revolution. Although dominated by the upper class, UDEL was joined by the middle-class Independent Liberal Party (PLI), as well as Conservative dissidents, the Social Christian Party, the Moscow-line Socialist Democratic Party (PSN), and trade union federations associated with the latter two organizations. UDEL hoped to get U.S. support for the 1981 elections. It was, however, fragmented, and concentrated almost exclusively on electoral strategies rather than on developing a program for a post-Somoza government.[28]

The left-of-center Frente Sandinista de Liberacion Nacional (FSLN), since its inception in 1961, had been engaged in several small-scale military operations, particularly in the countryside. In December 1974, the FSLN raided a Christmas party held in honor of U.S. Ambassador Turner Shelton. The operation proved to be a major propaganda coup for the movement.

In response to the attack, Somoza imposed martial law and press restrictions. By September 1977, the state of siege was lifted in an apparent effort to deflect pressures from the Carter administration. As was the case in Iran, and as would be the case in the Philippines, the easing of restrictions led to public demonstrations of discontent. *La Prensa* reported on corruption in the Somoza administration, Conservative and Social Christian factions increased demands for political reform, and the FSLN stepped up its military attacks.

Changes in the tax laws in 1977 led to an increasing rift between business and government. In association with the Catholic Church, the two business organizations, COSIP (the former COSEP) and INDE, sought to encourage a "national dialogue" to resolve the political crisis. The resolution sought was not a radical one: business interests hoped to eliminate Somoza while maintaining the same political structures, including the National Guard and the National Liberal Party. *La Prensa* publisher and opposition leader Pedro Joaquin Chamorro, representing the moderate UDEL coalition, held secret meetings with the Sandinistas to learn more about them and possibly form a united front with the group.[29] Moderate forces made several efforts to resolve political tensions during the fall of 1977. Although Somoza remained adamant about completing his term to 1981, he was persuaded by the Americans to agree to talks.

Apparent U.S. attempts to move Nicaragua toward democracy and the end of martial law were not welcomed by the Sandinistas who perceived the moves "as a threat, not an opportunity."[30] Their goal was the destruction of the National Guard and the Somoza regime, not the pursuit of moderate reform. On October 13, 1977, the FSLN attacked several National Guard barracks and police stations. Humberto Ortega, minister of defense in the post-revolution FSLN government, later remarked that the Sandinistas "took note of the fact that the enemy had taken a step forward by lifting the state of siege and was considering an amnesty, and saw that if this happened, we would be in a difficult position. So we decided to speed up the offensive."[31]

Two days after the attack, a statement was issued simultaneously in Costa Rica and in Washington, D.C., warning that, "There can be no permanent solution to the escalating armed conflict, which now threatens to envelop all of Nicaragua, without the participation of the Sandinista National Liberation Front." The statement was signed by twelve prominent Nicaraguan businessmen, lawyers, priests, and educators who had been organized clandestinely by the FSLN. The October attacks and the document issued by this Group of Twelve established the military viability and political legitimacy of the FSLN.[32]

In January 1978, *La Prensa's* publisher Pedro Joaquin Chamorro was assassinated. Anastasio Somoza Debayle was not directly implicated in the murder. His son, however, was found to have played a role in the assassination in retaliation for a *La Prensa* exposé incriminating him in business fraud. Somoza's corruption, made salient in the aftermath of the 1972 earthquake, had antagonized the private sector; Chamorro's assassination, however, "was the catalyst that moved the private sector toward political action."[33] If Pedro Joaquin Chamorro could be killed, so could they; and if Somoza could not assure public order, business interests would be harmed.[34]

In reaction to the assassination, demonstrations broke out throughout the country. Alfonso Robelo Callejas, president of COSEP, called for a general strike. The three-week strike was 90 percent effective. "For the first time, businessmen, as an organized and cohesive political group, issued a public demand for Somoza's resignation."[35]

This time, Somoza responded with concessions rather than repression. On February 26, 1978, he announced that he would resign as president and as commander of the National Guard when his term concluded in 1981. He promised an investigation of the Chamorro assassination and that he would permit participation by new political parties. Somoza also agreed to discuss reform of the television and radio code, the rights of labor unions, and the reorganization of the National Guard.[36]

Reform, which had long been the goal of the opposition, was now no longer enough. Popular discontent with the 1981 resignation date led to continued riots, demonstrations, and fighting. In March 1978, Alfonso Robelo joined with a group of young professionals to establish the Nicaraguan Democratic Movement (MDN); in May, a fragmented opposition comprised of sixteen groups united under the umbrella of the Broad Opposition Front (FAO). The union was encouraged by the United States.[37]

Pressure from the Unites States and from regional neighbors led to further concessions from Somoza. In June, he invited the Organization of American States Inter-American Commission on Human Rights (IAHCR) to visit the country and permitted the return of the Group of Twelve. (Members of the Group had fled in October 1977 after being identified as members of the FSLN revolutionary cabinet.)[38]

Despite the concessions, a one-day strike was called by the FAO in July 1978; it was honored by 70 percent of Nicaragua's business (and 90 percent of businesses in Managua). In early August, Archbishop Obando y Bravo and members of the Bishops' Conference issued a declaration calling for Somoza's resignation, for the National Guard to be reorganized into a non-political force, and for the formation of a transition government.[39] The private sector, represented by the Nicaraguan Development Institute (INDE), issued a statement supporting the church's demands. The Broad Opposition Front (FAO) released a sixteen-point plan urging Somoza to resign and calling for the organization of a national unity government. Control of the National Guard, the plan proposed, should be transferred to officers not associated with the Somozas. The FAO also declared another nationwide strike, which brought Nicaragua to a standstill for almost a month.[40]

While the moderate opposition pursued its aims via public pronouncements, strikes, and demonstrations, the FSLN pursued its goals by military means. Having learned of an imminent coup by the National Guard, it acted to protect its political interests. Fearing that such a coup would clear the way for the installation of a moderate government, the FSLN sought to forestall the plan by attacking the National Palace. The attack on the seat of the Congress and several government ministries occurred on August 22, 1978. Humberto Ortega later explained,

> We knew that the mass movement was developing, and preferred that it come rather than not come. The important thing was to block an imperialist junta that would undercut the revolutionary struggle. . . . We knew that because we lacked a great partisan organization and because we didn't have the working classes organized in a block, the only way to establish a political presence was with arms. . . . Thus it was a military action, but it obeyed the necessities of the political rather than military, situation.[41]

The Sandinistas took more than two thousand hostages. They demanded and received half a million dollars in ransom, the release of sixty Sandinista prisoners, and unrestricted passage to Panama for the FSLN attack team. Among those who left for Panama was the man in charge of the operation, a moderate, Eden Pastora. Pastora met with Presidents Torrijos of Panama and Perez of Venezuela. Both were impressed by him and became convinced that the Sandinista mission ought to be supported. An FSLN victory, they believed, would not necessarily result in a Marxist Nicaragua. As a result, political and military assistance to the FSLN increased from both countries.[42]

The National Palace attack was a political, military, and propaganda success for the guerrillas. It was followed by attacks on National Guard detachments throughout the country and by civil uprisings in several cities. The civil rebellions were coordinated by Nicaragua's moderates and the FSLN.[43]

Somoza was no longer prepared to respond with concessions. He ordered the arrest of some fifty moderate opposition leaders, recalled Central Bank loans to businessmen who had been strike organizers, and revoked the charter of the most prominent business associations.[44] Eventually, six to eight hundred people were imprisoned. The Guard cracked down throughout Nicaragua, leveling large sections of several cities. Widespread atrocities committed by the National Guard were reported. The Red Cross estimated that the civil strife had caused fifteen hundred to three thousand deaths, that a half-dozen cities had been devastated, and that thirty thousand people had lost their homes.[45]

By the end of September 1978, pressure from the United States, Venezuela, and countries in Central America again forced concessions from Somoza. He agreed to an IACHR inspection, "released 350 political prisoners," and accepted OAS mediation led by the United States, Guatemala, and the Dominican Republic.[46]

Negotiations Begin

The OAS-mediated negotiation began in October 1978. Opposition members from the FAO and FSLN refused to participate in direct talks with Somoza and demanded his "resignation and exile." They also insisted on the reorganization of the National Guard and demanded that a Government of National Unity, which would include members of Somoza's Liberal Party, be established to implement the FAO political program.[47]

Although acting only as a mediator, the United States hoped to achieve a solution acceptable to its own interests. Afraid that a post-Somoza government without a strong military base would be vulnerable to FSLN usurpation, Washington supported the continued existence of the National Guard, albeit with a more acceptable commander.[48]

While Somoza agreed to discuss the 1981 elections, he refused to negotiate his resignation. He did, however, reduce censorship and curfew restrictions, limit the use of military courts, and agree to an FAO demand that he negotiate through mediators.[49]

The negotiations, as well as the opposition FSLN and FAO, broke down within two months. The FSLN objected to the participation of foreign mediators, principally the United States. Furthermore, a successful mediation would be contrary to FSLN interests because it would entail installation of a moderate government.[50] The Sandinistas, "who had more guns and fewer votes than the moderates in the FAO," needed a military struggle to take power.[51] Thus, on October 25, 1978, the FSLN's Group of Twelve disassociated itself from the FAO in protest of a U.S.-supported plan to include members of Somoza's National Liberal Party and the National Guard in the new junta. It complained that any plan that allowed the National Guard to remain was, in effect, "Somocismo sin [without] Somoza."[52]

FSLN hostilities resumed in November 1978 while mediators pressed Somoza for further concessions so that talks could continue. By the end of

November, both sides had agreed to a plebiscite proposal in which Nicaraguans would vote for or against Somoza's continued tenure in office. In December 1978, Somoza lifted the state of siege, announced a general amnesty for Sandinistas who gave up their weapons, and rescinded censorship restrictions for radio and television. In exchange, he insisted on and got direct talks with the FAO.[53]

Conciliatory steps, however, did not bring peace any closer. The FAO had abandoned its principal demand of no direct negotiations. As a result, moderates who had been opposed to the concession abandoned both the FAO and the talks. Somoza, who had decided that the plebiscite was unacceptable because he was likely to lose, stalled the talks by arguing about the constitutionality of such a vote.[54] By the end of December 1978, negotiations had in effect collapsed.

In addition to contributing to the breakup of the moderate opposition, the effort to reconcile Somoza and the FAO also served to unite the FSLN, which had become divided on issues of strategy and tactics after the 1974 raid. Fearing a mediation success, the various factions of the FSLN united in early December 1978.

A final effort to revive the fading talks was made with another proposal. On January 12, 1979, U.S. negotiator William Bowdler warned Somoza that American support "was out of the question" and that he should accept the most recent proposal. Somoza's representatives, however, demanded more changes. On January 19, 1979, the FAO issued a communiqué declaring that the negotiations had ended and condemning "the brutal intransigence of the dictator."[55]

Following the collapse of negotiations, the FAO virtually disintegrated. Many moderates lost hope, and perceiving the FSLN to be more moderate than it really was, joined with it. The merged groups formed the United People's Movement (MPU) and the National Patriotic Front (FPN).[56] Latin American leaders, believing that only through the FSLN would Somoza be ousted, supported the Sandinistas.[57] Alfonso Robelo of COSEP and the Nicaraguan Democratic Movement later acknowledged that he had joined the opposition junta because of "the support" given to the FSLN by Presidents Omar Torrijos of Panama, Carlos Andres Perez of Venezuela, and Rodrigo Carazo of Costa Rica. That support, he said, gave him the "confidence that it was the right thing to do."[58]

In the spring of 1979, the FSLN launched a series of attacks on National Guard outposts, occupied public office buildings in several cities, and launched a "final offensive." Fighting was reported in several cities, and Nicaragua's second-largest city, Leon, came under FSLN control. In desperation, Somoza again imposed a state of siege in early June. Nonetheless, the FSLN continued its military offensive and announced the formation of a five-man junta as the "provisional government." Its members included representatives of the moderate opposition and the FSLN.[59]

The Andean Pact nations condemned Somoza at the end of May 1979, and on June 16, the day the provisional government was announced, recognized the FSLN as the legitimate government of Nicaragua.[60] The United States, however, continued efforts to find a moderate solution.

On July 17, 1979, Somoza brought the family dynasty to an end by announcing his resignation. The revolution was won. Shortly after Somoza's announcement, the FSLN advanced on Managua. The National Guard was informed that U.S. assistance would not be forthcoming, and Guard commanders decided to give up the fight.[61] On July 19, with the U.S. negotiator looking on, the new FSLN-led government in Managua was sworn in.

Opposition Factions: The FSLN and the Catholic Church

The moderate political and business sectors were essential participants in the anti-Somoza movement. The Catholic Church, too, played a significant role in the revolution, while the FSLN served as its central catalyst.

The Church. Nicaragua's Catholic hierarchy supported the Somoza regime through much of its reign. The lower ranks of the clergy, however, denounced and fought Somoza's repression with various tactics. Catholic religious orders organized "Christian base communities" (comunidades evangelicas de base, or CEBs), which helped the rural and urban poor improve their lives and put their demands before the government. The CEBs played a central role in mobilizing antiregime elements after the 1972 earthquake.

Political and philosophical agreement tied the lower ranks of the clergy to the FSLN. Christian groups provided organizational and logistical support, and church buildings were often used as sanctuaries. The tie between clergy and the FSLN was clearly evidenced even after the revolution, when members of the clergy were appointed to government posts: Miguel D'Escoto Brockman, a Maryknoll priest, served as minister of foreign relations, and Ernesto Cardenal, a Trappist father, became minister of culture.[62]

In response to the clergy's "subversive" activities, the National Guard murdered Christian organizers and community workers. The violence moved the church hierarchy and a number of orders to denounce the human rights violations of the Somoza regime. In June 1976, thirty-five American Capuchin priests serving in Nicaragua sent a letter to Somoza complaining about human rights abuses. In January 1977, three weeks before the Carter inauguration, seven bishops from the Nicaragua Episcopal Conference issued a pastoral letter calling for civil rights and due process of law for criminal and political offenders.[63]

Official Catholic Church policy began to change in 1968 with the appointment of Miguel Obando y Bravo as archbishop. In 1971, the archbishop issued a statement denying church support for the Somoza-Auguerro agreement in which Congress was dissolved and executive power given to a three-man junta acting for Somoza. Obando and other bishops boycotted the inaugural ceremonies for the three-man executive in 1972 and, in 1974, boycotted the presidential elections and inaugural ceremonies in which Somoza ran and won through constitutional manipulation and election fraud. The archbishop also refused to register for a 1971 municipal election so that he would not "dignify" the expected and inevitable fraud.[64]

Although opposed to the regime, the archbishop was not supportive of the violent tactics and Marxist ideology of the FSLN. Thus, in the fall of 1977, as head of the Coordinating Commission for National Dialogue, Archbishop Obando urged that the conflicting parties resolve the crisis through mediation. Such a process, he hoped, would replace Somoza with a moderate government and preempt an FSLN military victory. In the summer of 1978, as the situation in Nicaragua deteriorated further, Archbishop Obando again called for a "national government of transition."[65]

The church also acted as a buffer between the guerrillas and the regime. It negotiated the release of hostages following the 1974 and 1978 FSLN attacks. During the 1978 state of siege, it threatened the National Guard with excommunication if it again behaved as it had during the 1974–1977 martial-law period.[66]

The Frente Sandinista de Liberacion Nacional (FSLN)

FSLN ideology. The FSLN derived its ideological impetus from the anti-imperialist Sandino movement of the late 1920s and early 1930s. Augusto Cesar Sandino's movement centered on a concern for the rural poor and on antagonism toward foreign intervention in Nicaragua (particularly U.S. involvement); it was not motivated by the Marxist thinking. Sandino's anti-Americanism intensified after the U.S. occupation of Nicaragua in 1927. He and the others involved in his cause persisted in hostilities against the Americans until the United States withdrew its forces in 1933. In February 1934, the Somoza-led National Guard murdered Sandino.[67]

Whereas Sandino was impelled by anti-Americanism and concern for Nicaragua's peasants, the FSLN embraced, as part of its orientation, elements of Marxist thought. The FSLN was founded in July 1961, taking political and tactical inspiration from the Cuban experience. Its foreign policy perspective centered on an anti-imperialism generally limited to a vehement antagonism toward the United States.[68]

In 1969, the FSLN announced what was considered to be its definitive policy statement:

> The people of Nicaragua suffer under subjugation to a reactionary and fascist clique imposed by Yankee imperialism in 1932, the year Anastasio Somoza Garcia was named commander in chief of the so-called National Guard.
>
> The Somozaist clique had reduced Nicaragua to the status of a neocolony exploited by the Yankee monopolies and the country's oligarchic groups.
>
> The present regime is politically unpopular and juridically illegal. The recognition and aid it gets from the North Americans is irrefutable proof of foreign interference in the affairs of Nicaragua.
>
> [In foreign policy], the new revolutionary government will refuse to honor the loans imposed on the country by the Yankee monopolies or those of any other power.
>
> The Sandinista people's revolution will . . . put an end to the Yankee interference in the internal problems of Nicaragua and will practice a policy of mutual respect with other countries and fraternal collaboration between peoples.
>
> It will accept economic and technical aid from any country, but always and only when this does not involve political compromises.[69]

The radical rhetoric of the guerrillas did not, however, prove completely commensurate with the policies they would pursue as a government.

FSLN structure. From its inception, the FSLN functioned with a relatively small cadre; its success, therefore, was not inevitable. In 1961, the FSLN numbered approximately twenty guerrillas; by 1967, it had no more than one hundred armed men. During its early years, the organization was active primarily in rural Nicaragua and, until 1970, engaged unsuccessfully in a number of small-scale guerrilla activities and major military operations. In 1970, with the aid of local peasants, the FSLN launched a successful military campaign against National Guard outposts in northern Nicaragua. The Guard attempted to destroy the guerrillas by using intimidation and violence against suspected peasant supporters. The tactic proved counterproductive, turning peasants away from the regime and toward the FSLN. By 1978, the Sandinistas had organized "rural workers and landless peasants in workers' committees"; these were united within the national Rural Workers' Association.[70]

In the urban areas, young people from the barrios who were opposed to Somoza's repression, or who were associated with self-help organizations, entered the ranks of the FSLN. A growing student movement in the 1970s also created a pool of potential sympathizers. The massive corruption of the Somoza regime, particularly after the 1972 earthquake, prompted the children of middle-and upper-class families to join the FSLN as well.[71]

At the time of the December 1974 assault, the FSLN's Henry Ruiz estimated its cadres to number only about 150.[72] Although the National Guard virtually destroyed the FSLN membership after the December 1974 raid, the incident served to enhance the military stature and prestige of the guerrillas and to attract more adherents from the middle and upper classes. Indeed, following the October 1977 assaults on National Guard barracks and police stations, Somoza commented on the fact that "sons of solid Conservative families participated in the battles."[73]

The August 1978 attack on the National Palace increased the ranks of the FSLN. By mid-1978, FSLN membership had grown to an estimated five hundred to one thousand armed guerrillas.[74] (U.S. government estimates in January 1978, however, reported the numbers at fifty to one hundred fifty men; State Department estimates for mid-1978 put its numbers at only fifty fighting men.)[75] Humberto Ortega explained in 1980 that FSLN military activity in mid-1978, and Somoza's crackdown which followed, created more recruits. "Everybody had a relative or friend killed in the struggle and there was a great thirst for revenge."[76] By the time the revolution ended in July 1979, the FSLN estimated that three to five thousand people had participated in the fighting against Somoza, in addition to an approximate ten thousand *muchachos* (young boys who joined in the fighting).[77]

Disintegration of the FAO made it possible for the FSLN to establish a united broad-based political opposition centered on the United People's Movement (MPU) and the National Patriotic Front (FPN). Under the umbrella of the FPN, the Sandinistas brought together the MPU, Independent Liberals, the Popular Social Christian faction, the Group of Twelve (Sandinista), and several unions. By spearheading a united opposition front, the FSLN was able to forge for itself a central role in the anti-Somoza struggle.[78]

Nicaragua after Somoza

Because of the FSLN's prerevolutionary alliances with moderates and the Catholic Church, the structure of Nicaragua's postrevolutionary politics represented a mix of sectors, ideologies, and political orientations. Economic and political constraints forced the FSLN-led government to pursue policies which, despite the movement's Marxist leanings, were more pragmatic than the 1969 statement of principles would have indicated.

Immediately after the revolution, the political and military configurations of the new regime were still unclear. The junta, composed of five members, headed the Government of National Reconciliation. Its membership included two moderates, two Sandinistas, and one former Sandinista viewed by many as a moderate social democratic. The eighteen-member cabinet included a former National Guardsman as minister of defense, and a number of moderates who were particularly well represented in the economic ministries. Predictions on where the revolution would go varied. One observer noted,

> American conservatives saw the Sandinistas as committed Marxist-Leninists who served the Soviet Union. On the other hand, several well-known Marxists visited Nicaragua in the months after the revolution and returned distressed that the more pragmatic elements of the Sandinistas appeared to have mortgaged the future of the revolution to cope with the immediate needs for the people.[79]

Despite the participation of moderates in the postrevolutionary regime, the Sandinistas unobtrusively insinuated themselves as the predominant force in the government. The businessman Alfonso Robelo later admitted that several months had passed before he realized that " 'someone in olive green,' a representative of the nine-member Directorate [the military Commandantes], was present at every junta meeting." The views of the Commandantes generally prevailed on important decisions.[80] With the assistance of Cuban advisers, the FSLN Directorate concentrated on organizing the army, police, internal security, and "popular" mass organizations such as the Sandinista Defense Committees.[81]

In April 1980, the junta announced that membership in the legislative body, the Council of State, would be increased. The expansion was deemed necessary to give representation to the new mass organizations created by the FSLN. It also, however, established an FSLN majority. The junta approved the measure despite the vetoes of moderates Alfonso Robelo and Violeta de Chamorro. Both resigned in protest.[82]

Although the FSLN attempted to dominate the politics of postrevolutionary Nicaragua, opportunities existed for non-Sandinista groups to participate actively in government. As independent groups appeared, the FSLN tried to co-opt them. If it met with resistance to its "inducements and harassment," however, the FSLN yielded.[83] The MDN, for example, which had been established by Robelo as a middle-class, anti-Somoza opposition group, was transformed into a political opposition party.[84] COSEP, the business association, continued to represent private-sector interests, and labor unions were able to organize. By mid-1986, seven of twelve independent parties were represented in Nicaragua's National Assembly.[85] Many parties that emerged during the first six years of the new regime faded, however, because they "lacked leadership, organizational capacity, and, most important, grassroots support."[86]

The mix represented in Nicaragua's domestic politics in the early years of the revolution also became apparent in its economic policies. The Sandinistas honored Somoza's $1.6 billion foreign debt in an effort to maintain creditworthiness within the international financial community.[87] It was only in 1983 that economic hardship forced the government to "begin to prioritize the servicing of some debts while renegotiating others."[88]

Contrary to earlier policy statements, the Nicaraguan economy was not completely socialized. Banking, insurance, agricultural trade, and mineral companies were nationalized, however, as were the private properties of many individuals. Property owned by Somoza and his associates, comprising approximately 20 percent of Nicaragua's arable land, was confiscated.[89]

Civil rights were given ostensible protection. When it entered office, the FSLN government decreed a bill of rights, ended the death penalty, and lifted restrictions on the news media.[90] The human rights situation was, nonetheless, marred by abuses. An IACHR team visited Nicaragua in 1980 and gave a generally favorable report; the independent Nicaraguan Human Rights Commission, however, was shut down in 1980. It was permitted to reopen following protests from Amnesty International and the IACHR.

In late 1981, the Nicaraguan government responded to U.S.-supported *contra* activity along the Rio Coco by ordering the "involuntary evacuation" of eighty-five thousand to ten thousand Miskito Indians.[91] Following the disclosure of Reagan-approved CIA-sponsored paramilitary operations against Nicaragua, and *contra* attacks inside Nicaragua in 1982, a state of emergency was declared. Short-term preventive detention of suspected "subversives," already in force, was followed by the suspension of civil and political rights, including freedom of the press.

Nicaragua's Foreign Policy after the Revolution

Although vehemently anti-American, the foreign policy orientation of the revolutionary Sandinista regime was declared to be nonaligned. In reality, Nicaragua's relations tilted toward the communist bloc. Its relations with the United States were initially neutral and, indeed, disposed toward cooperation in the interest of economic development. In the summer of 1979, before the FSLN "final offensive," Sergio Ramirez, who would become a member of the junta and vice-president in the postrevolutionary government, wrote:

> To think that a new, democratic government in Nicaragua might be hostile to the United States is a perverse fantasy. To think that a new and truly representative Nicaraguan government is going to insist on dignified relations with the more powerful countries . . . is to think correctly. . . . We aspire to dignity, integrity, and international respect. . . . The United States should learn not to fear the ghosts of its past mistakes.[92]

Foreign Minister Miguel D'Escoto said in 1980, "we wish to be friends, but we will never sell out, nor will we compromise in our sacred task of building of a new, free, sovereign Nicaragua."[93]

In its diplomatic relations, the new government showed flexibility. It joined the movement of nonaligned states and devoted considerable efforts to cultivating cordial relations with Latin America and Western Europe. The Nicaraguans established close ties with Cuba immediately after the revolution, but the Soviet ambassador arrived only in 1980. In November 1981, Daniel Ortega signed an agreement with the Soviet Union allowing it use of the port of San Juan del Sur. Such agreements in other countries gave the Soviet Union the opportunity to conduct naval surveillance and to use available facilities for other military purposes. Nicaragua became an observer in the Council of Mutual Economic Assistance (CEMA), the Soviet bloc's major economic organization, in September 1983. Other countries with similar status were socialist states such as Yugoslavia, or "socialist-oriented" nations such as Angola, Afghanistan, and Ethiopia.[94]

In the United Nations, the Sandinista-led government abstained from votes condemning the Soviet invasion of Afghanistan and the downing of a Korean airliner. It did, however, oppose the Soviet Union in 1984, siding with the West on a resolution to send UN peacekeeping troops to Lebanon. Nicaragua sent teams to Moscow for the 1980 Olympics, when the United States and many of its Western allies joined in a boycott against the event; however, it also participated in the Los Angeles games in 1984 when the Soviet Union, Cuba, and the socialist bloc would not.[95]

In its economic relations, ideological inclinations moved post-Somoza Nicaragua closer to the Soviet Union and the Eastern bloc. On March 17, 1980, the first major Sandinista delegation arrived in Moscow. An economic protocol, signed in September 1981, assured that the Soviet

Union would provide Nicaragua with $50 million in Soviet credit; the sum would supplement $100 million from Libya and $64 million from Cuba. Sandinista leaders visited the Soviet Union eight times between May 1982 and mid-1983. The May 1982 meeting led to an additional $150 million in credit for Nicaragua.[96]

Despite the ideological ties, the Soviet Union "made it clear that it was not willing to underwrite a 'second Cuba' "; neither hard currency nor military support could be expected. Moscow was "reluctant to take on the economic burden of Nicaragua as it did in Cuba. The USSR's failure to rush in as it had in Cuba to take up Nicaragua's sugar quota when it was dropped by the United States (in May 1983) . . . [was] symbolic of Moscow's reluctant approach."[97]

Extensive associations with the Soviet Union did not make Nicaragua a client state of the superpower. To assure its economic stability, Nicaragua sought to establish economic relations with all nations; the United States, as well as the socialist bloc, were acceptable partners. Central to its trade policy, however, was the principle of equality, which required that economic relations not be encumbered by conditional arrangements.[98] Between 1978 and 1982, Nicaragua's "exports to and imports from the socialist bloc rose from 0 and 1 percent, respectively, to 7 and 11 percent." By mid-1985, "the overall value of trade with the socialist bloc stood at 20 percent." Figures for Nicaragua's exports and imports to and from the United States stood at 23 and 31 percent, respectively, for 1978, and at 24 and 19 percent for 1982.[99] A *Pravda* report on Nicaragua's import figures for the first half of 1983 showed that 15 percent of its imports came from Central America, 27 percent from other Latin American countries, 14 percent from the Common Market, 19 percent from the United States; 8 percent from other developed capitalist countries, and 12 percent from the socialist bloc.[100]

Economic assistance was sought from various sources. Although Reagan had cut off aid after his inauguration in 1981, other nations—including Argentina, Austria, Brazil, Canada, Denmark, Libya, Mexico, Peru, Sweden, and members of the socialist bloc—provided the Sandinista government with economic assistance. Data from the American embassy in Managua showed that in 1982, the Soviet bloc provided 47 percent of the foreign assistance flowing to Nicaragua; in 1981, foreign aid from the Soviet bloc amounted to 15 percent.[101] In 1985, economic assistance from the socialist bloc and Yugoslavia totaled $202 million; Western Europe provided $198 million. The FSLN initiated a literacy campaign with the help of twelve hundred volunteers from Cuba, as well as volunteers from Costa Rica (40), Spain (70), and the Dominican Republic (39). Peace Corps volunteers were not accepted because they were suspected of being CIA agents.[102]

As was the case with trade and aid, Nicaragua sought military assistance throughout the world, including the United States. Concerned that if it did not cooperate the Sandinistas would look toward the communist world, Washington offered "nonlethal" military equipment (e.g., trucks, medical supplies, communications equipment) on condition that the United States provide Nicaragua with military training.[103] Washington's refusal to supply equipment without providing military training led the Sandinistas to seek other sources; Panama, France, Cuba, and Eastern Europe filled the gap. In 1980, 850 tons of armaments were shipped to Nicaragua from the Soviet bloc; in 1985, 18,000 tons of weapons were supplied. The FSLN also accepted military advisers from the Soviet Union, East Germany, and Cuba.[104]

Sandinista hostility toward the United States was based on a history of U.S. intervention in Nicaragua's affairs. As events unfolded after the revolution, and as the Reagan administration intensified anti-FSLN efforts, distrust and antagonism were exacerbated and U.S.–Nicaraguan relations deteriorated further.

United States–Nicaraguan Relations before the Revolution

American involvement in Nicaragua had spanned well over a century by the time the FSLN successfully routed the Somoza dynasty. Nicaragua had been a colony of Spain, a domain of the Mexican Empire, and subsequently part of the Central American Federation; it became an independent state in 1838 and fell under U.S. influence shortly thereafter.

American interests in Nicaragua were geographic and political: Nicaragua was "located in the center of the U.S. sphere of influence in Central America" and "provided an ideal location for a transisthmian canal."[105] In 1849, Nicaragua granted concessions to Cornelius Vanderbilt to build a transit route across Nicaragua. The exclusive concession was lost in 1850 when the United States and Great Britain signed the Clayton-Bulwer Treaty, an agreement that gave the two nations joint control of any transisthmian canal located on Nicaraguan territory. Nicaragua was neither asked to participate in the treaty talks, nor consulted about its arrangements.[106]

In 1914, Nicaragua's ambassador to Washington, General Emiliano Chamorro Vargas, signed the Chamorro-Bryan Treaty. The treaty was unfavorable to Nicaragua, stipulating that "The Government of Nicaragua grants in perpetuity to the Government of the United States, forever free from all taxation or other public charge, the exclusive propriety rights necessary and convenient for the construction, operation, and maintenance of an inter-oceanic canal."[107] The Americans were given a "renewable ninety-nine-year option'' to construct a naval base in the Gulf of Fonseca, and a ''renewable ninety-nine-year lease to the Great and Little Corn Islands in the Caribbean.'' Nicaragua, in return, was to receive three million dollars in payment, much of which went to pay foreign creditors.[108] In 1916, two years after the treaty was signed, Emiliano Chamorro was elected president of Nicaragua—an event that was generally viewed as suspiciously coincidental.[109]

American involvement in Nicaragua's domestic affairs became common. In 1855, William Walker, an American, joined the Nicaraguan Liberals in defeating the Conservatives. He became president of Nicaragua and was quickly recognized as such by Washington. Walker's popularity waned as he exiled and executed Conservatives and began to turn against Liberals whose loyalty he suspected. Confronted by disaffection, rebellion, and finally military defeat, Walker accepted a U.S.-brokered surrender and escaped to the United States under U.S. navy protection.[110]

In 1909, the United States joined with Great Britain and Nicaragua's Conservatives to overthrow the reformist president, José Santos Zelaya. Zelaya had provoked the United States by antagonizing U.S. business interests and by seeking a canal treaty with Japan and Germany after the United States had decided to build a canal through Panama. Fighting between Conservatives and Liberals provided Washington with an excuse to dispatch marines to ''protect U.S. lives and property.'' Zelaya resigned, but the U.S. Marines remained in Nicaragua until 1933.[111]

American intervention in Nicaragua's domestic politics continued as successive American administrations supported or deposed the country's leaders as U.S. interests dictated. Such interventions occurred in 1911, 1919, 1927, and in 1936, when Anastasio Somoza Garcia became president. Following the 1910 election of Conservative President Juan Estrada, for example, the United States assumed virtual control over the structure and course of Nicaragua's government and finances. American troops, which had arrived in Nicaragua in 1909 grew to 2,700 by 1912, when they were used to bolster the government of President Adolfo Diaz. When the United States again defended his regime in 1927, more than 5,400 marines were stationed in the country's principal cities, and eleven U.S. cruisers and destroyers were docked in Nicaraguan ports. After mediating a peace between Conservatives and Liberals in 1928, the United States supervised Nicaragua's presidential elections.[112]

In addition to its direct military presence, American influence in Nicaragua was achieved through its control of the High Commission of Customs and of the National Guard (which the United States helped establish in 1925 and which it continued to train). The United States was also represented on the directorships of the railway and the national bank.[113]

In 1932, the United States supported the appointment of Anastasio Somoza García as commander of the National Guard; he used his position to climb to the presidency in 1936. U.S. foreign relations in Latin America were at the time defined by a policy of noninterference. As a consequence, Washington recognized Somoza, despite the fraud and manipulation he had used to achieve the presidency. Opposition to Somoza became evident, and a second term was impossible under Nicaragua's constitution. In 1945, with a presidential election expected, U.S. Assistant Secretary of State for Inter-American Affairs Nelson Rockefeller warned Nicaragua's ambassador that a reelection attempt by Somoza might lead to "difficulties" both for him, and for U.S.–Nicaraguan relations.[114]

Domestic opposition and warnings from the United States did not stop Somoza. He revised the Constitution to allow himself to stay in office until 1947, and then ran for reelection. The United States refused to support these maneuvers and, in response, denied Somoza's request for arms for the National Guard. In an effort to gain American endorsement, Somoza engineered the election of a puppet Liberal Dr. Leonardo Arguello. The new Liberal president did not prove as malleable as Somoza had expected, and fired Somoza from his position as commander of the National Guard. Somoza overthrew Arguello and subsequently installed two more puppet presidents in succession.[115]

The United States continued in its refusal to recognize Somoza's puppets, and withdrew the chief of the U.S. military mission and the American director of the Nicaraguan Military Academy. At the Rio Pact negotiations of 1947, the U.S. representative suggested that the Nicaraguan regime was "oppressive," "a puppet," and a "creature of Somoza"; he urged the Latin American nations not to recognize the Nicaraguan regime. Nevertheless, Washington did agree to accede to majority sentiment, and in 1948, under pressure from Latin America, recognized to Somoza's puppet president, Victor Manuel Roman y Reyes. Roman's death in 1950 gave Somoza another opportunity to rewrite the constitution and, consequently, another term in the presidency.[116] He remained in office until his assassination in 1956.

U.S.–Nicaraguan Economic Relations

In the early years of this century, U.S. interests dominated the most significant sectors of Nicaragua's economy. Nicaragua's finances and budget were organized and supervised by Americans, and its customs revenues collected by them. The Nicaraguan railroad and its national bank were managed by U.S. banks, and the State Department approved nominations for the collector general of the customs.[117] During World War II, the American-directed Price and Commerce Control Board ran Nicaragua's economy in conformance with U.S. needs. Nicaragua produced raw materials for the U.S. war effort: it replaced rubber and citronella from Asia and provided mahogany for U.S. naval vessels. By mid-1943, Nicaragua sent 95 percent of its exports to the United States.[118]

U.S. economic assistance to Nicaragua increased steadily between 1953 and 1975. Between 1953 to 1961, Nicaragua received $41.4 million in aid; its economic-assistance package from 1962 to 1975 totaled $237.3 million.[119] During the Alliance for Progress, the U.S. Agency for International Development (AID) assisted in the formation of three reformist institutions whose purpose it was to reduce socioeconomic disparities by supporting community development projects, cooperatives, education, expansion of public services, and community-government cooperation.[120] (See Table 4-1 for a breakdown of economic assistance to Nicaragua from 1967 to 1980.)

U.S. business investment in the late 1970s reached over $100 million, and American businesses operated 76 percent of all foreign-controlled enterprises. Sixty-three American transnationals and seventy American subsidiaries operated in Nicaragua, including Exxon, Hercules, Pennwalt, United Brands, Nabisco, General Foods, U.S. Steel, and Sears, Roebuck and Company.[121]

U.S. Military Assistance

The Nicaraguan National Guard. U.S. military assistance to Nicaragua ranged from military training to the provision of equipment. When it was ready to withdraw the marines from Nicaragua in 1925, the United States hoped to get as a replacement a nonpartisan Nicaraguan force which could maintain the peace. The government of Nicaragua contracted with retired U.S. Army Major Calvin B. Carter to head its new national constabulary, the National Guard, and its training school. U.S. marines, who left Nicaragua in 1925, and returned in 1927 to support the presidency of Conservative Adolfo Diaz, stayed until 1933 to train, organize, and supervise the operations of the Guard.[122]

In addition to the U.S. funds used to support the National Guard, 4,897 Guardsmen participated in U.S. military training programs between 1950 and 1975. Of these, 4,089 were trained locally. Between 1970 and 1975, 52 Nicaraguans, the highest number of trainees for all of Latin America, trained in the U.S. Army Infantry and Ranger School, Army

Civil Affairs School, Military Police School, and Army Command and General Staff School (see Table 4-2).[123]

CIA involvement in the National Guard was reported to be entrenched. It was generally understood that the National Guard high command was infiltrated by CIA agents and that CIA intelligence was provided to the Guard "in exchange for a free hand in Nicaragua." Indeed, it was rumored that as the FSLN marched on Managua in July 1979, a CIA "adventurer" assisted the escape of over a hundred Guard officers.[124]

U.S. Military Aid. With U.S. assistance, the Office of National Security (Oficina de Seguridad, or OSN) was established to spy on Nicaraguan dissidents. In 1939, Somoza convinced President Roosevelt to help Nicaragua reestablish a military academy; by 1944, academy cadets were receiving their final year of training in Fort Gulick in the Canal Zone. An American military mission in Managua was opened in 1953; in 1954, American fears of communism, prompted by President Arbenz of Guatemala, led to the establishment of a Military Assistance Program (MAP).[125]

Military assistance was forthcoming, despite the domestic policies pursued by the Somozas and the persistent view in Nicaragua that the United States was arming a dictator. Thomas Whelan, the U.S. ambassador to Nicaragua, wrote in 1952:

> The political opposition to Somoza in Nicaragua harps upon the charge that the United States created the Nicaraguan army which, according to this opposition, is the force that has kept Somoza in power. . . . Repeatedly oppositionists have called upon this embassy to help break the chains which they claim we forged to bind them under Somoza's domination. It is possible that the restoration of a military mission would intensify this complaint and be interpreted as our lining up more strongly with the Somoza government. . . . This is the sole political objection I see to the restoration of the mission. I do not regard it as particularly important.[126]

The ambassador later cabled Washington that Nicaragua was stable "for the first time during this century, despite the widespread impression to the contrary." Somoza, he wrote, "is not a dictator in the true sense of the word."[127]

Nicaragua joined the Central American Defense Council (Consejo de Defensa Centroamericano, or CONDECA) in 1961. Council members participated in a U.S.-supported regional defense plan whose purpose it was

Table 4-1
U.S. Economic Assistance to Nicaragua, 1967–1980 (in millions of U.S. dollars)

Fiscal Year	Total Economic Commitments[a]	Direct Economic Assistance			Other Economic Assistance		
		AID		Ex-Im Bank Loans[b]	Other U.S. Loans/Grants[c]	Multilateral Development Banks	
		Funds Committed	Funds Delivered			Loans Approved[d]	Abstentions[e]
1967	$12.2	$11.4	$7.3	$0.0	$0.0		
1968	25.7	25.5	8.8	4.9	0.0		
1969	2.4	1.9	12.4	0.0	0.0		
1970	3.1	2.3	18.2	0.0	0.1		
1971	13.2	12.5	11.5	1.1	0.0		
1972	4.7	2.5	6.0	0.1	0.0		
1973	26.8	22.5	13.1	0.0	0.5	$ 0.0	
1974	15.5	12.4	16.2	3.4	1.7	18.3	
1975	42.2	40.1	11.6	>.05*	0.3	9.0	$ 0.0
1976[f]	20.2	17.7	10.1	12.4	0.0	32.5	0.0
1977	3.3	1.4	13.7	3.4	0.0	71.8	0.0
1978	14.0	12.5	24.3	0.2	0.0	65.1	0.0
1979	26.5	17.7	19.3	0.0	0.0	36.5	0.0
1980	39.8	20.5	63.9	0.0	0.0	52.0	0.0
1981		14.7			11.7	0.0	0.0
1982		6.2					

1983	3.4
1984	1.0
1985	-1.9

[a] Includes AID grants and loans and AID Economic Support Funds (ESF); PL-480 Titles I and II (Sales and Grants); International Narcotics Control. ESF is given for security purposes. In the Philippines, ESF expenditures were committed as follows (in millions of U.S. dollars): FY1973—$49.3; 1974—$0.5; 1975—$0.3; 1980—$20.0; 1981—$30.0; 1982—$50.0; 1983—$50.0; 1984—$50.0; 1985—$140.0; 1986—$300.3; ESF for Nicaragua; FY1979—$80.0; 1980—$1.1.

[b] Does not include export credit insurance and guarantees.

[c] Short-term credit granted by U.S. Department of Agriculture under the Commodity Credit Corporation Charter Act; OPIC direct loans and private trade agreements; PL-480 (I) private-sales agreements financed by the act.

[d] World Bank Group—International Bank for Reconstruction and Development, International Development Association, and International Finance Corporation; Asian Development Bank; Inter-American Development Bank; African Development Bank.

[e] U.S. vetoes or abstentions on human rights grounds. U.S. votes recorded as of 1975. U.S. abstentions/vetoes related to human rights, against any country, began in FY 1977.

[f] 1976 numbers include additional fifth transitional quarter 1976–1977, covering the period July 1, 1976, to September 30, 1976.

*Less than $50,000.

Sources: *Development Issues: U.S. Actions Affecting the Development of Low-Income Countries: Annual Report of the Chairman of the Development Coordination Committee Transmitted to the Congress.* (1979–1983.)

International Finance: The National Advisory Council on International Monetary and Financial Policies Annual Report to the President and the Congress. (Washington, D.C.: U.S. Government Printing Office, n.d.). (1979–1985.)

U.S. Agency for International Development, Office of Planning and Budget, Bureau for Program and Policy Coordination, *U.S. Overseas Loans and Grants and Assistance from International Organizations.* (1976–1987.)

U.S. Department of Commerce, Bureau of Economic Analysis, Balance of Payments Division, Government Grants and Capital Branch, unpublished data, letter dated 7 November 1990.

Notes: Figures are rounded off to the nearest $100,000.

Table 4-2

U.S. Military Assistance and Sales to Nicaragua, 1967–1980 (in millions of U.S. dollars)

Fiscal Year	U.S. Government		Commercial Sales Deliveries[c]	Number of Students in International Military Education and Training Program
	Military Aid Approved[a]	Military Deliveries[b]		
1967	$ 1.1	$1.0	$0.2	272
1968	1.1	1.4	0.2	244
1969	0.8	.8	0.1	179
1970	1.2	1.3	0.2	242
1971	1.6	2.1	0.3	216
1972	1.0	1.3	0.2	197
1973	3.0	1.9	0.2	92
1974	2.1	2.7	0.2	154
1975	4.3	1.3	0.4	253
1976	3.8	2.3	0.8	242
1977	3.1	1.2	1.6	234
1978	0.4	1.5	0.6	275
1979	>.05*	0.1	0.01	6
1980	0.0	0.2	0.0	0

[a] Includes Foreign Military Sales grants/credits, MAP, IMET, and EDA.

[b] Includes Foreign Military Sales for cash or credit, MAP, IMET, and EDA.

[c] Munitions purchased directly from U.S. manufacturers and requiring a U.S. export license.

* Less than $50,000.

Sources: *Foreign Military Sales, Foreign Military Construction Sales, and Military Assistance Facts*: December 1976; December 1978; December 1979; December 1980; September 1981; September 1982; 30 September 1983; 30 September 1984; 30 September 1985; 30 September 1986; 30 September 1987. (Washington, D.C.: Data Management Division, Comptroller, Defense Security Assistance Agency).

to "protect against a possible Cuban invasion, to secure regional supply and communication routes, and to conduct anticommunist counterinsurgency and 'civic action.' " Members, which included all Central American states except Costa Rica, worked in coordination with the U.S. Army's Panama-based Southern Command. The United States trained and equipped the military of all member states.[128]

Military aid to Nicaragua in the period from 1953 to 1961 totaled $1.9 million; from 1962 to 1965, military assistance increased to a total of $6.1 million. Between 1966 and 1972, Nicaragua's average annual military aid package totaled a little over $1.1 million. The sums increased substantially thereafter.[129] In 1977–1978, however, the first year of the Carter presidency, aid was cut as part of the administration's human rights agenda (see Table 4-2).

Changing U.S. Diplomacy in Nicaragua

As geographic interests receded, U.S. objectives in Nicaragua were dominated by a number of preeminent interests. These included precluding "the emergence of a regime . . . hostile to the United States and friendly to its adversary," preventing "instability from being exploited by a rival power," deterring Nicaraguan interference in the affairs of its neighbors, and promoting "peaceful change" via economic and political development.[130] The manner in which the United States pursued these interests varied with administrations, the state of internal politics in Nicaragua, and the vagaries of regional politics.

American involvement in Nicaragua had historically been quite blatant and, at times, heavy-handed. Under President Roosevelt's "Good Neighbor Policy," however, a strategy of "noninvolvement" was instituted, making it feasible for the United States to recognize Anastasio Somoza Garcia's presidency in 1936. Secretary of State Cordell Hull explained this changed foreign policy perspective:

> It has for many years been said that the United States has sought to impose its own views upon the Central American states, and that to this end, it has not hesitated to interfere in their internal affairs. This criticism has been made particularly in regard to our relations with Nicaragua. We therefore desire not only to refrain in fact from any interference, but also from any measure which might seem to give the appearance of such interference.[131]

In the case of Nicaragua, this policy was pursued even against the advice of the U.S. ambassador in Managua who urged U.S. intervention to stop Somoza. Indeed, so involved had the United States become in the affairs of Nicaragua, that even a policy of nonintervention served to implicate the United States in the minds of its Latin neighbors. The Mexican chargé d'affaires in Managua warned, for example, that "if Somoza, the man 'responsible for the death of Sandino, a hero in Latin America yet a mortal enemy of the United States' took power, it would appear as though the United States 'had put him in power as a reward for having killed Sandino.' ''[132]

Under the Somozas, close U.S.-Nicaraguan relations were deliberately pursued. Anastasio Somoza Garcia began to cultivate an association with the United States even before he became commander of the Guard in 1932; his efforts intensified after becoming president. A Somoza visit to Washington in 1939 was accompanied by full state honors and a promise of two million dollars in credit—a fact that Somoza would use to prove, both at home and abroad, that he had the support of the United States.[133]

Once in power, Somoza and his sons consistently endorsed American policy in an attempt to manipulate U.S. support. In May 1939, Anastasio Somoza Garcia announced, "I consider every Nicaraguan aviator and soldier as a potential fighting man for the United States."[134] Two days after the U.S. declaration of war on the Axis powers, Somoza, too, declared war. The tactic tied Nicaragua to the United States even more closely, providing the country with military aid in exchange for bases.[135] The relationship was succinctly described in a 1950 New York Times article: "In the United Nations, the Organization of American States and other international bodies, Nicaraguan delegates support U.S. policies so quickly and enthusiastically that they had given a new meaning to the phrase 'me too.' ''[136]

Although Somoza faced difficulties when the Truman administration refused to recognize his puppet presidents, he again found himself in the good graces of the United States when Dwight D. Eisenhower assumed the presidency. A 1949 State Department report indicated that the Nicaraguan people suffered "repression, widespread illiteracy, intimidation, and poverty."[137] The Eisenhower administration nevertheless focused its attention on the threats of communism, rather than on criticism of Somoza's domestic policies. (Indeed, after the death of Anastasio Somoza Garcia in 1956, U.S. Ambassador Whelan became involved in arranging the "dynastic succession.")[138]

Somoza used American concerns about communism as an opportunity to develop stronger bonds between the two nations. He offered to send Nicaraguan troops to Korea, and, in 1954, allowed the use of Nicaraguan territory as a training ground for the CIA-organized overthrow of Guatemala's President Arbenz. Somoza's son, Luis, permitted the use of Nicaraguan soil for the Bay of Pigs invasion in 1961: Cuban exiles were trained in Nicaragua, and the operation was launched from its shores. Nicaraguan troops were also offered for the Vietnam conflict. Although that offer was not accepted, the Nicaraguan military was used in 1965 when American forces occupied the Dominican Republic.[139] Nicaragua's cooperation was rewarded by the Kennedy and Johnson administrations with $6.2 million in military assistance between 1962 and 1965 alone.[140]

The Nixon administration seemed particularly sympathetic to Somoza's anticommunist rhetoric. U.S. Ambassador Turner Shelton became a confidant of Anastasio Somoza Debayle, irritating many with his evident subservience to the Nicaraguan president. "Under Turner Shelton. . . . the main function of the embassy had been to hold the hands of Somoza's followers while the ambassador held Somoza's. Shelton had actively discouraged meetings with Somoza's opponents and tried to block reports by embassy officers that appeared critical of the regime."[141] In 1971, when unrest led Somoza to cede presidential power, Shelton assisted in arranging a compromise that would help Somoza retain command of the National Guard. After the December 1972 earthquake, he encouraged Somoza to retake executive power. Indeed, Shelton had become so identified with Somoza, that he was depicted on a Nicaraguan commemorative coin with his head bowed to the dictator.[142]

Shelton was only one example in a history of obsequious American ambassadors. The close relationship and political support that had become the hallmark of U.S.–Nicaraguan relations did, however, begin to change with the end of the Nixon administration. Somoza's great supporter and confidant, Ambassador Shelton, was replaced by James Theberge. Assistant Secretary of State for Inter-American Affairs William D. Rogers explained the new American policy directly to Somoza. The United States, he said, was "absolutely neutral both publicly and privately in all its actions with regard to Somoza and the opposition, and would begin a dialogue with the opposition." Rogers also warned that Nicaragua's expenditure of AID funds would be more carefully scrutinized "to ensure that money was not misspent."[143]

Somoza was understandably disappointed with the new U.S. policy and the erosion of political support it would entail. He later complained in his autobiography that "Ambassador Theberge began to associate with Pedro Joaquin Chamorro, a known Sandinista. He was entertained by those people [Conservatives] in Granada and . . . was bent on establishing a close relation with the wrong side—an opposition coalition."[144]

President Carter and the Somoza Dictatorship

The Carter administration increased the pressure on Somoza. The president had vowed his commitment to human rights abroad and sought targets for his policy. Nicaragua seemed an appropriate case for such an initiative. Five days after Carter assumed the presidency, export licenses to Nicaragua for the sale of ammunition for sporting arms were canceled. Although not of major consequence, the ban nonetheless gave Somoza a clear message that, as his friend U.S. Representative John Murphy noted, "He was out of favor with the United States."[145] In a speech at Notre Dame University in May 1977, Carter announced, "Being confident, we are now free of that inordinate fear of Communism, which once led us to embrace any dictator who joined us in that fear."[146] Reports that the Sandinista threat had been dissipated by forceful government action in 1976, made Carter confident that he could pressure Somoza for reform without threatening the stability of an ally or the U.S. national interest.[147]

In June 1977, the administration announced that it would not sign a military aid agreement with Nicaragua unless the human rights situation improved. Somoza lifted martial law in September, but the administration continued to withhold economic and military assistance as a means of leverage. Requirements for the fiscal year, however, demanded that the administration sign a military agreement if it hoped to conclude one with Nicaragua at any time during the following twelve months. A military aid agreement was signed as a precautionary measure; the document was not intended for implementation. The decision, however, sent mixed signals at home and abroad.[148]

Evidence of deep-rooted problems and mounting discontent in Nicaragua became increasingly prominent. In June 1976, the Reverend Father Fernando Cardenal of Nicaragua (a future Sandinista minister) testified before the U.S. Congress about human rights abuse and repression in his country. He asked that the United States withdraw its military personnel from Nicaragua, suspend all aid and military assistance, and cut off financial credits and foreign aid funding. The same month, a U.S. Congressional committee investigating the human rights situation in Nicaragua received a letter from thirty-five North American Capuchin missionaries documenting torture, rape, and the disappearances of peasants on the Atlantic coast. In January 1977, Managua's Archbishop Obando y Bravo and the Nicaragua Bishops' Conference issued a statement confirming the existence of human rights violations in Nicaragua, including "summary executions of civilians."[149] U.S. Ambassador Theberge acknowledged the accusation in March, stating, "We have reason to believe that some of the allegations of human rights violations are accurate and our concern has been made clear to the Nicaraguan government on various occasions in the past year."[150] In August 1977, Amnesty International released a report highly critical of the National Guard and of martial-law abuses from December 1974 to January 1977: The report stated:

> The violation of human rights reported—political imprisonment, torture, executions—are to a great extent, directly or indirectly related to the decree of suspension of guarantees of December 1974. . . . The aspects of the decree bearing most directly on these human rights problems

are the extension of the jurisdiction of military courts to civilians, and the granting of the right to censor the news media to the executive. . . . The military courts . . . do not offer guarantees of due process and trial. Many low-level union and political party activists were found to suffer repeated short-term imprisonment, of up to 180 days . . . formally charged and sentenced . . . with offences of conscience. . . . Many campesinos are reported to have been shot in cold blood by military forces, and those simply detained . . . have reported severe torture. There is considerable evidence supporting allegations of the torture of prisoners in the custody of the National Guard.[151]

Although the specific abuses had apparently ended by the time the report was released, violations would continue in varying degrees of severity until Somoza's fall in July 1979.

Miguel D'Escoto, the future FSLN foreign minister and member of the pro-Sandinista Group of Twelve, visited Washington in November 1977; he warned Robert Pastor of the National Security Council (NSC) that "Nicaraguans are tired of living on Somoza's 'national farm' and would overthrow" him and his regime. He asked, that Washington not involve itself in Nicaragua's affairs, but that it instead "take a neutral position."[152]

By early 1978, with the fall of Somoza only a year and a half away, the United States still seemed to have the opportunity to influence events. U.S. government agencies were reporting FSLN numbers at only fifty to one hundred and fifty members. Even more generous estimates in mid-1978 calculated the number of FSLN cadre at five-hundred to one thousand men.[153] The moderate opposition at the time was urging a halt in U.S. support of Somoza. At a January 29, 1978, press conference, opposition leaders criticized U.S. support of Somoza, but gave President Carter credit for spurring the January strike. An opposition spokesperson explained, "We have heard President Carter's statements on human rights and we know that nowhere in the world are human rights violated more than in Nicaragua. . . . We cannot ask that Carter support us directly, but if the United States government ends its support of Somoza, that will be enough to assure our triumph."[154] Several days later, William Baez, executive director of the politically active business organization Nicaraguan Development Institute (INDE), remarked that it was "important . . . that for once the United States has kept its hands off. Tacho [Anastasio Somoza Debayle] does not have Ambassador Mauricio Solaun in his pocket as he did many of the American ambassadors in the past."[155] The moderate opposition asked the American ambassador for the U.S. position on Nicaragua. He responded by proposing a "statement of support for democracy," which was subsequently issued by the State Department on February 6, 1978.[156]

Despite Carter's pronounced commitment to human rights, the president insisted on a policy of noninterference. As such, the possibility of direct and unilateral U.S. involvement in the growing Nicaraguan crisis would not be entertained. In response to a January 1978 request by Venezuela's President Carlos Perez that the United States focus on the Nicaragua situation, President Carter stated that he would try to persuade Somoza to allow a visit by the Inter-American Human Rights Commission. Carter wrote to Perez in February, "We can and will voice our preference for increased democratization. . . . But we will not intervene or impose specific political solutions for individual countries."[157]

Carter's policy of non-intervention, the NSC's Robert Pastor explained,

> had two dimensions. First, the United States should encourage democracy and dialogue among competing groups within a country but should not mediate or arbitrate that dialogue. Decisions on the political future on Nicaragua should be made by Nicaraguans, not only by the United States.
>
> The second dimension stemmed from the same interest in balance, but it was aimed at international rather than national politics. The United States sought to forge regional relationships that were respectful and allowed greater autonomy. . . . This meant that if the Nicaraguan crisis required international help, the United States should consult and coordinate its response with friendly democratic governments in the region.[158]

This perspective would continue to instruct U.S. policy for several critical months.

By May 1978, Somoza had implemented some reforms and, despite strikes and demonstrations, had not reimposed martial law. After a year's delay, and under pressure from U.S. Representative Charles Wilson, a friend and staunch supporter of Somoza, the administration approved $10.5 million in basic human needs loans to Nicaragua. The State Department announced that "approval of AID projects for the needy is not intended as an expression of political support."[159]

Reforms announced by Somoza in June were followed by a Carter letter that expressed support for the proposed measures and encouraged their fulfillment. Similar encouragement is often given in such cases; in neither the United States nor in Nicaragua, however, was the Carter letter perceived as an effort to encourage further liberalization. One report from Nicaragua noted:

The moderate opposition leaders here . . . feel betrayed by the United States in their effort to effect a moderate transition.

At first they were encouraged when the Carter administration pressured General Somoza into making human rights concessions. Then, when the United States cut off most military aid to the regime, these moderates (who were privately encouraged by State Department officials) mistakenly thought open U.S. support of their cause was just around the corner.[160]

They were, however, "agog at this public pat on the back of their foe" which the Carter letter seemed to represent.[161]

The August 1978 crackdown, which followed the FSLN attack on the National Palace, created concern in Washington. Clergy from Nicaragua sent a letter to President Carter in which the Somoza government was labeled a "death-dealing regime" guilty of "indiscriminate machine-gunning of the population in different cities; . . . killing by torture of imprisoned persons; [and] illegal raids on a large number of homes."[162] Presidents Perez of Venezuela and Torrijos of Panama, along with Nicaragua's moderate opposition, urged the United States to replace the Nicaraguan president. The two Latin American presidents urged Somoza to resign. The Nicaraguan moderates asked the United States to halt the $10.5 million loan that had been allocated to Nicaragua, claiming that it only benefited Somoza's politicians. U.S. Ambassador Solaun reported from Managua in early September that he had met with business leaders and with Archbishop Obando y Bravo, and that all had urged U.S. mediation.[163]

Ambassador Solaun was instructed to protest the crackdown and the alleged atrocities of the National Guard. By September 1978, President Carazo of Costa Rica had proposed a regional mediation effort. Although the administration was still officially adhering to a policy of noninterference, it supported Carazo's proposal because it was devised by a government other than the United States, and represented a multilateral effort to be pursued within a regional framework. Washington asked the moderate Nicaraguan opposition, now united in the FAO, to issue an appeal for mediation. The appeal was issued on September 15 and was immediately followed by a statement of support from the Department of State. Central America, however, responded coolly, and Carazo withdrew the mediation initiative.[164]

Despite the collapse of the Costa Rica proposal, Washington remained sanguine about the Nicaraguan situation. President Carter told reporters, "We don't want to intervene in the affairs of a sovereign country. . . . [But] we are trying to work with our friends and well-meaning neighbors of Nicaragua to perhaps mediate the disputes . . . using the OAS vehicle wherever possible."[165] National Security Adviser Zbigniew Brzezinski explained that U.S. policy was neither neutralist nor interventionist. He expressed support for an immediate mediation effort so that the development of "extremism" would be halted.[166]

Under pressure from Panama, Central America, and Venezuela, President Carter finally approved a more active strategy. The State Department called for a truce, for OAS mediation, and for an investigation of the human rights situation. Somoza responded on American television that he would not accept mediation and would not leave office until 1981.[167]

It was becoming increasingly clear that a U.S. policy designed only to coax Somoza to move on reforms would not be enough. A U.S. emissary, William Jorden, was dispatched in September 1978 to convince Somoza of the need for negotiation. He suggested that in the administration's view, the situation was becoming "dangerously polarized," and advised that Somoza's "departure from office before 1981 is one of the possibilities that has to be considered." A direct request for Somoza's resignation, however, was not made.[168]

Somoza finally acceded to negotiations and, on October 3, 1978, mediators from the United States, Guatemala, and the Dominican Republic arrived. With the negotiations underway, U.S. strategy sought to assure the ascendance of a moderate leadership, while preserving the National Guard without Somoza. Events in Nicaragua, however, would not conform to the plans devised in Washington. As the mediations progressed, it became evident that Somoza was not negotiating in good faith, but merely temporizing. In November 1978, the OAS Inter-American Commission on Human Rights issued an incriminating human rights report on Nicaragua. The United States responded by vetoing a $20 million IMF loan; it also criticized Somoza's human rights record and announced that it hoped for his resignation.[169]

As the fruitless negotiations dragged on into December 1978, Somoza sent a representative to Washington to inquire about conditions of resignation should he choose to leave. He requested asylum in the United States, assurance against extradition, and a guarantee that his assets would not be seized. The administration was being handed an opportunity to use the asylum negotiations as leverage in the talks. Instead, Somoza was given responses without any conditions attached: yes to asylum, and maybe to protection against extradition and the freezing of assets.[170]

U.S. efforts continued. General Dennis McAuliffe, head of the U.S. Southern Command in Panama, met with Somoza in December 1978. He told Somoza,

The reason that I'm here, is that we [in the Pentagon] perceive that the cooperation you have given to the negotiating team is no longer evident. . . . We on the military side of the United States recognize that we have had strong and very effective friendship with . . . you in particular. We do not want to throw that over so to speak. . . . But we recognize . . . that the situation has changed. . . . It is our view that peace will not come to Nicaragua until you have removed yourself from the presidency and the scene.[171]

After the mediation talks collapsed in January 1979, the State Department warned Somoza that his relations with Washington would be affected by the "violence," "polarization," and human rights abuses which would likely erupt again. The United States, however, was willing to "resume the conciliation efforts should conditions and circumstances warrant."[172]

To demonstrate its dissatisfaction, the United States announced the imposition of "symbolic" military and political sanctions. CIA Director Stansfield Turner had reported in late January that, "The chances were better than fifty-fifty that Somoza would remain in power until 1981. The National Guard . . . had been strengthened [and] the Sandinistas were preparing for a long-term struggle."[173] It was assumed, therefore, that the sanctions would not destabilize Somoza's regime. A cut-off of all forms of economic aid, however, was not deemed acceptable by the administration; U.S. assistance, it was hoped, would provide some leverage. Sanctions that were decided upon, therefore, included:

1. Termination of the suspended military assistance program.
2. A halt to the consideration of new programs.
3. Suspension of two loan programs (although aid programs aimed at "basic human needs," which had already been implemented, continued).
4. Withdrawal of the U.S. military group.
5. Withdrawal of all Peace Corps volunteers.
6. Reduction of embassy staff to half (from 82 to 37).[174]

Ambassador Solaun was recalled for consultations in late February 1979 (and would not return). Many observers viewed the limited sanctions as a demonstration of the caution with which Washington moved to prevent both the destabilization of Somoza and a radical takeover by the FSLN. *La Prensa* and the FAO, however, supported the measures, glad that the United States had finally acted.[175]

Even with sanctions, the situation changed little. Limited U.S. sanctions proved an insufficient cause for Somoza's resignation, and he persisted in believing that the Guard would keep him in power. Continuing domestic turmoil in Nicaragua and the collapse of a regional effort at negotiation did not change the administration's fundamentally optimistic view of the situation. At a February 18, 1979, press conference, President Carter expressed the administration's views of the situation.

> The United States wants to note again its willingness to resume the conciliation efforts should conditions and circumstances warrant. . . .
>
> We call upon other governments in the region to avoid contributing to the continuation or spread of violence. We will continue to work closely with the OAS to the end that we can assist in promoting peace, democracy and full respect for human rights in Nicaragua.[176]

The administration could see little reason to become more intensively involved. The CIA reported in mid-May 1979 that Cuba had ceased to have faith in an FSLN victory before 1981.[177] There was consensus in the State Department and the CIA that the National Guard was a formidable force and that the Sandinistas were not a great threat. Although they were recruiting approximately one-hundred and fifty men each month, the Sandinistas had lost substantial numbers in the fighting and could only count on a 2,000-man fighting force.[178]

Contrary to administration perceptions, however, discontent and rebellion in Nicaragua had not receded. In May 1979, Somoza arrested members of the FAO leadership as they organized another strike; no charges, however, were lodged against them. Nonetheless, the United States approved a $66 million IMF loan to Nicaragua. The vote was accompanied by a statement from the State Department explaining that, "The U.S. position on this request should not be interpreted as an act of political support for the Government of Nicaragua."[179] This was, however, precisely the view taken by the Nicaraguan opposition.[180]

By the end of May 1979, Mexico had broken diplomatic relations with Nicaragua. The situation had deteriorated to a point where the Andean Pact nations (Venezuela, Colombia, Ecuador, Peru, and Bolivia) declared the situation in Nicaragua "a threat to the peace of the Americas," and sent a delegation to Managua to urge Somoza to resign. The next day, May 29, the Sandinistas launched the "final offensive," which the CIA determined would not be sufficient to overthrow Somoza. In June, Somoza again imposed a state of siege.[181]

An American Presidential Review Memorandum on Central America, prepared early in June 1979, suggested that the National Guard probably could resist current FSLN offensives, but that Somoza most likely would be ousted before his term of office concluded.[182] By June 12, the CIA reassessed the situation. The Guard, it warned, "was weaker and the Sandinistas stronger" than previously believed; Somoza could resist only for a short period of time. In the following days, the CIA reported that Cuba had sent eight to eleven planeloads of arms to the FSLN during May.[183]

The Culmination of the Revolution

On June 16, 1979, the Sandinistas announced the formation of a five-member provisional government. The FSLN stated its interest in maintaining good relations with the United States, and promised that representative democracy would be instituted under its rule.[184] On the same day, the Andean Pact foreign ministers condemned the Somoza government and called on "all nations to assist in 'the installation of a truly representative, democratic regime' " in Nicaragua.[185]

It was becoming clear that the Sandinistas were likely to rule post-Somoza Nicaragua. Fearing the consequences of such an outcome, Washington was forced to reevaluate its strategy. The administration agreed to act as an arbitrator in the search for a new Nicaraguan leadership. Washington informed Somoza that it expected an orderly resignation and transfer in which a government of national reconciliation would take power and the National Guard would be reformed. Somoza agreed under the condition that the process would be overseen by the Organization of American States (OAS), and that he would be given asylum in the United States.[186]

At an OAS meeting convened by the United States, Washington sought to encourage formation of an Executive Committee to serve as a buffer between the Sandinistas and the National Guard. The administration hoped to preserve the Guard, negotiate for free elections, and make certain that a post-Somoza provisional government would be established. Secretary of State Vance called for a cease-fire, and suggested that the OAS send a peace-keeping force to supervise the cease-fire and prevent a power vacuum from developing.[187]

The U.S. proposal was rejected by the FSLN and by the Latin American states. Mexico, Panama, and the Andean nations, in particular, did not share American anxieties about the Sandinistas. Panama broke relations with Somoza and recognized the Sandinistas provisional government. Mexico praised the Sandinistas and opposed negotiations with Somoza or any compromise that would lead to "Somocismo sin Somoza." The Latin Americans attempted to undermine the U.S. plan. Mexico's foreign minister, Jorge Castaneda, had been given instructions to "block U.S. interventionism." Mexico and the Andean countries worked on a resolution that would force Somoza to resign and make it possible for the

FSLN to step in. The resolution omitted reference to the peace-keeping force, the cease-fire, and to the demands for a halt in arms shipments.[188]

The final OAS resolution was, in effect, a defeat for the United States. Washington's strategy had been to minimize Sandinista influence in a post-Somoza government; the OAS, however, would not lend it support to such an outcome. The OAS resolution called for the "immediate and definitive replacement of the Somoza regime," which was deemed to be "the fundamental cause" of the revolution; "the installation . . . of a democratic government . . . [and] the holding of free elections as soon as possible." The United States was, however, able to include a passage permitting "member states to take steps that are within their reach to facilitate an enduring and peaceful solution of the Nicaraguan problem."[189] This clause would give Washington legitimacy in acting as negotiator.

On June 25, 1979, following receipt of a CIA report warning that Somoza would probably last only a week, the administration decided on a two-track policy: talk with the junta to broaden and moderate its structure and policy, and negotiate the establishment of an Executive Committee composed of moderates. In Managua, the U.S. chargé d'affaires met with FAO leaders who made clear their dissatisfaction with the OAS resolution and the legitimacy it had bestowed on the FSLN. They told the U.S. representative that the FAO hoped to continue as an independent organization rather than support the provisional government in San Jose. The FAO was, however, waiting for an indication of U.S. support.

The revised U.S. policy had not been clearly conveyed to the U.S. Embassy in Managua. As a consequence, the opportunity to move events in accordance with Washington's plans was lost. The U.S. chargé d'affaires advised the moderates that although there was no U.S. position on the matter at the time, it would be preferable that they maintain their independence from the provisional government.[190] Unaware of Washington's position, and disappointed with the minimal efforts made by the United States to contact them since February 1978, the opposition decided to unite with the leftist-dominated junta.[191]

On June 27, 1979, the day the FAO announced its support for the junta, U.S. Ambassador Lawrence Pezzullo warned Somoza, "We don't see the beginning of a solution without your departure." When Somoza agreed to step down, Pezzullo asked him not to "move too precipitously," because he needed time to "get organized a little bit." The ambassador admitted that the Americans had not yet "been able to pull . . . together" ideas on how a transition government would be assembled.[192] Washington's revised plan for Nicaragua was disclosed on June 28. It was rejected publicly by the junta, as well as by the FAO and COSEP, which reaffirmed their support for the FSLN.[193]

Despite the uncertainties of the situation at the end of June 1979, Pezzullo reported that the National Guard remained a "strong fighting force" and was likely to survive in a "reconstituted" form. Pezzullo did, however, note that the moderates would not join the proposed Executive Committee without firmer assurances from the United States and stronger indications that they would be supported by the National Guard.[194] President Carter would not give such assurances without support from the international community.[195]

As events unraveled, Washington's plans were revised: it abandoned the idea for an Executive Committee and sought to encourage a moderate junta. Assistant Secretary of State for Inter-American Affairs Viron Vaky was sent to Latin America to get an agreement on the plan. This plan, too, was rejected by the Sandinistas because it would preserve the Guard.[196]

The administration was no longer in a good position to influence events in Nicaragua. Its conduct had alienated moderate and radicals alike. Because it failed to give commitments in June 1979, the administration lost an opportunity to encourage FAO aspirations to remain independent; it also antagonized the opposition with proposals it had devised. The alienation was exacerbated on July 7, when the *Washington Post* reported that Somoza was ready to leave, but that the United States was "temporizing while negotiations were conducted with the junta in Costa Rica." COSEP, the organization representing anti-Somoza business leaders, and the editorial staff of *La Prensa,* responded by accusing the United States of prolonging the bloodshed.[197]

U.S. relations with the FSLN were not improving either. On June 20, 1979, Warren Christopher told U.S. Representative Tony Hall that the United States was not dealing "with them [Sandinistas] directly, but we just started to deal with them indirectly through the provisional government, through one person."[198] Later, an FSLN request to meet with President Carter was rejected. The Sandinistas were told they could only meet with Secretary of State Vance, as incentive for the provisional government to compromise on an expanded junta and on the nomination of a Guard commander. The Directorate and the junta refused the conditions.[199]

It was only a week before the FSLN victory that the United States made an effort to conduct a dialogue with the Sandinistas. A meeting was set up with Eden Pastora, one of the more independent members of the FSLN Directorate. Such an encounter had been encouraged for eight months by Carazo and Torrijos; they had been rebuffed because U.S. officials believed that the meeting would discourage Nicaragua's moderates. The meeting was a disappointment. Washington informed Pastora that it was willing to support social democracy in Nicaragua; Pastora, however, was suspicious and unwilling to cooperate.[200]

Anastasio Somoza Debayle resigned and left Nicaragua on July 17, 1979. According to plans devised by the United States, Francisco Urcuyo assumed temporary power as president. Urcuyo was to have handed over power to the provisional government in San José shortly after assuming his position. Once in power, however, he refused to abdicate. The junta was convinced that this was a U.S. plot. In an attempt to dissociate itself from Urcuyo, the Department of State announced the departure of Ambassador Pezzullo and most of his staff. The U.S. negotiator, William Bowdler, remained in Managua to witness the July 19 arrival of the Sandinistas and the inauguration of the new government.[201]

After the Revolution: United States–Nicaraguan Relations

The First Two Years: Carter and the Sandinista Government

Despite the mutual suspicions, the governments of the United States and Nicaragua sought to preserve their individual interests by constructing a nonhostile relationship. Foremost among those interests were the security concerns of each state. The FSLN wanted to prevent U.S. support of counterrevolutionary forces in Nicaragua, and the United States hoped to inhibit Nicaraguan support of revolutionary movements in Central America.[202] Thus, on July 23, 1979, less than two weeks after their victory, the new Sandinista government sent a note to Washington expressing its determination to conform to its international agreements and continue friendly relations with the United States. In response, the administration affirmed its willingness to maintain cordial relations with the new Nicaraguan regime.[203]

The rhetoric of cordiality was accompanied by action. Within two weeks of the Sandinista victory, the United States sent 1,732 metric tons of food, and 9,600 pounds of medical supplies, and contributed to other international relief efforts. President Carter also agreed to a Sandinista request for a September 1979 meeting during which the FSLN was assured of U.S. economic aid. Complaints about U.S. assistance to anti-FSLN forces were denied.[204]

In mid-September 1979, Assistant Secretary of State for Inter-American Affairs Viron Vaky presented the administration's Nicaragua policy to the House Subcommittee on Inter-American Affairs:

> While it is true that Marxist elements are well-positioned to exert power, they do not yet dominate the situation. Moderate democratic elements capable of exerting influence and power of their own also exist in key

places in the government and in society. . . . Nicaragua's future internal
policies and relationships with the outside world will, in fact, be determined by those Nicaraguans who best define and meet the country's
needs during the reconstruction period. . . . The course of the Nicaraguan revolution can thus be affected in no small way by how the United
States perceives it and relates to it.[205]

Congress received the administration's AID program request for Nicaragua in November 1979. Of the $80 million to be allocated for Economic
Support Funds for Central America and the Caribbean, $70 million in
loans was designated for Nicaragua (60 percent of which was to be given
to the private sector). Five million dollars of the total was to be used for
grants to private organizations working in the country. This aid represented "the first overt attempt to build up groups friendly to the United
States."[206]

The AID request was passed in May 1980 after much delay and with
numerous amendments. Congress stipulated that prior to the disbursal of
funds, the president would be required to submit certification confirming
that the Sandinistas were not supporting insurgents abroad and were protecting the civil liberties of Nicaraguans. President Carter signed the AID
bill on May 31. In September 1980, U.S. intentions to maintain good relations with Nicaragua were again made plainly evident. Despite lingering
questions about Sandinista support for the Salvadoran guerrillas, the administration issued Presidential Determination No. 82-26 which cleared
the way for fund disbursals to Nicaragua.[207] Congressional opponents,
however, used the appropriations process to further delay disbursal of
funds until October 1.[208]

After the certification had been signed, Deputy Assistant Secretary of
State James Cheek was reassured by the Sandinistas that the Farabundo
Marti National Liberation Front (FMLN) guerrillas in El Salvador would
not be given Nicaraguan support.[209] The assurances, it seems, were given
in good faith.[210] Arms were held back through October, although Nicaraguan territory was made available for use by a clandestine Salvadoran
rebel radio station.[211] Nicaragua's minister of interior, Tomas Borge, announced in October, "We have promised in all seriousness not to send
arms or troops to help the Salvadorans, and we have kept our promise. Mr.
Carter can rest assured that we are keeping our promise."[212]

President Carter continued to make every effort to extend the respect
the new government expected. He sent a senior delegation to the first-year
anniversary ceremonies in July 1980. Despite Congressional obstructions
and delaying tactics intended to impede the flow of economic aid to Nicaragua, a new proposal for a $75 million Nicaraguan Recovery Program

was submitted in November 1980. Assistance was designated for use for previously funded business organizations and for institutions with political interests. Thus, in addition to supporting organizations such as COSEP (Confederation of Business Associations) and FUNDE, an independent association of cooperatives, AID funds were also to be used for church community development projects, professional exchange programs, and for the American Institute for Free Labor Development (a representative of the AFL-CIO), which would funnel assistance to independent labor unions.[213] Washington also participated in a $189.1 million Inter-American Development Bank loan and a $102.7 million World Bank package (see Table 4-1).[214]

Despite the Carter administration's efforts, FSLN rhetoric was often ruled by its historic antagonism toward the United States. In a speech in the United Nations General Assembly on September 28, 1979, four days after meeting with Carter, Nicaragua's president, Daniel Ortega, complained about the imperialist policies of the United States.[215] In March 1980, Ortega attacked Washington for its hostility against Jamaica and for threatening intervention in El Salvador. Hugo Torres, the deputy minister for state security, accused the CIA of fomenting unrest inside Nicaragua.[216]

U.S.–Nicaraguan relations began to change dramatically, however, in November 1980. Ronald Reagan was elected president on a Republican platform that deplored "the Marxist Sandinista takeover of Nicaragua" and called for termination of aid to its new government. The antagonism manifested by Reagan and by the Republican Party platform prompted the Sandinistas to believe that they would be faced with a hostile U.S. administration, no matter what policy they pursued. Thus, whereas Nicaragua's new leaders had previously refrained from extending large-scale assistance to Salvadoran guerrillas in order to maintain peaceable relations with the Carter administration, they increased their assistance after Reagan's election.[217]

On January 6, 1981, the CIA submitted a report that, in Robert Pastor's opinion, established conclusively that the Sandinista government was supporting the FMLN.[218] Although U.S. law required that aid be cut off under such circumstances, President Carter only issued a warning. As had been the case in previous discussions, the Sandinistas denied their government's involvement in the Salvadoran conflict, but acknowledged that some government officials might have assisted the rebels. Continued evidence that aid had been moving from Nicaragua to the Salvadoran rebels during December 1980 and January 1981 forced President Carter to suspend $15 million of the $75 million economic aid package. The aid, however, was not canceled, and could be restored in the future.[219]

The warnings and the suspension of aid did not deter the FSLN from continuing its support of the Salvadoran guerrillas. Ambassador Pezzullo warned the junta that continued support of the Salvadoran rebels would lead to a break in relations. Nicaragua promised to close the Salvadoran rebel radio station and to prevent any further "unofficial" assistance. The FMLN's Radio Liberacion was shut down on January 20, 1981, and arms to El Salvador ceased to flow for several days until the first weeks of the Reagan administration.[220]

Reagan and the Revolutionaries

Under President Reagan, the goal of U.S. policy was to deter a growing leftist influence in Nicaragua. "From the outset," commented Carter's assistant secretary of state for inter-American affairs, Viron Vaky, "the Reagan administration conceptualized the Central American situation as essentially a Cold War problem. . . . This categorization of the Central American crisis as an East-West conflict was the result of the Reagan administration's conviction that Carter's 'liberal' human rights policies had destabilized the region; that the situation . . . reflected a loss of control in America's 'backyard' and a deterioration of U.S. power which could be reversed by the exercise of will."[221]

In March 1981, President Reagan signed a "Presidential Finding" directing the CIA to pursue covert actions in Central America for the purpose of interdicting arms flows to Marxist guerrillas. The CIA set up a meeting in Guatemala which culminated in the formation of the Nicaraguan Democratic Force (FDN). Participants included: U.S. officials, disgruntled Nicaraguans, National Guardsmen and their Argentine advisers.[222] On April 1, 1981, despite intelligence reports that Sandinista assistance to the FMLN had ceased, the Reagan administration accused Nicaragua of providing such aid, and terminated U.S. assistance.

U.S. policy in Central America, explained Vaky, expanded beyond "a single security issue." The revised policy now included U.S. support for "democracy, reform and freedom," along with American opposition to "the military challenge from Cuba and Nicaragua with support for the security of threatened nations."[223]

Although the anti-FSLN trend demonstrated by the Reagan administration was not conducive to continued trust, the Nicaraguans were being asked to show good faith by continuing a dialogue with the United States. Negotiations began in August with a visit by Assistant Secretary of State for Inter-American Affairs Thomas Enders. Enders suggested to the Sandinistas that Nicaragua cease to back "foreign insurgencies," that it cut down on its own military build-up, and that it reduce its armed forces from 23,000 to 15,000. In exchange, the United States would refrain from intervening in Nicaragua's internal affairs and would pledge to enforce U.S. neutrality laws. The Americans would also resume economic aid and expand cultural relations.[224]

An inherent skepticism about U.S. intentions had been exacerbated by the aid cut-off in April 1981; the Enders proposals, therefore, were not well received. Nicaragua denied assisting the FMLN and insisted that putting limitations on their military capabilities was a violation of sovereignty. The nonaggression pact promised by Enders, they complained, was meaningless because the Rio Treaty had already established that principle. The possibility of having economic aid restored also seemed implausible because, even under a far friendlier Carter administration, Congress only approved $75 million. Furthermore, the Reagan administration had canceled $7 million in economic support that had been only suspended by the Carter administration.

Communications based on the Enders proposal were exchanged until October 1981. The only agreement reached, however, was one in which both governments agreed to refrain from verbal attacks on each other.[225]

In September 1981, as negotiations proceeded, the Pentagon announced operation "Halcon Vista," a joint U.S.–Honduran naval and air exercise that was to run for three days in October. A warning from the Sandinistas that the exercise "would seriously affect" the negotiations brought a letter from Thomas Enders offering to discuss invitations for Nicaraguan observers. The FSLN was also visited by a U.S. army general who explained the aims of the maneuvers.[226]

Operation Halcon Vista went on as planned. In an October 1981 speech to the United Nations, it was denounced by Daniel Ortega as preparation for an assault on Nicaragua. At the end of October, complaints from Managua were delivered to Washington regarding the military exercises, the cancellation of aid, and the administration's support of exile groups. The antagonism evident in the U.N. speech gave administration officials a reason to doubt the seriousness of the Sandinistas in the bilateral negotiations. As a consequence, the administration perceived Nicaragua's complaints as a rejection of the Enders proposals.[227]

Relations further deteriorated in November 1981, when President Reagan signed National Security Decision Document 17. The document authorized support for anti-Sandinista activities, as well as an appropriation of $19 million for the CIA's Nicaragua-related activities and for financial support of a 500-man guerrilla force to be used in Nicaragua. In March 1982, the first major guerrilla assault on Nicaragua was launched and two bridges destroyed in the north of the country.[228]

In addition to its diplomatic and military offensive against Nicaragua, the Reagan administration also attempted to influence events by using economic sanctions. Bilateral aid had been sharply reduced by May 1983, and Nicaragua's sugar quota, valued at $18.5 million, was reduced by 90 percent. Nicaragua was excluded from participating in the Export-Import Bank and the Overseas Private Investment Corporation. As of November 1981, the United States had vetoed loans to Nicaragua in the World Bank and the Inter-American Development Bank. Because of the weight carried by the United States in these institutions, multilateral lending to Nicaragua also came to a virtual halt. Thus, whereas in 1979 Nicaragua received World Bank and Inter-American Bank loans totaling approximately $179 million, the banks extended only $30 million in assistance in 1983. Despite Sandinista efforts to repay Somoza's foreign debt on schedule, the U.S. Inter-Agency Exposure Review Committee downgraded Nicaragua's creditworthiness from "substandard" to "doubtful" in 1983. The purpose of the downgrade was to discourage private banks from extending loans to the country.[229]

U.S. sanctions and FSLN rhetoric, however, did not put a halt to bilateral negotiations. The United States continued its two-pronged approach of pursuing negotiation while planning, supporting, and participating in military offensives. In March 1982, Washington submitted an eight-point plan to the Nicaraguans that included a demand for free elections as an "essential element" in continuing relations between the two countries. It also offered financial aid and the cessation of U.S. assistance to the *contras* in exchange for an end to Nicaragua's involvement in El Salvador.[230]

Miguel D'Escoto, Nicaragua's foreign minister, complained that the plan's stipulation regarding elections was "an inexcusable position of interference in matters which are of Nicaragua's sole and exclusive competence."[231] Daniel Ortega complained at the United Nations:

> It is . . . inconceivable that the country that is carrying out the greatest arms build-up and spending the most money on weaponry in the history of mankind should seek to demand of us that we fail to fulfill the minimum requirements for the defence of our own country. Nicaragua rejects the attempt by the United States to impose humiliating restrictions on its inescapable prerogatives with respect to national defence. We are certain that no sovereign state in the world would accept such a thing. . . . We take this opportunity to reiterate this commitment as well as our willingness to sign non-aggression treaties and agreements with all the countries of the region.[232]

Nevertheless, the Sandinistas responded with a thirteen-point plan of their own. The effort concluded unsuccessfully when Washington failed to pursue a Nicaraguan proposal that combined the twenty-one points submitted by both nations, and that suggested that Mexico be invited to participate in the negotiations.

The October 1983 U.S. attack on Grenada created an opportunity for serious negotiations between Washington and Managua. It was wasted, however, by the Reagan administration's adamant hostility toward the FSLN. The Grenada attack had stirred fears within the Sandinista leadership that the United States might consider a similar offensive against Nicaragua. Because the stated reason for the Grenada invasion was to protect U.S. nationals, the junta assured Washington that U.S. citizens were safe and that plans had been drawn up for their protection and evacuation. In the fall of 1983, responding to the Grenada invasion and to the Central American peace effort then in progress under the Contadora negotiations, other efforts were made to accommodate the United States. The Nicaragua-based Salvadoran FMLN "command and control center" was shut down and most of its leadership asked to leave.[233] Daniel Ortega announced that he would agree to a number of concessions, including a "regional declaration" supporting "elections and democratic institutions," the removal of "outside military advisers," and the cessation of "military aid to the region."[234]

On October 20 and in early December 1983, Nicaragua presented proposals to the Contadora countries, to Central American governments, and to the United States; the proposals were designed to address the issues of security and nonaggression. The Sandinistas unilaterally relaxed human rights restrictions: censorship of La Prensa was partly lifted, some Miskito Indian political prisoners were released, and anti-Sandinista activists were given limited amnesty and the right to participate in the political system. Furthermore, a small number of Cuban personnel—not including military advisers—were sent home.[235]

The United States neglected to use this opening to press for an easing of U.S.–Nicaraguan tensions. Viron Vaky explained, "High officials questioned whether they [the Sandinista proposals] were really substantive and meaningful, or just tactical maneuvers to relieve pressure. Interior Minister Tomas Borge was refused a visa [to the United States] on the grounds that he was on a 'propaganda' mission. No response was made to the receipt of treaty drafts, other than to refer Nicaragua to the Contadora countries." Vaky added that the administration was not interested in exploring the "Nicaragua gambit. It . . . simply asked for more."[236]

Despite the suspicion and the lost opportunities, negotiations between the United States and Nicaragua continued intermittently throughout the Reagan years, as did official U.S. support for the contras and other anti-Somoza groups. Charges and countercharges between Washington and

Managua persisted. In the end, it was the Central American governments, working under the August 1987 Central American peace accord, Esquipulas II, which paved the way for free and open elections in Nicaragua, and for the reemergence of a pro-American government in Managua.

The United States in Nicaragua: Policy and Problems

The problems encountered and the policies pursued in Nicaragua were in many ways reminiscent of those in the Iranian case and portended those that would occur in the Philippines. In all the cases, political liberties and human rights had been set aside to further the power of a dictator; economies had grown, while disparities remained or increased between the rich and poor, and the rural and urban. Nationalist sentiment in all the cases became, or already had existed as an impelling force of revolutionary fervor. As discontent and protest increased in all three cases, Washington sought to maintain the political status quo by urging that reform be undertaken as a means of appeasement. Instead of opening avenues for participation, reform in all the cases led to intensified protest and, ultimately, to revolution. The United States had become so tied to the leaders of these nations, and the primacy of the relationship had become so paramount, that little assistance was given to moderate opposition forces.

Throughout much of Nicaragua's postindependence history, U.S. policy toward that country was characterized by military, political, and economic intervention. With the reins of power in the hands of the Somozas, Washington worked to support the dynasty on a fairly consistent basis. Although domestic discontent with economic and political conditions in Nicaragua was evident throughout most of the Somoza years, Washington began to react to the discontent only when the Ford administration came into office. Events in Nicaragua, however, would outpace decision making in Washington—just as they had in Iran, and would later in the Philippines. While U.S. policy would attempt to direct history, it would, in fact, be molded by ad hoc decisions devised to catch up with events. As such, American policy was neither timely, nor effective, nor well-informed.

The Nicaraguan revolution gained momentum as the Carter administration entered office. Maurice Solaun, Carter's ambassador to Nicaragua from September 1977 to April 1979, described U.S. policy during that period as evolving in three stages: from neutrality, to mediation, to partial withdrawal.[237] Referring to the neutrality phase, he explained,

> I had to implement our human rights policy. This initially implied a need
> to maintain proper relations with the Somoza government, while, at the

same time, opening broad contacts to the opposition and encouraging respect for human rights and the democratization of Nicaragua. . . .

   This policy became known among some supporters in the State Department and the National Security Council as a policy of "neutrality."
It was "neutral" in that, following the described interventionist constraints of our human rights policy, we were not to place ourselves entirely within either the camp of the government of Nicaragua or the
opposition. In effect, Washington was periodically critical in public of
the Somoza regime but the embassy was not to side with the opposition
to the extent of organizing the overthrow of the government, nor was it
to help organize the opposition or finance any of its factions. . . .

   Objectively, really, our policy was to avoid any commitment to either side. This is not to say that our policy was one of indifference to the
situation; hardly so, inasmuch as we were critical of the status quo, and
privately and publicly favored a change in Nicaragua. As we were not
committed to the overthrow of the government of Nicaragua the embassy was restricted from direct contact with virtually all groups organized to violently do so. . . .

   Nicaragua was a faithful client of the United States. The Somozas
were our friends.[238]

The stated goal of Carter's noninterventionist policy, of maintaining
distance while encouraging dialogue and reform, may well have represented a successful strategy through the mid-1970s. Reform during those
years was the ultimate goal of the existing opposition; overt disaffection
among the poor and the business elite had not yet become so intense as to
render compromise untenable. By the latter half of the 1970s, however,
such a policy was no longer sufficient. The poor had a champion in the
FSLN, and the business sector, discontented with deteriorating conditions, was calling for Somoza's resignation by 1977.

   While implementing its policy of noninterference, Washington also
lost valuable time in which the moderate opposition might have been organized and strengthened. Instead, while the United States temporized,
the radical elements gained strength and developed their organization. As
time elapsed frustrations grew in Nicaragua, military encounters between
the Guard and the FSLN increased, and the economy was battered. As was
the case during the Roosevelt administration, nonintervention in the
Carter administration led to disaster: under Roosevelt, it paved the way for
the presidency of Anastasio Somoza Garcia; under Carter, it contributed to
the anti-Somoza revolution and the ascendancy of the FSLN.

   By September 1978, U.S. policy had edged toward a greater willingness to participate more actively in the crisis. "The mediation phase developed when the potential for widespread bloodshed became more
apparent."[239] Positions by then, however, had become more rigid and the
possibilities of reaching compromise rendered virtually nonexistent.

When negotiations collapsed in January 1979, the imposition of sanctions against Somoza was viewed as a necessary measure to re-establish U.S. credibility among Nicaragua's moderates and across Latin America. The impact of the sanctions, however, was limited. The crisis atmosphere created by the Sandinista attacks had waned, and no new options were found or sought either by the United States or by Somoza. In Ambassador Solaun's assessment, the situation was one of "stale-mate": The government was "not strong enough to control the opposition and the opposition [was] not strong enough to overthrow the government. . . . The result was a process of disintegration, a 'situation of quasi-anarchy.' "[240]

As turmoil in Nicaragua increased in the spring of 1979, and as Nicaraguan moderates and Central American states pressed Washington to oust Somoza, the United States was again drawn into the crisis. However, none of the administration's tactics—its protestations to Somoza, its attempts to obtain regional cooperation in solving the crisis, or its effort to form an acceptable political configuration for a post-Somoza Nicaragua—would by then prove viable options. By the time the United States sought to create a moderate interim Executive Committee, many of the moderates had already joined the FSLN, believing that they had been abandoned by Washington. Those who were left would not join in Washington's plan without guarantees. Washington would not give guarantees without approval from Latin America, and Latin America would not join the United States. Washington proved neither able to contribute to a peaceful resolution of the crisis nor capable of orchestrating an outcome it could find acceptable.

While the policies Washington sought to enforce lagged behind events, they also carried insufficient weight to alter those events. For example, the very inactivity that defined the initial policy of neutrality would prove detrimental to U.S. interests. The policy neither promoted significant change that could appease an increasingly hostile population, nor did it give sufficient support for developing a moderate opposition. Indeed, despite its own guidelines, the administration tended to ignore the opposition in favor of Somoza.

As U.S. policy moved toward mediation, its influence on events was no more effective. Ambassador Solaun attributed the collapse of negotiations on Somoza's awareness of the unwillingness of the United States "to go all the way against him . . . to use overt or covert force . . . to change the government of Nicaragua."[241] Somoza's friend, U.S. Representative Charles Wilson, conceded this point too, when he noted that sanctions imposed before February 1979 would not have proven successful. Somoza, he said, "wasn't ready to go until [late June 1979 when] the situation made it impossible to stay." Wilson agreed, however, that a different ambassador or a different strategy might have convinced Somoza to resign earlier.[242]

In addition to being characterized by time lags and ineffectiveness U.S. foreign policy making was also plagued by a lack of critical information. Rebellion and protest had erupted throughout the years of the Somoza dynasty. As early as 1960, Conservative Party leader Fernando Aguero warned that if Somoza was permitted to remain, a "communist takeover in Nicaragua" would be possible. What was needed, he said, was a "democratic revolution," and "social and economic and reform."[243] The clergy and the opposition issued complaints throughout the 1970s.

As in Iran, however, information about the organization and activities of the opposition was scant. Inaccurate evaluations were submitted partly because the U.S. intelligence network had failed: the CIA presence in the region had been cut, and intelligence reports were written to conform to "the mood and view of those who read them."[244] Viron Vaky later recalled that the CIA view was "comforting" since it seemed to suggest "the absence of imminent crisis." Furthermore, the State Department and CIA hesitated to pursue contacts with the Sandinistas because such association might indicate U.S. recognition of the FSLN as a "legitimate contender for power."[245] As violence increased in 1978, embassy staff was also discouraged from traveling outside of the capital.

Gaps in intelligence gathering distorted the information upon which decisions were being made, and possibly misdirected U.S. policy. During the latter part of the revolution, for example, Washington was unaware of the full extent of assistance being given to the Sandinistas by Mexico, Panama, Venezuela, Costa Rica, and Cuba. Weapons which Panama's Torrijos solicited from Cuba on behalf of the Sandinistas, began to arrive in September 1978. Until his term concluded in March 1979, Venezuela's President Perez sent arms to Costa Rica, for use by Costa Rica and the FSLN. Costa Rica, which had long supported the Nicaraguan struggle against the Somozas, established a policy of "tolerance" toward FSLN activity. Mexico funneled funds to the Sandinistas beginning in the fall of 1978.[246] "As late as one month before" Somoza's fall, NSC member Robert Pastor wrote, Washington's ignorance about the FSLN "arsenal and logistics network" led to a mistaken belief that a "third force" might still be able to assume power. Furthermore, during June and July 1979, when plans were being made to preserve the National Guard under a new commander, most policymakers in Washington incorrectly assumed that "a wide range of contacts had been maintained with the Guard."[247]

Despite limited information, the United States could have promoted its own interests more aggressively by working more closely with the moderate opposition. The administration had a number of opportunities to help the moderates and, thereby, promote its own interests. Membership in the FSLN was low until the mid-1970s. A united moderate front, centered on Nicaragua's business sector, already existed. COSEP and INDE had called for political and economic reform in 1974, and moderate political activists united under UDEL to pursue reform in Nicaragua and avoid revolution. Had it had more support, the umbrella FAO, which was organized in May 1978, might have proven a viable political force able to take charge of the government. Indeed, even at the time of the August 1978 Sandinista attack on the National Palace, the FSLN later admitted, it was not in control of the situation in Nicaragua and was fearful of a moderate takeover of the government. Humberto Ortega recounted that during the September 1978 fighting, which had spread to five major cities, "The mass movement went beyond the vanguard's capacity to take the lead." "It was a spontaneous reaction on the part of the masses which, in the end, the Sandinista Front began to direct through its activists and a number of military units."[248] Interviews with FSLN leaders Henry Ruiz, Daniel Ortega, and Jaime Wheelock Roman pointed to the "fear" in all three FSLN factions that, even by the fall of 1978, the Nicaraguan bourgeoisie would rid the nation of Somoza and establish a moderate government before the Sandinistas could complete their revolution.[249]

Despite its diminishing influence, opportunities for the United States to encourage moderate political forces may have even lasted through July 1979. Moderates began to move into the FSLN camp following the failed negotiations in early 1979 and became alienated by Washington's unwillingness to support them in late June; nevertheless, it is conceivable that the Carter administration might still have been able to salvage the moderate option at that time. A number of moderates remained willing to discuss the American plan for an Executive Committee; what they needed was assurances from the United States. Hope for the "third force" died not because the possibility of forming an Executive Committee did not exist, but because Washington would not unilaterally commit itself to guarantees and Latin America would not give them. Indeed, Daniel Ortega and Alfonso Robelo later admitted that even one month before the fall of Somoza, they were unaware of how precarious Somoza's position was.[250]

The lack of contact with and assistance to the moderates, and the complete neglect of the FSLN and the moderates within it, proved fatal when the revolution came. Control of the military would be the source of power in the new government. William Bowdler, the U.S. negotiator, urged two moderate members of the junta, Alfonse Robelo and Alfredo Cesar, to seek a "counterweight" to the Guard. Confidence in the Americans, however, had by then been sorely tested and American advice not welcome.[251] Even the Latin Americans were unsuccessful in their efforts to get the moderate elements in the revolutionary movement to maintain their power. Panamanian and Venezuelan officials advised moderate FSLN member Eden Pastora to retain his supporters and their weapons. It was a suggestion Pastora would not heed. He was excluded from the Directorate after the revolution and later acknowledged that he had erred in neglecting the advice.[252]

Had the United States made a more concerted effort to support the moderates before the revolution, its influence on events in post-Somoza Nicaragua might have significantly increased. The political situation during the initial postrevolutionary period was sufficiently fluid to allow moderate opposition factions to assume greater power within the new system. Lack of organization among the moderates, however, meant that many factions would lose effectiveness and thus leave the way open for wider Sandinista infiltration.

Nicaragua and the U.S. National Interest

The Somoza dynasty left behind a stratified society where widespread poverty prevailed and where foreign economic aid was critical. In economic terms, neither the corruption that predominated during the Somoza reign nor the devastated economy over which the Somozas presided served the U.S. interest; indeed, Nicaragua's economic plight was in large measure the cause of revolution. The human and economic costs of the war that brought down the dynasty were calculated by the United Nations and the Inter-American Human Rights Commission. Approximately 10,000 were killed between September 1978 and July 19, 1979—most were civilians. In total, 45,000 people were killed (80 percent civilians), "up to 160,000 were wounded, and 40,000 orphaned." Approximately one million people were left in desperate need of food, and 250,000 required shelter. Government funds were depleted to pay for the war: Somoza had amassed a $1.5 billion debt and had plundered the Central Bank, leaving the public coffers with only $3 million. "Economic losses" caused by the war stood at about $2 billion, and the gross domestic product (GDP) decreased by 25.1 percent in 1979.[253] The loss and human suffering that accompanied the revolution, and which the United States might have done more to prevent, contributed nothing to the interests of the Americans.

The protection and support extended to the Somozas by the United States was in many ways comparable to that given to Shah Mohammad Reza Pahlavi and to Ferdinand Marcos. In Iran, U.S. strategic interests centered on resources, on Iran's proximity to the Persian Gulf and the Soviet Union, and on Iran's willingness to act as proxy policeman for the United States. U.S. military bases in the Philippines represented a major strategic concern for Washington. In the case of Nicaragua, however, no equally preeminent interest existed to warrant such a policy of support.

Washington's initial interests in Nicaragua had centered on geographic concerns, particularly as they related to the building of a transisthmian canal. As geographic considerations receded, U.S. interests moved toward issues of ideology and the threat of communism. The salience of that issue too, however, waned by the time the Carter administration took office in January 1976. Thus, by the latter half of the 1970s, the U.S. national interest in Nicaragua focused rather narrowly on the protection of a friend who, in the past, had supported and upheld U.S. policy in the region. The Somoza dynasty, however, was plainly corrupt—its policies heedless of the political aspirations, human rights, and economic needs of the Nicaraguan people. Opposition came primarily from a moderate, pro-Western business sector. To have ignored this opposition in favor of a dictator, when no immediate threats to American national interests existed and no viable radical alternative was present, would seem to have been a critical error.

As was the case in Iran and the Philippines, when Washington finally acted in the midst of revolution, it did too little too late, damaging both its short-term and long-term interests. In the short term, the United States gained little by supporting Somoza. Somoza was not, at the time, protecting any particular U.S. interests and, in fact, was creating a problem by fostering conditions for the expansion of a radical opposition. In the long run, the administration subverted the national interest by maintaining a distance from the moderates and by ignoring the FSLN. The domestic politics and foreign policy of the Sandinistas, in comparison to Somoza or an alternative moderate regime, proved the least acceptable to the U.S. interest. Under the FSLN-led government, private property was subject to confiscation and human rights were frequently restricted. In its foreign policy, the FSLN professed adherence to nonalignment. Nonetheless, Nicaragua established close ties to the Soviet Union and the Eastern bloc while exhibiting intense hostility toward the United States. Within the region, it supported the El Salvador guerrillas who threatened an American-supported government.

Despite its support of Somoza and its attempts to isolate the FSLN during the revolution, the United States did not completely lose in Nicaragua. In the interest of rebuilding their country, the Sandinistas allowed pragmatism to outweigh principle. They were willing to continue relations with the United States, although only under conditions of equality. Accusations of Sandinista support for the FMLN remain questionable. Documents received by the International Court of Justice, from a former CIA analyst, and from Sandinista defectors, showed that substantial transfers of arms occurred until early 1981. Any assistance extended after that period was minimal.[254]

Indeed, it was not even the conduct of the United States before or during the revolution that led to the increasing strains between Washington and Managua, but the postrevolutionary policies of the Reagan administration. The United States engaged in military, diplomatic, and economic assaults on Nicaragua. Anti-Sandinista *contras* were supported, military assistance to Honduras was increased, military exercise off the coast of Nicaragua were carried out, and the FSLN government was denounced for its human rights abuses and political inclinations. Although the Sandinistas often chided the United States for its imperialist history, it was the reaction of the Reagan administration to the Nicaraguan revolution that made antagonism and distrust inevitable. In an April 1982 speech, President Reagan identified Nicaragua as "the principal threat to the region and to U.S. interests."[255] U.S. officials criticized the FSLN and often made demands that would seem arrogant and indeed untenable to any sovereign state. Thus, although the Enders proposals of August 1981 may have been negotiable, they were rejected because of the distrust harbored by the Sandinistas and because of the offense they felt at Enders's style.[256] Bayardo Arce, an FSLN official and member of the Directorate explained, "At the time, we didn't think that Enders was very serious. In retrospect, we consider him as the most serious person who spoke with us." Daniel Ortega said about the failed talks, "I would say the principal problem that we had in the meeting with Enders was his arrogance."[257]

Secretary of State George Shultz also exhibited some of that arrogance in a 1986 address when he observed that:

> Our objectives in Nicaragua . . . are straightforward. We want the Nicaraguan regime to reverse its military buildup, to send its foreign advisers home, and to stop oppressing its citizens and subverting its neighbors. We want it to keep the promises of the coalition government that followed Somoza's fall: democratic pluralism at home and peaceful relations abroad. . . . Our goals are limited and reasonable. They are also essential for our values and our security and those of our neighbors.[258]

Former CIA official John Horton wrote in February 1985,

> This [Reagan] administration considers agreement with Marxist-Leninists to be risky . . . but it also finds them too distasteful and inconsistent with our tough posturing to be a serious option. The

administration did not simply fail to give sufficient hearing to a diplomatic strategy; it ideologically shackled its imagination and so was not free to use the informed pragmatism that enables a skilled diplomat to probe for solutions.[259]

Despite its history, however, cordial U.S.–Nicaraguan relations were reestablished when, under the auspices of the Arias plan, the governments of Central America negotiated free elections in Nicaragua, and Violeta Barrios de Chamorro was elected president.[260]

The Lessons of Neoconservatism Examined

In Nicaragua, as in the other cases, neither neoconservative nor neorealist prescriptions proved wholly prescient or effective. As in Iran and the Philippines, the United States was not, and could not be, the ultimate arbiter of affairs in a foreign nation. When the United States refused to sell equipment and planes to Somoza in the 1950s, he bought them from Brazil; when he was refused military arms in the late 1970s, he purchased equipment from Spain, France, Argentina, Israel, Guatemala, Honduras, El Salvador and the black markets in South Africa and the Bahamas.[261] Somoza refused to heed the admonitions of American diplomats during the OAS-mediated negotiations of 1978–1979, boasting on American television, "I even had your ambassador come and tell me that . . . President Carter and Secretary Vance wanted me to get off the presidency, and I said no."[262]

The United States sought gradual change in Nicaragua and hoped to pursue its goals through a policy of noninterference. Its plans were thwarted by events over which it had no control. Nicaragua would succumb to revolution and Washington would be forced to move from noninterference to direct mediation. Any resolution the United States hoped to implement was irrevocably hampered by the limitations of regional politics and the imprints of history. Venezuela, Panama, Costa Rica, Mexico, and the rest of Latin America supported the FSLN, while the United States was still seeking a moderate alternative. At least fifteen nations had recognized the junta or suspended relations with Somoza by mid-June 1979 as Washington was devising plans for a "third force."

Historical memory in Nicaragua also would limit U.S. options. The National Guard was widely despised for its corruption and its ties to the Somozas. As such, a post-Somoza government that preserved the National Guard would prove increasingly unacceptable. Furthermore, once the FSLN was in power, anti-Americanism that had resulted from decades of

U.S. interference could not be easily ameliorated. Indeed, had a less moderate FSLN faction taken control of the movement, even minimal relations with the United States would likely have been suspended.

The contention that the pursuit of U.S. interests leads to the protection of human rights abroad remains unconfirmed in this case, too. The Somozas frequently violated the political liberties and human rights of their people. Nonetheless, in the U.S. interest, Washington supported the Somozas and supplied them with the instruments of repression.

The neoconservative caveat proven correct, again, was that pressure for reform will lead to unknown consequences. As in Iran, liberalization eventually contributed to revolution. Following the lifting of martial law in September 1977, opposition activity burgeoned: *La Prensa* reported on corruption in the Somoza administration, Conservatives and Social Christians increased demands for political reform, strikes were called, and the FSLN attacked National Guard outposts in several cities. Somoza's response to the turmoil and discontent was concession rather than repression—a response designed to appease the Carter administration. Among the conciliatory steps announced by Somoza was a promise to resign at the end of his term in 1981. But frustrations had by then become too intense even for such a compromise, and protests again broke out in opposition to the 1981 resignation date. Although Somoza exchanged compromise for repression by August 1978, the opposition had by that time become more united and the population more determined to bring down the dynasty.

While the warnings that reform may lead to unknown consequences prove valid, the relationship between reform and revolution is not inevitable. The United States pressed for reform when frustrations had become intense and partial reform was no longer sufficient. Nicaraguans had long sought a more open political system and better economic conditions; the United States had the opportunity to urge such reforms in the 1960s and 1970s. By the time Washington became involved in the Nicaraguan crisis, the intensity of disaffection had become too great to be appeased by measured steps. Even in this situation, had the United States supported the development and organization of a moderate opposition, it might have avoided the negative consequences of revolution. A more unified alternative opposition might have urged reform more forcefully or, failing to do so, might have been in a better position to take hold of the reins of power. A September 1978 *Wall Street Journal* article reported, for example, that "politicians in the business community talked of including the Marxist-leaning Sandinista guerrillas in a government controlled by moderates; now they seem resigned to merely wanting a piece of the action in a 'national government' that they realize could well be dominated by leftist forces."[263]

U.S. pressures on Somoza also had consequences that were not fore-seen, but which might have been anticipated. Washington denied aid to Somoza forcing him to look elsewhere for the weapons and funds needed by the National Guard. Somoza was able to get needed ammunition else-where, but his resources dwindled and the Guard was weakened; Somoza's position became more tenuous. The United States thus may have hastened the final collapse of the Somoza dynasty and the ascendancy of a leftist regime by helping to subvert Somoza's strength while still seeking an al-ternative to it.

The central premise of the neoconservative argument, that commu-nism will follow revolution, is also only partially established in this case. In Nicaragua, as in Iran, the United States kept its distance from the mod-erate opposition in deference to the ruler. We neither knew enough about this opposition nor, more important, gave it enough support. Moderate forces that would have served the U.S. interest best were overwhelmed by a more organized and more radical opposition. A coherent policy, which would have supported the development, organization, and training of moderate organizations and parties, might have served to preempt the rad-ical victory.

Even with the radical alternative in Nicaragua, however, the threats posed by a communist regime, as perceived by the neoconservatives, were not especially evident. The foreign policy of the Sandinista government certainly was not comparable to that of the Somoza regime in terms of U.S. interests. The Sandinistas embraced Marxist philosophy, increased diplomatic, military, and economic relations with the Soviet Union and the Eastern bloc, and professed a virulent anti-Americanism. Nonetheless, they announced themselves to be a part of the nonaligned movement and were willing to subsume principle to pragmatism and continue economic, diplomatic, and even military relations with the United States. That little progress was made on these fronts may have been as much the responsi-bility of the Reagan administration as it was of the FSLN's professed an-tagonism. Indeed, the only significant national interest endangered by the FSLN victory related to its ostensible support of El Salvador's FMLN. Here too, however, the damage may not have been as severe as public pro-nouncements would have indicated.

The Neorealist Perspective Reviewed

As is the case with neoconservative prescriptions, results are also mixed when applying neorealist guidelines to empirical situations. The neoreal-ist formula is essentially designed to put the United States in good stead with the political opposition, thereby assuring that friendly relations will be maintained when the governing elite change. In Nicaragua, more so than in the other two cases, the United States pursued such a policy of dissociation; the efforts, however, were not rewarded with the expected cordiality. The problem lies in the assumptions made by the neorealist argument.

Diplomatic pressure and economic and military sanctions are encouraged by the neorealists as a means of achieving human rights reforms and as an instrument of dissociation. These measures, they assume, would not so antagonize a dependent leader as to impel him toward another camp and away from the U.S. sphere of influence. In Nicaragua, pressure and sanctions were imposed, and Somoza did not abandon his relationship with the United States.

The attitudes a new elite adopts toward the United States, neo-realists argue, are in part dependent on U.S. human rights policy in the period before the revolution. This argument, however, does not prove completely valid in the Nicaraguan case. While the moderate opposition in Nicaragua recognized the role U.S. human rights policy played in ameliorating human rights conditions in 1977, and thus in accelerating the demise of the Somoza dynasty,[264] it was at the same time also aware of U.S. involvement in Nicaragua's history and suspicious of its motives in the crisis. When Washington did not remove Somoza, the moderates perceived the United States as duplicitous, rather than ineffective. In September 1978, a member of the Conservative Party asserted that "Somoza is part of the American system, not ours." Conservative Congressman, Eduardo Chamorro Cornel, referring to U.S. military forces that had installed Somoza's father in 1933, complained, "Somoza is the last Marine. After so many of years of intervention, you say, 'We don't intervene.' That's the most sophisticated intervention we have seen."[265]

The New York Times reported in December 1978 that all but the most conservative Nicaraguans were bitter that,

> Washington, fearing "another Cuba," is searching for stability rather than for social and economic change or even human rights—repeating, as they see it, American policy during its occupation of Nicaragua between 1912 and 1933, and its subsequent support for the Somoza family. Nicaraguans note that the Carter administration was silent when the National Guard killed 3,000 people in crushing the September insurrection, but moved quickly when it recognized the popularity of the Sandinist guerrillas.[266]

In March 1979, Alfonso Robelo complained, "First the United States came and told everyone that they would put pressure on Somoza to go.

They created false expectations. When Somoza's reaction was to say 'Come do it physically,' they backed down. . . . It has a boomerang effect on the opposition, on the U.S. image."[267]

Despite the suspicion, the moderate forces invited American involvement in resolving the crisis. Their disappointment with the conduct of U.S. policy in Nicaragua, during the crisis and throughout Nicaragua's history, proved not even to have seriously affected their relations with the United States a decade later. Thus, under the presidency of the moderate Violeta Barrio de Chamorro, U.S.–Nicaraguan relations were reestablished.

Indeed, even under an FSLN government, the extent of antagonism that developed between the United States and Nicaragua was not inevitable. Eden Pastora admitted after the revolution that he, like others in the Sandinista leadership, understood that U.S. support for Somoza had been withdrawn early on.[268] Sandinista hostility was based on a nationalism provoked by a past in which the United States had been involved in virtually every aspect of Nicaraguan affairs. Thus, for example, Carlos Fonseca Amador, one of the founders of the FSLN wrote,

> The people of Nicaragua have been suffering under the yoke of a reactionary clique imposed by Yankee imperialism virtually since 1932, the year in which Anastasio Somoza Garcia was named commander in chief of the so-called National Guard, a post that had previously been filled by Yankee officials. This clique has reduced Nicaragua to the status of a neocolony—exploited by the Yankee monopolies and the local capitalist class.

Fonseca delineated U.S. involvement in Nicaragua since 1850 and accused the United States of "using Nicaragua's geographic position to make it a base for aggression against other Latin American peoples."[269]

Further exacerbating antagonisms engendered by the past was Washington's attitude toward the FSLN. Until the last moment, the Carter administration attempted to bar the possibility of Sandinista participation in a post-Somoza government. Indeed, even at the June 1979 OAS meeting, U.S. delegates unsuccessfully tried to prevent Miguel D'Escoto, foreign minister of the Provisional Government of National Reconstruction, from addressing the meeting.[270]

As the revolution took hold, and the Reagan administration took office, sanctions were imposed on Nicaragua and anti-FSLN activities were supported; the alienation and suspicion grew. Nicaragua's foreign minister, Miguel D'Escoto, explained in a 1986 interview:

> more than any other country in continental Latin America, we have suffered the consequences of U.S. official interventionism. We have been

invaded, we have been occupied time and time again. We suffered the imposition of one of the most hideous regimes in the history of Latin America for close to a half century, and we are at this present time experiencing a war that is characterized, even by the people in the U.S. Congress, as not only illegal, but also immoral. . . . I think we have reason to be concerned about the United States.[271]

The assumption that human rights is the core interest of opposition movements under right-wing regimes also stands on weak ground in Nicaragua, as it had in the case of Iran and would in the case of the Philippines. The forces that impelled revolution in Iran were based on economic and social discontent, as well as cultural and nationalist sentiment; in the Philippines, economic difficulties and nationalism fed the rebellion. Although criticism of Somoza's human rights abuses had been frequent, at the core of Nicaragua's revolution were issues related to economics, political rights, and nationalism. Particularly after the 1972 earthquake, the business community witnessed the corruption of Somoza and his associates; entrepreneurs, workers, and civil servants were incensed by the taxation and regulations Somoza had ostensibly imposed for the earthquake relief effort. As repression by the National Guard increased and prospects of Somoza's immediate departure waned, political demands became more prominent.

On the radical front, complaints voiced by the FSLN centered on the issue of economic exploitation. Support for the FSLN came from the rural and urban poor who were discontented with their economic lot, and from the children of Nicaragua's business community, who resented the venality of the Somoza regime after the 1972 earthquake. In addition, however, the FSLN criticized the inequities of the Nicaraguan political system and continued the rhetoric of anti-imperialism and anti-Americanism begun by Sandino.

That the impetus for revolution was primarily economic is perhaps demonstrated further by Nicaragua's more recent history. The economy of the nation under the Sandinistas deteriorated dramatically; by early 1990, private consumption fell by 70 percent and "real wages fell to less than 10 percent of their former value."[272] Primarily as a consequence of the failing economy, the Sandinista government was voted out of office. The American-supported Violeta de Chamorro won the presidency in 1990, and the United States reestablished its links to the country. A history of U.S. intervention, its support of a Somoza dynasty abusive of human rights, a decade of anti-American rhetoric, and a U.S. policy designed to destroy Nicaragua's economy and government, did not develop into a backlash that would isolate the United States permanently from Nicaraguan affairs. Pragmatism and economic necessity prevailed over political history.

The neorealist suggestion that the U.S. national interest be redefined in postrevolutionary situations to accommodate nonaligned foreign policy orientations does show validity in this case. Although it joined the non-aligned movement, the FSLN increased its diplomatic, economic, and military ties to the Soviet Union and Eastern bloc. Nonetheless, even under these circumstances, the U.S. interest was not irrevocably damaged. Nicaragua remained willing to pursue relations with the United States, as long as those relations were based on mutual respect and equality. Nicaraguan support of the FMLN in El Salvador was probably less extensive than was assumed. Furthermore, although when Somoza fell Washington may have lost an ally who would, at intervals, act on its behalf, no immediately apparent need for such assistance existed. Thus, the national interest was not placed in great jeopardy by the revolution.

In this case, as in the others, the neorealist caveat that misplaced loyalties lead to misguided policies rings true. It is, however, best exemplified in the Nicaraguan case. No immediate U.S. interest in Nicaragua required Somoza's support; nonetheless, a singular loyalty—based on an ideological congruence—led to a failure in intelligence gathering and to a critical loss of perspective among policymakers.

5   The Philippines:
U.S. Foreign Policy—
An Inadvertent Success

The Philippines under Ferdinand Marcos replicated in many ways the patterns of politics, repression, and U.S. involvement evident in the case of Iran: political liberties and human rights were trampled upon by an increasingly oppressive ruler, economic conditions deteriorated, corruption became rampant, and domestic discontent was exacerbated. As in Iran, the patterns of American political and economic involvement spanned decades, and military and economic ties were extensive. Warnings came from the Philippine opposition about internal conditions and their imminent effect on Philippine stability. In this case, too, despite the evidence, American administrations refused to abandon an ostensibly loyal and useful ally.

While ultimately not a revolution in theoretical terms, events in the Philippines nonetheless unfolded in much the same way as did the revolutions in Iran and Nicaragua. The causes that impelled the three revolutions were closely akin. Although little changed with the overthrow of the Marcos regime, initial hopes for the revolution centered on expectations for fundamental revisions in the economic and political structures of the nation.

The similarities, particularly between the Philippine and Iranian cases, did not, however, lead to analogous outcomes. Whereas American support of the Shah ultimately led to a rupture in U.S.–Iran relations, U.S. backing of Marcos did not lead to a rift between the United States and the Philippines. Postrevolutionary Philippines continued to maintain relatively friendly relations with Washington.

The U.S. Presence in the Philippines

Nearly half a century of American colonial administration in the Philippines created extensive and lasting influences. U.S. control of the Philippines was officially assumed in 1898 when a defeated Spain ceded the territory under the Treaty of Paris. Colonial status for the Philippines came to an end on July 4, 1946, when the nation achieved independence from the United States.

As a colony of the United States, the Philippines became an important market for U.S.-manufactured goods and was regarded as the U.S. outpost in the Far East; it served as a staging area for U.S. military contingents fighting in the Chinese Boxer Rebellion and was used as a base for U.S. intervention in Siberia during the Russian civil war early in the twentieth century. During its administration of the territory, the United States instituted free and universal public education (conducted in English), and attempted to inculcate its precepts of democratic government and economic liberalism. Americans opened the administrative bureaucracy and civil service to the Philippine elite and middle class, and opened a lower legislative house to elected Filipino representation. In public administration, law, jurisprudence, and education, American codes and norms prevailed. Philippine raw materials were given tariff-free access to the U.S. market. At independence, a new Philippine constitution was drawn up closely resembling that of the United States.[1]

Policies instituted by the United States served to co-opt the middle and upper classes; they did not, however, remedy the country's massive poverty. Thus, while a generally positive feeling toward the United States existed nationwide, discontent could still be stirred and nationalist feelings aroused among the poor. These were conditions that would give the Socialist and Communist parties the opportunity to develop in 1929 and 1930, respectively.

Postcolonial Philippines emulated, in some measure, the institutions and values Americans had attempted to develop and instill. By no means, however, did it conform to the measures of a paradigm democracy. America's colonial legacy had given the Philippines some semblance of constitutional democracy, where freedom of speech was honored and regular elections held. Philippine politics was characterized by a two-party system dominated by the Nationalist and Liberal parties.[2] Most Filipino political leaders sought close relations with the United States as a means of improving the nation's economy and enhancing its postwar security.

The United States, for its part, continued to view the Philippines as an ideal military and political outpost—an entity that had to be protected from external threat and internal subversion. To ensure these interests, postindependence treaties and agreements were signed. Many of the stipulations attached by the United States perpetuated Philippine economic dependence and ensured U.S. extraterritoriality on its military bases. The agreements underlined the unequal relationship between the two nations and provoked the kind of resentment that, as in Iran, ultimately led to widespread anti-Americanism.

Postindependence Agreements

The Philippine Trade Act of 1946. Among the treaties signed, one of the most grievous in the minds of Filipinos was the Philippine Trade Act of 1946. The agreement tied the economies of the two countries by establishing a system of preferential tariffs. It placed restraints on the government of the Philippines in controlling the nation's economy, and pegged the value of the peso to the U.S.dollar. Under the much-resented Parity Rights Amendment, the Philippines was required to amend its constitution to give U.S. citizens equal treatment in the Philippine economy. A constitutional amendment gave Americans the right to own up to 100 percent of Philippine corporations, development rights for public utilities, and exploitation rights for Philippine natural resources.[3] The United States was able to force acceptance of this amendment by tying it to much-needed rehabilitation aid and by arranging the illegal ouster of leftist members of the Philippine Congress who might have barred its passage.[4]

The Laurel-Langley Agreement (1955). The Laurel-Langley Agreement replaced the Philippine Trade Act of 1946.[5] It was, in part, designed to mollify Philippine opposition to restrictive clauses in the Trade Act by eliminating the pegged peso and by dropping a prohibition on the right of the Philippines to impose export tariffs. A schedule of declining tariffs was revised in favor of Philippine goods, and parity agreements were revised to establish ostensible reciprocity. Assurances for American business interests, however, continued, and U.S. investors were guaranteed equal treatment with Filipinos in all areas of the economy.

Military Base Agreement (1947). The 1947 Military Base Agreement underwent numerous revisions. In its original form the agreement gave the United States a ninety-nine year lease on extensive military facilities in the Philippines. The Philippines was prohibited from granting basing rights to any other country and from accepting military aid or advisers from other nations without U.S. approval. Under the terms of the agreement, the United States was not subject to any restrictions on the use of the bases, nor on the types of weapons it could deploy or store on them. In addition, Filipino volunteers could be recruited into U.S. forces.[6]

Military Assistance Agreement (1947). A week after signing the Military Base Agreement, the governments of the Philippines and the United States concluded a military assistance agreement.[7] In exchange for land areas occupied by the U.S. military bases, Washington promised to provide the Philippines with weapons and military advice through the Joint U.S. Military Advisory Group (JUSMAG). The aid was justified as a means of maintaining the U.S.-Philippine defense partnership in Southeast Asia, as well as of assisting with the internal defense of the Philippines. (A threat was perceived to exist in central Luzon, where a radicalized peasantry had developed.)

Mutual Defense Treaty (1951). The Mutual Defense Treaty stipulated that in the event of an armed attack on the Philippines, the United States would act to meet the common danger in accordance with the U.S. constitution. A guarantee of automatic assistance, however, was not given.

The U.S. Bases

The major U.S. installations in the Philippines were Clark Air Base and Subic Bay Naval Base. Smaller installations included San Miguel Communications Station in San Antonio, Zambales; Camp John Hay Air Base in Baguio City; a naval station at Poro Point, La Union; and a communications station at Camp O'Donnell in Capas, Tarlac.[8]

The role of the American bases changed as U.S. foreign policy evolved. They served as strategic assets in supporting the deployment of American forces in the Western Pacific, Indian Ocean, and Southeast Asia. Philippine-based forces played a major role in supporting U.S. military efforts in the Korean and Vietnam Wars; in the mid-1970s, they were used to project U.S. military power in the Middle East. U.S. carrier task forces were sent to the Indian Ocean and Arabian Sea from Subic Naval Base in 1979, at the time of the Iranian revolution, the North Yemen–South Yemen border war, and the Soviet intervention in Afghanistan. After the fall of the Shah, the United States assured the Middle East oil supply by dispatching its Philippine-based military to the Persian Gulf. Clark Air Base was used as a staging point for the 1980 Iranian hostage rescue mission,[9] and antisubmarine patrols and intelligence gathering were conducted from Subic Bay. Subic Bay also served as the navy's principal repair and supply station for the Asian fleet. In addition, U.S. bases in the Philippines were considered a point of departure for Middle East action by the Rapid Deployment Force.[10]

The U.S. bases created an American dependence on the Philippines that would prove difficult to dislodge. The flow of arms and aid in exchange for basing rights continued unabated throughout the postwar years, regardless of whether the administration in Washington was Republican or Democratic, conservative or liberal.

Ferdinand Marcos (1965–1986): From Weak Democracy to Dictatorship

In 1965, the Nationalist Party candidate, Ferdinand Marcos, was elected to the presidency. He was reelected in 1969 in a campaign characterized by unprecedented violence and widespread fraud. Challenges to the status quo became increasingly evident during the Marcos years as economic discontent and political radicalism took hold. The countryside was rendered virtually lawless: armed bandits worked for local politicians, landless tenants took actions against landlords and government authorities,[11] and rebellion was fomented by the Maoist New People's Army (NPA) and the Muslim Moro National Front. In the urban areas, laborers who had been denied the right to strike, voiced complaints; in Manila, students organized demonstrations.[12]

Martial Law and Beyond: 1972 to 1986

In September 1972, with less than a year left in his second term, Marcos declared martial law. The immediate justification given, was the lawlessness that prevailed in the country and an alleged assassination attempt on the life of Secretary of Defense Juan Ponce Enrille[13]—an incident that, it was subsequently learned, was perpetrated by Enrille himself. A year earlier, under pretense supplied by a bombing (later acknowledged to be the work of Marcos associates), Marcos suspended habeas corpus.

Under martial law, Congress was abolished and the president given unprecedented powers; a program aimed at achieving greater economic development was instituted under the banner of the "New Society." Initial domestic reaction to martial law was generally positive, if not enthusiastic. Loss of freedom was accepted in exchange for a remedy to widespread lawlessness. The business community adopted a wait-and-see attitude, while the promise of land reform under the New Society gave hope to the left.[14]

Martial law and the New Society, however, proved unlikely remedies for the ills of the Philippines; instead, they led to ever-increasing disaffection among all sectors. The political milieu deteriorated further, and the institutions of state were corrupted. Suspension of political and human rights, which began with the suspension of habeas corpus in 1971, reached extremes. Even after martial law was lifted in 1981, Marcos retained extensive emergency powers and repression continued.

Marcos destroyed the political institutions of democracy. A convention held in 1971 to revise the constitution "was purged" of Marcos rivals. In 1973, thirty thousand selected citizens voted to adopt a revised constitution by a show of hands. Among the provisions accepted at these meetings were those which gave President Marcos the right to stay in office indefinitely, and which temporarily suspended the constitution itself. By 1981, continued revisions of the constitution redefined politics in the Philippines. They provided for an elected president who could issue decrees in place of law, a prime minister and cabinet wholly dependent on the president's favor, and a weakened legislature that could neither block the president's emergency decrees nor control the prime minister and cabinet.[15]

Party politics and electoral competition became virtually nonexistent. Between 1972 and 1978, electoral competition was suspended. Instead, carefully staged plebiscites and referenda were conducted. Parliamentary and local elections held between 1978 and 1984 were denounced for fraudulence. In the 1981 presidential elections, no opposition candidates even bothered to run against Marcos. Almost all Marcos opponents were jailed at some point during martial law.[16]

Most forms of political participation were eliminated: Congress was suspended; the right to organize rallies, hold public meetings, and participate in other political activities was denied; strikes and other job actions by labor were banned. Organizations ostensibly created to represent the masses, such as citizens' assemblies, the National Assembly, and the KBL (Kilusan Bagong Lipunan, or New Society Movement), were neither genuinely "representative nor deliberative bodies."[17]

The conduct of law, too, was subject to Marcos's manipulations. In 1977, the International Commission of Jurists noted that, "judicial review which gave some semblance of constitutional legitimacy to the government was itself compromised, making the continued tenure of Supreme Court Justices depend on the whim of the president."[18]

Free speech was stifled, and Marcos associates acquired newspapers, as well as radio and television stations. The government set up a Martial Law Advisory Council to define guidelines for the media, and news agencies were censored. Licenses were required for all publications, and the registration of mimeograph machines with the military was made mandatory.[19]

Reports of human rights abuses, arbitrary arrests, torture, and murder were prominent. Soon after martial law was imposed, approximately thirty thousand people were arrested and detained. Among them were senators and prominent journalists. Amnesty International estimated that in the first three years of martial law, more than 50,000 were arrested, with many tortured and almost all detained without charge or trial.[20]

In 1975, Amnesty International reported that of 107 political prisoners it had interviewed, trials had been concluded for none. It further noted, "The conclusion is unavoidable that torture of prisoners is part of a general approach to the treatment of suspects."[21] In 1981, the organization found evidence of disappearances, arbitrary arrests, incommunicado detention, ill treatment, torture, and extrajudicial killings—acts carried out by the armed forces of the Philippines, the National Police, and irregular paramilitary units apparently operating with official sanction.[22]

Even when martial law was lifted in 1981, habeas corpus remained suspended and emergency rules remained in effect; Marcos still retained wide latitude in suspending law and legal procedure under Presidential Commitment Orders (PCOs). A vocal opposition composed of labor and human rights groups, jurists, and clergy denounced these conditions; the Catholic Bishops Conference of the Philippines called the PCOs "immoral."[23] In 1985, 119 medical personnel signed a document denouncing the human rights abuses of the Marcos regime and criticizing as "antidemocratic" such executive decrees as PCOs and PDOs (Presidential Detention Orders).[24]

A 1984 report to the U.N. Commission on Human Rights, submitted by a Filipino group, Task Force Detainees-Philippines, detailed human rights abuses which followed the lifting of martial law. The group found that arrests numbered 1,377 in 1981; "1,911 in 1982; 2,088 in 1983; and 3,033 in 1984." Extrajudicial killings numbered "321 in 1981; 210 in 1982; 368 in 1983; and 445 in 1984." The study reported 644 cases of torture in 1983.[25] In 1985, "hamletting," the practice of removing peasants from farmland in order to accommodate agribusiness interests or break up peasant organizations, was revealed by OXFAM to have become accepted practice.[26]

Despite evidence of such abuses, Marcos stated in 1974 that, "No one, but no one, has been tortured. . . . None has reason to complain that his dignity has been violated or that his convenience has not been looked after."[27] The Philippine government itself, however, admitted to human rights transgressions in 1982, when the Presidential Security Command reported to Marcos that, between 1972 and 1982, serious human rights infractions involving 4,228 persons had been reported.[28]

As evidence continued to be published about the human rights situation in the Philippines, Marcos justified any restrictions on human rights in terms of the greater good to be achieved by their imposition. "The error of human rightists," he said in 1984, "is that they think political [rights] are the only rights we have to take care of. But our historical experience dictates that we also think of economic rights. And when at times this clashes with other human rights . . . well, it is a matter of judgment."[29]

It was an argument few would accept. A 1980 World Bank report noted that,

> "While poverty is generally a politically sensitive subject, it is even more sensitive in the Philippines than in most of our borrowing countries. First, the skewedness of income distribution is worse in the Philippines than elsewhere in the region and is exceeded only in Latin America. Secondly, whereas military-dominated government in, for example, Thailand and Korea, has been justified on the basis of credible external threats, martial law in the Philippines has been justified considerably on the basis of its benefits for the poor."[30]

A 1985 report by the University of the Philippines stated that "the exercise of individual rights such as freedom of expression, freedom to organize, the access to information by citizens, etc., are themselves fundamental and . . . are economically valuable as channels of information by which to determine peoples' evolving preferences and behavior."[31]

Economic Conditions Under Marcos

Despite Marcos's attempt to attenuate the human rights issue with arguments about economic development, most Filipinos gained little in terms of economic advantage. Whereas land reform was ostensibly intended to change land ownership patterns, its real effect was minimal. The New Society program was designed to affect rice and corn land only; it excluded all landless rural workers, all tenant farmers working on crops other than rice and corn, and all tenants on plots of less than seventeen acres. When implemented, the policy affected only an estimated 5 percent of the target population, leaving three million landless agricultural workers as destitute as ever. Even those peasants who were to profit from the New Society land reform often did not gain much. They found themselves in debt and unable to discharge the responsibilities of ownership, such as upkeep of property, management of capital, cooperative marketing, and meeting the costs of fertilizers and pesticides. The government was not prepared to assist the farmers with these problems or to take on the costs of irrigation, reclamation, and highway construction necessary to the success of the program. The extent of frustration was evident in September 1985, when ten thousand farmers and their families marched into the town plaza of Escalante, Negros, to draw attention to the conditions of poverty in which they lived. (Twenty-seven were killed by paramilitary forces.)[32]

Rural residents moved into the cities, and the agricultural labor force declined from 61 percent of the total work force in 1960, to 46 percent in 1980. By 1980, the urban population had grown, with 34 percent of the Philippine population living in the nation's two largest cities (as compared to 27 percent living in Manila in 1960).[33] Despite the desperate need for low-cost housing, the government undertook massive building projects of luxury hotels in the hope of promoting tourism and generating profits for the friends and family of Marcos.[34] Working conditions deteriorated as government decrees abandoned labor regulations in an attempt to lure foreign investment. Child labor was legalized, strikes were outlawed, minimum wage requirements were weakened, and restrictions on foreign land holding and capital investment in extractive industries were relaxed.[35]

The gap in national income distribution between rich and poor widened. The poorest 60 percent, who had received only 27 percent of total national income in 1970, received only 22.4 percent in 1979. At the other end of the scale, the richest 10 percent of the population increased its share of the total national income from 38.5 percent to 41.7 percent.[36] Real wages declined, and "prices increased by about 7 percent between 1975 and 1976."[37] Between 1972 and 1980, average monthly earnings for wage earners declined approximately 20 percent; in agriculture, it fell 30 percent; and in commerce, 40 percent.[38] Decline in real wages in 1982 alone was 5.7 percent.[39] The unemployment rate deteriorated progressively, with three million people—approximately 15 percent of the total working-age population—unemployed in 1985.[40] The World Bank reported in 1985 that twenty million out of fifty-six million Filipinos lived in poverty; the Philippines was the only major non-communist country in Asia with a deteriorating economy.[41] Despite the massive poverty, government expenditures in 1979 allocated only two dollars per capita on health, in comparison to nine dollars per capita for defense.[42]

The economy was battered by external market forces and domestic tensions. Prices for raw material exports fell, with sugar, for example, dropping from sixty-five cents a pound in 1974 to eight cents a pound in 1976. External debt as a percentage of Gross National Product rose from 20.7 percent in 1970, to 40.3 percent in 1977, to 83 percent in 1980.[43]

The situation deteriorated further after the assassination of Benigno Aquino in August 1983.[44] Fear of instability led to massive capital flight ($700 million in the first three months after the assassination). In addition, several major firms ceased operations, the peso was devalued, the cost of oil and other imported products rose, and price increases led to further unrest.[45] An unstable environment discouraged foreign investment. The publication *Business Environment Risk Information* advised that because of prevailing "political instability," "no long-term commitments . . . in the Philippines" ought to be made "and even trade relationships should involve secure letters of credit."[46]

The Anti-Marcos Opposition

Marcos had written the scenario for rebellion. Armed and vocal opposition to the Philippine government had existed for decades. The increase in its numbers, however, was stimulated by conditions that had developed during the Marcos era: economic hardship, corruption, subversion of the political and judicial systems, and the suspension of even the most basic of human rights—the right to life.

The opposition spanned various sectors, economic interests, and political ideologies. In the 1960s, the Communist Party was revived, and the Maoist New People's Army (NPA) was formed. When martial law was declared in 1972, NPA fighters numbered approximately one thousand. By 1984, the government of the Philippines reported the well-armed NPA guerrillas to number eight thousand.[47] NPA supporters had increased "from a few thousand in 1972 to at least one hundred thousand" by 1982. Left-of-center antigovernment movements composed of students, journalists, laborers, and even some members of the business community became increasingly radicalized in the 1960s, leading to the organization of the National Youth Movement and the Free Peasant Union. By 1973, the National Democratic Front had been formed to represent leftist opposition groups, including the Communist Party of the Philippines, underground organizations of workers, and Christians for National Liberation. In 1969, the Moro National Liberation Front was created in response to the Muslim rebellion in Mindanao and the Sulu Archipelago. It was a rebellion that, although sectarian, had its roots in the economic deprivation experienced in these areas.[48]

Student opposition erupted in the early 1970s focusing on crime, widespread corruption, feudal economic conditions, and the abuses of imperialism. It also focused on election fraud, which was widely believed to have brought Marcos his second term. Indeed, in 1970, following his second election victory, Marcos faced twenty thousand taunting students, workers, and peasants, cynical about his two-million vote margin.[49] This was a development, *The New York Times* noted, which seemed "to be rapidly turning into a populist movement embracing workers, peasants, middle class intellectuals, clergy and moderate students, as well as radical revolutionary students."[50] Fraudulent elections for the National Assembly in April 1978 led to a number of protests in Manila, the majority of which were conducted by clergy-led students and workers.[51]

In the countryside, attempts by farmers, villagers, and town residents to negotiate with local elites and government officials were met with harassment, violence, and extortion by soldiers. Such military abuses, said a 1984 U.S. Congressional report, "are a key factor, if not the most important consideration, for . . . the degree of support people give the NPA."[52] Peasants increasingly lost faith in reform and joined the NPA as they were squeezed out by traditional landlords and multinational corporations. Even those who benefited directly from New Society land reform became disenchanted. Monopolies run by Marcos cronies continued to impinge upon these farmers, and the general business of farming became increasingly burdensome.[53] Martial law engendered opposition within the traditional Philippine economic and political elite as well. Landlords who had been negatively affected by the land reform, and the old oligarchy that felt dispossessed by Marcos's corrupt economic practices, became increasingly alienated. Marcos was criticized by former Philippine senator and foreign secretary Raul Manglapus, and by members of the United Democratic Opposition, an organization that included former president, Diosdado Macapagal (1961–1965), and former senators Benigno Aquino, Jr. and Salvador Laurel.[54] In 1976, S. P. Lopez—a former Marcos spokesman, ambassador to the United States, and president of the University of the Philippines—"rejected as untenable the claim that after four years, martial law was still necessary for social reform."[55]

Increasingly, too, the generally conservative business sector became disillusioned with the unfulfilled economic promises of the Marcos regime. Corruption and gross mismanagement had taken hold: Marcos's economic program destroyed businesses as the monopolies he created used profits or interest-free loans to absorb or bankrupt independent enterprises. As the political climate deteriorated and foreign investment fell, business people began to look for alternatives to Marcos—some even to the extent of lending support to the NPA. Discontent was reinforced, in October 1983, by reports that the nation's international debt was closer to $24 billion than the assumed $18 billion.[56] It had become evident that the country's economy had been virtually destroyed. Middle-class business groups provided direction and financing to anti-Marcos efforts after the Aquino assassination; they even released employees to join the anti-Marcos demonstrations. The Makati Business Club, "a private forum of business and economic leaders," called for reforms and for Marcos's resignation so that "international confidence in the political stability and integrity" of the nation could be restored.[57]

Slowest to turn against the Marcos regime was the military. It, too suffered from the corruption and mismanagement that permeated the country. Marcos had in large measure presented martial law as a necessary step to defeat the NPA, a strategy that was supported by the military. NPA numbers, however, instead increased. Morale and the quality of the military deteriorated as promotions became dependent upon friendships with Marcos or with General Fabian Ver, the chief of the armed forces. Comrades-in-arms were killed by the NPA as incompetent friends of Marcos supervised battles with the insurgents.[58]

In an attempt to restore professionalism in the armed forces, an informal group of field and company-grade officers established the Reform the Armed Forces Movement (RAM) in 1985. Defense Minister Juan Ponce Enrille and Vice Chief of Staff General Fidel V. Ramos associated themselves with the group, calculating it to be a potential source of political support.[59]

The discontent and antagonism evident in Philippine society were reflected in the Catholic Church as well. Martial law had restricted the rights of free speech and eliminated all institutional opposition; the Protestant and, in particular, the Catholic churches, however, remained autonomous.[60] Clerics advised the business community and political moderates on theological as well as political justifications for resistance; local priests, particularly in the rural areas, often acted as opinion leaders. The church had the power that could, and would, ultimately be used to defeat Marcos.[61]

Catholic Church opposition to Marcos developed slowly; it began with criticism from liberal members but eventually included moderate and conservative clergy. The lower ranks of the church, in particular, became progressively more disenchanted with Marcos's economic promises and abuses. As in Latin America, these clergy were protagonists of liberation theology and participated in "Christian-base communities," where rural and urban poor could discuss the Scriptures and their application to their lives. Some members of the clergy extended assistance to the NPA or even joined the guerrillas.[62]

Marcos's abuses, however, also prompted protests by influential moderate and conservative members of the Catholic hierarchy. Immediately after the proclamation of martial law, sixteen bishops wrote to Marcos expressing concern about the loss of fundamental rights and about the possibility of repression. Soon thereafter, members of the Association of Major Religious Superiors in the Philippines (AMRSP), an organization representing twenty-five hundred priests and seven thousand nuns, wrote to Marcos to voice their concerns. Reports of human rights abuses prompted AMRSP to establish the Task Force for Detainees in January

1974. In April 1974, the Second Mindanao-Sulu Pastoral Conference issued a statement denouncing the injustices and the torture inflicted under martial law. During the same year, the conservative Catholic Bishops Conference of the Philippines (CBCP) called for fair practices in response to the intimidating Marcos strategy of holding open-voting referenda. By February 1975, when the third such referendum was scheduled to be held, liberal Catholic Church leaders called for a nation-wide boycott and denounced the referendum as a "mockery of democracy" and a "Marcos gimmick to justify his unlawful stay in power." In cooperation with the People's Association for Freedom and other groups, liberal church members called for a boycott of a December 1977 referendum on whether Marcos should stay on as president and prime minister after an interim National Assembly had been organized. The CBCP issued a number of pastoral letters critical of the Marcos regime after 1979; a 1983 letter accused the government of graft, corruption, economic mismanagement, and repression. When President Marcos called for the snap presidential election of February 1986, the church again demanded that free elections be held. The CBCP worked closely with the National Committee for Free Elections (NAMFREL) and used its personnel and resources to protect the ballot.[63] Immediately after the 1986 elections, evident manipulation by Marcos led to a public statement by the CBCP in which the election was decried as "unparalleled in . . . fraudulence." The statement further urged a "non-violent struggle for justice," and complained that a "government that assumes or retains power through fraudulent means has no moral basis."[64]

Even the most conservative elements of the church eventually joined the anti-Marcos campaign. In November 1974, Manila's Jaimie Cardinal Sin, who had described himself as a "critical collaborator,"[65] criticized the "indefinite detention of prisoners" without formal charges. He characterized the June 1981 presidential elections as "a farce reminiscent of one-candidate elections in totalitarian states,"[66] and suggested in 1982, that Marcos had "lost the respect of the people" and should step down so that a "new leadership" could take power.[67] In the spring of 1983, the cardinal broke with Marcos by approving a church-sponsored weekly magazine, *Veritas*. The publication would supply the public with independent information. Cardinal Sin also called for fair and honest national elections in 1984, and in the interests of assuring a fair election in 1986, issued a widely publicized pastoral letter, condemning "a very sinister plot by some people and groups to frustrate the honest and orderly expression of the people's genuine will."[68] The cardinal was credited with helping Salvador Laurel and Benigno Aquino's wife, Corazon, forge an opposition alliance in preparation for the February 1986 elections, and thus was instrumental in achieving the Marcos defeat. Responding to the revolt being led by Minister of Defense Juan Ponce Enrille and Vice Chief of Staff Fidel Ramos, Sin urged Filipinos to show support for the military dissidents by converging on Camp Crane and Camp Aguinaldo.[69]

United States–Philippine Relations During the Marcos Years

Despite manifest evidence of economic mismanagement, institutional corruption, human rights abuses, and growing domestic disaffection, U.S. decision makers were slow to respond to deteriorating conditions and unfolding events in the Philippines. Whatever the problems, Washington focused on Marcos as the key to the solution: the alternatives were viewed as Marcos or communism. Support of the Marcos regime, therefore, remained a cornerstone of U.S. policy in Southeast Asia; responses designed to convey U.S. disapproval were often as cosmetic as Marcos's tactics to assuage his critics. Factors that tied the United States to the Philippines were summarized in a 1984 National Security Council Study Directive:

> The United States has extremely important interests in the Philippines:
> Politically . . . the Philippines must be a stable, democratically oriented ally. A radicalized Philippines would destabilize the whole region.
> Strategically, continued unhampered access to our bases at Subic and Clark is of prime importance because of the expanded Soviet and Vietnamese threat in the region. Fall-back positions would be much more expensive and less satisfactory.
> A strong ASEAN that includes a healthy Philippines allied to the U.S. is a buffer to communist presence in Southeast Asia and a model of what economic freedom and democratic progress can accomplish.
> Economically, we benefit from a strong investment and trade position.[70]

Military Relations

External threats to the security of the Philippines in the 1970s and 1980s were nonexistent, and internal threats were not severe. Nonetheless, U.S. national interests sustained a policy that supported continued military assistance in the form of arms, equipment, computers, and counterinsurgency training. Military aid was not necessarily conditioned on the level of internal or external threat; it was instead dependent upon the need to maintain close and friendly relations. Between 1969 and 1972, $89 million in U.S. military assistance was approved for the Philippines; the value of aid approvals was increased after the imposition of martial law, rising to $162.4 million in the period 1973 to 1976. The Carter administration allocated $182.6 in military aid to the Marcos regime (see Table 5-1).

Commercial arms sales also remained unaffected. In fiscal year 1977, for example, the Philippines was supplied with $14.1 million in weapons (see Table 5-1). In addition, U.S. arms companies established coproduction projects in the Philippines, thereby creating an industry over which U.S. government control would ultimately be limited or nonexistent. The U.S. Department of Defense and Colt Industries of Connecticut, for example, participated in the coproduction of arms in the Philippines in the mid-1970s. Between 1975 and 1979, the Philippines purchased 10,000 rifles and assembled 150,000 M16s.[71]

Indicative of the degree of U.S. dependence on the Philippines, was the policy pursued by President Carter, a vocal advocate of human rights. Despite the human rights abuses which by U.S. law would require that assistance be curtailed, U.S. military aid to the Philippines continued unabated during the Carter administration. When in 1977, U.S. Representative Yvonne Burke initiated an effort to reduce military aid to the Philippines, she was opposed. The administration issued an Executive Branch Position Paper on her bill, H.R. 7797, warning that cuts in military assistance "would have serious impact upon important programs with a treaty ally which allows us the use of valuable military facilities."[72] Carter also successfully fought off efforts to cut Philippine military aid in 1979 and 1980.

Military equipment and training provided by the United States to the Philippines was used for purposes of internal repression. As a consequence, the United States was linked with an increasingly dictatorial regime. Studies conducted in 1976 and 1977 by the General Accounting Office, the Friends of the Filipino People, and the Center for International Policy in Washington, D.C., found that U.S. arms-export policies served to perpetuate martial law in the Philippines and that U.S. arms were used for purposes of repression and counterinsurgency.[73]

American policymakers clearly understood that American-supplied equipment was being directed to uses antithetical to U.S. human rights concerns. A 1974 report by the Public Safety Project Report on the Philippines, published by the Office of Public Safety/Aid (Washington, D.C.), noted that "maintenance problems" with torture devices supplied by AID were not "anticipated since each city has technicians trained on the equipment and sufficient spare parts on hand."[74] Friends of the Filipino People, a U.S.-based organization composed primarily of clergy and former Peace Corps volunteers in the Philippines, reported in 1976 that the

Table 5-1

U.S. Military Assistance and Sales to the Philippines, 1967–1986 (in millions of U.S. dollars)

Fiscal Year	U.S. Government		Commercial Sales Deliveries[c]	Number of Students in International Military Education and Training Program
	Military Aid Approved[a]	Military Deliveries[b]		
1967	$ 33.0	$26.8	$ 0.1	456
1968	29.9	35.5	0.1	786
1969	21.9	23.9	0.3	664
1970	27.3	18.2	0.1	668
1971	18.7	19.3	0.6	433
1972	21.1	19.1	0.3	398
1973	50.4	20.0	0.2	344
1974	27.0	32.2	2.0	189
1975	36.3	19.6	3.0	327
1976	48.7	38.0	11.8	392
1977	38.1	37.0	14.1	126
1978	37.3	47.7	7.2	134
1979	31.7	32.5	5.6	106
1980	75.5	47.0	8.0	98
1981	75.6	31.7	1.0	272
1982	51.2	50.8	1.0	250
1983	51.4	31.3	5.9	296
1984	51.5	22.4	4.0	313
1985	42.2	21.7	11.6	449
1986	105.1	43.6	2.2	547

[a]Includes Foreign Military Sales grants/credits, MAP, IMET, and EDA.

[b]Includes Foreign Military Sales for cash or credit, MAP, IMET, and EDA.

[c]Munitions purchased directly from U.S. manufacturers and requiring a U.S. export license.

Sources: *Foreign Military Sales, Foreign Military Construction Sales, and Military Assistance Facts:* December 1976; December 1978; December 1979; December 1980; September 1981; September 1982; 30 September 1983; 30 September 1984; 30 September 1985; 30 September 1986; 30 September 1987. (Washington, D.C.: Data Management Division, Comptroller, Defense Security Assistance Agency).

Public Safety Project "can most probably take credit for helping to institutionalize the most advanced technique of information and confession-extraction from political suspects."[75] Indeed, half of the torturers identified in a 1976 Amnesty International report were graduates of the U.S. International Military Education and Training Program (IMET). The United States had so incriminated itself by supplying Marcos with security equipment and expertise, that Cardinal Sin protested in 1985 that the "United States should stop sending military aid to the Philippines because it only goes to slaughter Filipinos.[76]

Economic Ties

A willingness to accommodate Marcos in the interests of maintaining the U.S. bases not only affected American policy in relation to military assistance, but also affected the goals and the course of U.S. development assistance in the Philippines. Total economic assistance went up from $135.5 million in the period between 1970 and 1972, to $237.4 million in 1973–1974. Between 1975 and 1985, Marcos received $1,474.4 million in U.S. economic assistance (see Table 5-2). Corruption in Marcos's circle, however, meant that much of the aid would never reach the poor.

In addition to direct U.S. economic aid, private American investment in the Philippines was quite extensive. The growing tide of nationalism during Marcos's first term, however, led to judicial decisions inimical to the interests of U.S. business. U.S. citizens and corporations were prohibited from owning agricultural lands, and foreigners' rights to the exploitation of raw materials, including oil, were restricted. In addition, it was announced that after the 1974 expiration of the Laurel-Langley agreement, foreigners would no longer be permitted to hold positions in management or sit on boards of directors of Philippine corporations.

Marcos assured American companies that he would "annul" these rulings. Following imposition of martial law, he kept his word; in addition, he implemented a decree, previously rejected by the Philippine Congress, providing "lucrative incentives" to foreign oil companies.[77] So enamored of Marcos was the U.S. business community that, five days after his declaration of martial law, it sent a note of congratulations that said, "The American Chamber of Commerce wishes you every success in your endeavors to restore peace and order, business confidence, economic growth, and the well-being of the Filipino people and nation. We assure you of our confidence and cooperation in achieving these objectives. We are communicating these feelings to our associates and affiliates in the United States."[78]

When martial law was proclaimed in 1972, more Americans than all other foreign nationalities combined resided and worked in the Philippines, U.S. multinationals had invested over $2 billion in Philippine assets, and twenty-four of the country's fifty largest enterprises were American-owned.[79] U.S. investment in 1974 totaled 45 percent of total foreign investments; in 1977 and 1980, the investment ratio stood at 54 percent and 53 percent, respectively. Even as total foreign investment declined precipitously in the two years before the revolution, the U.S. proportion of foreign investment rose reaching 59 percent and 67 percent of total investment in 1984 and 1985, respectively.[80] In addition, between 1.7 and 3.0 percent of the Philippine GNP was generated by U.S. military spending; base-related Philippine employment accounted for $96 million, and annual purchases of local supplies and services amounted to approximately five hundred million dollars.[81]

Marcos and U.S. Interests

The United States could not be certain that it had a faithful ally in the Philippines—despite the substantial military assistance, economic aid, and business investment it had directed to the country. Neither a continued U.S. presence on the bases, nor Philippine conformity to U.S. foreign policy interests, could be assured.

Under Marcos, and with his tacit approval, anti-Americanism was fanned in the Philippine press. The United States was accused of exploiting the Philippines and of treating its people with arrogance. During the Johnson administration and into Marcos's second term, Philippine policy demonstrated respect toward the United States, coupled with complaints about Washington's failure to stabilize Southeast Asia. The United States and other affluent nations were criticized for not giving sufficient assistance to smaller nations in their struggles against communism.[82]

In foreign policy, Marcos pursued strategies not necessarily in conformance with the U.S. agenda. President Johnson's effort to gain wider participation by Asian allies in the Vietnam War, gave Marcos an opportunity to exact large payments for minimal cooperation. Marcos was given a much-sought invitation to Washington in 1966, and received $6 million to sustain Philippine units that were to go to Vietnam, but which in fact stayed at home. (Only one out of ten promised battalions were sent to Vietnam.) A U.S. Congressional investigation was unable to determine where the funds had gone. Marcos was also given $80 million in economic aid, which included $3 million for a cultural center supported by his wife, Imelda.[83]

Table 5-2
U.S. Economic Assistance to the Philippines, 1967–1985 (in millions of U.S. dollars)

Fiscal Year	Total Economic Commitments[a]	Direct Economic Assistance AID		Other Economic Assistance		Multilateral Development Banks	
		Funds Committed	Funds Delivered	Ex-Im Bank Loans[b]	Other U.S. Loans/Grants[c]	Loans Approved[d]	Absentions[e]
1967	$ 44.2	$ 11.3	$ 5.5	$ 0.0	$ 0.0		
1968	19.2	10.3	7.3	0.0	0.4		
1969	18.7	5.6	9.6	21.2	0.0		
1970	25.1	9.0	9.4	9.6	18.9		
1971	40.5	11.1	14.6	45.2	39.0		
1972	69.9	30.5	16.7	7.3	34.2		
1973	173.3	135.0	41.4	23.5	51.1		
1974	64.1	45.0	31.0	9.5	9.7	$170.9	
1975	68.8	55.6	48.9	9.9	15.0	302.3	$ 0.0
1976[f]	86.1	61.5	35.8	296.4	42.8	387.0	0.0
1977	86.8	34.9	36.4	0.0	49.6	384.5	0.0
1978	83.9	52.8	41.4	4.7	49.6	662.5	161.1
1979	72.0	43.7	37.1	0.6	0.0	431.2	0.1
1980	103.3	79.7	28.1	27.8	0.0	903.5	79.2
1981	127.6	98.5	36.5	69.3	0.0	457.5	81.5
1982	157.1	139.4	47.0	8.4	0.0	719.5	0.0

1983	152.8	136.8	128.4	0.0	0.0	639.9	0.0
1984	156.3	134.3	99.4	78.8	0.0	671.0	0.0
1985	379.7	322.9	93.8	0.0	0.3	249.9	0.0
1986	699.4	651.7	334.1	0.0	1.2		

[a] Includes AID grants and loans and AID Economic Support Funds (ESF); PL–480 Titles I and II (Sales and Grants); International Narcotics Control. ESF is given for security purposes. In the Philippines, ESF expenditures were committed as follows (in millions of U.S. dollars): FY 1973—$49.3; 1974—$0.5; 1975—$0.3; 1980—$20.0; 1981—$30.0; 1982—$50.0; 1983—$50.0; 1984—$50.0; 1985—$140.0; 1986—$300.3; ESF for Nicaragua: FY 1979—$80.0; 1980—$1.1.

[b] Does not include export credit insurance and guarantees.

[c] Short-term credit granted by U.S. Department of Agriculture under the Commodity Credit Corporation Charter Act; OPIC direct loans and private trade agreements; PL–480 (I) private-sales agreements financed by the act.

[d] World Bank Group—International Bank for Reconstruction and Development, International Development Association, and International Finance Corporation; Asian Development Bank; Inter-American Development Bank; African Development Bank.

[e] U.S. vetoes or abstentions on human rights grounds. U.S. votes recorded as of 1975. U.S. abstentions/vetoes related human rights, against any country, began in FY 1977.

[f] 1976 numbers include additional fifth transitional quarter 1976–1977, covering the period July 1, 1976, to September 30, 1976.

Sources: *Development Issues: U.S. Actions Affecting the Development of Low-Income Countries: Annual Report of the Chairman of the Development Coordination Committee Transmitted to the Congress.* (1979–1983.)

International Finance: The National Advisory Council on International Monetary and Financial Policies Annual Report to the President and the Congress. (Washington, D.C.: U.S. Government Printing Office, n.d.). (1979–1985.)

U.S. Agency for International Development, Office of Planning and Budget, Bureau for Program and Policy Coordination, *U.S. Overseas Loans and Grants and Assistance from International Organizations.* (1976–1987.)

U.S. Department of Commerce, Bureau of Economic Analysis, Balance of Payments Division, Government Grants and Capital Branch, unpublished data, letter dated 7 November 1990.

Notes: Figures are rounded off to the nearest $100,000, except for total amounts less than that.

In 1969, Marcos announced his New Developmental Diplomacy—a policy designed to free the Philippines from excessive reliance on the United States. Foreign Secretary Romulo suggested that the U.S.–Philippine economic relationship be reevaluated and that agreements on parity and the bases be renegotiated to eliminate the "symbols of lingering enslavement."[84] The Philippines began to open doors to the Soviet Union and Communist bloc. In April 1975, when it was becoming apparent that Cambodia would fall, a Philippine government press release announced that, "Developments in Indochina have compelled the government to review its policies on security and development. . . . This review included a hard-headed reassessment of security ties with the United States, especially the presence of American bases."[85] Mrs. Marcos visited Cuba in 1975, and the Philippines was among the first nations to recognize the united Peoples Republic of Vietnam. In 1982, along with about half of the Marcos cabinet, Imelda Marcos visited the Soviet Union, Reagan's "evil empire." Several agreements were signed, including one for the finance and construction of a $1 million cement plant, which included the presence of up to fifty Soviet workers (assumed to be KGB agents).[86]

Full U.S. control of affairs on the military bases was also not to be taken for granted. The original 1947 base agreement had been subject to intermittent renegotiation and revision; in most cases, U.S. base-related rights were increasingly ceded to the Philippines. Marcos perceived the U.S. presence on the bases to be an infringement upon Philippine sovereignty and an insult to Philippine dignity. He wanted Philippine control of the bases and the right to rent them to the highest bidder, including the Soviet Union.[87] In 1966, the lease-termination date for the bases was moved from the year 2046 to 1991.[88] Marcos demanded and got revisions of U.S.-dictated criminal code provisions, military base labor relations, and customs procedures. In an agreement reached in 1979, Philippine sovereignty over the military bases was recognized. Provisions of the agreement included placing command of each base under a Philippine base commander, the right of the Philippine flag to be flown alone on each base, and the transfer of responsibility for base-perimeter security to the Philippines. A five-year review process for the agreement was also instituted, and $500 million in military aid was promised for a five-year period.[89] A 1983 agreement assured that the United States would consult with the government of the Philippines before placing long-range missiles on the bases. It was also agreed that Philippine base commanders would be informed of U.S. armed forces activities in the Philippines and would have access to all but highly sensitive locations on the military facilities. The United States was to enumerate for the government of the Philippines all personnel, equipment, and weapons systems present. In return for its use of the bases, the United States raised its promised aid to $900 million for a five-year period. This was to include $425 million in military assistance and foreign military sales credit, and $475 million in economic support.[90]

Anti-Americanism in the Philippines

Beyond its official dealings in the Philippines, the United States employed covert operations in pursuit of its national interest. In the belief that non-Americans had greater credibility in Asia than did Americans, the CIA enlisted Filipinos to work in its Asian operations. The CIA assisted President Magsaysay (1953 to 1957) by offering advice, writing his speeches, and orchestrating the domestic Philippine press on his behalf. In 1957, when the anti-American Nationalist Party candidate Claro M. Recto ran for the presidency, the CIA entered into the process to assure his defeat.[91] Diosdado Macapagal was paid $50,000 during his term as Philippine vice president (1957–1961); when he ran for the presidency in 1961, Macapagal's campaign was partly underwritten by the CIA. The 1961 Senate campaign of Raul Manglapus was also funded, in part, by the CIA.[92]

The degree to which the United States made itself felt in all sectors of Philippine society opened possibilities for the development of anti-American sentiment. A relationship perceived as unequal and exploitive, and a policy that supported a manifestly undemocratic ruler, gave rise to such sentiment.

Filipinos held the United States responsible for the social and cultural changes they were experiencing: American individualism was blamed for the weakening of the "traditional family system"; American materialism and Protestantism were held responsible for corrupting the Catholic Church; and American permissiveness was blamed for a declining morale. Americans were accused of implementing a self-serving aid program, which perpetuated a low standard of living and was designed to keep the Filipinos as "hewers of wood and drawers of water." Anti-American sentiment was also harbored among the newly developing middle class: Filipino lawyers and business people were often dependent on their U.S. connections, and new technocrats and managers believed positions they ought to hold were being occupied by Americans.[93] Non-Marxists complained about Washington's obvious hesitancy to distance itself from Marcos; ultranationalists and leftists implicated the United States in Marcos's decision to declare martial law, claiming that Marcos could only stay in power with U.S. support. The United States was further criticized for supplying Marcos with aid that gave him the military means to avoid seeking resolution of massive economic problems.[94] Despite the resentment, however, most Filipinos saw a need, indeed an obligation, for continued U.S. assistance to help them escape these conditions.

While the overwhelming sentiment in the Philippines was pro-American, nationalist fervor led to several demonstrations of anti-American sentiment. Even the moderate opposition became increasingly agitated by U.S. support of Marcos. A 1975 petition, asking that U.S. military aid be suspended until civil and human rights were restored, gathered 21,000 signatures.[95] The Civil Liberties Union of the Philippines, chaired by former Philippine senator José Diokno, complained that the United States had assisted Marcos in the suppression of political and civil rights in order "to protect the privileged position of foreign . . . capital, and the interests of the U.S. government." U.S. "foreign investments," the group announced, exploited the Philippine economy and made "it harder to achieve economic independence."[96] In January 1981, immediately prior to the lifting of marital law, the Union wrote:

[Marcos] has used 8 years of martial law to build and perfect a pervasive infrastructure of personal power which he can dismantle only by stepping down, and leaving this country in peace.

Short of that, he fools no one—not even the U.S. government who, from the very start, has been in collusion with his regime. Together, Mr. Marcos and the U.S. government have obviously decided that it is time to deodorize their joint conspiracy against the Filipino people with the ultimate cosmetic: the removal, in name, of the hated martial rule which, for 8 years has enabled Mr. Marcos and American transnational corporations to ravage the economy and place the country under their complete control, while allowing the U.S. government to obtain a new bases agreement, unhampered by the vexatious queries which an independent Congress would at least have made possible.[97]

On a trip to Manila in May 1978, U.S. Vice President Walter Mondale refused to meet with opposition leader Benigno Aquino because Marcos had let it be known that such a meeting would be "absolutely unacceptable." Meetings with Cardinal Sin and other members of the opposition were kept as quiet as possible so that Marcos would not be offended. Diosdado Macapagal, a former president and an opponent of Marcos who met with Mondale, complained that the Filipino people had been "misled." Instead of "promoting democracy" during his visit, the vice president brought Marcos assurances of President Carter's support. The Carter administration, Macapagal contended, had done "nothing" to relieve martial law abuses.[98] So disgruntled was the opposition with Mondale, that most members ceased to speak with U.S. embassy personnel and few agreed to meet with U.N. Ambassador Andrew Young when he visited Manila a year later. [99]

Antagonisms toward the United States also centered on the issue of the American bases. As early as 1956, Philippine Senator Claro Recto complained that:

> by granting America extra-territorial rights in the bases, we surrendered to her the power, the jurisdiction, and the sovereignty of the Republic over portions of the national territory whose integrity is guaranteed by Article I of the Constitution. . . . The 99-year term . . . [is an] odious peacetime military occupation by a friendly country with immunity from our laws and our courts.[100]

Nationalist fervor, and the anti-Americanism which was often fueled by the U.S. presence on the bases, were heightened as opposition grew both against Marcos and the U.S. government that supported him. Objections to the base agreements continued to be centered on issues of sovereignty and security (e.g. that the bases might draw fire in time of conflict). When Marcos and the U.S. government reached an agreement on the bases in late 1978, forty-two members of the opposition sent a letter of complaint. Among them were clergy and seven former senators, including Benigno Aquino and Ramon Mitra, later a member of Corazon Aquino's cabinet. The letter criticized "the Marcos martial law regime for bartering the survival, the development, and the welfare of the Filipino people for compensation which will help perpetuate it in power without the free consent of our people." It also stated, "We denounce the Carter administration for advocating respect for human rights while at the same time generously subsidizing a dictator and imposing the continued presence of its bases upon a people shackled by martial law, thereby denying them the most basic of all human rights, namely, their right to survival."[101]

A statement of political principles calling for removal of U.S. bases was signed in December 1984 by a number of potential presidential candidates. The signatories included Corazon Aquino; Jaimie Ongpin, a prominent business executive; and former senators Lorenzo Tanada, Jose Diokno, and Raul Manglapus. However, two potential presidential candidates, Salvador Laurel, chairman of the largest opposition party, UNIDO, and Vice-Chair Eva Estrada Kalaw, refused to sign.[102]

In 1985, former Senator Jose Diokno chaired an International Conference on Peace and Removal of Foreign Bases in Quezon City, Philippines. The Conference declaration stated:

> In the Philippines, in the early '70s, there was a clamor for reform, nationalist in character, that demanded among other things the dismantling of the U.S. bases. To quell these demands, martial law was imposed. After martial law, U.S. military and economic aid more than doubled.

Martial law resulted in the dismantling of the institutions of democracy in the Philippines—an independent judiciary, a freely elected legislature, a free press, and freedom of assembly and expression. They have resulted in unjustified arrests, torture, unexplained disappearances and extra-legal executions. [103]

Washington Ignores a Deteriorating Philippines

U.S. dependence on the Philippines meant that the very problems and issues that could serve to undermine the U.S.–Philippine relationship would have to be ignored. A deteriorating economy, corruption of the political process, abuse of human rights, and growing anti-American sentiment were problems that were either left unacknowledged, or were dismissed in deference to President Marcos and the relationship he was evidently willing to continue with the United States. The imposition of martial law did not call forth the kind of protest that might have been expected: it would be easier for the United States to deal with a Marcos unrestrained by political strictures and a growing nationalism.

The advantages of martial law were proven during the 1979 military base negotiations, when generous concessions were made by the Philippines despite the addition of provisions granting greater sovereign rights to the Philippine government. Marcos gave the United States the right to conduct military operations from the bases without prior consultation, and to store nuclear weapons on Philippine soil without prior consultation or notification. These concessions reversed previously established agreements. [104]

Marcos made it easy for the United States to extend its support to his martial-law administration by raising the specter of chaos and communism. In his Proclamation of Martial Law of 24 September 1972, Marcos explained that "lawless elements" and "ruthless groups of men" were

waging an armed insurrection and rebellion against the Government of the Republic of the Philippines in order to forcibly seize political and state power in this country, overthrow the duly constituted government, and supplant our existing political, social, economic, and legal order with an entirely new one whose form of government, whose system of laws, whose conceptions of God and religion, whose notion of individual rights and common relations . . . are based on Marxist-Leninist-Maoist teachings and beliefs. [105]

Despite the imposition of martial law and ample evidence that domestic problems were increasing, Marcos continued to receive U.S. military and economic assistance without attendant efforts to extract reform. Within a year of the declaration, he was publicly supported by the State Department.[106]

Warnings of Impending Collapse

As early as 1969, hearings conducted by Senator Stuart Symington showed U.S. policy to be either misdirected, or at least in need of serious reexamination. The following brief exchange took place between Senator Symington and Lt. General Robert H. Warren, deputy assistant secretary of defense for military assistance and sales.

> SENATOR SYMINGTON: The truth of the matter is that the principal threat to the government of the Philippines comes from the Filipinos who do not agree with the government of the Philippines. . . .
>
> Yesterday we had testimony that the external threat to the Philippines was very little. Today we have testimony that the United States support of counterinsurgency is minimum. What, therefore, is the real purpose of this military assistance? Doesn't it come down to a quid pro quo for the bases and a means of contributing to the Filipino government? . . .
>
> Isn't this really a means of keeping the government satisfied?
>
> LT. GENERAL WARREN: In my opinion, to a degree, yes, sir. But it is also to help the Filipino forces to physically protect U.S. forces in the Philippines.
>
> SENATOR SYMINGTON: From whom?
>
> LT. GENERAL WARREN: Internally, sir, to maintain security and stability and, thereby, make our own activities over there more secure.
>
> SENATOR SYMINGTON: In other words, we are paying the Philippine government to protect us from the Philippine people who do not agree with the policies of the government or do not like Americans.
>
> LT. GENERAL WARREN: To a degree, yes, sir.[107]

Apprehensions about U.S. policy continued. Five weeks after Marcos's imposition of martial law in 1972, a critical report by the State Department Bureau of Intelligence and Research noted, "Marcos' security measures so far appear aimed more at his own political opponents than at communists, and his 'reforms' [are] little more than conventional bids for popular support which could have been initiated without martial law." The proposed land reforms were "not much of a bargain for the tenant" since the 700,000 eligible peasants would be required to make annual payments for a period of fifteen years, at "25 percent of the farmer's harvest income." "What [Marcos] is clearly doing," the report concluded, "is erecting a one-man constitutional regime which permits him to stay in office indefinitely, with almost unlimited powers, under a veneer of parliamentary democracy."[108]

A 1972 Rand Corporation report also questioned the validity of Marcos's contention that a communist threat required the imposition of martial law. It revealed that contrary to Marcos's estimates of 8,000 NPA guerrillas, 10,000 "active cadres," and 100,000 "sympathizers," the real numbers were closer to one thousand guerrillas and perhaps "another five to six thousand part-time militia," none of whom were "well-armed."[109]

A 1972 U.S. Senate staff report outlined the contradictions in which U.S. policy was involved:

We found few, if any, Americans who took the position that the demise of individual rights and democratic institutions would adversely affect U.S. interests. In the first place, these democratic institutions were considered to be severely deficient. In the second place, whatever U.S. interests were—or are—they apparently are not thought to be related to the preservation of democratic process. . . . Thus, U.S. officials appear prepared to accept that the strengthening of presidential authority will . . . enable President Marcos to introduce needed stability; that these objectives are in our interest; and that . . . military bases and a familiar government in the Philippines are more important than the preservation of democratic institutions which were imperfect at best.

At the same time, there is some apprehension on the part of American officials about the future. . . . [An official] in the Philippines stated that if President Marcos obtained the power he sought "the only alternative his opponents will have will be to go to the hills."[110]

So corrupt had the political system become under Marcos that six weeks before the 1978 Assembly elections, the U.S. embassy in Manila cabled Washington that "the results of the forthcoming legislative elections are virtually certain. Oppositionists will likely win but a few seats, and President Marcos will be assured of an overwhelming majority in the new interim parliament."[111]

Warnings also came from numerous anti-Marcos organizations that lobbied the U.S. Congress to withhold economic and military support from the Marcos regime. These included the Movement for a Free Philippines, the Union of Democratic Filipinos, the National Committee for the Restoration of Civil Liberties in the Philippines, the National Association of Filipinos in the United States, and Friends of the Filipino People.

The 1983 assassination of Benigno Aquino served to accelerate discontent with Marcos both in the Philippines and in the United States. As the economy declined and the political atmosphere grew more tense in 1984, the U.S. embassy warned, "There is little optimism that the Marcos Government is capable of turning the situation around . . . ultimate defeat and a communist takeover of the Philippines—a very possible scenario."[112]

A 1985 staff report to the U.S. Senate Select Committee on Intelligence noted:

> The recent rapid growth of the CPP/NPA is attributable to its skillful exploitation of a growing catalog of popular grievances against the Marcos regime.
>
> Political and economic power are monopolized at the top by a small oligarchy, while at the bottom, the mass of Filipinos live in poverty without real input into the political process. A few favored Marcos cronies have been given control of large agricultural and industrial monopolies that dominate the economy. They retain their favored position by demonstration of loyalty to the president and financial support for his political machine. Political corruption and human rights abuses, particularly by the armed forces, have fueled popular resentment. The 1983 assassination of President Marcos' strongest political opponent, which the Agrava Commission concluded was committed by Philippine military personnel, greatly hastened the decline in popular support for the regime while stimulating recruitment for the NPA. . . .
>
> . . . The NPA has established itself throughout the Philippines. . . . The roots and causes of the NPA insurgency are more varied, including economic deprivation, social injustice, government corruption and abuse of power, and the decrepitude of existing public institutions. . . .
>
> In the 2 years since the Aquino assassination, the NPA has expanded so rapidly that it now poses a credible threat to the survival of the Philippines government. From a total force of a few thousand armed guerrillas in 1980, the NPA has grown to probably over 15,000 regulars and a somewhat larger number of part-time irregulars. . . . Some level of NPA activity now exists in almost all of the country's 73 provinces.[113]

Protecting U.S. Interests: The Role of Diplomacy

Marcos's sometimes questionable loyalty to the United States, evidence of his economic and political decline, and his increasing anti-Americanism, did not deter the United States from reinforcing its military and economic support of Marcos via public and private diplomacy. Administration concerns about human rights were most often conveyed via "quiet diplomacy" that, at times, was almost silent. President Nixon visited the Philippines in 1969, six months before the Philippine presidential elections. Marcos was running for reelection in a country where no president had previously achieved such a success. The U.S. embassy reported that "the visit itself is a domestic political windfall for Marcos" and that "President Nixon's mere presence in Manila will convey to the average voter a U.S. endorsement and protect Marcos from opposition charges that he is not a good friend of the U.S."[114] While in Manila, Nixon made certain to stress the close ties between the United States and the Philippines, noting that "we have a special relationship with the Philippines which will always be in our hearts, but we also recognize the force of nationalism which is the wave of the future."[115]

Within a year of the martial-law declaration, Assistant Secretary for East Asian Affairs Marshall Greene publicly expressed U.S. support for Marcos.[116] In a note to Marcos in August 1974, President Gerald Ford pledged continued support for the security, independence, and economic development of the Philippines. Ford also assured Marcos that the United States considered its relationship with the Philippines to be of great importance.[117]

Despite its rhetorical emphasis on human rights, the Carter administration continued the Philippine–American relationship with little modification. Some initial efforts were, however, made to effect changes. In 1977, Lee T. Stull, the U.S. chargé d'affaires in Manila, discussed the human rights interests of the new American president with President and Mrs. Marcos. Embassy personnel also extended contacts to various opposition groups. In 1978, the assistant secretary of state for human rights, Patricia Derian, met with Marcos and his defense minister, Juan Ponce Enrille, to present the administration's concerns about human rights.[118]

The diplomacy of human rights, however, was constrained by the pragmatism of national interest. Richard Holbrooke, Carter's assistant secretary of state for East Asia, responded to Stull's 1977 human rights diplomacy with a cable notifying him that "the intensity of our dialogue with Marcos on human rights is all that the traffic will bear at the present time."[119] In the spring of 1977, the administration supported an $88 million World Bank loan to the Philippines. Prior to the April 1978 National Assembly elections, the administration attempted to move Marcos toward some reform with less-than-forceful persuasion. U.S. Ambassador Newsom was instructed to tell Marcos that "real progress in human rights" would be likely to reduce Congressional and press criticism, and could lead to improved bilateral relations. The instructions specified that Marcos should be asked to "move in a clear, credible way on elections and martial law," and that he be persuaded to "temporarily release" Benigno Aquino and other "nonradical detainees" so that they might participate in the campaign. The ambassador, however, was advised not to "press so hard" for the lifting of martial law "as to not upset the chances of its being done at the time of the vice-president's visit," scheduled for May 1978.[120]

The April 1978 election proved fraudulent, and Aquino was not released; nonetheless, the Carter administration announced the elections to be "a step toward eventual restoration of representative government." A scheduled visit by Vice President Mondale went on as planned. Although the vice president met with members of the anti-Marcos opposition, and discussed with Marcos the administration's concerns about human rights, the visit itself signaled support for the Marcos regime. Furthermore, Mondale deferred to Marcos's political sensibilities: he did not meet with the imprisoned Benigno Aquino, and kept publicity about meetings with opposition leaders at a minimum. Following the elections, the administration approved three aid packages which provided, in part, for $17 million in bullets, armored vehicles, and patrol boats.[121]

On a visit to Hawaii in 1980, Marcos was greeted by Carter's designated personal representatives, Dean Rusk and Richard Holbrooke. The emissaries brought with them a letter from the president, which thanked Marcos for his support of the American position on the summer Olympic Games in Moscow, and praised the solid and continuing U.S.–Philippine relationship.[122] Mrs. Marcos visited the White House five or six times during Carter's tenure to meet with Vice President Mondale.[123]

That the politics of pragmatism had taken precedence over the rhetoric of morality in the Carter administration became evident to Marcos. He soon surmised that the human rights issue could be deflected with gratuitous concessions. Undersecretary for Economic Affairs Richard Cooper confirmed this view at a September 1977 meeting of the Association of Southeast Asian Nations, where he noted that "human rights are not the 'be all and end all' of [American] government objectives."[124] So confident had Marcos become, it took him three years to respond to the administration's request for Aquino's release. When it did come, it was less as a result of Carter administration efforts than of Marcos's sense of survival. Aquino's failing health and Marcos's fear that Aquino's death might lead to rebellion were the more salient motives for the move.

The Reagan administration sought to strengthen the U.S.-Philippine alliance. Benigno Aquino, by then in exile in the United States, lost access to administration officials with whom he had had contact during the Carter period. In December 1980, then President-elect Reagan met with Imelda Marcos and urged her to advise President Marcos not to lift martial law if it would affect the country's stability. He entertained the Marcoses in Washington in 1982, extending an invitation that had been denied them by previous administrations. In 1983, Reagan increased the Philippine aid package twofold, promising $900 million for a five-year period.[125] After winning a fraudulent presidential reelection in June 1981, Marcos received a personal note of congratulation from President Reagan. Vice President Bush was sent to attend the inauguration in Manila where, in a toast, he complimented Marcos for his "adherence to the democratic principles and the democratic process."[126]

It was only after the Aquino assassination in August 1983 that a greater ambiguity toward Marcos became evident. This increasing concern, however, was prompted more by a perceived threat to U.S. interests, than by an interest in promoting human rights. In addition to economic deterioration, public protests became more evident, and were supported by members of the middle class, the church, and some of the business elite. The NPA gained in strength and influence.

The Reagan Administration and the Revolution

Immediately following the Aquino murder, the administration issued statements noting that it would be "prepared to dissociate itself" from the Marcos regime should it be implicated in the assassination.[127] Despite this announcement, President Reagan stated on the day following the murder that plans for his Philippine trip would not be altered. Reports of domestic U.S. opposition to the trip forced its cancellation six weeks later. The president, however, canceled his entire Asian itinerary so that Marcos would not be singled out. Reagan also sent a handwritten letter, delivered personally by Michael Deaver, in which he wrote, "I've always had confidence in your ability to handle things. . . . Our friendship for you remains as warm and firm as does our feeling for the people of the Philippines."[128] In early October 1983, Vice President Bush reconfirmed U.S. support of Marcos in comments to the press. He warned that the United States could "not cut away from a person who, imperfect though he may be on human rights, has worked with us." Bush further stated, "The United States does not want to have another Khomeini."[129]

U.S. policy toward Marcos is outlined in a 1984 National Security Council Study Directive. It serves as a summary statement of American policy in the Philippines.

> The communist New People's Army, taking advantage of the depressed economy, the weakness of the Philippine military and its abuse of civilians, popular fear and resentment of the military, and the government's

inability to deliver economic and social development programs, has continued to expand significantly. This threat will doubtless continue to grow in the absence of progress toward credible democratic institutions, military reform including the curbing of abuse, and basic economic reform. . . .

While President Marcos at this stage is part of the problem he is also necessarily part of the solution. . . .

The U.S. does not want to remove Marcos from power to destabilize the GOP [Government of the Philippines]. Rather, we are urging the revitalization of democratic institutions, dismantling 'crony' capitalism and allowing the economy to respond to free market forces, and restoring professional, apolitical leadership to the Philippine military to deal with the growing communist insurgency. . . .

Our assets include not only the economic and military assistance that we are able to provide, but also the respect and sympathy that we continue to enjoy with most segments of the Philippine population. Our support is one of Marcos's largest remaining strengths. Our assets, particularly at the people-to-people level, could be lost if we come to be seen as favoring a continuation of the Marcos regime to the exclusion of other democratic alternatives. . . .

Our active public and private diplomacy has been aimed at demonstrating to the Philippine public that we stand with them in their time of troubles, but that we are encouraging the basic reforms necessary to the survival of their democratic institutions. . . .

In the Philippine cultural context, the way we convey our policy messages to the government leadership, the opposition, the Church, and the business community is almost as important as the policy.

An effective, low-key approach involves no special efforts at communication other than the normal—an occasional presidential letter, regular visits by administration officials, close embassy contact, and regular one-on-one meetings between President Marcos and Ambassador Bosworth.[130]

By 1985, evidence of increasing instability rendered the situation in the Philippines sufficiently precarious as to prompt high-level visits by U.S. presidential emissaries. The visitors, who urged Marcos to make needed reforms, included in their numbers Paul Wolfowitz, assistant secretary of state for East Asia; Richard Childress of the National Security Council; Richard Armitage, assistant secretary of defense for international security; William Casey, director of the CIA; and Admiral William Crowe, commander of the Pacific fleet (subsequently appointed chairman of the Joint Chiefs of Staff). Members of Congress, including Stephen Solarz and Jack Kemp, visited as well.[131]

Support for Marcos began to wane in Washington. Admiral Crowe submitted a secret report to President Reagan warning that the Philippine military was corrupt, demoralized, and incapable of fighting the counter-insurgency. He concluded that the "NPA was a serious threat," and advised the president to pursue a policy designed to convince Marcos to step down.[132] As conditions in the Philippines deteriorated, an anti-Marcos bias began to develop in the State Department and public criticism of Marcos was heard. In February 1985, Paul Wolfowitz explained that "military abuse against civilians" was "one of the most commonly cited factors in explaining the alarming growth of the communist insurgency throughout the islands."[133] He told the House Subcommittee on Asian and Pacific Affairs in March 1985, "The Philippines cannot afford a business-as-usual approach to the insurgency or the urgent need to deal with its root problems."[134] Richard Armitage warned at the same time that the NPA guerrillas could "force a 'strategic stalemate' in three to five years."[135]

By August 1985, many conservatives in the State Department, particularly below the level of assistant secretary, joined the anti-Marcos camp: U.S. long-term interests in the Philippines could not be protected if Marcos's failing health and domestic policies threatened Philippine stability. It appeared to these policymakers that Marcos was likely to continue to exploit and destroy the Philippine economy and corrupt its military in pursuit of personal advantage—even if it meant the eventual victory of communism.[136]

Executive Support and Congressional Dissent. In the Congress, criticism of Marcos's human rights violations had been raised since 1973. Discussion about possible cuts in foreign aid continued until 1976, when both houses of Congress passed a concurrent resolution disapproving the sale of certain defense articles to the Philippines.[137] In 1977, military appropriations for fiscal year 1978 were cut by $3 million.[138] Stipulations were added to PL-480 (Title 1) agreements requiring that the Philippines "describe how the commodities or the sale proceeds would be used for projects or programs directly benefiting needy people."[139] Congress also cut administration funding requests for international lending institutions based on past U.S. votes for loan approvals to countries, including the Philippines, that had abused human rights.[140] The Philippines was warned that future U.S. approval of international financial institution loans would be contingent upon the human rights situation in that country.[141] Congressional attempts to cut direct U.S. aid to the Philippines in 1979 and 1980, however, were unsuccessful.

Following the Aquino assassination in August 1983, the House of Representatives passed a resolution praising Benigno Aquino and calling for an unbiased investigation of his murder. It also called for U.S. support of free parliamentary elections in 1984 and linked U.S. policy to

Philippine efforts in achieving these goals.[142] In 1984 and 1985, Congress demonstrated its displeasure with Marcos's human rights violations by transferring military assistance funds to economic aid programs. In 1984, $45 million in military aid was transferred to the economic assistance fund, and in December 1985, a $55 million cap was placed on military aid for fiscal year 1986.[143] These cuts were only "symbolic"; aid agreements with the Philippines in effect constituted "unofficial rent" for the bases and were thus not seriously vulnerable to actual budget cuts.[144] In May 1985, the Senate passed an amendment to the fiscal year 1986 Foreign Authorization Bill expressing a sense of the Congress that aid to the Philippines be approved contingent upon "significant progress" in human rights reform.[145]

Administration support, however, remained firm. When Congress sought to cut military aid in July 1985, General Teddy Allen, head of the U.S. Military Advisory Group in Manila, was flown to Washington to warn against such action.[146] U.S. policy developed a schizophrenia upon which Marcos relied. President Reagan and close conservative advisers, including Secretary of Defense Caspar Weinberger and CIA Director William Casey, demonstrated support for Marcos, seeking only those reforms that would assuage the volatile domestic situation. But many in the State Department and Congress saw no solution but to have Marcos leave.

As a consequence of the apparent divisions in Washington, Marcos's responses were only cosmetic. In August 1985, Marcos told an interviewer,

> Your government is divided into bureaucratic factions. There is one faction there which closes its eyes to reality and has come out openly against my administration. There is another trying to help us. . . . The story in diplomatic circles of course is that in Washington you need two ambassadors—one for Congress and another for the executive department.[147]

The *Christian Science Monitor* reported in February 1986,

> Behind the consensus for reform were differing views within the Reagan Administration on the Philippine crisis. At one end of the spectrum was the White House, where support for Marcos was strongest. At the other end were mid-level policy analysts at the State and Defense Departments and the intelligence community who, months before the Aquino assassination, became concerned about the durability of the Marcos regime.[148]

American Diplomacy and Revolution in the Philippines. By October 1985, it seemed evident to the administration that Marcos was not giving sufficient credence to its concerns and that he was relying on the support he perceived he had in the White House. As a consequence, Senator Paul Laxalt was sent on a publicized visit to bring Marcos a personal message from the president. The publicity, it was hoped, would maximize the pressure on Marcos.[149]

Reinforcing the show of increased concern was a November 1, 1985, statement by Senator David Durenberger, chairman of the Senate Select Committee on Intelligence. Senator Durenberger quoted a staff report which asserted that "democracy was doomed" in the Philippines because of declining economic conditions and the spread of the communist insurgency. He further stated that Marcos could not or would not institute necessary reform and should therefore resign.[150]

Two weeks after the Laxalt visit and two days after the Durenberger statement, Marcos called for snap elections to be held in February 1986. Marcos had decided earlier to hold elections in order to silence American critics by demonstrating the continued support he had in the Philippines— support he was sure to be able to claim by manipulating the election results. The brief period between the announcement and election would give little time for the opposition to mobilize.[151]

The opposition, however, was galvanized into a formidable force. Cardinal Sin worked to unite the two major opposition contenders for the presidency, Corazon Aquino and Salvador Laurel. Support for the ticket came from the business sector, the church, and segments of the military. On January 7, 1986, fifteen military officers from the Reform the Armed Forces Movement announced their intention to support "honest, clean, and fair" elections.[152]

The dual approach pursued by the American administrations—working with Marcos in the interests of keeping him in power, while maintaining varying degrees of contact with the opposition—was ultimately outrun by events. U.S. policy could no longer manipulate events easily and was instead more likely to be shaped by them.

Marcos lost the February 7, 1986, election—a loss witnessed and verified by international observers, including Senator Richard G. Lugar and a delegation of U.S. observers. Reagan's singular support of Marcos would be virtually impossible to continue. Senator Lugar was convinced that Marcos had cheated and that Aquino had won. When Lugar returned on February 11, he told Reagan that despite all the fraud committed by Marcos supporters, Marcos had "failed to emerge as a clear-cut winner."[153] Reagan nonetheless would not concede a Marcos defeat. He told a news conference that evening that "fraud and violence may have been occurring on both sides."[154]

Philip Habib, who visited the Philippines after the election as a Reagan emissary, informed the president that he concurred with Lugar's opinion. Nonetheless, it was February 15 before Reagan even admitted that the "ruling party"—although not Marcos himself—had been largely responsible for "widespread fraud and violence" so "extreme that the election's credibility had been called into question."[155] On February 22, 1986, with the military rebellion under way and "people power" clearly on its side, the White House issued another statement in which the election fraud was again blamed on the Marcos party. This statement warned that the "extreme" fraud would "impair the capacity of the government of the Philippines to cope with the growing insurgency and troubled economy."[156] In neither statement was Marcos asked to step down.

Events within the Philippines, however, forced U.S. policy in a direction Reagan had not initially been prepared to accept. A *Wall Street Journal* article reported on March 3, 1986, that the U.S. embassy in Manila had begun to help the anti-Marcos forces. In order to make certain that sufficient publicity was generated for the February 22, 1986, press conference in which Defense Minister Juan Ponce Enrille and General Fidel Ramos would announce the anti-Marcos military rebellion, the U.S. embassy notified correspondents about the meeting. Washington also applied pressure in support of the rebels and "people power" by dissuading Marcos from using force to quell the opposition. Messages were sent to Marcos on February 23 and 24 warning him that there would be costly consequences if violence was employed against the armed forces.[157] Attempts to resolve the situation "by force," a White House statement said, "would cause untold damage to the relationship between our governments," and would lead to a halt in U.S. military assistance.[158] U.S. Ambassador Bosworth told Marcos that his "time was up" and that the United States "will make the transition as peaceful as possible."[159] U.S. intelligence advised rebels of instructions Marcos was giving to his men, and rebel forces were given access to Clark Air Base to refuel helicopters and rearm with Philippine weapons stored on the bases.

Marcos's refusal to concede finally forced President Reagan to become directly involved in moving events to a resolution. On February 24, 1986, Reagan made a public and explicit statement in which Marcos was asked to step down. "Attempts to prolong the life of the present regime by violence are futile," he said. "A solution to this crisis can only be achieved through a peaceful transition to a new government."[160] Marcos called Senator Laxalt to confirm that these were, indeed, the president's sentiments. When the U.S. position became clear, when he realized that his support even from the President had dissipated, Marcos conceded and went into exile on February 26. The Americans flew Marcos and his entourage to Clark Air Base and then to Hawaii.

U.S. Policy and the Postrevolutionary Philippines

Reagan's loyalty to Ferdinand Marcos, and his consequent ambivalence toward the opposition, led to a policy that might have alienated the anti-Marcos forces. In reaction to Reagan's initial postelection statement, claiming that both sides had participated in fraud, Corazon Aquino retorted, "I wonder at the motives of a friend of democracy who chose to conspire with Mr. Marcos to cheat the Filipino people of their liberation."[161] President Reagan waited until April 1986, two months after her victory, to congratulate President Aquino. The evident ambivalence signaled from the White House put in doubt the strength of American support for the new Philippine president.[162]

Despite Reagan's obvious displeasure with events in the Philippines, support for the Philippine opposition, which would attenuate antagonisms toward the United States, was forthcoming from various U.S. officials. Immediately after news of Benigno Aquino's death reached Washington, John Maisto, the Philippine desk officer at the State Department, called Corazon Aquino with condolences; he then called the anti-Marcos opposition in the United States. The U.S. ambassador to Manila, Michael Armacost, visited Benigno Aquino's wife and mother to express his sympathies. He attended the funeral mass, despite notification from the Philippine Foreign Ministry that attendance would be considered an "affront to Marcos."[163]

Although the extent of association with the anti-Marcos opposition was inconsistent during the Marcos years, Aquino's assassination led to an intensification of contacts by U.S. embassy staff. Whereas prior to the assassination U.S. Ambassador Armacost had maintained only formal relations with Cardinal Sin, meetings were scheduled frequently after the event. Indeed, President Reagan was even convinced to make a conciliatory comment toward the opposition, stating in a February 1985 interview, "We realize there is an opposition party that we believe is also pledged to democracy."[164]

A February 1986 article in the *Far East Economic Review,* which appeared before the revolt, revealed that "the U.S. embassy . . . was engaged in intense secret contacts with the opposition, Marcos' ruling party, and the military in an effort to bring about a reconciliation of the two political groups, without Marcos."[165]

The United States supported the Reform the Armed Forces Movement (RAM). It secretly funneled funds to the group and brought its officers to the United States to demonstrate to members of Congress and opinion leaders that possibilities existed for reforming the military. AID funds were diverted through the Asia Foundation to support an opposition station, Radio Veritas. Washington also gave financial assistance to an independent election monitoring group, the National Movement for Free Elections (NAMFREL), and pressured Marcos to allow the organization to participate in the election process.[166]

Reagan's apparently antagonistic comment that election fraud may have been committed by both sides, was vitiated by Senator Lugar's statement that, "The president was not well informed when he made the statement."[167] The U.S. ambassador to Manila visited a disgruntled Corazon Aquino to say, "That wasn't the full U.S. position you heard. Be patient."[168] Secretary of State George Shultz asked Aquino's friend, Bob Jones, to convey a similar message.[169]

The Reagan administration did, however, eventually accede to the course history had taken, and publicly proclaimed its support for the inevitable revolution. Within two hours of Marcos's departure, Secretary of State Shultz went on television to announce U.S. recognition of the new government and to assure the Aquino administration that,

> The United States stands ready, as always, to cooperate and assist the Philippines as the government of President Aquino engages the problems of economic development and national security.[170]

In her first hundred days as president, Aquino was visited by Secretary of Defense Weinberger, Secretary of State Shultz, senior U.S. civil servants, and U.S. military officers. In March, U.S. Representative Solarz brought her an invitation to address a joint session of Congress.[171] During her visit to Washington in September 1986, Aquino received an enthusiastic reception from virtually the entire Washington political community. She was hailed in Congress and complimented by the State Department. Despite the Gramm-Rudman Act, Congress voted a $200 million grant in additional assistance for the Philippines; it also increased the Philippine sugar quota.[172] Following his meeting with President Aquino on September 17, Reagan said, "The United States stands ready to assist President Aquino in her quest to create a stable and secure land, as well as in her commitment to invigorate the Philippine economy."[173] He also told the press, "I'm bullish on the Philippines."[174] Reagan's comments, explained Philippines Ambassador Pelaez, "put to rest for many people, any questions about Reagan's continued support of Marcos."[175]

Realpolitik in the Philippines

U.S. policies in the Philippines, as in Iran, were primarily designed to protect the U.S. national interest. In the Philippines, that interest centered on the American military bases. By becoming so dependent on that presence, American policy became hostage to the vagaries of Philippine politics.

Marcos was perceived to be the only protector of U.S. interests and communism the only likely alternative to his rule. Even as conditions deteriorated, policymakers sought panaceas rather than alternatives. In 1984, when Reagan responded to a question about the Philippines becoming another Nicaragua, the president said, "I know there are things there in the Philippines that do not look good to us from the standpoint right now of democratic rights, but what is the alternative? It is a large communist movement."[176] Even as late as February 23, 1986—in the aftermath of the Philippine presidential election and the subsequent army rebellion, and after receiving advice from State Department and White House staff that Marcos would have to go—Reagan could not perceive that a Philippines without Marcos would be in the U.S. interest. He still opposed dissociation from Marcos, warning against creating opportunities for communism.[177]

Under such assumptions, U.S. administrations could do nothing but give Marcos economic support, military assistance, and diplomatic backing throughout his rule. The constant infusion of aid and the rhetoric of alliance continued, despite the flagrant and persistent abuse of political and human rights, and the destruction of the nation's economy. When the United States finally responded to the demands of the Filipinos, it did so only at the last moment and under duress. It was only after the February 22, 1986, Enrille-Ramos press conference that Secretary of State Shultz admitted clearly that Marcos was "unraveling," and would have to be told that his position was no longer tenable.[178] In its general outline, therefore, U.S. policy in the Philippines seems much akin to the one followed in Iran.

If maintaining the U.S. presence on the bases in the Philippines was the only consideration, the U.S. national interest, in the short term, was not significantly damaged by its support of Marcos. The support ensured Marcos's malleability and served to preserve the U.S. interest. Indeed, despite its past support of Marcos, Washington continued to maintain friendly relations with the postrevolutionary Aquino regime. Demands made in 1991 for U.S. withdrawal from the bases were impelled by Philippine nationalist sentiment, not by antagonism engendered by U.S. support of Marcos. Marcos himself had increased his demands in exchange for the continued use of the bases, particularly during the 1979 and 1983 negotiations. It is, therefore, quite possible that a scenario similar to that which occurred during the Aquino presidency might also have occurred under a Marcos administration.

It may not, however, be possible to isolate and protect a single element of the U.S. interest without affecting its other aspects. In the case of the Philippines, the U.S. worked against its own interest in several ways. U.S. support contributed to conditions that proved economically costly and potentially damaging to the United States. It supported a leader who devastated his nation's economy and bled its treasury. In 1972, when martial law was imposed, the Philippine foreign debt was approximately $2 million; at the end of Marcos's rule, it had increased to $26 billion.[179] By buttressing the Marcos regime and allowing it to drain the nation's economic vitality, the United States helped create a nation dependent upon massive outside economic assistance and threatened by a growing communist insurgency. If Marcos had not been deposed, the United States could ultimately have been confronted by a communist regime, or at least a revolutionary elite resentful of U.S. support of Marcos. It is doubtful that an amicable working relationship with the United States would have continued under either scenario.

Postrevolutionary Philippines and the U.S. National Interest

Under the Aquino administration, human rights violations committed both by the government and leftist elements continued, and widespread poverty and unemployment continued to fuel the communist insurgency.[180] Discontent with government corruption and the course of the anticommunist campaign led to at least seven coups. Nonetheless, habeas corpus was reinstituted and political participation invited. In contrast to Iran, Washington's unfailing and public support of the Marcos dictatorship did not lead to an avalanche of anti-American sentiment. The new post-Marcos government of the Philippines maintained generally cordial relations with the United States, and U.S. economic interests remained protected. By 1991, however, Philippine nationalism forced the United States to begin withdrawal from the bases.

President Aquino's ambassador to the United States, Emmanuel Pelaez, stated two months after the revolution:

> The new government of President Aquino has chosen the path of what might be known as the moderate nationalist option, under which the Philippines will maintain close relations with the United States on the basis of mutual respect and benefit. . . .
> Underlying this option . . . is the fact that nationalism is a powerful force in the Philippines today, that the Philippines, like any other independent state, has its interests to pursue, that the Philippines wishes to

stress its nature as an Asian nation, that it desires treatment as an equal, and that it needs to assert the authenticity of its independence, sovereignty, and dignity. This the Philippines can do without necessarily becoming anti-American or breaking the historic friendship that has bound the two countries and peoples together for much of this century. Instead, the Philippines would like to believe that its historic encounter with the United States constitutes a comparative advantage giving it an edge over others in getting the assistance it now seeks.[181]

Vocal opposition to the American influence and presence dominated the Philippine Congress, however, and limited Aquino's ability to maneuver in her relations with the United States. During October 1988 discussions about the status of the U.S. bases, Philippine Foreign Secretary Raul Manglapus assured the U.S. administration of President Aquino's support if she could get a package "she could sell to the people."[182] The agreement reached for 1990–1991 required that the United States get approval before chemical or nuclear weapons were stored on the bases. It also provided for $962 million in direct aid for the two-year period, with $200 million earmarked for military assistance. An additional $500 million in indirect aid, dependent on private American investment, was also included. Although this fell short of Philippine demands for $1.2 billion, it was substantially above the $180 million per year previously allocated.[183]

Criticism of the agreement nonetheless came from both the Philippine Left and Right. An editorial in the left-wing paper, *Malaya,* complained that Foreign Secretary Manglapus "has sold out his country and grossly deceived his people. For these treasonous acts he ought never to show his face again in Manila." A right-wing editorial in *The Philippine Daily Globe* criticized the terms of the agreement as the "wages of attaching a price tag to one's society and self-respect."[184]

In August 1991, a ten-year treaty governing the use of American bases was agreed to contingent upon approval by the Philippine Congress. It provided for $203 million in annual military aid and additional economic assistance estimated to total $3.5 billion in the course of the decade. The economic advantages attributed to the U.S. presence, in terms of economic aid and employment, led President Aquino and much of the Philippine public to support the agreement. The Philippine military, fearing the loss of its substantial U.S. military assistance, also gave it its backing. Nonetheless, nationalist sentiment in the Philippine Senate, and objections to what was considered an unacceptable compensation package, derailed the treaty. In a 12–11 vote, the U.S. lease for Subic Bay was voted down. (Clark Air Base was abandoned after the June 1991 eruption of Mt. Pinatubo.)

Even with a U.S. withdrawal, however, American strategic interests, which the bases ensured, were not irrevocably damaged. Options long existed for the transfer of the Philippine-based operations to Singapore, Guam, Japan, and Hawaii. Furthermore, realignments in post–Cold War political and strategic configurations meant that cutbacks in the U.S. military presence worldwide were feasible. Dramatic reductions in naval operations conducted out of Subic Bay were being planned for the Philippines even before the U.S. withdrawal was demanded. Indeed, the security value of the Philippine installations were downgraded from "vital" to "important" before the 1991 base negotiations began.[185]

Although the U.S.–Philippine military relationship has been transformed, and economic aid consequently slashed, cordial bilateral relations continue. President Fidel V. Ramos, who was elected to succeed President Aquino in 1992, is an advocate of close U.S.–Philippine relations. In November 1992, he assured Washington that the Philippines had a "continuing community of strategic and economic interests" with the United States based, in part, on trade interests and on a commitment to democracy.[186] Indeed, in early November 1992, as the last contingent of U.S. Marines prepared to leave the Philippines, an agreement to give U.S. fighting ships, aircraft, and troops continued access to Philippine military installations was announced. An American official characterized the agreement as giving the United States continued use of "Philippine facilities in a fairly liberal manner." President Ramos made clear, a month earlier, that "despite constitutional restrictions," he was willing to find a way for U.S. troops to remain in the Philippines.[187]

U.S. Policy in the Philippines: An Inadvertent Success

Particularly after the 1972 imposition of martial law, increasing economic exploitation, human rights abuse, and growing opposition in the Philippines became plainly evident to U.S. policymakers. Marcos's role in assuring the continued presence of U.S. bases on Philippine territory and his pro-business policies made it easy for Washington to overlook the rapidly deteriorating situation.

Although martial law was initially unopposed by a majority of the Philippine population, including business and the Left, its shortcomings led to growing opposition among all sectors of Philippine society. Martial law had failed to establish the promised tranquility and economic prosperity the business sector had expected; its New Society land reforms did not improve the lot of the rural poor. Martial law did, however, increase the abuse of civil and political rights, antagonize the landed elite who had been affected by land reform, and create discontent within a business sector that had suffered from the corruption of the Marcos regime. Throughout the 1970s, however, the aim of the moderate opposition was reform rather than revolution. Although Marcos's resignation was demanded by members of the business sector in 1982, and by Cardinal Sin in 1983, the demands were not likely to lead to revolutionary changes in the Philippines. Only the NPA, which was increasing in numbers as Marcos's repression and corruption continued, sought to foment rebellion.

The U.S. Congress condemned abuses in the Philippines and, on occasion, tried to cut or manipulate U.S. aid; American administrations, however, publicly proclaimed strong support for Marcos throughout his tenure. The Reagan administration began a quiet campaign to urge reform only in 1985, when the stability of the Marcos regime appeared to be threatened. It was, however, in February 1986 that U.S. support for Marcos was finally withdrawn. This occurred only after Marcos was defeated in national elections, when a military rebellion was imminent, and when there were few alternatives left by which to respond to the widespread upheaval.

Fortunately for the United States, rebellion erupted at a time when the NPA had not established a sufficiently extensive network to assume a leading role in the revolution. By 1985, a U.S. intelligence report noted that the NPA had 15,000 armed full-time guerrillas and an equal number of irregulars. Unlike other leftist movements, the guerrillas did not receive outside assistance and acquired their weapons by capturing Philippine army supplies. Had Marcos remained in power without drastically improving conditions, pro-NPA sympathies would likely have increased. Given time to consolidate its numbers and improve its organization, an NPA revolution, similar to that which had occurred in Nicaragua, might well have occurred—or might still be possible. Indeed, a 1985 State Department report predicted a possible NPA victory within three to five years.[188] (By mid-1990, the Congressional Research Service reported NPA numbers at twenty to twenty-five thousand regulars.)[189]

It was not, therefore, the policies of the Carter or Reagan administrations—policies largely akin to those pursued in Iran—which led to a moderate, pro-U.S. revolution in the Philippines. It was rather a fortuitous concatenation of events, leading to the eruption of revolution before the NPA was ready to take control, which led to a foreign policy success for the United States.

The Lessons of Neoconservatism Examined

The Philippine case adheres, in a very significant way, to neoconservative prescriptions related to human rights and the U.S. interest. Marcos was protected and supported throughout his presidency despite any abuses he may have inflicted upon his nation or its people. Any policies or criticisms emanating from the Congress or the White House regarding human rights abuses left him virtually unscathed. Washington poured funds and arms into the Philippines to protect Marcos, and stood by him until left with little alternative but to abandon his regime. Yet the efforts proved futile. In this case, as in Iran, intolerable domestic conditions led to a popular revolt; the power to mold events, which neoconservatives assume the United States to possess, proved insufficient to ensure that politics and history in the Philippines would be written by the United States. U.S. policy, in this case too, became subject to external events.

Contrary to neoconservative arguments, the regime that arose after the fall of Marcos was not communist, but pro-Western and generally pro-American. Indeed, if the United States had not, at the end of the day, encouraged Marcos to leave, and assisted the moderate opposition to power, the eventual outcome could have been a communist revolution or one led by a vehemently anti-American elite.

Unsubstantiated in the Philippine case, too, is the neoconservative proposition that the pursuit and protection of the U.S. national interest abroad serves to enhance human rights. Such rights were plainly destroyed in the Philippines under Marcos, with little protest forthcoming from the United States. Indeed, the United States supplied the preponderance of equipment used to destroy those rights. Although Marcos did take occasional cosmetic actions to mollify criticisms directed at him by Congress, the State Department, or U.S. administrations, he felt confident in stepping over the boundaries of law because the United States relied on him as the protector of its interests.

The neoconservative caveat that U.S. pressure for reform may lead to unknown consequences has again been borne out. As in Iran and Nicaragua, reform led to a revolution that the United States did not seek or foresee. This does not, however, preclude the possibility that a U.S. policy to stimulate change in nations subject to dictatorial rule is not both pragmatic and necessary for the pursuit of the U.S. national interest. As in the previous cases, U.S. pressures for, and regime concessions to, political liberalization came only when the situation had reached crisis proportions and when disaffection had reached almost all sectors of society. Domestic demands in the Philippines initially centered on requests for more extensive and meaningful economic and political reform. When such reform was not forthcoming, the call for change was replaced by a clamor for revolution. Had the United States pursued efforts to move Marcos, the Shah, or Somoza toward reform when early demands for liberalization were being made, it might have contributed to a more stable political environment—one in which revolution would not be perceived as the only alternative, and one where the United States could continue its relatively stable bilateral relationships.

U.S. support of Marcos did serve the short-term interests of the nation—but the policy was also shortsighted. It allowed economic and political conditions to deteriorate, creating an environment in which opposition grew and leftist movements developed; the United States took every opportunity to identify itself with a ruler who was quickly losing popular support. As circumstances developed, the Philippine revolution was led by moderates; the protection of U.S. interests was thereby assured. Had Marcos stayed in power—allowing the condition that antagonized the Filipino people to be perpetuated and giving the NPA more time to organize—the United States may have found its long-term interests sacrificed to its short-term goals.

The Neorealist Perspective Reviewed

The Philippine case also conforms, in some ways, to neorealist assumptions. Marcos did not sever relations with the United States in reaction to any of the minimal sanctions it imposed to signify discontent with his human rights abuses. The effect of those sanctions and of U.S. human rights policy on opposition perceptions, is not, however, clear.

As in Iran, anti-Americanism was initially triggered not by the role the United States played vis-à-vis human rights, but by sentiments of growing nationalism, and by economic and social problems for which the United States was in large measure blamed. As a former colonial power, as a nation that maintained a special and dominant relationship with the Philippines and its corrupt dictator, the United States was criticized for exploiting the people, economy, and sovereignty of the Philippines.

The United States was often criticized, even by the moderate opposition, for supporting Marcos and supplying him with weapons. In December 1977, former Philippine president, Diosado Macapagal said, "we do not want the United States to intervene. We can take care of the democratic situation ourselves. We are just requesting one thing, that is, that the United States not aid the government, not lend its prestige to the Marcos government by providing military aid."[190] In 1978, Macapagal complained that the Carter administration had done "nothing" to relieve the martial law conditions.[191] During a 1984 trip to Washington, the opposition leader Salvador Laurel lamented that the United States "has supported and continues to support with money, arms, and fulsome praise the dictatorship of the Philippines."[192] U.S. refusal to condemn Marcos's election fraud in 1985 prompted one business executive to complain, "America is not willing to follow through. . . . He [Marcos] has called your bluff time after time. Fire and thunder from Washington, and then what do you get? A whimper."[193] A pro-Aquino human rights lawyer observed, "the U.S. is running true to form. Its only interest is in safeguarding its bases, not in restoring democracy."[194] Diane Orentlich, deputy director of the Lawyer's Committee for Human Rights, visited the Philippines during the 1986 elections and testified in Congress that

> Filipinos, on the whole, felt that they had done everything humanly possible to try to reclaim democracy, and that they needed outside help. They were looking to President Reagan for that support. Not only was the support not forthcoming immediately, but when President Reagan finally spoke, he literally pulled the floor out from under them, and I think it will take a long time for the Filipino public to recover from that wound.[195]

Positive attitudes toward the United States nonetheless persisted and a pro-American policy prevailed. Interviews conducted at the time showed that a widely held sentiment was that "Carter's talk of human rights has made talk of human rights here legitimate."[196] Upon his release from prison in May 1980, Benigno Aquino told an interviewer, "When Carter came onto the scene and spoke about human rights it gave us new hope. . . . It was the best thing that ever happened to the Third World."[197]

The pro-American foreign policy pursued by the new Philippine government thus may have derived from influences other than the official human rights policies of U.S. administrations. Contacts with opposition leaders, for example, had been expanded during the Carter administration. Although they were again limited during the Reagan presidency, members of the U.S. Congress continued to associate with the Philippine opposition, and U.S. embassy contacts were extended after the Aquino assassination. In addition, the moderate opposition, which had been at the forefront of the revolution, was composed of an elite that was politically and ideologically Western in orientation and thus inclined to embrace the United States.

U.S. acceptance of nonaligned foreign policy orientations, which developing nations often seek to adopt, is urged by the neorealists; it seems to represent a pragmatic approach for the pursuit of U.S. foreign policy and its national interest in the Philippines. The United States must now deal with a Philippine government and people that are still pro-American and still willing to pursue friendly relations, but who are not willing to be dominated by the United States. Nationalist sentiment that led the Philippine Congress, courts, and even Marcos, to demand economic, territorial and sovereign rights for the nation have increased. The United States cannot impose its will or lure a people inspired by nationalism with promises of economic assistance. Even among those who opposed the 1991 bases treaty, it was nationalism rather than anti-U.S. sentiment that formed their view. Juan Ponce Enrille, former defense minister in the Marcos and Aquino governments, opposed the agreement because "it perpetuated the reputation of the Philippines as a 'mendicant' nation dependent on the United States for protection and support." He explained, "This is not a question of liking Americans or not liking Americans. . . . I like the United States of America. But it is time for the nation to put its own interest first."[198]

The fall of Marcos did not lead to the end of the U.S.–Philippine alliance. Despite the U.S. departure from the bases, the Philippines remains a nation that has proven its desire for democracy, that seeks to maintain cordial relations with the United States, and that will likely serve as a political asset.

The case for the Philippines underscores the limited effect U.S. policy may have on events abroad. Washington could not, as prescribed by the neoconservatives, save a ruler destined to fall by virtue of his own policies. Neither did it damage its interests by supporting a dictator, against the wishes of the opposition, as the neorealists would expect. Thus, while a number of assumptions related to both schools have been validated in the Philippine case, the hypotheses of neither has been proven correct.

6   Summary and Conclusion

Instruments of Foreign Policy
to Support Human Rights

Instruments of foreign policy may vary in form and force depending upon the message being sent and the relationship that exists between the initiating and target states. Sanctions, the most severe and ostensibly most effective of instruments, may not, however, represent the optimum strategy in achieving foreign policy goals. Stanley J. Heginbotham of the Congressional Research Service testified to this effect in 1979. The use of leverage, he stated, was useful in "a number of cases drawn from countries as diverse as Guinea, the Dominican Republic, Indonesia, Korea, and Tanzania," where an interest in "obtaining some form of benefit from the United States" led to "an effort to improve its human rights conditions." Heginbotham admitted, however, that "the record on direct and explicit use of foreign assistance to bring about specific improvements in human rights conditions . . . is not impressive." In fact, "direct pressures seem often to provoke counterproductive reaction," as they did in Chile, Argentina, and Ethiopia.[1]

In the cases of Iran, Nicaragua, and the Philippines, foreign policy instruments were little used in defense of human rights. Reforms, when implemented, came in the absence of punitive measures or before their impact was felt. Similarly, the tools of U.S. foreign policy proved ineffective in protecting rulers upon which the United States depended.

Iran

In the case of Iran, U.S. sanctions were neither used nor contemplated; the Shah was supported throughout his reign with aid, trade, and diplomacy. U.S. economic aid between 1960 and 1967 totaled $301.1 million; total military assistance grew from $421.2 million in the period 1960 to 1965, to $602.9 million in the period between 1966 and 1969.[2] Iran ceased to receive U.S. economic and military assistance in 1967 and 1969, respectively. Thereafter, Iran became a major trading partner and principal customer of military weapons. Iran's military purchases from the U.S. government, given in terms of value of deliveries, rose from $469.8 million in the period 1972 to 1973, to $4.3 billion in 1977 to 1978 (see Table 3-1).

In the manner in which the Shah was supported, U.S. policy in Iran was essentially neoconservative. Human rights was not a significant issue in bilateral relations, and there was little debate on the floor of Congress about the issue between 1971 and 1979. A letter related to human rights abuses was inserted into the *Congressional Record* in 1971; in 1975, U.S. Representative Stark suggested that U.S. relations with Iran be reevaluated in the light of Iran's unacceptable human rights record.[3] In August and September 1976, and in October 1977, the House Foreign Affairs Subcommittee on International Relations held hearings specifically focused on human rights in Iran.[4] Senator Hubert H. Humphrey, chairman of the Senate Foreign Relations Assistance Subcommittee, informed Secretary of State Kissinger in September 1976, that the committee intended to examine the human rights situation in that country.[5] Criticism of Iran's human rights record by the House International Relations Subcommittee in 1977, led to a State Department request that U.S. policy toward Iran not be changed. Iran was nonetheless informed that its human rights record would be evaluated before U.S. support was given for international financial institution loans.[6] Of five Iran-related discussions on the floor of Congress in 1978, only two condemned the country's human rights abuses.[7]

Congressional debate about conditions in Iran was relatively minimal in comparison to that about other U.S. allies, such as the Philippines. Nonetheless, in 1976, even prior to the inauguration of President Carter, the Shah proceeded on a program of liberalization.

Reforms were introduced for a number of reasons: the Shah hoped to defuse international condemnation of human rights abuses in Iran; he sought to assure the stability of the throne for his son; and, he anticipated the human rights priorities of the Carter administration. U.S. pressure, however, was neither applied nor threatened at the time liberalization was implemented. Indeed, the Carter administration encouraged the Shah to take forceful action in quelling the expanding rebellion. When it came to office, the Carter administration most significantly contributed to revolution in Iran through its universal advocacy of human rights and through the environment such rhetoric created in encouraging manifestations of discontent. Thus, one analyst wrote, "the irony is that Carter's human rights advocacy has had a major impact on the history of Iran and that that impact was entirely unintended."[8]

Nicaragua

Nicaragua had been under martial law at various times during the Somoza reign: during World War II, in 1960, 1972, 1974, and 1978. In September 1977, Anastasio Somoza Debayle lifted a state of siege imposed in 1974. Although U.S. economic and military sanctions were more stringently enforced in the case of Nicaragua than in the other cases, their actual influence on Somoza's September 1977 decision is difficult to gauge.

Martial law was lifted following President Carter's symbolic cancellation of sporting arms export licenses to Nicaragua, and after the administration's June 1977 announcement that a military aid agreement would not be signed without improvements in the human rights situation. Over $3 million in fiscal year 1977 military assistance was also delayed.[9] Nonetheless, military, and particularly economic aid disbursements, continued through 1978 at levels comparable to previous years (see Tables 4-1 and 4-2).[10] In addition, commercial sales of U.S. munitions continued to be approved through mid-1978. In 1977 and 1978, a total of $2.7 million in arms were delivered, and as of October 1978, a four-man U.S. military team was still stationed in Nicaragua.[11] Douglas J. Bennet, assistant secretary of defense for Congressional relations, explained in September 1978, "we have not approved any licenses for the commercial export of any Munitions List item to Nicaragua since July 1978. We have recently halted all military shipment," both "government and commercial, that might contribute to hostilities." For fiscal year 1978, Bennet noted, "$400,000 was appropriated and has been obligated for training."[12]

Multilateral development bank (MDB) loans increased through 1978 at rates sufficient to compensate for U.S. aid cuts. Thus, for example, while total U.S. direct aid between 1976 and 1977 fell by $17.6 million, MDB loans rose by $39.3 million. By 1979, military deliveries from the United States had decreased substantially; economic assistance, however, began to increase (see Tables 4-1 and 4-2).

As with military and economic aid, diplomatic pressure was not effectively utilized in 1977; it began in earnest in the fall of 1978 with the visit of William Jorden and with the OAS-sponsored talks. U.S. diplomacy, as Ambassador Solaun described it, was "neutral," but with an obvious bias toward Somoza. Congressional debate about Nicaragua had begun in 1976, but was divided.

Efforts by Latin American neighbors may have contributed as much, or more, to developments in Nicaragua than did U.S. activities. By mid-1978, prior to any such initiative by the United States, the presidents of Venezuela and Panama asked Somoza to resign. By the fall of that year, military assistance and/or territorial privileges were extended to the FSLN by Mexico, Panama, Venezuela, Cuba, and Costa Rica. Latin America would not allow the United States to use the OAS to save Somoza or the institutions of his government. The Andean Pact countries asked for Somoza's resignation in May 1979, the same month the United States approved a $66 million IMF loan for Nicaragua. In June, the Andean Pact nations, along with Panama, recognized the FSLN as the legitimate government of Nicaragua; this, at a time when Washington was still trying to find a "moderate" solution.[13]

Without Latin American assistance to the FSLN and the increasing violence mounted by the Sandinistas, Somoza might have retained power. Without the fears engendered by FSLN expansion, the United States might not have ultimately become so directly involved in Nicaragua. The impact of the Latin American states on the course of Nicaragua's history may, therefore, have been at least as great, if not greater, than that of the United States. As in Iran, President Carter's pronouncements about human rights created an environment where opposition forces would confront dictatorship; as in Iran, too, U.S. policy could not take the credit, or responsibility, for either the the 1977 liberalization or the outcome of the Nicaraguan revolution.

Philippines

Similar to the case of Iran, the February 1986 presidential elections and the ultimate resignation of President Marcos came as a result of factors other than U.S. economic or military sanctions. Human rights conditions in the Philippines had been a subject of U.S. Congressional debate since 1973. Aid cuts (attempted and successful) were made in Congress from 1977 through 1980; multilateral development bank loans were rejected on human rights grounds between 1978 and 1981. By 1984, Congressional discontent with conditions in the Philippines led to symbolic cuts in military aid, in the form of fund transfers, for fiscal years 1985 and 1986. The growing debate and the transfers of funds, however, had little impact. Military and economic aid to the Philippines continued to be approved. Actual military disbursements declined in 1984 and 1985, but military aid approvals assured that future arms deliveries would continue on a scale equal to the past. MDB loan requests received approval, and appropriations for economic assistance increased, as did AID fund distributions (see Tables 5-1 and 5-2).

Marcos, in fact, had little to fear. The United States was dependent upon him for the military bases. Even if a decision was made to cut aid and evacuate the bases, the logistics of such an operation, and the need to locate alternative facilities, would make it a long-term project. Furthermore, the symbolic transfer of military aid to economic assistance funds was not likely to hurt Marcos. As was the case in the late 1960s, Marcos could conceivably transfer economic aid funds to pay for military needs. Indeed, if Congressional condemnation and economic or military sanctions were to act as the impetus for Marcos's behavior, the Philippine president ought to have conceded to U.S. human rights concerns in the latter half of the 1970s, when the debate in Congress was intense and actual cuts were either made or attempted.

Marcos's conduct, it seems, was in a much more significant way shaped by his perceptions of White House support. Although Marcos was approached on the issue of human rights during the first two years of the Carter administration, the démarches were low key and presented little threat. By 1985, however, support for Marcos within the Reagan administration began to wane. Although President Reagan himself was a staunch supporter, State and Defense Department apprehensions about Philippine stability led to public criticism of the Marcos regime. A steady stream of administration envoys visited Marcos to urge reform.

The snap election called by Marcos in November 1985 apparently came in reaction to these pressures. This does not directly indicate, however, that Marcos was ready to make any major concessions. He had held presidential elections before and had rigged them to assure his success. This election, too, was to follow that pattern. International observer teams, including a U.S. delegation and a determined Philippine election-monitoring group, the National Movement for Free Elections, revealed the manipulation with which Marcos's victory was achieved. Despite public denunciations in the Philippines and the United States, Marcos seemed to have every intention of remaining in office until, and only until, he was convinced he had lost the personal support of President Reagan.

Various instruments of U.S. foreign policy had been utilized in the Philippines, if only minimally, since 1973. However, neither economic sanctions, nor the threat of their use in the late 1970s, nor Congressional condemnation, moved Marcos toward reform. It was the personal intervention of President Reagan that was apparently the most significant policy instrument effecting change in the Philippines.

In sum, the most effective instrument of U.S. foreign policy, as it emerges from these cases, was the public diplomacy of the Carter administration in support of human rights: the rhetoric of freedom proved to be a seminal influence in moving events toward revolution, particularly in Iran and Nicaragua. Other available instruments of foreign policy were generally neither utilized nor effectively applied. Sanctions related to military or economic assistance were applied in the Philippines and Nicaragua. In neither case, however, did they prove significantly effective. When diplomacy (public or private, executive or congressional) was used to criticize human rights abuses, the messages were contradicted by other policies such as foreign aid approvals that demonstrated support. Thus, neither the U.S. interest nor the cause of human rights were ultimately well served by the manner in which U.S. foreign policy instruments were utilized.

U.S. Human Rights Policy Abroad: The Cases Summarized

Specific questions related to U.S. human rights policy and its impact on the national interest are enumerated in Chapter 2. These questions deal with conditions that impelled revolutions, how such political disruptions affected U.S. policy and interests abroad, the kinds of human rights policies the United States pursued, and the effect such policies had on long term U.S. interests. Details related to the questions form the greater part of each case study. A summary of the findings follows:

1. *What was the nature of the civil and political rights situation under each regime?*

In all three cases, repression of civil and political rights was prominent and well documented. While periods of intermittent liberalization occurred in each case, they were often cosmetic and of short duration. Civil rights were often nonexistent, and political participation was generally limited to voting for government-approved parties in rigged elections. Dismissing the will of their people, the presidents of Nicaragua and the Philippines remained in power by manipulating constitutional limitations; in Iran, the Shah retained powers that the 1906 constitution had restricted. The legitimacy of these rulers waned as civil and political abuses continued and political exploitation persisted.

2. *What, if any, manifestations of discontent were present? What were the ideological and class orientations of the opposition groups? What were the causes of their dissatisfaction and how did they make their opposition known? What was the strength of the opposition in terms of members and sympathizers among the general public?*

Discontent with domestic conditions, and with the regimes that perpetuated them, was evident throughout the years and cases examined. Particularly when reforms allowed such expressions, discontent was manifested in public protests and press criticism; it was also publicized by international human rights organizations and exile opposition groups. Political and civil rights abuse and massive poverty existed in all three cases, as did disparities between rich and poor, the rural and urban. By the time revolution overtook each nation, the opposition had grown to include virtually all segments of society.

In Iran, the liberalization of the early 1960s saw an eruption of criticism. The Islamic clergy abhorred the Westernization associated with the White Revolution and also joined with members of the landed aristocracy in opposition to land reform. Poor farmers who gained little from land reforms also entered the ranks of the discontent, as did members of the middle class and intellectuals who resented the limitations the Shah had imposed on political participation. By the mid-1970s, the bazaari merchants and the urban poor would be included in the opposition: bazaaris were disgruntled with economic policies that threatened their livelihoods, and the urban poor, who lived in squalid conditions, faced unemployment and rising inflation.

Iran's opposition, which had its roots in the early 1960s, made relatively moderate demands. It primarily sought economic reform along with the continued existence of the monarchy under the provisions of the 1906 constitution. As protest grew and revolution intensified, Iran's moderate opposition, which in particular represented middle-class and business interests, lost its position as a leading force. Decades of oppression under the Shah's repressive policies rendered it organizationally weak and incapable of uniting and spearheading an opposition movement. As a consequence, the opposition joined with the clergy, the only institution that retained organizational viability and maintained ties to all sectors of the population, especially the urban poor and bazaaris. Radical demands for the abolition of the monarchy emerged as non-negotiable once the opposition movement was put in the hands of the clergy and its revolutionary leader, Ayatollah Khomeini. Anti-Americanism, which manifested itself during the revolution, intensified under the leadership of the clerics.

Opposition in Nicaragua, particularly as it related to repressive political conditions, had been exhibited throughout the Somoza dynasty in public protests and coup attempts. Such demonstrations of discontent often came from moderate opponents of the regime. As in the Philippines, however, a unified opposition movement to Somoza initially centered on a leftist, rural-based FSLN. The Sandinistas gained adherents among peasants who suffered poverty and who had been mistreated by Somoza's National Guard. Widespread sympathy for the FSLN also came from the lower ranks of the clergy who hoped to improve economic conditions of the poor, and who opposed Somoza's repressive policies. As economic conditions declined, as repression continued, and as Somoza's corrupt practices became more prominent, opposition grew to include Nicaragua's middle and upper classes, including its business sector. A large majority of the opposition focused on moderate demands; it sought reform and the ouster of Somoza, but expected to retain the institutions of government. Military successes of the FSLN, the inability of moderates to reach an agreement with Somoza, and the moderate opposition's belief that it did not have full U.S. support, led to a collapse of the moderate opposition and the ascendance of the FSLN.

Anti-Marcos opposition in the Philippines initially centered on the communist New Peoples Army (NPA). As Marcos's repression continued unabated, as the economy declined, and as corruption from within the Marcos camp increased, opposition grew. It came from the lower ranks of the Catholic clergy, who opposed the abuses of civil rights and the degradations of poverty suffered by the majority of Filipinos; it manifested itself among members of the landed aristocracy affected by the New Society land reforms, and among the moderate political opposition and students who resented the lack of free political participation. The business community joined the opposition in force following the Aquino assassination. The murder exacerbated tensions already extant because of the declining economy and Marcos's corruption.

The majority of the Philippine opposition was composed of political moderates who at first only sought major economic reform and greater political participation. Marcos's intransigence and the declining economy led to demands for his expulsion. The victory of Philippine moderates, however, came as a consequence of the relative weakness of the NPA, rather than the organizational strength or unity of the moderates.

3. *To what extent were U.S. policymakers aware of problems and the existence of opposition in each case?*

Evidence of growing opposition and of consequent threats to the stability of the regimes were apparent in all three cases. Information was made available by regime opponents operating from within and outside these countries, by international human rights monitors, by the CIA, and by embassy reports. The evidence was frequently ignored, however, so that immediate U.S. foreign policy goals and long-term ideological agendas could be accommodated.

4. *What was U.S. policy in relation to human rights and the target regime, in each case? What policy instruments did the United States utilize in implementing its human rights foreign policy objective, and what was the extent of their use? Were economic and/or military inducements or sanctions used? Was diplomatic support given or public condemnation issued?*

See the opening section of this Chapter, "Instruments of Foreign Policy."

5. *What was the U.S. role during the revolutionary crises in each country? Did it intervene in the process, and, if so, how and on behalf of which interests in the target state?*

U.S. involvement in the revolutionary crises represented by the three cases ranged from "nonintervention" to direct participation. In no case did the United States make direct, concerted efforts to organize and support the moderate opposition; in no case did it even approach the nonmoderate opposition before a collapse of the status quo became inevitable.

In Iran, U.S. support of the Shah remained generally steadfast during the entire revolutionary period: public and private diplomacy exhibited unwavering faith in the viability of the Shah's regime, military equipment continued to arrive from the United States, and U.S. General Huyser was initially sent to assure the continued support of Iran's military for the Shah's appointed government. Because of its attachment to the monarch throughout Mohammad Reza Pahlavi's reign, the United States had little contact with the moderate opposition or the clergy. During the last months of the revolution, however, the U.S. embassy did conduct negotiations with the moderate Freedom Movement to discuss resolution of the crisis. Washington sought to keep Khomeini out of Iran and did not make contact with the clerical opposition until January 15, 1979—one day before the Shah went into exile.

In the Philippines, domestic antagonism grew sharply as a consequence of the 1983 Aquino assassination and the deteriorating economy. Apprehensions in Washington about the stability of the Marcos regime and possible threats of communist revolution prompted the Reagan administration to urge reform. Congressional disapproval of Marcos had been made plainly evident, and State and Defense Department officials began to criticize Marcos publicly. The president himself, however, maintained his unstinting loyalty to Marcos. Administration support was removed only when there was little recourse left, when it became evident that the United States would be tying itself to a fallen leader and to a blatantly corrupt election process. U.S. intervention on behalf of the moderate coalition—composed of Manila's middle class, the clergy, and elements of the military—came only on the eve of an anti-Marcos military coup, which was acting in association with the moderate opposition.

The rather unidimensional character of U.S. policy in Iran and the Philippines, in extending support until the virtual collapse of the respective regimes, was less apparent in the case of Nicaragua. Although economic support for Somoza began to decline in 1977, Washington did not directly support the moderate opposition. U.S. involvement ranged from "noninterference" in the early stages of the crisis, to direct mediation between Somoza and the moderates. The United States did not communicate with the FSLN even as the moderates disintegrated and joined with the Sandinistas. Indeed, until Somoza's departure and the FSLN's triumphant entry into Managua, American policy was geared to staving off a leftist takeover and engineering a moderate government for Nicaragua.

In all cases, members of the moderate opposition conceded that Carter's human rights policy created an atmosphere in which public protest

could develop. Many, however, sharply criticized the president for not acting in accord with his rhetoric: he neither extended assistance to the opposition, nor refrained from giving support to the governments in question.

6. *What were the ideological foreign policy orientations of the postrevolutionary regimes? Were they pro– or anti–American, pro– or anti–
Soviet Union, or nonaligned? What policies did these regimes pursue in
relation to the United States?*

The foreign policy orientations of the postrevolutionary governments
differed in each case. In Iran, the ruling Islamic Republic Party (IRP) was
hostile both toward the United States and the Soviet Union. Suspicion toward the United States led to strained relations; after the November 1979
U.S. embassy takeover, relations between the two nations ceased to exist.
Pragmatic considerations, however, superseded ideological or religious
biases, even in the case of Iran. When weapons were needed for an anti-
Kurd campaign soon after the revolution, or for fighting on the Iraqi front
in 1985, Iranians seemed willing to deal with the United States. Indeed, at
the end of 1991, after a decade of vituperation, Iran's Islamic government
expressed a willingness to consider renewed ties with the United States.

In Nicaragua, a leftist FSLN joined the nonaligned movement, established close ties to the Communist block, and made public statements denouncing the United States. It was willing, however, at least initially, to
continue trading with the United States, to have a dialogue with Washington, and even to limit its support of the FMLN in El Salvador. Hostility
demonstrated by the Reagan administration in diplomatic statements, as
well as economic and military offensives, led to deteriorating relations.
Bilateral relations remained uneasy until the 1990 election of Violeta de
Chamorro.

The postrevolutionary government of the Philippines continued to
maintain friendly relations with Washington: U.S. economic and military
assistance continued to flow, trade remained unaffected, and the U.S. military bases in the Philippines continued to operate. By 1991, however,
growing nationalist sentiment led to U.S. withdrawal from the bases. Amicable relations nonetheless continue.

7. *What was U.S. policy in relation to the postrevolutionary governments? Was diplomatic recognition immediately given? Were public pronouncements sympathetic or antagonistic toward the new regimes? Was
economic or military aid extended? Were sanctions imposed?*

U.S. policy toward the postrevolutionary governments varied in the
three cases. In Iran, the alienation that had characterized U.S. relations
with the clergy before the revolution, continued after their victory; direct
contact with Ayatollah Khomeini still had not been established eight
months after the revolution. Nonetheless, when moderates held senior

government positions during the initial postrevolutionary period, relatively cordial U.S.–Iran relations were maintained. Strains developed in the relationship as a consequence of a number of provocations. These included Congressional condemnation of the human rights situation in post-revolutionary Iran, a perceived reticence by the United States to deliver and sell arms to Iran, and the asylum given to the Shah and his associates. The November 1979 U.S. embassy takeover and the ouster of moderate politicians from the government led to a further decline in relations. The deterioration culminated in a cutoff of diplomatic relations, the imposition of economic sanctions, and a U.S. tilt toward Iraq in the Iran–Iraq conflict.

In Nicaragua, as in Iran, opposition forces that would eventually rule the country were neglected by U.S. officials; as in Iran, Washington had difficulties with the new government once it took power. Although the United States had made every effort to keep the Sandinistas from achieving a political success, once the FSLN entered office, the Carter administration extended diplomatic recognition and economic aid. Suspicion between the two governments, however, persisted. In the United States, conservative members of Congress held up a proposed aid package to Nicaragua, and the administration remained uncertain about the extent of FSLN support for the Salvadoran guerrillas. Although relations remained relatively cordial during the Carter administration (despite denunciations by the FSLN), the election of Ronald Reagan led to a precipitous deterioration. Under Reagan, diplomacy and trade were exchanged for military offensives and economic sanctions.

In the Philippines, moderates who took power with U.S. assistance continued the cordial relationship that had characterized the Marcos regime. The administration and Congress extended financial and diplomatic support to the new regime and enthusiastically welcomed President Aquino.

8. *What was the history of U.S. involvement in each case?*

In Iran and the Philippines, U.S. involvement was initially perceived in positive terms. In both cases, however, increasing numbers of U.S. expatriate workers, and treaties viewed as contrary to the principles of sovereignty, aggravated nationalist sentiment. In addition, the United States was associated with unpopular rulers who allowed urban and rural poverty to increase, political and civil repression to continue, and negative Western influences to prevail. As a consequence, the benign image of the United States began to erode. U.S. involvement in Nicaragua was, from the beginning, generally viewed as exploitive and contrary to the sovereign rights of the nation. Unfair treaties, and U.S. support of favored Nicaraguan politicians—including the Somozas—served to reinforce generally negative perceptions.

9. Could U.S. policy have been more effective in achieving its national interest goals in each case?

Despite differences in administrations and the foreign policy instruments used, striking similarities in the failures of U.S. human rights policy exist across the cases. These similarities served to undermine both neoconservative and neorealist policies.

In all cases, the U.S. interest was defined in terms of a single figure or dynasty. U.S. policymakers ignored domestic problems that might lead to turmoil in the countries in question and disregarded warnings that came from U.S. embassies, intelligence reports, and opposition figures. Information transmitted to Washington was often contradictory or deceptive; it was frequently limited because of a dependence on intelligence from target states (SAVAK or the National Guard), or because embassy personnel would not, in deference to the host government, pursue contacts with all sectors of society. Intelligence analysis very often reflected Washington's prejudices rather than political realities.[14]

Lack of contact with the opposition, in all the cases, proved to be a critical error. Contact with radical forces was eschewed for ideological reasons, or because Washington did not wish to offend an ally or undermine the confidence of moderate opposition forces. U.S. support for moderate opposition groups was limited because of Washington's allegiance to a particular ruler or, in the case of Nicaragua, because it was pursuing a policy of nonintervention, which was a de facto policy of support for Somoza.

Particularly during the Carter administration, policy pronouncements—if not policy in fact—led to increased opposition criticism in all three countries; the eventual eruption of revolution came, in part, as a result of this atmosphere. When moderates began to call for the resignation of their rulers, rather than just liberalization (Iran, 1978; Nicaragua, 1977; Philippines, 1984), the United States temporized and lost opportunities to mediate compromises and peaceful transitions. When it did enter the process, its interventions came too late and had little effect.

In all cases, the clergy played an important, and sometimes critical, role in the course of revolution. In Iran, the Islamic clerics unified the opposition and carried out the revolution. In Nicaragua and the Philippines, local Catholic clergy supported the radical movements; as events deteriorated in the two countries, higher levels of the Catholic hierarchy joined with moderate and business groups to find solutions and ultimately to oust the ruler. U.S. contacts with the clergy had been nonexistent or minimal in all three cases. In their roles as opinion makers and mediators, religious institutions may carry great political weight. The United States might be well advised, therefore, to maintain and develop contacts with the clergy in those countries where religion is still a powerful institution.

The section on "Alternative Approaches" later in the chapter further elaborates on U.S. policy options.

Realpolitik Reassessed

Evidence from the three cases indicates that neither the neoconservative nor the neorealist prescriptions would serve well as pragmatic, comprehensive guides for a U.S. human rights foreign policy. In the three cases studied, empirical examination does not confirm the prescriptions or the assumptions proffered by either school.

The Neoconservative Prescription: A Failed Policy

The neoconservative thesis proposes that if the U.S. national interest is to be safeguarded, right-wing repressive rulers, who are allied with the United States, must be protected. Although the validity of this thesis is established for short-term U.S. interests, American support of dictators may serve to undermine U.S. interests in the longer term. By extending such support, the United States is identified with an unpopular ruler who may be perpetuating unacceptable economic, social, and political conditions. Such conditions may also serve as fertile ground for rebellion—the consequence of which may be damaging to the United States.

Contrary to the neoconservative assumption, military equipment, economic aid, and diplomatic support could not prevent revolutions from erupting. As events in Iran and Nicaragua have shown, policies that made use of these instruments to support dictatorship ill-served the U.S. interest. American interests were preserved in the case of the Philippines as the result of a fortuitous concatenation of events, not because of U.S. policy: most significantly, anti-Marcos sentiment culminated in revolution before the communist NPA was sufficiently organized to take advantage of the situation.

Neoconservative admonitions that support of human rights reform may lead to revolution are, in these cases, verified. An inevitable causal connection between the two does not, however, exist. Where reform is implemented before disaffection reaches crisis proportions, and before demands for compromise are superseded by intransigence, continuation of moderate government is more likely than is revolution. In the cases of Iran and Nicaragua, reforms implemented in the late 1970s were neither sufficiently comprehensive nor timely enough in addressing popular demand. As such, relaxation of repression merely gave opponents an opportunity to express their frustrations and rally a discontented populace. When no satisfactory responses were forthcoming, the call for revolution became almost inevitable. (In the Philippines, a similar program of reform was not implemented prior to the revolution. The upheaval was sparked by one event—the 1986 presidential election.) It would, indeed, be difficult for the United States to foment revolution unless conditions for its eruption already existed. Increased pressure on Marcos in the late 1970s, for example, did not lead to revolution, while despite Reagan's staunch support of Marcos, revolution did erupt in 1986.

Also unsubstantiated is the neoconservative assumption that once revolution takes place, communism will follow. Two of the three cases indicate that this is not in fact the case. In Iran, a conservative government came to power. Although vehemently anti-American, it also opposed the Soviet Union and in no way harbored a propensity toward embracing communist ideology. As it enters its second decade, economic necessity and the end of the Cold War are moving the government of Iran toward accommodation with the West and the United States. The elite in the post-revolutionary Philippines retained friendly relations with the United States. Indeed, despite rejection of the 1991 base treaty, U.S.–Philippines relations continue to remain cordial. Even in Nicaragua, where a leftist, pro-communist regime took office, relatively amicable relations were maintained with Washington. U.S. hostility toward the Sandinista-led government during the Reagan administration—its diplomatic, economic, and eventually military offensives—insured, however, that friendly relations would not continue. Neoconservative admonitions that socialist or communist governments are not amenable to democratization is, in this case, refuted as well. The leftist government of Nicaragua allowed free elections in 1990 and gave up the reins of power to a popularly elected moderate, pro-American regime.

Ironically, the very fear the United States traditionally exhibited in relation to communist subversion, a fear that is central to the neoconservative world view, made it possible for allied states to manipulate U.S. foreign policy in their favor and in opposition to U.S. interests. Marcos, for example, could impose martial law and continue repressive rule by calling up the specter of communist rebellion. In Nicaragua, a perceived communist threat inside the country, and the role Nicaragua could play in fomenting or preventing communist insurgency in neighboring countries, served Somoza's interests. In Iran, U.S. fears of Soviet expansion, a fear of which the Shah made use, worked to keep U.S. policy in line with the monarch's ambitions.

Furthermore, the fear of communism may in itself have led to self-fulfilling prophecies. Reagan administration hostility toward the Sandinista government, for example, led to U.S. condemnations and sanctions;

the policy exacerbated Nicaragua's antagonisms toward the United States and forced the new government to become increasingly dependent on the Communist bloc for trade and assistance.

In no case did the protection of democracy at home and U.S. interests abroad preserve or increase human rights in allied countries. In neither Iran nor the Philippines, where neoconservative prescriptions framed the course of U.S. foreign policy, was the U.S. national interest protected because of that policy.

Neorealism: A Narrow Pragmatism

As with the neoconservative argument, the assumptions and prescriptions of the neorealist school do not emerge unchallenged when applied to the three cases.

Despite some prescience, central neorealist assumptions are not borne out by the case studies. The neorealists are proven correct in their assumption that dissociation from right-wing dictators, a policy most prominently implemented in the Nicaragua case, would not lead to severed ties between the United States and the regime under fire. The issue of human rights, however, proved not to be the core revolutionary impulse in any of these cases, nor did U.S. policy in relation to human rights ultimately shape perceptions about the United States.

While political issues significantly influenced the course taken by the revolutions, initial opposition demands in all three cases centered on issues of economics, social disintegration, and nationalist sentiment—not human rights. Furthermore, no matter what role the United States played in supporting a dictator, the moderate opposition in each case was willing to continue friendly relations with the U.S. government. American interests in Iran and Nicaragua were demolished as a result of factors other than U.S. human rights policy: most critically, disorganization within the moderate camp gave radical anti-American groups the opportunity to assume leading roles in the revolutions. Had conditions allowed moderates to control the institutions of government after the revolutions in Iran and Nicaragua, amicable relations with the United States would have continued, and U.S. interests would have been better served.

Neorealist admonitions about the limits of U.S. influence in shaping events abroad are corroborated. The intensity of domestic discontent in the three states, along with regional and international constraints, particularly in relation to Iran and Nicaragua, assured that Washington could neither shape events nor protect rulers upon whom it relied.

Also reinforced by the cases, is the view that the adoption of nonaligned foreign policies among U.S. allies would not be detrimental to the U.S. interests. Secretary of State John Foster Dulles encouraged such a perspective as early as 1953, when he announced, "we do not want weak or subservient allies. Our friends and allies are dependable just because they are unwilling to be anyone's satellites. . . . they will no more be subservient to the United States than they will be subservient to Soviet Russia.[15]

East-West ideological friction that engendered the nonaligned movement, however, have dissipated with the collapse of the Soviet Union and its empire. A reconstituted non-aligned movement may, nonetheless, survive. Its focus in the post–Cold War era is likely to be on problems of development, and on other issues which divide North and South. Concern about the effects of nonaligned foreign policies on U.S. interests, therefore, need to be re-evaluated. The implications of this changing international environment were summarized by a State Department official who remarked in July 1990, "When you had a Stalinist in power in Moscow, everything in the world was dichotomized. Anyone who was with them was against us." Now such allegiances no longer exist. "For the first time in years you really have to think about what your interests are."[16]

In sum, neither neoconservative nor neorealist prescriptions are, on the whole, proven correct by the three cases. The national interest is too narrowly defined by the neoconservatives: it is often viewed in terms of a unique personality whose existence is presumed to ensure the U.S. national interest. The human rights foreign policy of this school is too short-sighted, in that it seeks only to preserve the position of particular individuals, rather than improve and protect the conditions that would help maintain the U.S. national interest.

The neorealist perception of the national interest is broader and its prescriptions more focused on the longer-term preservation of U.S. interests. This policy is most likely to be successful if implemented before political demands and opposition movements become radicalized—when what is being sought is compromise and reform, not revolution. However, when demands begin to escalate and popular discontent begins to mount, a neorealist policy of U.S. dissociation from despots may prove too narrow, and perhaps too dangerous, for the long-term interests of the United States. By encouraging reform at such a point, Washington may be supporting revolution and inviting unknown, perhaps unwanted, consequences. Indeed, in his memoirs, President Carter argued for a foreign policy geared toward urging more timely reform.

> There is no doubt, [he wrote,] that a few of these [oppressive regimes] could have been spared both embarrassment and the danger of being overthrown if they had strengthened themselves by eliminating the

abuses. For those who did not survive, it may be that our emphasis on human rights was not wrong, but too late. Had America argued for these principles sooner, such foreign leaders might not have allowed themselves to become too isolated to correct the abuses without violence.[17]

Targeting the Moderates: An Alternative Realpolitik Human Rights Foreign Policy

In addition to the neoconservative and neorealist prescriptions, another policy, one that considers direct U.S. intervention in mediating revolutionary situations, has been implicitly incorporated throughout this book. In each case, a chronology of events, as well as the ideological positions and relative organizational strengths of the various opposition movements are examined. Opportunities are reviewed where the United States might have made more direct efforts to find solutions and support compromise between dictator and the moderate opposition. This last-minute approach to human rights and the preservation of the U.S. national interest, however, is also encumbered by difficulty. The United States seems historically unwilling to find compromises with radical opposition groups unless it perceives no alternative. If conditions have so deteriorated that discussions with a radical opposition is necessary, it is likely (as in the case of Iran and Nicaragua), that the radical groups will have gained enough of an edge to render negotiations with the United States or domestic moderate forces unattractive or unnecessary. (Under either scenario, the ruler himself might also refuse to negotiate a compromise. Neither the Shah, Marcos, nor Somoza would agree to make necessary reforms in a timely fashion.)

Encouraging reform, a policy suggested by the neorealists, may, as the cases indicate, contribute to revolutions that the United States neither seeks, nor for which it is prepared. The use of sanctions and dissociation, one of the central neorealist prescriptions for encouraging reform, may thus prove antithetical to the U.S. interest if implemented independently of other strategies. A fourth alternative, introduced in Chapter 1, might serve to fill the gap in the neorealist prescription.

Under the alternative approach, U.S. human rights policy would go beyond the unitary "state as actor" approach prescribed by both schools, in order to conduct human rights foreign policy via nonstate actors, particularly moderate opposition forces.[18]

It becomes evident from the three cases that the conditions and institutions that preserve the U.S. interest ought to be protected, not individual leaders who claim to do so. U.S. policy should, therefore, focus more directly on developing, organizing, and training moderate opposition forces in target countries. Such a strategy would prepare moderate opposition groups to participate in a reformed system and/or take a leading role should a revolution develop. The alternative program does not exclude the neorealist prescription for dissociation from oppressive regimes, but takes into account the need to assure that a viable moderate opposition exists to take advantage of liberalization, and that reform does not lead to radical takeover. The relevance of such a policy prescription is particularly evident in the cases of Iran and Nicaragua. Disorganization among the moderates in these countries made it possible for radical forces to take the lead during both the revolutionary and postrevolutionary periods. The decline of the moderate opposition virtually assured the destruction of U.S. interests in both countries.

Access required to pursue such a strategy in a target country may be gained covertly, or overtly, by promising inducements or threatening sanctions. The popularity of covert operations among the American public is not high, and pursuit of policy via covert methods is much maligned. This strategy, however, may be suited to an era where military power may no longer bear primacy as a foreign policy tool, and where, as Secretary of State Shultz noted in 1984, "as one nation among many, we do not have the power to remake the planet."[19] It may be argued too, that "if one agrees that there are external objectives that America simply cannot abandon, and if furthermore, they cannot be successfully pursued by diplomacy, or without bribery, one is left with the choice of relying on either military force or informal penetration. Since the former is so costly and risky, the latter may be the only course of action left."[20]

This solution, of course, does not address all U.S. human rights foreign policy needs. There are dangers in pursuing covert operations both to the American system of government and to the target state. Furthermore, the neorealist caveat which relates to the limitations of power, applies here as well. "As with military force," warns Miroslav Nincic, "it is naïve to think that external subversion is a reliable means of affecting the course of a nation's politics in a desired direction. Political reality is usually too complex to be shaped by the projects of foreign bureaucrats and covert operatives."[21]

Moderate groups may also be supported through other channels, both official and unofficial. The American labor movement, for example, has in the past worked to strengthen labor unions abroad, "giving support and advice, teaching the skills of organizing and operating." Secretary of State Shultz noted in 1984 that, "In Western Europe after World War II, it was the free labor unions, helped in many cases by free unions here, that communist parties from taking over in several countries. Today, free political parties in Western Europe give similar fraternal assistance to budding parties and political groups in developing countries. . . ."[22] The 1984 Kissinger Commission report suggested that democratic institutions and leadership training might be achieved by encouraging "neighborhood groups, community improvement organizations, and producer cooperatives which provide a training ground for democratic participation and help make governments more responsive to citizen demands."[23] Such support, as well as advice about election organization, election campaigning, and legal reform is being given, for example, through the National Democratic Institute for International Affairs, the International Republican Institute, and the bipartisan National Endowment for Democracy.[24] The U.S. Information Agency and the U.S. Agency for International Development also support labor unions, train journalists, and help strengthen judicial institutions and procedures. (In the Philippines, for example, AID funds were covertly funneled to the opposition Radio Veritas.)[25]

In conforming to the prescriptions of the alternative realpolitik human rights strategy, the U.S. interest may be better served both in the short term and the long term. Pressures created by U.S. support for moderate groups might lead to some measure of reform in target states. Furthermore, with the end of the Cold War, tactics that in the past may have proven successful for Third World leaders—for example, playing one superpower against the other—are no longer effective. Because states can no longer seek economic advantages from competing political or ideological blocs, political leaders are less likely to abandon their association with Washington, even if it imposes pressures for reform. Under such circumstances, the short-term U.S. interest will have been served: the government upon which the United States depends will remain in power, while at the same time the causes of discontent, which might have led to revolution, are addressed.

In the medium term, if the United States encourages and assists moderate opposition groups as alternative power centers, Washington might prove less dependent on abusive governments that are perceived to protect American interests, and more likely to discontinue unquestioning support for them. In the longer term, should revolution in fact erupt, U.S. support for a moderate opposition would have contributed to creating a viable alternative governing elite that would be more likely to maintain cordial working relations with the United States.

Alternative Approaches to the Study of Democratic Transition and Human Rights

A broad domain of issues and questions remains for further study of democratic transition and U.S. foreign policy. Sanctions have had a less-than-successful record for effecting change. As such, an alternative study of the potential and effectiveness of inducements in encouraging reform might be useful. Human rights as an economic issue might also be examined: the salience of economics in impelling revolution and in incriminating the United States with unpopular regimes is evident in the three cases. Even the essentially neoconservative Kissinger Commission report on Latin America warned that "unless rapid progress can be made on the political, economic and social fronts, peace on the military front will be elusive and would be fragile. The encroachments of poverty must be stopped, recession reversed, and prosperity advanced."[26] Although a foreign policy strategy focused on economic development would encounter formidable problems such as high financial costs and opposition from vested interests in target states, the problems created by economic neglect make it imperative that a policy centered around development be considered as an alternative.

Other factors may affect the impact of U.S. human rights efforts as well, and other instruments may contribute to a more effective human rights policy. What, for example, is the effect on regime and opposition when a U.S. human rights policy is not clearly stated or stringently applied (e.g., Carter's human rights policy in Iran and Nicaragua)? When opinions are divided between the U.S. executive branch and Congress, what is the impact on the players in target states?[27] What role can regional and/or international programs and institutions play in support of human rights? How may the intercession of regional and international agencies in the domestic affairs of other nations affect the U.S. national interest? What role can or should the United States play in supporting such efforts? The Conference on Security and Cooperation in Europe, for example, produced the Helsinki Accords: as a consequence, a human rights movement in a Soviet-dominated Eastern Europe was created. Regional efforts in Latin America pursued via the Contadora and Arias (Esquipulas II) plans, attempted to settle domestic political conflicts that had in part resulted in deteriorating human rights conditions. Would an approach modeled after the Contadora or Arias plans be useful in other circumstances and regions? Can regional organizations such as the Organization of American States (OAS) or Organization of African Unity (OAU) work more creatively in aiding peace and promoting human rights? Past OAS efforts may bode well for the evolution of a proactive regional organization for human rights and democracy. OAS involvement in election monitoring in Haiti, Surinam, El Salvador, Paraguay, and Panama; its adoption of the June 1991 "Santiago Committment to Democracy and the Renewal of the Inter-American System"; and its efforts—albeit less than successful—to restore to power Haiti's democratically elected president, Jean-Bertrand Aristide, suggest such an evolution.

The United Nations is also increasingly playing a more direct role in resolving domestic political conflicts and fostering democratic development. It oversaw the first elections in Namibia, negotiated a resolution to El Salvador's civil war, and became the central actor in the Cambodian peace process.[28] In 1991, the U.N. Development Programme issued its *Human Development Report*. It included, for the first time, a Human Freedom Index which ranked countries according to their political, civil, social, and personal freedoms.[29]

As promising as are these examples of U.N. involvement in the area of democracy and human rights, Third World reactions to such efforts must inject some pessimism about the potential of the United Nations. A binding U.N. resolution "condemning the [September 1991] military takeover" in Haiti and "supporting OAS efforts to restore democracy" was derailed by China and several nonaligned countries. They were concerned that the "Security Council, at the urging of Western nations, is becoming increasingly involved in domestic issues that are the private affairs of member states."[30] The Human Freedom Index was criticized by Third World states as inaccurate, irrelevant to their development needs, and a form of "interference" in their internal affairs. Apprehension was expressed that such ranking "would encourage industrialized countries to tie development aid to recipients' human rights records." As a consequence, efforts were mounted to ban further publication of the Index.[31] In February 1991, a request by Human Rights Watch for accreditation for consultative status in the United Nations was blocked by Cuba, Syria, Iraq, Sudan, Libya, and Algeria. Human Rights Watch is the "second largest monitoring organization in the world."[32]

The traditionally apolitical role of international financial institutions is also evolving. Although economic reforms are generally the critical determinant for receipt of funds from international lending institutions, a move to link the political and human rights situations of recipient states to financial assistance is becoming apparent. The European Bank for Reconstruction and Development, for example, has been mandated to approve financial assistance to the former Soviet republics and the governments of Eastern Europe only on condition that they are "committed to the principles of multiparty democracy, pluralism and market economics."[33] At a November 1991 meeting of twelve Western donors including the United States, Great Britain, Canada, France, Germany, and Japan, a six-month probation was imposed on Kenya linking full aid to political reforms and improvement in human rights. The communiqué issued by the donor governments stated that "good government is a prerequisite for equitable economic development and would therefore be a major factor influencing aid allocations."[34] Within a week, a fragile and tentative process of democratization was begun with an announcement by Kenya's President Daniel arap Moi that multiparty politics would be legalized and that elections would be held. Many Kenyans believed that the reforms were prompted by the action of the twelve donors.[35] In May 1992, similar conditions were set for Malawi by the World Bank and leading Western donor nations.[36]

In addition to the potential role of regional and international institutions in promoting democracy and human rights, communications technologies have proven to be valuable tools in effecting political change in cases ranging from Iran to Eastern Europe, and from Panama to China. Such technologies have been used to spread new ideas, mobilize discontented masses, and link opposition groups to supporters on the outside.[37] Their impact both on domestic politics and on the international system underlines the significance of factors other than the traditional instruments of power in interstate relations; it also reinforces the relevance of the complex interdependence approach to the study of international politics and the issue of human rights.

U.S. human rights policy analyzed in terms of various approaches associated with decision-making theory could also prove useful. The bureaucratic politics model[38] could determine the degree to which such policy is affected by the pressures of government institutions. In the cases reviewed in this book, policy was affected by the Department of State, the National Security Council, the Department of Defense, the Department of Energy, the Central Intelligence Agency, and the Treasury Department. Other, less formal influences on foreign policy should be accounted for as well. In the cases of Iran and the Philippines, for example, U.S. business interests lobbied on behalf of the Shah and Marcos.

Perceptual models analyze decision making as a process that, at least in part, is dependent upon subjective interpretation.[39] In this study, for example, U.S. policy toward the opposition, reform, and revolution was strongly affected by Washington's perception of its dependence on individual leaders. The willingness of leaders in target states to make concessions on human rights also seemed to depend on their perceptions of U.S. support (or lack of it). Marcos would concede little while he perceived strong support from the executive branch; Somoza looked to his Congressional supporters for help. On the other hand, it has been argued that despite U.S. support for the Shah, the monarch perceived his support within the Carter administration to be lacking.[40] It might also prove useful to examine how perceptions held by leaders in target states are formed and, more important, how they could be altered so that negative signals would be understood if and when they are sent from Washington.

The rational-actor model focuses on decision making in terms of choices calculated to best serve the particular goals and values of an actor.[41] Policy failures experienced by the United States in the three cases would make the study of U.S. human rights foreign policy in terms of the rational-actor model quite valuable. For example, given the long-term interests of the United States in preserving stability abroad and ensuring that pro-American regimes survive, it might be asked, if support of dictators is rational. Is it rational to encourage reform without assuring that a moderate alternative is available, or to ignore opposition factions—no matter what their ideology? In target states, is it rational for leaders to implement reform without exceptional domestic pressure and/or without direct demands from the United States.

Protecting Human Rights Abroad: Moral Pursuit in the Interest of Realpolitik

Chapter 1 of this book delineates several questions relating to U.S. human rights foreign policy and the national interest. The intent of the study has been, in part, to find whether U.S. interests are best served by a policy of realpolitik pragmatism devoid of ethical considerations, and whether the preservation of human rights at home requires that it be abandoned abroad.

Secretary of State Shultz discussed the problems of choice in foreign policy in the context of human rights in a 1984 speech:

> Any foreign policy must weave together diverse strands of national interest: political objectives, military security, economic management. All these goals . . . have moral validity, and they often confront us with real choices to make. . . . Foreign policy thus often presents us with moral issues that are not easy to resolve.
>
> The dilemmas we face are many. What for instance, is the relationship between human rights concerns and the considerations of regional or international security on which the independence and freedom of so many nations directly depend? . . .
>
> There are countries whose internal practices we sometimes question but which face genuine security threats from outside—like South Korea—or whose cooperation with us helps protect the security of scores of other nations—like the Philippines. . . . There are also cases where regional insecurity weakens the chances for liberalization and where American assurance of security support provides a better climate for an evolution to democracy. Human rights issues occur in a context, and there is no simple answer. . . .

> If we distance ourselves from a friendly but repressive government, in a fluid situation, will this help strengthen forces of moderation, or might it make things worse?[42]

The principles of democracy and of human rights that would define a "moral" U.S. foreign policy may not contradict the interests of realpolitik, as Secretary of State Shultz suggested. The "dilemma of effective choice"[43] between human rights and realpolitik may be amenable to resolution without discounting either.

The importance of human rights as part of a pragmatic foreign policy has been argued by a number of policymakers and scholars. At the opening of the United Nations in 1948, Secretary of State George Marshall suggested to his audience that, "Governments which systematically disregard the rights of their own people are not likely to respect the rights of other nations and other people, and are likely to seek their objectives by coercion and force in the international field."[44] The salutary effect that democratic states have on the international system was demonstrated, for example, by Zeev Maoz and Narsin Abdolali, who found that among 1,666 pairs of states involved in 960 disputes, democratic states were less likely to engage in conflict with one another.[45] In testimony given in 1979, Warren Christopher, deputy secretary of state during the Carter administration, noted that U.S. security is enhanced when U.S. foreign relations are based on "a shared commitment to democratic values" rather than on temporary "accommodation" with repressive but useful regimes.[46] Even the Reagan administration's secretary of state, George Shultz, admitted to a similar perspective when he stated that "in many cases a concern for human rights on our part may be the best guarantee of a long-term friendly relationship with that country. There are countries whose long-term security will probably be enhanced if they have a more solid base of popular support and domestic unity."[47]

The association between morality and the U.S. national interest, as it pertains to Central America, was outlined in the 1984 Kissinger Commission report. The document conceded that

> in Central America today, our strategic and moral interest coincide. . . . Experience has destroyed the argument of the old dictators that a strong hand is essential to avoid anarchy and communism, and that order and progress can be achieved only through authoritarianism. . . . The modern experience of Latin America suggests that order is more often threatened when people have no voice in their own destinies.[48]

According to the report, a principal of U.S. policy in the hemisphere ought, therefore, to be to encourage "democratic self-determination" among member nations; to support the development and preservation of "political pluralism, freedom of expression, respect for human rights, the maintenance of an independent and effective system of justice, and the right of people to choose their destiny in free election without repression, coercion, or foreign manipulation."[49]

How U.S. interests are viewed, the extent to which U.S. interests are seen to be threatened, and the magnitude of Washington's responses to events abroad, are likely to be re-evaluated and redefined in the post-Cold War world. U.S. involvement in a violently disintegrating Yugoslavia, for example, remained conspicuously constrained. For more than a year, the bloodshed and chaos that engulfed Somalia at the end of the Cold War elicited little more than a minimal U.S. humanitarian response. During the Cold War, by contrast, Somalia had been assured of receiving generous U.S. military assistance because of its strategic "location on the Indian Ocean and Gulf of Aden."[50]

U.S. obligations and the factors that comprise its national interest are being debated within the liberal and conservative camps. In both camps, internationalist prescriptions for intervention clash with demands for isolationism.[51] While perspectives may vary widely, a convergence of policy prescriptions, if not rationales, often becomes evident among isolationists and interventionists within both ideological camps. Liberal isolationists argue for the use of American resources at home in support of social and economic programs; liberal internationalists advocate an American mission in support of global human rights.[52] Among conservatives, isolationists focus almost exclusively on domestic agendas, often defined in terms of national security,[53] while internationalists advocate the pursuit of a worldwide crusade for democratic capitalism.[54] Between these sharply divergent perspectives, proponents of "selective intervention" advocate limited U.S. involvement, both because the country's power requires this, and because its economic well-being demands it.[55]

Perspectives also vary as to what U.S. human rights commitments should be. Among conservatives, for example, the spectrum ranges from antagonism toward any measure of support for democracy,[56] to proposals for varying standards of intervention depending upon U.S. interests,[57] to an across-the-board embrace of U.S. support for—if not extensive and direct involvement in—processes of democratization throughout the world.[58] The three cases in this book indicate, however, not only that the preservation of human rights at home does not require its disregard abroad, but that it indeed demands its protection and expansion elsewhere. In two of the three cases, Iran and Nicaragua, U.S. national interest was damaged because Washington failed to press for sufficient liberalization when reform was demanded. A similar scenario might have occurred in the Philippines had the Marcos regime continued in power for another two to three years.

The question of whether a realpolitik policy devoid of ethical considerations best serves the U.S. interest is thus, perhaps, irrelevant. The protection and expansion of human rights abroad may be considered desirable not just because of its moral implications per se, but because of its positive consequences in terms of the long-term U.S. national interest.

NOTES

Introduction

1. Thomas L. Friedman, "U.S. to Counter Iran in Central Asia," *New York Times*, 6 February 1992, A3; Thomas L. Friedman, "Republics Promise to Protect Rights," *New York Times*, 13 February 1992, A:12; Thomas L. Friedman, "Uzbek Says Yes to Democracy, Of Course," *New York Times*, 17 February 1992, A:7.

Chapter 1

1. In its broadest sense, the term "authoritarian regime" encompasses "totalitarian states, dictatorships, and regimes in which opposition is suppressed" (see Marshall D. Shulman, "On Learning to Live with Authoritarian Regimes," *Foreign Affairs* 55, no. 2 [January 1977], 326). Within the context of U.S. foreign policy discussion, however, distinctions between authoritarianism and totalitarianism are clearly evident. Authoritarian regimes are generally described as not being destructive of "alternative power basis in a society" (see Jeane J. Kirkpatrick in "Human Rights and American Foreign Policy: A Symposium," *Commentary* 72, no. 5 [November 1981], 44). Such power bases may include opposition parties, a restricted press, the church, independent business enterprises, labor union movements, or voluntary organizations. Antiregime opposition is forbidden, although private dissent is tolerated and public affirmation of the regime not required. Totalitarian states, on the other hand, "claim [complete] jurisdiction over . . . society" and do not allow for the existence of independent sources of authority, knowledge, or power (see Jeane J. Kirkpatrick, "Dictatorships and Double Standards," reprinted in Howard Wiarda, ed., *Human Rights and U.S. Human Rights Policy: Theoretical Approaches and Some Perspectives on Latin America* [Washington, D.C.: American Enterprise Institute for Public Policy Research, 1982], 26, and Nathan Glazer in "Human Rights and American Foreign Policy: A Symposium," *Commentary* 72, no. 5 [November 1981], 36). The "raison d'etre" of these regimes is "systematic and complete regimentation" (see William Barrett in "Human Rights and American Foreign Policy: A Symposium," *Commentary* 72, no. 5 [November 1981] 26). See also Ernest W. Lefever, "The Trivialization of Human

213

Rights," *Policy Review* (Winter 1978), 15–16; Seymour Martin Lipset in "Human Rights and American Foreign Policy," *Commentary* (November 1981), 48.

2. Robert O. Keohane, "Theory of World Politics: Structural Realism and Beyond," in Robert O. Keohane, ed., *Neorealism and Its Critics* (New York: Columbia University Press, 1986), 165; Cecil V. Crabb, Jr., *Policy-Makers and Critics: Conflicting Theories of American Foreign Policy* (New York: Praeger, 1976), 167.

3. Hans Morgenthau, *Politics Among Nations: The Struggle for Power and Peace,* 4th Edition, (New York: Knopf, 1967), 5.

4. Morgenthau, 5.

5. Keohane, "Theory of World Politics," 165.

6. Kenneth N. Waltz, "Anarchic Orders and Balances of Power," in *Neorealism and Its Critics,* 98–130.

7. Michael Joseph Smith, *Realist Thought from Weber to Kissinger* (Baton Rouge: Louisiana State University Press, 1986), 4, 9.

8. Neorealism in the human rights debate is not related to the "neorealism," or structural realism, of international political theory as developed by Kenneth Waltz. See Robert O. Keohane, "Realism, Neorealism and the Study of Politics," in Keohane, *Neorealism and its Critics,* 15.

9. Alan Tonelson, "Human Rights: The Bias We Need," *Foreign Policy* (Winter 1982–83), 52–74.

10. U.S. Congress, House Committee on International Relations, Subcommittee on International Organizations, *Human Rights and U.S. Foreign Policy,* 96th Cong., 1st sess., 10 May 1979, Statement of Ernest W. Lefever, 216; Ernest W. Lefever, "The Trivialization of Human Rights," 11–34; see also Robert W. Tucker, "The American Outlook," in H. Bliss and G. M. Johnson, eds., *Consensus at the Crossroads: Dialogues in American Foreign Policy* (New York: Dodd, Mead, 1972), 14–43; Tucker, "The Purposes of American Power," *Foreign Affairs* (Winter 1980–81), 241–74.

11. Jeane J. Kirkpatrick, "Dictatorship and Double Standards." *Commentary* (November 1979), reprinted in Howard J. Wiarda, ed., *Human Rights and U.S. Human Rights Policy: Theoretical Approaches and Some Perspectives on Latin America* (Washington, D.C.: American Enterprise Institute for Public Policy Research, 1982), 5–29.

12. Kirkpatrick, "Human Rights and American Foreign Policy: A Symposium," 43; see also Lefever, "The Trivialization of Human Rights."

13. Lefever, "The Trivialization of Human Rights."

14. *Washington Post,* 25 September 1977, C3 quoted in Lars Schoultz, *Human Rights and U.S. Policy Toward Latin America* (Princeton, N.J.: Princeton University Press, 1981), 112.

15. Samuel P. Huntington, "Human Rights and American Power," *Commentary* 72, no. 3 (September 1981), 41, 38, 39, 40; see also Huntington, "American Ideals versus American Interests," *Political Science Quarterly* 97, no. 1 (Spring

1982, reprinted in G. John Ikenberry, ed., *American Foreign Policy: Theoretical Essays* (Glenview, Ill.: Scott, Foresman, 1989), 223–58.

16. Kirkpatrick, "Dictatorship and Double Standards," 12.

17. Warren Christopher, "Lessons of Iran," address delivered to the Los Angeles County Bar Association, 26 May 1981, reprinted in Warren Christopher, "Diplomacy: The Neglected Imperative," bound pamphlet, n.d., quoted in Richard E. Feinberg, *The Intemperate Zone: The Third World Challenge to U.S. Foreign Policy* (New York: Norton, 1983), 245; see also William P. Bundy, "Who Lost Patagonia? Foreign Policy in the 1980 Campaign," *Foreign Affairs* 50, no. 1 (Fall 1979), 1–27.

18. Feinberg, *The Intemperate Zone*, 188.

19. Sandra Vogelgesang, "Diplomacy of Human Rights," *International Studies Quarterly* 72, no. 2 (June 1979), 216–45.

20. Tucker, "The American Outlook," 38–39.

21. Feinberg, *The Intemperate Zone*, ch. 4.

22. Tom J. Farer, "On a Collision Course: The American Campaign for Human Rights and the Anti-Radical Bias in the Third World," in D. Kommers and G. Loescher, eds., *Human Rights and Foreign Policy* (Notre Dame, Ind.: University of Notre Dame Press, 1979), 263–270.

23. Farer.

24. Eric Schmitt, "U.S. and Kuwait Sign Pact on Troops," *New York Times*, 20 September 1991, A10; Peter Green, "New Kuwait Pact Symbolizes U.S. Stake in Mideast," *Christian Science Monitor*, 23 September 1991, 1.; Youssef M. Ibrahim, "Gulf Nations Said to be Committed to U.S. Alliance," *New York Times*, 25 October 1991, A9.

25. Elaine Sciolino, "The Sun May Not Set on More and More U.S. Bases Abroad," *New York Times*, 24 January 1988, sec. 4, 2.

26. Youssef M. Ibrahim, "Iran's Leaders Ask Wide Cooperation and Ties to West," *New York Times*, 28 May 1991, A1; William Claiborne, "U.S.-Iranian Cooperation Possible," *Washington Post*, 19 September 1991, A39; Geraldine Brooks, "Radical Islamic Groups in Lebanon Tone Down Anti-Western Fervor," *Wall Street Journal*, 19 November 1991, A1; Elaine Sciolino, "U.S. Nears Deal to Settle Claims by the Iranians," *New York Times*, 21 November 1991, A1; "Iran Woos Investors," *Wall Street Journal*, 27 November 1991, A6.

27. Discussions related to definitions of human rights may be found in the following: *Annals of the American Academy of Political and Social Science* 4, no. 3 (September 1977), 60–63; William P. Bundy, "Dictatorships and American Foreign Policy," *Foreign Affairs* 54, no. 1 (October 1975), 51–60; Rupert Emerson, "The Fate of Human Rights in the Third World," *World Politics* 26 (January 1975), 201–226; Jeane J. Kirkpatrick, "Human Rights and Foreign Policy," in Fred E. Bauman, ed., *Human Rights and American Foreign Policy* (Gambier, Ohio: Public Affairs Conference Center, Kenyon College, 1982), 1–11; Daniel Patrick Moynihan, "The Politics of Human Rights," *Commentary* 64, no. 2 (August 1977), 19–26.

28. Cyrus R. Vance, "Human Rights and Foreign Policy," address by the Secretary of State at Law Day Ceremonies, 30 April 1977, University of Georgia School of Law at Athens, Georgia, *Department of State Bulletin* 76, no. 1978 (23 May 1977), 505.

29. See the "Vienna Declaration and Program of Action," adopted by the World Conference on Human Rights, 25 June 1993. A/Conf. 157/23, 12 July 1993; quoted Vogelgesang, *American Dream/Global Nightmare* (New York: Norton, 1980), 188.

30. U.S. Congress, *Human Rights and U.S. Foreign Policy*, 12 July 1979, statement by Raymond Gastil, 266; see also Alan Riding, "A Bleak Assessment as Rights Meeting Nears," *New York Times*, 23 April 1993, sec. 1, 11.

31. Vogelgesang, *American Dream/Global Nightmare*, 196.

32. Vogelgesang, *American Dream/Global Nightmare*, 198.

33. United Nations Development Programme, *Human Development Report 1991* (New York: Oxford University Press, 1991), 21.

34. Jane Perlez, "Will Kenya's Bad Habits Jeopardize Its Aid?" *New York Times*, 17 November 1991, sec. 4, 5.

35. The focus is on discontent manifested on a national scale, not on demands of national minorities who might seek greater autonomy or national liberation.

36. Miroslav Nincic, *United States Foreign Policy: Choices and Tradeoffs* (Washington, D.C.: Congressional Quarterly Press, 1988), xiii.

37. Lars Schoultz, *Human Rights and U.S. Policy*, 109–110.

38. Crabb, 96.

39. U.S. Congress, Senate Committee on Foreign Relations, Subcommittee on Western Hemisphere Affairs, *United States Policies and Programs in Brazil*, 92d Cong., 1st sess., 4, 5, 11 May 1971, quoted in Lars Schoultz, "U.S. Economic Aid as an Instrument of Foreign Policy: The Case of Human Rights in Latin America," in Jack L. Nelson and Vera M. Green, eds., *International Human Rights: Contemporary Issues* (Stanfordville, N.Y.: Human Rights Publishers Groups, 1980), 319.

40. U.S. Congress, House Committee on Foreign Affairs, Subcommittee on International Organizations and Movements, *International Protection of Human Rights*, 93rd Cong., 1st sess., 1973, 507, quoted in Schoultz, *Human Rights and U.S. Policy*, 110.

41. Schoultz, *Human Rights and U.S. Policy*, 111.

42. Robert A. Pastor, *Condemned to Repetition: The United States in Nicaragua* (Princeton, N.J.: Princeton University Press, 1987), 50.

43. Jimmy Carter, *Keeping Faith: Memoirs of a President* (New York: Bantam Books, 1982), 150.

44. U.S. Congress, Senate Committee on Appropriations, Subcommittee on Foreign Assistance and Related Programs, *Foreign Assistance and Related Programs Appropriations Fiscal Year 1978*, 95th Cong., 1st sess., 1977, 196, quoted in Schoultz, *Human Rights and U.S. Policy*, 114.

45. George P. Schultz, "Human Rights and the Moral Dimension of U.S. Foreign Policy," address by the Secretary of State at the 86th Annual Washington Day Banquet of the Creve Coeur Club of Illinois, Peoria, Illinois, 22 February 1984, *Department of State Bulletin*, no. 2085 (April 1984), 16.

46. The alternative hybrid approach conforms to Robert Keohane's "modified structural research program." Keohane's program attempts to construct an approach which combines the assumptions of complex interdependence with those of structural realism, which focuses on the impact of the international system on interstate behavior. Thus, although Keohane accepts the assumption that states are the principal actors in international politics, he gives greater weight than do most realists to the role of "non-state actors, intergovernmental organizations, and transnational and transgovernmental relations" in the analysis of state interaction. (See Keohane, "Theory of World Politics), 192–94.

47. Robert O. Keohane and Joseph S. Nye, *Power and Interdependence: World Politics in Transition* (Boston: Little, Brown and Company, 1977), 37; see also Keohane, "Theory of World Politics," 192–193.

Chapter 2

1. Miroslav Nincic, *United States Foreign Policy: Choices and Tradeoffs* (Washington, D.C.: Congressional Quarterly Press, 1988), 14; Lars Schoultz, *Human Rights and United States Policy Toward Latin America* (Princeton, N.J.: Princeton University Press, 1981), 134.

2. A. Glenn Mower, Jr., *The United States, the United Nations and Human Rights: The Eleanor Roosevelt and Jimmy Carter Eras* (Westport, Conn.: Greenwood Press, 1979), 144.

3. David D. Newsom, "The Diplomacy of Human Rights: A Diplomat's View," in David D. Newsom, ed., *The Diplomacy of Human Rights* (Lanham, Md.: University Press of America, 1986), 6.

4. Schoultz, *Human Rights and U.S. Policy*, 117.

5. Nincic, 17, 18.

6. "The Carter Administration and Latin America, Africa, and Asia: State Department Reports," in Judith F. Buncher, ed., *Human Rights and American Diplomacy: 1975–1977* (New York: Facts on File, 1977), 175–77.

7. Miroslav Nincic and Peter Wallensteen, "Economic Coercion and Foreign Policy," in Miroslav Nincic and Peter Wallensteen, eds., *Dilemmas of Economic Coercion: Sanctions in World Politics* (New York: Praeger, 1983), 9, 10.

8. Nincic and Wallensteen, 6; see also Stephen Kinzer, "The Serbs Pick Milosevic, and the World Is Baffled," *New York Times*, 27 December 1992, sec. 4, 3.

9. Quoted in "The Carter Administration: State Department Reports," in Buncher, 177.

10. Nincic and Wallensteen, 3.

11. Richard R. Fagen, "The Carter Administration and Latin America: Business as Usual?" *Foreign Affairs - America and the World 1978* 57, no. 3, 652–69.

12. U.S. Congress, House Committee on International Relations, Subcommittee on International Organizations, *Human Rights and U.S. Foreign Policy,* 96th Cong., 1st sess., 2 and 10 May, 21 June, 2 August 1979, 333.

13. U.S. Congress, *Human Rights and U.S. Foreign Policy,* 321.

14. Schoultz, *Human Rights and U.S. Policy,* 341.

15. Alan Tonelson, "The Bias We Need," *Foreign Policy* (Winter 1982–1983), 52–74.

16. U.S. Congress, *Human Rights and U.S. Foreign Policy,* 71

17. Quoted in U.S. Congress, *Human Rights and U.S. Foreign Policy,* statement by Richard B. Lillich, 89.

18. Harry R. Strack, *Sanctions: The Case of Rhodesia* (Syracuse, N.Y.: Syracuse University Press, 1978), xi-xii; Gunnar Adler-Karlsson, *Western Economic Warfare, 1947–1967: A Case Study in Foreign Economic Policy* (Stockholm: Almqvist and Wiksell, 1968), 10; James A. Blessing, "The Suspension of Foreign Aid: A Macro-Analysis," *Polity* 13 (Spring 1981), 533. All quoted in David A. Baldwin, ed., *Economic Statecraft* (Princeton, N.J.: Princeton University Press, 1985), 55.

19. Nincic, *United States Foreign Policy,* 17.

20. U.S. Congress Senate Committee on Foreign Relations, Hearing, PTI, 91st Cong., 1st sess., 1969, 249, quoted in U.S. Congress, Senate, Senator Abourezk, "Problems of the Philippines," 93d Cong., 2d sess., *Congressional Record* 120, pt. 13 (4 June 1974), 17453.

21. International Financial Institutions Act, section 701(a) and 701(f).

22. Eighth Annual Report Submitted to Congress in Response to Title VII — Human Rights — of the International Financial Institutions Act (Public Law 95–118, as Amended), in U.S. Congress, House Committee on International Relations, Subcommittee on Human Rights and International Organizations, *Status of U.S. Human Rights Policy, 1987,* 100th Cong., 1st sess., 2 February 1987, 46.

23. Mower, 154.

24. Congress, *Human Rights and U.S. Foreign Policy,* 86.

25. Direct military intervention to preserve the status quo or effect change is, of course, also a policy alternative; it is one which neoconservatives would likely support. This policy, however, was neither used nor considered in any of the three cases.

26. Cyrus Vance, "Secretary Vance Gives Overview of Foreign Assistance Program," *Department of State Bulletin* 176, no. 1970, 28 March 1977, 284–89.

27. In June 1975, a State Department spokesman testified to the Senate Foreign Assistance Subcommittee that "even if it is not the law, we apply the same kind of policy considerations to commercial sales as we do to FMS [Foreign Mil-

itary Sales] cases," quoted in Walden Bello and Severina Rivera, "The Logistics of Repression," in Walden Bello and Severina Rivera, eds., *The Logistics of Repression and Other Essays,* (Washington, D.C.: Friends of the Filipino People, 1977), 7–12, reprinted in Daniel B. Schirmer and Stephen Rosskamm Shalom, eds., *The Philippine Reader: A History of Colonialism, Dictatorship and Resistance* (Boston: South End Press, 1987), 249–53.

28. Michael T. Klare, *American Arms Supermarket,* (Austin, Texas: University of Texas Press, 1984), 186.

29. Klare, 186, 260, 264.

30. Congress, House Committee on International Relations, Subcommittee on International Organizations, *Human Rights in Indonesia and the Philippines,* 94th Cong., 1st and 2d sessions, 18 December 1975 and 3 May 1976, 110.

31. Quoted in Lars Schoultz, "U.S. Economic Aid as an Instrument of Foreign Policy: The Case of Human Rights in Latin America," in Jack L. Nelson and Vera M. Green, eds., *International Human Rights: Contemporary Issues* (Stanfordville, N.Y.: Human Rights Publishers Group, 1980), 319.

32. Schoultz, *Human Rights and U.S. Policy,* 249.

33. *The Report of the President's National Bipartisan Commission on Central America,* (New York: Macmillan, [1984], 114, 115.

34. R. K. Ramazani, *The United States and Iran: The Patterns of Influence* (New York: Praeger, 1982), 27; see also Barry Rubin, *Paved with Good Intentions* (New York: Oxford University Press, 1980), 130.

35. U.S. Congress, House Committee on Foreign Affairs, Subcommittee on Inter-American Affairs, *Aircraft Sales in Latin America,* 91st Cong., 2d sess., April 1970, 3 (Bowdler), and U.S. Congress, House Committee on International Relations, *Foreign Assistance Legislation for Fiscal Year 1978,* 95th Cong., 1st sess., 1977, pt. 7: 80, 67 (Fish), both quoted in Schoultz, *Human Rights and U.S. Policy,* 248.

36. Schoultz, *Human Rights and U.S. Policy,* 46–47.

37. Richard P. Claude, "Human Rights in the Philippines and U.S. Responsibility," in Peter G. Brown and Douglas MacLean, eds., *Human Rights and U.S. Foreign Policy: Principles and Applications* (Lexington, Mass.: D. C. Heath, 1979), 239.

Chapter 3

1. Richard W. Cottam, *Nationalism in Iran,* updated through 1978, (Pittsburgh, Pa.: University of Pittsburgh Press, 1979), 268; Nikkie R. Keddie, *Roots of Revolution: An Interpretive History of Modern Iran* (New Haven, Conn.: Yale University Press, 1981), 133.

2. Fred Halliday, *Iran: Dictatorship and Development* (New York: Penguin Books, 1979), 80.

3. Michael Ledeen and William Lewis, *Debacle: The American Failure in Iran* (New York: Knopf, 1981), 55.

4. "A Report by the United States State Department on Human Rights Practices in Iran (in Accordance with Sections of the Foreign Assistance Act of 1961, as Amended) to the Senate Committee on Foreign Relations and House Committee on International Relations, 3 February 1978," reprinted in Yonah Alexander and Alan Nanes, eds., *The United States and Iran: A Documentary History* (Frederick, Md.: University Publications of America, prepared in association with the World Power Studies Program, Center for Strategic and International Studies, Georgetown University, 1980), 458.

5. Halliday, 205, 49.

6. James A. Bill, *The Eagle and the Lion: The Tragedy of American-Iranian Relations* (New Haven, Conn.: Yale University Press, 1988), 99; Richard W. Cottam, *Iran and the United States: A Cold War Case Study* (Pittsburgh, Pa.: University of Pittsburgh Press, 1988), 123; Keddie, *Roots of Revolution*, 150, 152; Hossein Bashiriyeh, *The State and Revolution in Iran, 1962–1982* (London: Croom Helm, 1984), 20.

7. *Kayhan International* (Tehran), 3 March 1975, p. 2, quoted in Bill, 196.

8. "State Department Report on Human Rights in Iran (Pursuant to the Arms Export Control Act of 1976) to the House Committee on International Relations, 31 December 1976," reprinted in Alexander and Nanes, 429–34.

9. Quoted in Bill, 187.

10. U.S. Congress, House Committee on International Relations, Subcommittee on International Organizations, *Human Rights Conditions in Selected Countries and the U.S. Response*, 95th Cong., 2d sess., 25 July 1978, 30.

11. "A Report by the United States State Department on Human Rights Practices in Iran (in Accordance with Sections of the Foreign Assistance Act of 1961, as Amended) to the Senate Foreign Relations and House Committee on International Relations, 3 February 1978," reprinted in Alexander and Nanes, 455.

12. U.S. Congress, *Human Rights Conditions*, 129.

13. Gerard de Villiers, *The Imperial Shah: An Informal Biography* (Boston: Little, Brown, 1976), 259.

14. Amir Abbos Hoveida, interview with James Bill, 30 June 1974, Tehran, in Bill, 186.

15. The "White Revolution," a national program instituted by the Shah, was ostensibly designed to improve the lot of the poor and impose a Western lifestyle on Iranian society.

16. Misagh Parsa, *Social Origins of the Iranian Revolution* (New Brunswick, N.J.: Rutgers University Press, 1989), 73.

17. World Bank, *World Development Report 1979* (New York: Oxford University Press, 1979), 163.

18. Farhad Kazemi, *Poverty and Revolution in Iran: The Migrant Poor, Urban Marginality and Politics* (New York: New York University Press, 1980), 42, 40.

19. Ledeen and Lewis, *Debacle*, 28.

20. World Bank, 165.

21. Kazemi, 89, 91.

22. Kazemi, 89. By 1972, 428 squatter settlements comprising 3,780 households had been identified in Tehran. While conditions in these residences were wholly inadequate, even the ''non-squatting migrant poor'' in Tehran lived under crowded conditions and ''lacked basic urban services such as piped water or electricity'' (Kazemi 47, 50).

23. Bill, 100; Cottam, *Cold War*, 127.

24. Cottam, *Cold War*, 130–31; Keddie, *Roots of Revolution*, 156.

25. Cottam, *Cold War*, 127, 129, 139; Keddie, *Roots of Revolution*, 161–63; Sepehr Zabih, *Iran's Revolutionary Upheaval: An Interpretive Essay* (San Francisco: Alchemy Press, 1979), 32.

26. Bill, 219–220; Keddie, *Roots of Revolution*, 232.

27. Bill, 222; Parsa, 54; Richard W. Cottam, ''American Arms Sales and Human Rights: The Case of Iran,'' in Peter G. Brown and Douglas MacLean, eds., *Human Rights and United States Foreign Policy: Principles and Applications* (Lexington, Mass.: Heath, 1979), 281–301. Saikal, 191–92; Cottam, ''American Policy and the Iranian Crisis,'' 296.

28. Halliday, 289.

29. Cottam, *Cold War; Keddie, Roots of Revolution*, 242–43.

30. Cottam, ''Arms Sales and Human Rights,'' 281–301; Cottam, *Cold War*, 172; Keddie, *Roots of Revolution*, 249–250.

31. Ledeen, 138; see also Cottam, *Cold War*, 172.

32. Gary Sick, *All Fall Down: America's Tragic Encounter with Iran* (New York: Random House, 1985), 62, 63; see also Keddie, *Roots of Revolution*, 252; Cottam, *Cold War*, 164, 179.

33. Quoted in Sepehr Zabih, *The Iranian Military in Revolution and War* (New York: Routledge Press, 1988), 27–28.

34. Amin Saikal, *The Rise and Fall of the Shah* (Princeton, N.J.: Princeton University Press, 1980), 194; Keddie, *Roots of Revolution*, 251, 246; Kazemi, 89; Bashiriyeh, 88–89.

35. Bill, 237; see also Robert E. Huyser, *Mission to Tehran* (New York: Harper and Row, 1986), 78, 79.

36. Cottam, *Cold War*, 184; Keddie, *Roots of Revolution*, 256.

37. Parsa, 241; Zabih, *Iranian Military*, 38; Sick, 140.

38. Zabih, *Iranian Military*, 64–70, 78–79; see also Sick, 156.

39. Bill, 96; Richard W. Cottam, ''American Policy and the Iranian Crisis,'' *Iranian Studies* 12, nos. 1–4 (1980), 279–305.

40. Ruhallah Khomeini, trans. Hamid Algar, *Islam and Revolution* (Berkeley, Calif.: Mizan Press, 1981), 24.

41. Kazemi, 91; see also Bashiriyeh, 113; Halliday, 219; Bill, 238.

42. Kazemi, 92.

43. Kazemi, 91–92; see also Keddie, *Roots of Revolution*, 181–82, 244–45.

44. *Kayhan*, 2 November 1978, quoted in Parsa, 201–02.

45. Parsa, 203.

46. Keddie, *Roots of Revolution*, 248.

47. Hedayat Matin Daftari, "Mossadeq's Legacy Today," interview in *MERIP Reports*, no. 113 (March-April 1983), 24.

48. Bill, 265; Sick, 188; Cottam, *Cold War*, 174.

49. Bill, 265; Ledeen and Lewis, 198; Parsa, 252; Cottam, *Cold War*, 191, 199–200.

50. Bill, 265; Ledeen and Lewis, 202–03.

51. Bill, 267–69; see also Cottam, *Cold War*, 229.

52. Ledeen and Lewis, 203–5.

53. Mehdi Bazargan, interview with Oriana Fallaci, in *New York Times Magazine*, 28 October 1979, quoted in Ledeen and Lewis, 196.

54. Bill, 280.

55. John Graves to USICA Washington, "A Major Public Affairs Concern," 4 September 1979 (Asnad, 16:65), and John D. Stempel, interview with James Bill, 2 September 1980, Washington, D.C., quoted in Bill, 280.

56. Bill 287–88, 290–91, 293–94; Cottam, *Cold War*, 210; Keddie, *Roots of Revolution*, 262.

57. "Message from the Persian Minister [Alai] to the Secretary of State," 21 February 1924, Washington, D.C., reprinted in Alexander and Nanes, 45.

58. "The Under Secretary of State [Welles] to President Roosevelt," 20 October, 1942, Washington, D.C., reprinted in Alexander and Nanes, 111.

59. "The Iranian Ambassador [Alai] to the Secretary of State," no. 2936, 5 March 1946, Washington, D.C., reprinted in Alexander and Nanes, 161.

60. Shapur Bahktiar, "The Americans Played a Disgusting Role," interview in *MERIP Reports*, no. 104 (March-April 1982), 11.

61. Robert B. Stobaugh, "The Evolution of Iranian Oil Policy, 1925–1975," in George Lenczowski, ed., *Iran Under the Pahlavis* (Stanford, Calif.: Hoover Institution Press, 1978), 201–52.

62. Khomeini, 182.

63. "Message from the Secretary of State to President Roosevelt," 16 August 1943, Washington, D.C., reprinted in Alexander and Nanes, 103–4.

64. "Message from the Acting Secretary of State to the Embassy in Iran," 3 January 1948, Washington, D.C., reprinted in Alexander and Nanes, 189–91.

65. "Memorandum for the President by the Central Intelligence Agency," 27 July 1950, reprinted in Alexander and Nanes, 195–96.

66. Ann Tibbitts Schulz, *Buying Security: Iran Under the Monarchy* (Boulder, Colo.: Westview Press, 1989), 15–16.

67. "Agreement of Defense Cooperation between the Government of the United States of America and the Imperial Government of Iran," 5 March 1959, reprinted in Alexander and Nanes, 306–7.

68. Bill, 171.

69. U.S. Congress, *Human Rights Conditions*, 125.

70. Bill, 401; Cottam, *Cold War*, 148.

71. Schulz, 17.

72. The "twin pillar" policy was a corollary of the 1969 Nixon Doctrine. The doctrine sought to establish "indirect [U.S.] power through specified Third World allies," and was designed to allow the United States to become the "arsenal rather than the policeman of the non-communist world." See Barry Rubin, *Paved with Good Intentions* (New York: Oxford University Press, 1980), 128.

73. "Statement of Secretary Kissinger upon the Conclusion of the United States-Iran Joint Commission," 6 August 1976, reprinted in Alexander and Nanes, 402–4.

74. "Agreement Establishing a United States Military Mission with Iranian Gendarmerie," 27 November 1943, Tehran, reprinted in Alexander and Nanes, 122–127.

75. "Message from the Acting Secretary of State to the Ambassador in Iran [Morris]," 25 October 1944, Washington, D.C., reprinted in Alexander and Nanes, 119.

76. "The Secretary of State to the Secretary of War [Patterson] on Interest of United States in Maintaining Postwar Military Missions in Iran," 17 October 1945, Washington D.C., reprinted in Alexander and Nanes, 153.

77. In 1947, the United States agreed to cooperate with the Iranian Ministry of War and the Iranian Army to increase the efficiency of Iran's military. See "Agreement between the United States and Iran on the Establishment of a Postwar Military Mission in Iran," 6 October 1947, Tehran, reprinted in Alexander and Nanes, 155–61; Zabih, *Iranian Military*, 43.

78. U.S. Agency for International Development, Office of Planning and Budgeting, Bureau for Program and Policy Coordination, *U.S. Overseas Loans and Grants and Assistance from International Organizations*, 1969 Report.

79. Military assistance which had already entered the pipeline, however, continued through 1973; see Table 3-1.

80. "A Staff Report to the Subcommittee on Foreign Assistance of the Committee on Foreign Relations, United States Senate: United States Military Sales to Iran," July 1976, reprinted in Alexander and Nanes, 406–19.

81. Michael T. Klare, *American Arms Supermarket* (Austin, Tx.: University of Texas Press, 1984), 118; R. K. Ramazani: *The United States and Iran: The Patterns of Influence* (New York: Praeger 1982), 49.

82. World Bank, *World Development Report 1982*, (New York: Oxford University Press, 1982), 157.

83. AID, *U.S. Overseas Loans*, 1968 Report.

84. Bill, 114–15.

85. "Communique of United States-Iran Joint Commission Issued at Tehran," 7 August 1976, reprinted in Alexander and Nanes, 397–400.

86. Saikal, 54.

87. "Statement by Secretary of State Kissinger upon the Conclusion of the United States-Iran Joint Commission," 6 August 1976, reprinted in Alexander and Nanes, 402–4.

88. U.S. Congress, Senate Committee of Foreign Relations, "United States Military Sales to Iran," Staff Report, July 1976, reprinted in Alexander and Nanes, 409.

89. Saikal, 207.

90. Keddie, 177.

91. "Address by President Eisenhower to the Members of Parliament of Iran," 14 December 1959, reprinted in Alexander and Nanes, 309.

92. Quoted in Sick, 52.

93. "President Johnson and the Shah Exchange Greetings upon the Shah's Arrival in Washington," 22 August 1967, reprinted in Alexander and Nanes, 362.

94. "National Security Council Report on United States Strategy for Iran," 1973, reprinted in Alexander and Nanes, 353–61.

95. "National Security Council Report on United States Strategy in Iran."

96. "State Department Report on Human Rights in Iran," 3 December 1976, reprinted in Alexander and Nanes, 430.

97. U.S. Congress, House Committee on International Relations, Subcommittee on International Organizations, *Human Rights in Iran*, 94th Cong., 2d sess, 3 August and 8 September 1976.

98. "State Department Report on Human Rights in Iran," 433.

99. Bill 227, 233; Cottam, "American Policy and the Iranian Crisis," 298.

100. Cottam, "American Policy and the Iranian Crisis," 298–99; see also Cottam, *Cold War*, 162.

101. Ramazani, 136; Sick, 49, 50.

102. Sick, 51; see also Cottam, *Cold War*, 176; Zbigniew Brzezinski, *Power and Principle: Memoirs of the National Security Adviser 1977–1981* (New York: Farrar, Straus, Giroux, 1983), 361.

On September 8, 1978, following the imposition of martial law, demonstrators in Tehran clashed with troops. Death toll estimates for that day ranged from 95 to 2,000 dead. See Rubin, *Paved with Good Intentions*, 14, and Nicholas M. Nikazmerad, "A Chronological Survey of the Iranian Revolution," *Iranian Studies—Iran's Revolution in Perspective* 13, nos. 1–4 (1980), 327–68.

103. Bill, 258. Richard Cottam, however, states that "Iranian oppositionists were aware of differences in the Carter administration" and some, therefore, remained hopeful that U.S. policy would change (*Cold War*, 176).

104. Sick, 54, 55.

105. Quoted in Sick, 62; see also President Jimmy Carter, News Conference, 10 October 1978, reprinted in Alexander and Nanes, 460–61.

106. Sick, 68.

107. Secretary of State Cyus Vance, News Conference, 3 November 1978, reprinted in Alexander and Nanes, 461–62.

108. Sick, 72; Brzezinski, 365.

109. Ledeen and Lewis, 146.

110. Brzezinski, 372; President Jimmy Carter, News Conference, 12 December 1978, reprinted in Alexander and Nanes, 463–64.

111. Quoted in Ledeen and Lewis, 170.

112. Sick, 126; see also Brzezinski, 375.

113. Sick, 126; Brzezinski, 376.

114. Sick, 126–32.

115. Secretary of State Cyrus Vance, News Conference, 11 January 1979, reprinted in Alexander and Nanes, 474.

116. Carter, 10 October 1978, 460–61.

117. President Jimmy Carter, "Question and Answer Session at a Breakfast with Members of the White House Correspondents Association," 7 December, 1978; see also News Conference, 17 January 1979, reprinted in Alexander and Nanes, 463–64 and 476–78, respectively.

118. Zabih, *Iranian Military,* 109; see also Sick, 139–40; Huyser, 38–42, 44; Brzezinski, 376, 378.

119. Zabih, *Iranian Military,* 47; Sick, 240; Huyser, 102; Brzezinski, 387, 388.

120. Zabih, *Iranian Military,* 58, 59.

121. Sick, 132–33; Cottam, *Cold War,* 174–75; Keddie, *Roots of Revolution,* 253; Huyser, 89, 92.

122. Sick, 137; Huyser, 99; Brzezinski, 381.

123. Sick, 140.

124. Sick, 143, 146.

125. Barry Rubin, "America's Relations with the Islamic Republic of Iran," *Iranian Studies* 13, nos. 1–4 (1980), 307–26.

126. Cyrus Vance, *Hard Choices: Critical Years in America's Foreign Policy* (New York: Simon and Schuster, 1983), 343.

127. President Jimmy Carter, New Conference, 27 February 1979, reprinted in Alexander and Nanes, 478–79.

128. Bill, 282–83; Cottam, *Cold War,* 209; Rubin, "American Relations."

129. Vance, 343.

130. Ledeen and Lewis, 227.

131. Rubin, *Paved with Good Intentions,* 372; Bill, 306–7; Rubin, "American Relations," 317.

132. L. Bruce Laingen to Secretary of State, "Iran Policy Overview," 20 August 1979 (Asnad 16:48), quoted in Bill, 282.

133. Harold H. Saunders to Secretary of State Cyrus Vance, "Policy toward Iran," 5 September 1979 (Asnad 16:72), quoted in Bill, 281–82.

134. Bill, 236.

135. President Jimmy Carter, Address, Georgia Institute of Technology, 20 February 1979, reprinted in Alexander and Nanes, 479.

136. Carter, 17 January 1979, 477.

137. Carter, 27 February 1979, 478–79.

138. National Security Adviser Zbigniew Brzezinski subsequently wrote that "though we encouraged the Shah to move toward a more representative system, we did not have, nor did we feel we should have, a detailed blueprint for how quick and extensive such policy change ought to be" (Brzezinski, 357).

139. Brzezinski, for example, noted in his memoirs the "the record does show that the Shah had enough encouragement from Carter and me to have taken . . . the tougher line" (Brzezinski, 356, 357).

140. "The Current Internal Political Situation in Iran: A Report by the Deputy Director of the Office of Greek, Turkish, and Iranian Affairs [John W. Bowling], United States Department of State, to the President," 11 February 1961, reprinted in Alexander and Nanes, 315–21.

141. "Political Characteristics of the Iranian Urban Middle-Class and Implications Thereof for United States Policy: A Report by the Deputy Director of Greek, Turkish, and Iranian Affairs [Bowling], United States Department of State, to the President," reprinted in Alexander and Nanes, 322–29.

142. Bill, 211.

143. Sick, 81.

144. Michael A. G. Michaud, "Communications and Controversy: Thoughts on the Future of Foreign Service Reporting," *Foreign Service Journal* (October 1969), 24, quoted in Bill, 396.

145. Brzezinski, 359.

146. Zabih, *Iranian Military*, 99; Brzezinski, 395.

147. Bill, 404.

148. Quoted in Sick, 32.

149. Harold Saunders, "The Situation in Iran and its Implications: Statement before the Subcommittee on Europe and the Middle East of the House Committee on International Relations," 17 January 1979, reprinted in Alexander and Nanes, 468.

150. See Brzezinski, 367, 394, 396, 397.

151. Bill, 402; Cottam, *Cold War*, 148.

152. U.S. Congress, House Subcommittee on Evaluation, Permanent Select Committee on Intelligence, *Iran: Evaluation of U.S. Intelligence Performance Prior to November 1978*, Staff Report, (Washington, D.C.: U.S. Government Printing Office, January 1979), 6, quoted in Ramazani, 126.

153. Quoted in Ledeen and Lewis, 124.

154. "Henry Precht, Director of Office of Iranian Affairs, to L. Bruce Laingen, Chargé d'affaires a.i., American Embassy, Tehran, 20 July 1979 (Asnad, 15:127), quoted in Bill, 276.

155. Sick, 171.

156. Quoted in Rubin, *Paved with Good Intentions,* 257.

157. Sick, 171.

158. Warren Christopher, "Lessons of Iran," speech delivered to the Los Angeles County Bar Association, 26 May 1981, reprinted in Warren Christopher, "Diplomacy: The Neglected Imperative," bound pamphlet, n.d., quoted in Richard Feinberg, *The Intemperate Zone: The Third World Challenge to U.S. Foreign Policy* (New York: Norton, 1983), 245.

159. *Washington Post,* 19 November 1978, quoted in Ledeen and Lewis, 163; see also Brzezinski, 369.

The Russo-Iran Treaty of 1921 permitted "Russia to intervene against the troops of any power using Iran as a base of operation against Russia" (Keddie, *Roots of Revolution,* 87–88).

160. *The Washington Post,* 20 November 1978, quoted in Ledeen and Lewis, 164.

161. Brzezinski, 355.

162. Bill, 150, 171–72; Keddie, *Roots of Revolution,* 236; Cottam, *Cold War,* 121.

163. Parsa, 1–13; see also M. Tehranian, "Communication and Revolution in Iran: The Passing of a Paradigm," *Iranian Studies* 13 (1980), 5–30; J. Green, "Pseudoparticipation and Counter-Mobilization: Roots of the Iranian Revolution," *Iranian Studies,* 13 (1980), 31–53; A. Saikal, *Rise and Fall of the Shah;* N. Momayezi. "Economic Correlates of Political Violence: The Case of Iran," *Middle East Journal* 40 (1986), 68–81; Sick, *All Fall Down;* N. Keddie, "The Iranian Revolution in Comparative Perspective," *American Historical Review* 88 (1983), 579–98; J. Stempel, *Inside the Iranian Revolution* (Bloomington: Indiana University Press, 1981).

164. Harold H. Saunders, "The Situation in Iran and Its Implications," 469.

165. Bakhtiar, *MERIP,* (March-April 1982), 11.

166. Mat McCarthy, "Iran's Rising Opposition," *Washington Post,* 9 July 1978, B3.

167. *Washington Post,* 2 January 1979, and *Le Monde,* 10 January 1979, quoted in Rubin, *Paved with Good Intentions,* 241.

168. Vance, 339.

169. Vance, 347.

170. Youssef M. Ibrahim, "Iran's Leaders Ask Wide Cooperation and Ties to West," *New York Times,* 28 May 1991, A1.

171. Elaine Sciolino, "Distrust of U.S. Hinders Iran Chief," *New York Times,* 10 April 1992, A3.

172. William Claiborne, "U.S.-Iranian Cooperation Possible," *Washington Post*, 19 September 1991, A39.

173. Bill, 178, 214.

174. Department of State, Bureau of Intelligence and Research, "Iranian Outlook," 4 May 1976, Report no. 411, quoted in Bill, 214.

Chapter 4

1. Anastasio Somoza Garcia, President, 1936–1947 and 1950–1956; Luis Somoza, 1956–1963; Anastasio Somoza Debayle, 1967–1971, 1972–1979.

2. In 1963–67, unrest led Luis Somoza to pass the presidency to two puppets, Rene Schick and Lorenzo Guerrero. Anastasio Somoza Debayle remained at the center of power as commander of the National Guard. After assuming the presidency in 1967, political unrest in 1971 led Anastasio Somoza to cede presidential power to a three-man junta. He nonetheless retained command of the Guard—a compromise arranged with the assistance of U.S. Ambassador Turner Shelton. A December 1972 earthquake gave Anastasio Somoza another opportunity to seize executive power. "He ruled by decree" until 1974 and formally resumed title to the presidency in 1974 for a term to conclude in 1981. This arrangement, too, was encouraged by Ambassador Shelton. See John A. Booth, *The End and the Beginning: The Nicaraguan Revolution* (Boulder, Colo.: Westview Press, 1982), 73, 75–76; Thomas W. Walker, *Nicaragua: The Land of Sandino*, 2nd edition, (Boulder, Colo.: Westview Press, 1986), 30; Anthony Lake, *Somoza Falling* (Boston: Houghton Mifflin, 1989), 19.

3. Karl Bermann, *Under the Big Stick: Nicaragua and the United States Since 1848* (Boston: South End Press, 1986), 237.

4. Booth, 89, 61.

5. Walker, *Nicaragua: The Land of Sandino*, 29.

6. Walker, *Nicaragua: The Land of Sandino*, 29; Booth, 75.

7. Bernard Diederich, *Somoza and the Legacy of U.S. Involvement in Central America* (New York: Dutton, 1981), 31.

8. Booth, 103–04.

9. Walker, *Nicaragua: The Land of Sandino*, 102.

10. Booth, 219, 113.

11. Booth, 92, 56, 57, 55; Diederich, 34; Walker, 27; Richard R. Fagen, "Dateline Nicaragua: The End of the Affair," *Foreign Policy*, no. 36 (Fall 1979), 178–91; Walter LeFeber, *Inevitable Revolutions: The United States in Central America*, expanded ed. (New York: Norton, Inc., 1984), 226.

12. Booth, 57, 94; LeFeber, *Inevitable Revolutions*, 226.

13. Booth, 94, 95; LeFeber, *Inevitable Revolutions*, 227–28.

14. Diederich, 25.

15. Robert A. Pastor, *Condemned to Repetition: The United States and Nicaragua* (Princeton, N.J.: Princeton University Press, 1987), 43, 44; Booth, 110; Walker, *Inevitable Revolutions*, 29.

16. World Bank, *World Development Report 1979* (New York: Oxford University Press, 1979), 162.

17. Booth, 218, 84; Diederich, 128; Pastor, 44; Food and Agriculture Organization, *Nicaragua: Mission de Identificacion y Formulacion de Proyectos* (Managua: Programa de Cooperacion Tecnica, 1979), 9, cited in David Kaimowitz and Joseph R. Thome, "Nicaragua's Agrarian Reform: The First Year (1979–1980)," in Thomas W. Walker, ed., *Nicaragua in Revolution* (New York: Praeger, 1982), 223–40.

18. Booth, 122, 83, 85; William LeoGrande, "The United States and the Nicaraguan Revolution," in Walker, *Nicaragua in Revolution*, 63–77.

19. Booth, 81; Diederich, 100; Pastor, 36; Fagen, "Dateline Nicaragua"; LaFeber, *Inevitable Revolutions*, 228; Richard C. Schroeder, "Roots of Current Antagonism" in *Editorial Research Reports* 1, no. 8 (1986): 154–59, reprinted in Andrew C. Kimmens, ed., *Nicaragua and the United States, The Reference Shelf* 59, no. 2 (New York: Wilson Company, 1987), 6–12.

20. Booth, 168.

21. Booth, 168–69, 69, 80; World Bank, 1979, 154.

22. Booth, 99, 105; Diederich, 23, 60, 61.

23. Diederich, 52, 23, 61, 80, 101, 102; Pastor, 36.

24. Diederich, 26, 30, 45, 58, 61.

25. Diederich, 83–84; LaFeber, *Inevitable Revolutions*, 228.

26. Booth, 102.

27. Lake, 20.

28. Booth, 83, 152, 106; Pastor, 37; Lake, 20; George Black, *Triumph of the People: The Sandinista Revolution in Nicaragua* (London: Zed Press, 1981), 65–66.

29. Booth, 102, 157; Pastor, 59; Fagen, "Dateline Nicaragua."

30. Pastor, 57.

31. Humberto Ortega, interview with Marta Harnecker, in *Granma*, 27 January 1980, reprinted as Humberto Ortega, "Nicaragua — The Strategy of Victory," in Tomas Borge, et al., *Sandinistas Speak* (New York: Pathfinder Press, 1982), 53–84.

32. Quoted in Pastor, 58.

33. Pastor, 59; Booth, 157.

34. Shirley Christian, *Nicaragua: Revolution in the Family* (New York: Random House, 1985), 49; Richard R. Fagen, "The Carter Administration and Latin America: Business as Usual," in *Foreign Affairs - America and the World 1978* 57, no. 3 (1979), 652–69.

35. Pastor, 59.

36. Pastor, 64.

37. Pastor, 63–64, 95; Booth, 153; Christian, 59.

38. Booth, 157

39. Pastor, 72, 59; Christian, 59; Walker, *Nicaragua: The Land of Sandino*, 36.

40. Booth, 161, 103; Pastor, 72; Christian, 59; Walker, *Nicaragua: The Land of Sandino*, 37.

41. Humberto Ortega Saavedra, "La insurreccion nacional victoriosa," interview in Nicarauac 1 (May–June 1980): 44–45, quoted in Booth, 161.

42. Christian, 70; Pastor, 71, 126.

43. Booth, 144; Pastor, 73; LeoGrande, "The United States and the Nicaraguan Revolution"; Walker, *The Land of Sandino*, 37.

44. Pastor, 77.

45. Pastor, 93; Walker, *Nicaragua: The Land of Sandino*, 37.

46. In early September 1978, Venezuela and the OAS again called on Somoza to allow a visit by the Inter-American Commission on Human Rights (IACHR). Costa Rica made repeated protests about violations of its territorial integrity committed by Nicaraguan troops pursuing FSLN guerillas. On September 15, Venezuela and Costa Rica signed a defense pact: Costa Rica was permitted to borrow sophisticated weaponry from Venezuela and Panama to deter Nicaraguan transgressions over its border (Booth, 165).

47. Booth, 165–66; Pastor, 101; Lake, 148.

48. Pastor, 107; Booth, 165.

49. Pastor, 101; Booth, 166–67.

50. Booth, 166–67; Pastor, 102.

51. Lake, 148.

52. Booth, 166; Pastor, 102; Lake, 148.

53. Pastor, 108–10; Booth, 167.

54. Booth, 167; Pastor, 111.

55. Pastor, 114, 115.

56. Pastor 122; Henri Weber, "The Struggle for Power," in Peter Rosset and John Vandermeer, eds., *The Nicaraguan Reader: Documents of a Revolution Under Fire* (New York: Grove Press, 1983), 151–66 and reprinted from Henri Weber, *Nicaragua: The Sandinist Revolution*, Patrick Camiller, trans. (London: Verso Editions and NLB, 1981).

57. Pastor, 267.

58. Alfonso Robelo, interviews with Robert Pastor, 29–30 July 1983, San Jose, Costa Rica, in Pastor, 267.

59. Alfonso Robelo from the business community; Sergio Ramirez from the Group of Twelve; Violeta D. Chamorro widow of Pedro Joaquin Chamorro, from La Prensa; Moises Hassan a Sandinista who held a Ph.D. in physics from North Carolina State University; and Daniel Ortega Saavedra from the FSLN Directorate.

60. Pastor, 138; Weber.

61. Pastor, 185.

62. Booth, 118, 125, 135–36, 202; Michael Dodson and T.S. Montgomery, "The Churches in the Nicaraguan Revolution," 161–80, and Luis Serra, "The Sandinist Mass Organization," both in Walker, *Nicaragua in Revolution*, 161–80, 95–113, respectively.

63. Booth, 134–35; Walker, *Nicaragua: The Land of Sandino*, 42; Diederich, 124; Dodson and Montgomery.

64. Lake, 20; see also Pastor, 36–37; Booth, 135.

65. Pastor, 72, Booth, 137, 102, 157; Christian, 59.

66. Booth, 164.

67. Lake, 56; Conor Cruise O'Brien, "God and Man in Nicaragua," *The Atlantic Monthly* (August 1986), 66–69, reprinted as "The Protomartyr," in Kimmens, 12–16; Booth, 42.

68. Walker, *Nicaragua: The Land of Sandino*, 40; Booth 138–39; Ricardo E. Chavarria, "The Nicaraguan Insurrection: An Appraisal of its Originality," in Walker, *Nicaragua in Revolution*, 25–40.

69. FSLN, "The Historic Program of the FSLN," in Borge, 13–22.

70. Booth, 139, 147, 140–41; Walker, *Nicaragua: The Land of Sandino*, 102; Serra; Fagen, "Dateline Nicaragua."

71. Booth, 141, 150; Pastor, 37.

72. Pastor, 40.

73. Anastasio Somoza (as told to Jack Cox), *Nicaragua Betrayed* (Boston: Western Islands Publishers, 1980), 86.

74. Booth, 145.

75. *U.S. Government Intelligence Fact Book*, cited in Diederich, 152; U.S. Congress, House Appropriations Committee, *Foreign Assistance and Related Program Appropriations Bill, 1978*, Report no. 95–417, 15 June 1977, 65, cited in Pastor, 49.

76. Humberto Ortega, 72.

77. Robert Matthews, "The Limits of Friendship," in North American Congress on Latin America (NACLA), *Report of the Americas* May–June 1985, 25, in Pastor, 352, ftn. 12.

78. Booth, 154, 145.

79. Pastor, 197.

80. Robelo, interview with Pastor, 29–39, July 1983, in Pastor, 198.

81. Pastor, 199; see also Theodore Schwab and Harold Sims, "Relations with the Communist States," in Thomas W. Walker ed., *Nicaragua: The First Five Years* (New York: Praeger Publishers, 1985), 447–66.

82. Pastor, 211.

83. Pastor, 201; see also Assistant Secretary of State for Inter-American Affairs Viron Vaky, "Testimony in Congress, House Subcommittee on Inter-American Affairs and the Foreign Affairs Committee," *Central America at the*

Crossroads, 11–12 September 1979, in Robert S. Leiken, ed., *Central America: Anatomy of a Conflict* (New York: Pergamon Press, Inc., published in cooperation with the Carnegie Endowment for International Peace, 1984), 1–20.

84. Booth, 194.

85. Pastor, 201; Saul Landau, "The Way of the Sandinistas," *The Progressive* August 1988, 21–25, reprinted in Kimmens, 141–54.

86. Walker, *Nicaragua: The Land of Sandino*, 114.

87. Walker, *Nicaragua: The Land of Sandino*, 44, 67; Richard E. Feinberg, "Central America: No Easy Answer," *Foreign Affairs* 59, no. 5 (1981): 1121–46.

88. Walker, *Nicaragua: The Land of Sandino*, 67.

89. Pastor, 201; Walker, *Nicaragua: The Land of Sandino*, 68.

90. Pastor, 200.

91. Booth, 198; Walker, *Nicaragua: The Land of Sandino*, 47.

92. Sergio Ramirez, "What the Sandinistas Want," *Caribbean Review* 7, no. 3 (Summer 1979), 50–51, quoted in Walker, *Nicaragua: The Land of Sandino*, 131.

93. Speech by Miguel D'Escoto, Naciones Unidas Asamblea General, *Acta Taqugrafica Provisional* (A/35/pv. 28) 8 October 1980, quoted in Alejandro Bendana, "The Foreign Policy of the Nicaraguan Revolution," in Walker, *Nicaragua in Revolution*, 328.

94. Pastor, 201; Morris Rothenberg, "The Soviets and Central America," in Robert S. Leiken, ed., *Central America: Anatomy of Conflict* (New York: Pergamon Press, Inc., published in cooperation with the Carnegie Endowment for International Peace, 1984), 131–49.

95. Pastor, 201; Walker, *Nicaragua: The Land of Sandino*, 132.

96. Rothenberg; see also Schwab and Sims.

97. Rothenberg, 141.

98. Walker, *Nicaragua: The Land of Sandino*, 43; Feinberg, "Central America: No Easy Answer."

99. Figures for 1978 and 1982 from "Lunes Socio-Economico," *Barricada*, 23 May 1983; figures for 1985 from "Reagan Wields a Double-Edged Sword," *Central American Report* 12, no. 17 (10 May 1985), 129, both cited in Walker, *Nicaragua: The Land of Sandino*, 67.

100. Rothenberg, 141; see also E. Bradford Burns, *At War in Nicaragua: The Reagan Doctrine and the Politics of Nostalgia* (New York: Harper and Row, 1987), 103.

101. U.S. Embassy Managua, *Foreign Economic Trends Report 1983*, 3, cited in Rothenberg, 135.

102. Walker, *Nicaragua: The Land of Sandino*, 68; Pastor, 215; see also Nadia Malley, "Relations with Western Europe and the Socialist International," in Walker, *Nicaragua: The First Five Years*, 485–98.

103. Pastor, 25.

104. Pastor, 254.

105. Booth, 18.

106. Booth, 17; LaFeber, *Inevitable Revolutions*, 29–31.

107. Quoted in Jinesta, *El canal de Nicaragua*, 62, quoted in Booth, 34.

108. Walker, *Nicaragua: The Land of Sandino*, 20; Booth, 34.

109. Booth, 35.

110. Booth, 18, 20; see also Schroeder.

111. The Marines were absent from Nicaragua between August 1925 and January 1927. See also Booth 24, 27; Harry E. Vanden, "The Ideology of the Insurrection," in Walker *Nicaragua in Revolution*, 41–62.

112. Booth, 30–32, 39–41; David Howard Bain, "The Man Who Made the Yanquis Go Home," in *American Heritage* 36, no. 5 (August–September 1985), 50–61, in Kimmens, 16–35.

113. Walker, *Nicaragua: The Land of Sandino*, 21.

114. Pastor, 28.

115. Pastor, 28; Booth, 59.

116. Pastor, 29.

117. Pastor, 22.

118. Booth, 59; Bermann, 232.

119. U.S. Agency for International Development, Bureau for Program and Policy Coordination, Office of Planning and Budget, *U.S. Overseas Loans and Grants and Assistance from International Organizations*, reports for 1968 to 1975. Economic assistance rose substantially in response to the December 1972 earthquake; see also Table 4-1.

120. Booth, 101–102.

121. Pastor, 44; Black, 39; Burns, 21.

122. Booth, 38, 40–43.

123. Black, 48.

124. Landau, 146.

125. Booth, 55, 56; Black, 47.

126. U.S. Department of State, *Foreign Relations of the United States, 1952*, 4 (Washington, D.C.: U.S. Government Printing Office, 1983), 1372, quoted in Lake, 16–17.

127. U.S. State Department, 1375, quoted in Lake, 17.

128. Booth, 76.

129. U.S. AID, *U.S. Overseas Loans*, reports for 1968–1972.

130. Pastor, 269.

131. U.S. Department of State, "The Secretary of State to the Minister in Nicaragua [Lane]," *Foreign Relations of the United States 1934* 5, 26 February 1934, 538–39, quoted in Pastor, 26–27.

132. U.S. Department of State, "The Minister in Nicaragua [Lane] to the Secretary of State," *Foreign Relations of the United States, 1935* 4, 14 May 1935, 855–61, quoted in Pastor, 27.

133. Black, 35; Diederich, 22; LaFeber, *Inevitable Revolutions*, 69.

134. Quoted in Diederich, 22.

135. Booth, 59; Pastor, 30.

136. *New York Times*, 9 May 1950, quoted in Bermann, 239.

137. U.S. Office of Intelligence, "Political Developments in the Other American Republics in the Twentieth Century," Research Report no. 4,780, Group 59 (Washington, D.C.: National Archives, 1 October 1949), 2–3, quoted in Walter LaFeber, "The Burdens of the Past," in Leiken, 57.

138. Bermann, 242.

139. Lake, 17; Pastor, 30; Fagen, "Dateline Nicaragua."

140. U.S. AID, *U.S. Overseas Loans*, 1968 report.

141. Lake, 97.

142. Pastor, 36; Diederich, 116.

143. Pastor, 38–39.

144. Somoza, 58.

145. U.S. Representative John Murphy, interview with WGBH, 15 May 1984, Danbury, Conn., quoted in Pastor, 53.

146. President Jimmy Carter, "Power of Humane Purpose," speech at University of Notre Dame, 22 May 1977, reprinted in Ernest Lefever, ed., *Morality and Foreign Policy: A Symposium on President Carter's Stance* (Washington, D.C.: Ethics and Public Policy Center of Georgetown University, 1977), 3–10.

147. LeoGrande, "The United States and the Nicaraguan Revolution."

148. John M. Goshko and Karen De Young, "Decisions Send Nicaragua 'Garbled' Rights Message," *Washington Post*, 25 October 1977; Alan Riding, "In Nicaragua, This May Be the Twilight of the Somoza's," *New York Times*, 30 October 1977, Sec.4, 3.

149. Diederich, 123, 124; Bermann, 259; see also Dodson and Montgomery.

150. *Time*, (14 March 1977) 30, quoted in Bermann, 262.

151. Amnesty International, *The Republic of Nicaragua: An Amnesty International Report Including the Findings of a Mission to Nicaragua 10–15 May 1976* (London: Amnesty International Publications, 1977), 38–39.

152. Pastor, 64.

153. Diederich, 152; Booth, 145.

154. Quoted in Diederich, 161.

155. Quoted in Diederich, 163.

156. Pastor, 63.

157. Pastor, 62–63.

158. Pastor, 77, 78.

159. Quoted in Pastor, 65–66.

160. John Huey, "Human Rights and Nicaragua," *Wall Street Journal*, 19 September 1978, reprinted in U.S. Congress, House, 95th Cong., 2d sess., *Congressional Record* 124, pt. 25 (4 October 1978), 33677.

161. Huey, 33677.

162. Quoted in Diederich, 203.

163. Pastor, 73; Diederich, 196; Lake, 137.

164. Pastor, 73, 85.

165. *Public Papers of the Presidents of the United States, Jimmy Carter, 1978* 2, 1596–1602, quoted in Pastor, 89.

166. Zbigniew Brzezinski, interview with Latin American editors, 22 September 1978, White House transcript, quoted in Pastor, 87.

167. Pastor, 87; see also LeoGrande, "The U.S. and the Nicaraguan Revolution."

168. Somoza, 314, 318. Somoza places this conversation in November 1978; Robert Pastor has written that it occurred in September. See Pastor, 91.

169. Pastor, 175; Booth, 167; see also LeoGrande, "The United States and the Nicaraguan Revolution."

170. Pastor, 109; Lake, 159.

171. General Dennis McAuliffe, tape of conversation with Somoza, 21 December 1978, Managua, Nicaragua, in Somoza, 328, 329.

172. *Department of State Bulletin*, April 1979, 66, quoted in Pastor, 119.

173. Lake, 166.

174. Pastor, 116, 119.

175. Pastor, 120; Diederich, 230.

176. Quoted in Lake, 172.

177. U.S. Congress, Senate *Congressional Record* (19 May 1980), 11653–55, quoted in Pastor, 130.

178. Pastor, 130; see also LeoGrande, "The United States and the Nicaraguan Revolution."

179. Quoted in Pastor, 129.

180. Pastor, 124, 129; Diederich, 24; Walker, *Nicaragua: The Land of Sandino*, 38; LaFeber, *Inevitable Revolutions*, 233; see also LeoGrande, "The United States and the Nicaraguan Revolution," and LeoGrande, "The United States and Nicaragua," in Walker, *Nicaragua: The First Five Years*, 425–456.

181. Pastor, 132, 134, 138; see also Weber, LaFeber, *Inevitable Revolutions*, 233.

182. Pastor, 134–35.

183. Pastor, 137, 143.

184. Alan Riding, "Rebels in Nicaragua Name Five to Form Provisional Junta," *New York Times*, 18 June 1979, A1; and William Long, "Key Rebel

Dreams of New Nicaragua with 'Democracy'," *Miami Herald*, 23 June 1979, both cited in Pastor, 143.

185. Lake, 219; see also Weber.

186. Lake, 230.

187. Pastor, 145–46; see also LeoGrande, "The United States and the Nicaraguan Revolution"; LaFeber, *Inevitable Revolutions*, 234.

188. Pastor, 148; see also Weber; Lake, 225.

189. OAS Resolution II, 23 June 1979, reprinted in John Norton Moore, *The Secret War in Central America: Sandinista Assault on World Order* (Frederick, Md.: University Publications of America, 1987), 161–162.

190. Pastor, 150.

191. Pastor, 154; see also LeoGrande, "The United States and the Nicaragua Revolution."

192. Anastasio Somoza, tape of meeting with Ambassador Pezzullo, 27 June 1979, Managua, Nicaragua, in Somoza, 334, 335, 344, 349.

193. Pastor, 158; see also LeoGrande, "The United States and the Nicaragua Revolution."

194. "National Guard Survival," and "Nicaraguan Scenario," declassified cables from U.S. Embassy, Managua, to Secretary of State, 30 June 1979, Managua 3,914 and 2,929, respectively, quoted in Pastor, 157, 158.

195. Pastor, 166.

196. Pastor, 163–65, 168; Fagen, "Dateline Nicaragua"; LaFeber, *Inevitable Revolutions*, 236; Jeff M. McConnel, "Counterrevolution in Nicaragua: The U.S. Connection," in Rosset and Vandermeer, 175–89.

197. Lake, 248.

198. U.S. Congress, House Committee on International Relations, Subcommittee on International Organizations, *Human Rights and U.S. Foreign Policy*, 96th Cong., 1st sess., 21 June 1979, 203.

199. Pastor, 169.

200. Pastor, 173–74, 197.

201. Pastor, 186.

202. Pastor, 216; Moore, 13; LeoGrande, "The U.S. and Nicaragua," 425.

203. Pastor, 195; see also LeoGrande, "The United States and Nicaragua.

204. Christian, 142; Pastor, 196; Moore, 12.

205. Vaky, 'Testimony in Congress, House Committee Foreign Affairs, Subcommittee on Inter-American Affairs, *Central America at the Crossroads*, 96th Cong., 1st sess., 11–12 September 1979, in Leiken, 3–4.

206. McConnel, 179; see also Burns, 20.

207. Presidential Determination no. 82–26 of 12 September 1980 in *Federal Reporter* 45, no. 185, 22 September 1980, 62779, cited in Pastor, 217; see also Burns, 20.

208. Pastor, 210; see also LeoGrande, "The United States and the Nicaraguan Revolution."

209. Pastor, 218; Moore, 24.

210. Pastor, 218.

211. Pastor, 220; Moore, 24.

212. Tomas Borge, "Presentation Made to the Inter-American Human Rights Commission," 10 October 1980, in Borge, *Sandinistas Speak*, 85–104.

213. Pastor, 214; McConnel. Nicaragua stopped distribution of AID grants in late 1982 because it disapproved of the purposes for which they were being used (McConnel, 182).

214. Arturo Cruz Sequeira, "The Origins of Sandinista Foreign Policy," in Leiken, 95–109.

215. Pastor, 207.

216. FBIS, "Security Chief Discussed CIA Activities in Country," 10 March 1980, p. 16, cited in Pastor, 211.

217. LeoGrande, "The United States and Nicaragua.

218. Pastor, 225–26; Moore, 24.

219. Pastor, 226–27; Moore, 2; see also LeoGrande, "The United States and Nicaragua."

220. Pastor, 227, 232; Moore, 24.

221. Viron Vaky, "Reagan's Central American Policy: An Isthmus Restored," in Leiken, 235.

222. Pastor, 237; Burns, 52.

223. Vaky, 236.

224. Booth, 214; Pastor, 233–34; Roy Gutman, *Banana Diplomacy: The Making of American Public Policy in Nicaragua, 1981–1987* (New York: Simon and Schuster, 1988), 70; LeoGrande, "The United States and Nicaragua."

225. LeoGrande, "The United States and Nicaragua"; Pastor, 234; Gutman, 74.

226. Gutman, 73; see also LeoGrande, "The United States and Nicaragua"; McConnell.

227. Gutman, 73; LeoGrande, "The United States and Nicaragua"; Pastor, 235; Christian, 191–92.

228. Pastor, 236–238; Gutman, 85; Burns, 53.

229. LeoGrande, "The United States and Nicaragua"; see also Burns, 30.

230. Barry Rubin, "Reagan Administration Policymaking and Central America," in Leiken, 299–318.

231. Quoted in Gutman, 96–97.

232. Daniel Ortega Saavedra, "Statement to the United Nations Security Council," United Nations, *Security Council Official Records, Thirty-Seventh Year*, 2,335th Meeting, 25 March 1982, S/P.V. 2335, p. 7.

233. Roger Fontaine, "Choices on Nicaragua," *Global Affairs* 1, Summer 1986, 113, quoted in Pastor, 248.

234. Hedrick Smith, "Arms Aid to Nicaragua Still Rising, U.S. Says," *New York Times*, 5 October 1983, A11, quoted in Pastor, 247.

235. Vaky, "Reagan's Central America Policy."

236. Vaky, "Reagan's Central America Policy," 250.

237. Diederich, 243.

238. Ambassador Mauricio Solaun, speech at the University of Illinois at Champaign-Urbana, April 1979.

239. Diederich, 243.

240. Quoted in Diederich, 243.

241. Don Bohning, *Miami Herald*, 7 May 1979, quoted in Diederich, 243.

242. U.S. Representative Charles Wilson, interview with Robert Pastor, 31 July 1985, in Pastor, 289.

243. Diederich, 72.

244. Lake, 217, 238.

245. Lake, 238.

246. Christian, 52, 59; Pastor, 130, 290.

247. Pastor, 274, 290, 175.

248. Humberto Ortega, 66, 62.

249. Henry Ruiz, Daniel Ortega, and Jaime Wheelock Roman, interviewed in *Latin American Perspectives* 6, no. 1 (Winter 1979): 108–28, cited in Pastor, 42.

250. Pastor, 274.

251. Robelo, interview with Pastor, in Pastor 186.

252. Eden Pastora, interview with Robert Pastor, 14 November 1983, Washington, D.C., in Pastor, 197; see also Feinberg, "Central America: No Easy Answer."

253. Christian, 117; Pastor, 195–96; Walker, *Nicaragua: The Land of Sandino*, 103; Bendana, 319–328.

254. Philip Taubman, "The CIA: In from the Cold War and Hot for the Truth, *New York Times*, 11 June 1984, B6; Don Oberdorfer and John M. Goshko, "Ex-CIA Analyst Disputes U.S. Aides on Nicaragua," *Washington Post*, 13 June 1984, A1, A28; "Arms Flow Largely Stopped," *Times of the Americas*, 10 December 1986, 7, all cited in Pastor, 256; Moore, 24; see also LeoGrande, "The United State and Nicaragua."

255. President Reagan's Address on Central America to Joint Session of Congress," *New York Times*, 28 April 1982, A12.

256. LeoGrande, "The United States and Nicaragua."

257. Bayordo Arce, interview with Gutman, July 1985, Managua, Nicaragua; Daniel Ortega Saavedra, interview with Gutman, August 1986, Managua, Nicaragua, in Gutman, 73.

258. Secretary of State Shultz, "Nicaragua and the Future of Central America," address before the Veterans of Foreign Wars, 15 March 1986, Washington, D.C., in *Department of State Bulletin* 86 (May 1986): 37–40, reprinted in Kimmens, 67.

259. John Horton, "The Real Intelligence Failure," *Foreign Service Journal* (February 1985), 24, quoted in Pastor, 246–247.

260. Despite the euphoria that followed President Chamorro's election in 1990, U.S. aid funds were frozen because of concerns in Congress about political and economic conditions in post-Sandinista Nicaragua. Concerns centered on continued Sandinista participation in Nicaragua's military and police forces, on the lack of significant judicial reform, and on the unsatisfactory pace of progress on compensation for private property seized from U.S. and Nicaraguan nationals, by the Sandinistas. See Jesse Helms, Washington, D.C., unpublished letters to Ronald Roskens, Administrator, Agency for International Development, Washington, D.C., 22 May 1992 and 22 June 1992; Barbara Crossette, "Ire in Congress Delays Nicaraguan Aid as U.S. Resumes Help for Peru," *New York Times,* 4 June 1992, A9; see also Steven A. Holmes, "Nicaragua to Get Blocked U.S. Aid," *New York Times,* 3 April 1993, A3.

261. Booth, 55; Walker, *Nicaragua: The Land of Sandino,* 38; Christian, 91, 92; Colonel D. Heinl, Jr., "U.S. Aid Cutoff a Major Boost for Nicaragua's Reds," reprinted in U.S. Congress, House, 95th Cong., 2d sess., *Congressional Record* 124, pt. 25 (5 October 1978), 24057.

262. Anastasio Somoza, interview with "Face the Nation," Easter 1979, quoted in Pastor, 123.

263. John Huey, "Human Rights and Nicaragua," *Wall Street Journal,* 19 September 1978, reprinted in U.S. Congress, House, 95th Cong., 2d sess., *Congressional Record* 124, pt. 25 (4 October 1978), 33677.

264. Even Somoza acknowledged Carter's role in the escalating revolution during a September 1978 interview. "The human rights policy of the Administration," he said, "has given the opposition in many countries the idea that they can overthrow the government by force." Anastasio Somoza, interview on the MacNeil-Lehrer Report, WETA/PBS Network, 19 September 1978.

265. *Time,* 25 September 1978, 32, quoted in Diederich, 196.

266. Alan Riding, "U.S. Strategy in Nicaragua Keeps the Time Bomb Ticking," *New York Times,* 17 December 1978, sec. 4, 3.

267. Quoted in Diederich, 236.

268. Pastora, interview with Pastor, in Pastor, 72.

269. Carlos Fonseca Amador, "Nicaragua: Zero Hour," *Tricontinental,* no. 14 (1969), reprinted in Borge, 23, 26–28.

270. LeoGrande, "The United States and the Nicaraguan Revolution."

271. Miguel D'Escoto Brockman, interview with Thomas H. Stahel, *America,* no. 16 (1986): 318–23, reprinted in Kimmens, 132.

272. Mark Uhlig, "Opposing Ortega," *New York Times Magazine,* 11 February 1990, 72.

Chapter 5

1. Claude A. Buss, *The United States and the Philippines: Background for Policy* (Washington, D.C.: American Enterprise Institute, 1977), 6–7.

2. This was not American-style politics, but a Philippine hybrid. Candidates competed on the bases of experience and ability rather than party platform; "national elections were won by promises or favors." The executive and legislative branches represented the same upper-and/or middle-class interests. Buss, 23; see also Carl H. Lande, "The Political Crisis," in John Bresnan, ed., *Crisis in the Philippines: The Marcos Era and Beyond*, (Princeton, N.J.: Princeton University Press, 1986), 122–23.

3. Daniel B. Schirmer and Stephen Rosskamm Shalom, eds., *The Philippines Reader: A History of Colonialism, Neocolonialism, Dictatorship and Resistance* (Boston: South End Press, 1987), 87.

4. Buss, 22.

5. "Parity Provisions, Laurel-Langley Agreement," in *Department of State Bulletin*, 19 September 1955, 469–70, reprinted in Schirmer and Shalom, 94–96.

6. "Military Bases: Agreement Between the United States and the Republic of the Philippines, 14 March 1947," in U.S. Congress, Senate, *A Decade of American Foreign Policy: Basic Documents, 1941–1949*, 81st Cong., 1st sess., 1950, Sen. Doc. 123, 869–81, reprinted in Schirmer and Shalom, 96–100.

7. Buss, 127–28; "Military Assistance to the Philippines: Agreement Between the United States and the Republic of the Philippines, 21 March 1947 in U.S. Congress, Senate, *Decade of American Foreign Policy*, 881–85, reprinted in Schirmer and Shalom, 100–103.

8. Buss, 120.

9. U.S. Congress, House Committee on Foreign Affairs, Subcommittee on Asian and Pacific Affairs, *United States Relations and the New Base and Aid Agreement*, 98th Cong., 1st sess., June 1983, 7–12 (Testimony of Admiral L. J. Long, Commander-in-Chief of U.S. Naval Forces in the Pacific), reprinted in Schirmer and Shalom, 243–247; Alva M. Bowen, Jr., "The Philippine-American Defense Partnership," in Carl H. Lande, ed., *Rebuilding a Nation: Philippine Challenges and American Policy* (Washington, D.C.: Washington Institute Press, 1987), 449–89.

10. Robyn Lim, "Foreign Policy," in R. J. May and Francisco Nemenzo, eds., *The Philippines After Marcos*, (New York: St. Martin's Press, 1985), 210–11.

11. Buss, 59.

12. A. James Gregor, "Some Policy Considerations," in A. James Gregor, ed., *The U.S. and the Philippines: A Challenge to a Special Relationship* (Washington, D.C.: The Heritage Foundation, 1983), 67–84; Schirmer and Shalom, eds., 163–64.

13. "General Order No. 1, That President Ferdinand E. Marcos Will Govern the Nation and Direct the Operation of the Entire Government," reprinted in

David A. Rosenberg, ed., *Marcos and Martial Law in the Philippines* (Ithaca, N.Y.: Cornell University Press, 1989), 241–242.

14. Carl H. Lande, "Introduction: Retrospect and Prospect," in Carl H. Lande, ed., *Rebuilding a Nation: Philippine Challenges and American Policy* (Washington, D.C.: Washington Institute Press, 1987), 7–44; William H. Overholt, "Pressures and Policies: Prospects for Cory Aquino's Philippines," in Lande, ed., *Rebuilding a Nation*, 89–110; Buss, 68; "A Statement of the Civil Liberties Union of the Philippines," in David A. Rosenberg, ed., *Marcos and Martial Law in the Philippines* (Ithaca, N.Y.: Cornell University Press, 1989), 291.

15. Richard Pierre Claude, "The Philippines," in Jack Donnelly and Rhoda E. Howard, eds., *International Handbook of Human Rights* (New York: Greenwood Press, 1987), 279–300; Buss, 67; Raymond Bonner, *Waltzing with a Dictator: The Marcoses and the Making of American Foreign Policy* (New York: Times Books, 1987), 302; "Report of the National Committee for the Restoration of Civil Liberties in the Philippines," reprinted in David A. Rosenberg, ed., *Marcos and Martial Law in the Philippines* (Ithaca, N.Y.: Cornell University Press, 1989), 264–70.

16. Lande, "Introduction," 20; Claude, "Philippines," 282; "Proclamation No. 1103, Declaring that the Interim National Assembly Provided for in Article XVII (transitory provisions) of the New Constitution Not to be Convened," reprinted in Rosenberg, *Marcos and Martial Law*, 250–251.

17. David A. Rosenberg, "The Changing Structure of Philippine Government from Marcos to Aquino," in Lande, *Rebuilding a Nation*, 329–350; Raul P. de Guzman, "The Evolution of Filipino Political Institutions: Prospects for Normalization in the Philippines," in A. James Gregor, ed., *The U.S. and the Philippines: A Challenge to a Special Relationship* (Washington, D.C.: The Heritage Foundation, 1983), 17–31; Jose Veloso Abueva, "Ideology and Practice in the 'New Society,' " in Rosenberg, *Marcos and Martial Law*, 36–57.

18. Claude, "Philippines," 282; see also "A Statement of the Civil Liberties Union," "Report of the National Committee for the Restoration of Civil Liberties," "General Order No. 3, on the Continuous Operations of All Government Instrumentalities Under Their Present Officers and Employees; on Limitations on the Jurisdiction of the Judiciary," "General Order No. 8, on the Creation of Military Tribunals," "General Order No., 12, on the Jurisdictions of Civil Courts and Military Tribunals;" Rolando V. Del Carmen, "Constitutionality and Judicial Politics," all reprinted in Rosenberg, *Marcos and Martial Law*, 287–88, 254–55, 242–48, 85–112, respectively.

19. Buss, 74; David A. Rosenberg, "Liberty Versus Loyalty: The Transformation of the Philippine News Media Under Martial Law," in Rosenberg, *Marcos and Martial Law*, 153–76.

20. Buss 67; Amnesty International, *Report of the Amnesty International Mission to the Republic of the Philippines, 1975* (London: Amnesty International Publications, 1976), cited in Claude, "Philippines," 282.

21. Amnesty International, *Report of an Amnesty International Mission to the Republic of the Philippines, 22 November-5 December 1975*, 2d edition, (London: Amnesty International Publications, 1977), 13–19, reprinted in Schirmer and Shalom, 188–91.

22. Amnesty International, *Report of an Amnesty International Mission to the Republic of the Philippines, 11–28 November 1981*, (London: Amnesty International Publications, 1982), 10–14, reprinted in Daniel and Shalom, 221–23.

23. Claude, "Philippines," 283.

24. Veritas, "Call for Repeal of PD 169," *MAG Bulletin* 1, no. 4, 17 March 1985, 13, quoted in Claude, "Philippines," 288.

25. Task Force Detainees-Philippines, *Human Rights Situation and Militarization in the Philippines: Trends and Analysis 1984, Report to the United Nations Commission on Human Rights, 41st Session, 1985* (Manila: Association of Major Religious Superiors, 1985), cited in Claude, "Philippines," 283.

26. Kathy McAfee, "The Philippines: A Harvest of Anger," *Facts for Action*, no. 15 (Boston: An Oxfam America Educational Publication, October 1985), reprinted Schirmer and Shalom, 292–301.

27. *Manila Bulletin Today*, 12 December 1974, quoted in Richard P. Claude, "Human Rights in the Philippines and U.S. Responsibility," in Peter G. Brown and Douglas MacLean, eds., *Human Rights and U.S. Foreign Policy: Principles and Applications* (Lexington, Mass.: D. C. Heath, 1979), 230.

28. A. James Gregor, *Crisis in the Philippines: A Threat to U.S. Interest* (Washington, D.C.: Ethics and Public Policy Center, 1984), 31.

29. "Embattled President Comes Out Fighting," *South*, no. 56 (Wellington, New Zealand), June 1985, 20, quoted in Claude, "Philippines," 290.

30. World Bank, "Philippines-Working Level Draft Country Program Paper" (Washington, D.C.: World Bank, August 29, 1980), 17, quoted in Claude, "Philippines," 286.

31. Florian A. Alburo, Dante B. Canlas, Emmanuel S. De Dios, et al., "Towards Recovery and Sustainable Growth" (Quezon City: University of the Philippines, 1985), 4, quoted in Claude, "Philippines," 290; see also "A Statement of the Civil Liberties Union of the Philippines on the State of the Nation After Three Years of Martial Law, (21 September 1975)," reprinted in Rosenberg, *Marcos and Martial Law*, 286–97.

32. Lande, "Introduction" 11; U.S. Congress, Senate Committee on Foreign Relations, *Korea and the Philippines: November 1972*, Staff Report, Committee Print, 93d Cong., 1st sess. (18 February 1973), 1–2, 31–33, 37, 41, 45–46, reprinted in Schirmer and Shalom, 166–69; Buss, 69; Karin Aguilar-San Juan, "Labor Movement Sparks Philippine Resistance," *Resist Newsletter* (Somerville, Mass.), January 1986, "Statement of the Civil Liberties Union," 292, Benedict J. Kerkvliet, "Land Reform: Emancipation or Counterinsurgency?" all reprinted in Rosenberg, *Marcos and Martial Law*, 113–117, 129–132, 134–140, respectively.

33. World Bank, *World Development Report 1982* (New York: Oxford University Press, 1982), 146; World Bank, *World Development Report 1990* (New York: Oxford University Press, 1990), 148.

34. Senate, *Korea and the Philippines*, reprinted in Schirmer and Shalom, 166–69.

35. Buss, 93; *New York Times*, 28 July 1974, F5; Abueva, 57–68.

36. World Bank, *World Development, 1982*, 158.

37. Buss, 71.

38. Schirmer and Shalom, 176.

39. Gerald Sussman, David O'Connor, and Charles W. Lindsey, "The Philippines, 1984: The Political Economy of a Dying Dictatorship," *Philippine Research Bulletin* (Durham, N.C.: Friends of the Filipino People, Summer 1984), reprinted in Schirmer and Shalom, 284–89.

40. Claude, "Philippines," 286; Hal Hill and Sisira Jayasuriya, "The Economy," in R. J. May and Francisco Nemenzo, eds., *The Philippines After Marcos* (New York: St. Martin's Press, 1985), 132–46; Bernardo Villegas, "The Economic Crisis," in Bresnan, 145–46.

41. "Marcos, Under U.S. Pressure, Heads for Test," *Congressional Quarterly Weekly Report*, (9 November 1985), 2287–91.

42. World Bank, *World Development 1982*, 156.

43. World Bank, *World Development Report 1979* (New York: Oxford University Press, 1979), 154; World Bank, *World Development 1982*, 138.

44. Benigno Aquino, a Philippine opposition leader, was jailed by Marcos from 1972 to 1980. In August 1983, Aquino returned to the Philippines from political exile in the United States and was assassinated at the airport by the Marcos regime.

45. Schirmer and Shalom, 275; Gregor, *Crisis in the Philippines*, 65; Stanley Karnow, *In Our Image: America's Empire in the Philippines* (New York: Random House, 1989), 385, 406.

46. Noel D. De Luna, "Country-Risk Analysis Sees Political Scene Positively," *Business Day* (7 December 1983): 2, quoted in Gregor, *Crisis in the Philippines*, 56.

47. The NPA reported that it had 12,000 guerrillas; the United States estimated NPA strength at 15,000 to 20,000 (Bonner, 359).

48. Bonner, 359, 237; Lande, "Introduction," 18; Buss, 74, 75.

49. Bonner, 78; Lande, "Political Crisis," 126.

50. Philip Shabecoff, "Protest Movement in the Philippines Widening Rapidly," *New York Times*, 12 March 1970, 10, reprinted in Schirmer and Shalom, 157–61.

51. Bonner, 237; Rosenberg, "Liberty versus Loyalty," 156.

52. U.S. Congress, Senate Committee on Foreign Relations, *Situation in the Philippines*, 1984, quoted, Benedict J. Kerkvliet, "Peasants and Agricultural

Workers: Implications for United States Policy," in Carl H. Lande, ed., *Rebuilding a Nation: Philippine Challenges and American Policy* (Washington, D.C.: Washington Institute Press, 1987), 212.

53. "Statement of the Civil Liberties Union," 292–93.

54. Buss, 69; Carl H. Lande, "Philippine Prospects After Martial Law," *Foreign Affairs* 59, no. 5 (Summer 1981): 1147–68. Manglapus would become foreign secretary in the Aquino regime; Salvador Laurel served as her first vice president.

55. Buss, 83.

56. William H. Overholt, "Pressures and Policies: Prospects for Cory Aquino's Philippines," in Lande, *Rebuilding a Nation*, 95; Gregor, *Crisis in the Philippines*, 65.

57. Gregor, *Crisis in the Philippines*, 81; David Wurfel, "The Succession Struggle," in R. J. May and Francisco Nemenzo, eds., *The Philippines After Marcos* (New York: St. Martin's Press, 1985), 28–29; Overholt, 95.

58. Overholt, 97; Lande, "Political Crisis," 137.

59. Lande, "Introduction," 15; Lande, "Political Crisis," 137.

60. Robert L. Youngblood, "Church Opposition to Martial Law in the Philippines," *Asian Survey* 18, no. 5 (May 1978): 505–20, reprinted in Schirmer and Shalom, 211–18; Buss, 73; Robert L. Youngblood, "Church and State in the Philippines: Some Implications for United States Policy," in Carl H. Lande, ed., *Rebuilding a Nation: Philippine Challenges and American Policy* (Washington, D.C.: Washington Institute Press, 1987), 351–68.

Eighty-five percent of the Philippine population professes Catholicism; the church was still able to use its authority, power, and extensive network of pulpits to question Marcos' policies.

61. Overholt, 95; Youngblood, "Church Opposition," 211.

62. Kathy McAfee, "The Philippines: A Harvest of Anger," in *Facts for Action*, no. 15 (Boston: An Oxfam America Educational Publication, October 1985), reprinted in Schirmer and Shalom, 292–301, see also 165; Overholt, 94–95.

63. Youngblood, "Church Opposition"; Youngblood, "Church and State"; Wurfel, 30–32; "Philippine Church-State Relations since Martial Law," in Rosenberg, *Marcos and Martial Law*, 298–302.

64. Catholic Bishops Conference of the Philippines, "Post-Election Statement," 13 February 1986 (n.p: Claretian Publications, 1986), quoted in Youngblood, "Church and State," 351.

65. Bonner, 242.

66. Foreign Broadcast Information Service, IV, 24 April 1981, 5, quoted in Youngblood, "Church and State," 356.

67. *Philippine News*, 28 July–3 August 1982, 1–2, 8, quoted in Youngblood, "Church and State," 356.

68. Jaimie Cardinal Sin, "A Call to Conscience," *Bulletin Today*, 19 January 1986, 10, in Robert L. Youngblood, *Marcos Against the Church: Economic De-*

velopment and Political Repression in the Philippines (Ithaca, N.Y.: Cornell University Press, 1991), 199; see also, Youngblood, "Church and State."

69. Youngblood, "Church and State," 351–52.

70. *Philippine News,* 3–9 April 1985, reprinted in Schirmer and Shalom, 322–26.

71. Stockholm International Peace Research Institute, *World Armaments and Disarmament, SIPRI Yearbook, 1976* (Cambridge, Mass.: M.I.T. Press, 1976), 36, cited in Claude, "Human Rights," 243.

72. Executive Branch Position Paper on HR-7797 (Senate Amendment 74), 18 October 1977, quoted in Claude, "Human Rights," 238.

73. Comptroller General of the United States, "Stopping U.S. Assistance to Foreign Police and Prisons," *Report to the Congress* (Washington, D.C.: General Accounting Office, 1976), 1; Walden Bello and Severina Rivera, eds., *Logistics of Repression* (Washington, D.C.: Friends of the Filipino People, 1977), 30; Center for International Policy, *Human Rights and the U.S. Assistance Program, Fiscal 1978, Part 2-East Asia* (Washington, D.C.: Center for International Policy, 1977), 34, all cited in Claude, "Human Rights," 242; "Report of the National Committee for the Restoration of Civil Liberties," 276–84.

74. Peter Williamson and Paul Katz, Evaluation Team, *Termination Phase-Out Study, Public Safety Project, Philippines* (Washington, D.C.: Office of Public Safety, 1974), 52–55, quoted in Claude, "Human Rights," 236.

75. Bello and Rivera, 30, quoted in Claude, "Human Rights," 235.

76. "Statement of U.S. Church Leaders and the Church Coalition for Human Rights in the Philippines," PHIDOC, *Philippine Information and Documentation* (Washington, D.C.: Church Coalition for Human Rights in the Philippines, 1985), 5, quoted in Claude, "The Philippines," 284; see also Robert B. Stauffer, "The Political Economy of Refeudalization," in Rosenberg, *Marcos and Martial Law,* 192.

77. Bonner, 134; Stauffer, 210–11; "Statement of the Civil Liberties Union," 290; "Statement of the National Committee for the Restoration of Civil Liberties," 271–72.

78. Chamber of Commerce Telegram: Manila 9198, 27 September 1972, in Bonner, 135–36; see also, Stauffer, 195–96.

79. Schirmer and Shalom, 141; "Report of the National Committee for the Restoration of Civil Liberties" 273–74.

80. United Nations Center on Transnational Corporations, Policy Analysis and Research Division, Data Base, n.d., unpublished. Figures for U.S. and total foreign investment given in Philippine pesos: 1974—416.6 million in U.S. investment/919 million total; 1977—706.3 million in U.S. investment/1,317.7 million total; 1980—1,022.7 in U.S. investment/1,938.5 million total; 1984—8,772.5 million in U.S. investment/15,604.9 million total; 1985—1,997.4 million in U.S. investment/2,985.5 million total.

81. Bernard E. Trainor, "As Manila Resists, the U.S. Looks at a Depleted Network of Bases," *New York Times,* 11 September 1988, sec. 4, 3; "Dollars Are Leaving Philippines, Too," *New York Times,* 29 December 1991, A6.

82. Buss, 148, 63.

83. Karnow, *In Our Image*, 377.

84. Quoted in Buss, 53.

85. Philippine Government Press Release, 13 April 1975, quoted in U.S. Congress, House, "Vietnam Contingency Act of 1975," 94th Cong., 1st sess., *Congressional Record* 121, pt. 9 (22 April 1975), 11239.

86. Buss, 87; Bonner, 313; Lim, 208.

87. Buss, 91; Lim, 209; William J. Barnds, "Political and Security Relations," in Bresnan, 234–38.

88. "Military Bases: Agreement Between the United States and the Republic of the Philippines, 14 March 1947," reprinted in Schirmer and Shalom, 96–100.

89. "Military Bases Agreement, March 14, 1947—Amendment, 7 January 1979," and Letter from Jimmy Carter to President Marcos, 4 January 1979, reprinted in Lande, *Rebuilding a Nation*, 474, 479; "Foreign Aid Funding Caught in Budget Crunch," *Congressional Quarterly Weekly Report*, 8 March 1980, 701.

90. "Military Bases Agreement, 14 March 1947—Amendment 1 January 1983," and Letter from President Ronald Reagan to President Marcos, 31 May 1983, in Lande, *Rebuilding a Nation*, 484–86; "Marcos, Under U.S. Pressure," *Congressional Quarterly*, 9 November 1985.

91. Raymond Bonner, *Waltzing with a Dictator: The Marcoses and the Making of American Foreign Policy* (New York: Times Books, 1987), 41–42; James Burkholder Smith, *Portrait of a Cold Warrior* (New York: G. P. Putnam's, 1976), 109–10; 250–55, 279–80, reprinted in Schirmer and Shalom, 149–52.

92. Bonner, 43, 143.

93. Buss, 54, 137, 144.

94. Lande, "Introduction," 38; Lande, "The Political Crisis," 124; Buss, 63.

95. Bonner, 64; U.S. Congress, Senate, "Mr. Cranston Talks," 94th Cong., 1st sess., *Congressional Record* 121, pt. 14 (12 June 1975), 18581–82.

96. "A Statement of the Civil Liberties Union," 296–98.

97. Civil Liberties Union of the Philippines, "Tuloy Ang Ligaya [On with the Circus]," 1 January 1981, reprinted in Schirmer and Shalom, 219–20.

98. Diosdado Macapagal, interview with Raymond Bonner, 22 November 1985, Manila, in Bonner, 244.

99. Bonner, 242, 245.

100. Claro M. Recto, "American Bases and National Freedom and Security," 29 October 1956, in Renato Constantino, ed., *The Recto Reader* (Manila: Recto Memorial Foundation, 1965), 96–97, quoted in Schirmer and Shalom, 153.

101. Quoted in Bonner, 251; see also "Statement of the Civil Liberties Union," 290; "Report of the National Committee for the Restoration of Civil Liberties" 284–85.

102. "The Convenor's Statement," *Philippine News* (San Francisco), 2–8 January 1985, reprinted in Schirmer and Shalom, 306–8.

103. "Declaration of the 1983 International Conference on Peace and the Removal of Foreign Bases," reprinted in Schirmer and Shalom, 301–5.

104. U.S. Congress, House Committee on Foreign Affairs, Subcommittee on Asian and Pacific Affairs, *United States-Philippine Relations and the New Base and Aid Agreement* (excerpt), 98th Cong., 1st sess. (June 1983) 7–12, reprinted in Schirmer and Shalom, 244–247.

105. "Proclamation No. 1081, Proclaiming A State of Martial Law in the Philippines," 24 September, 1972, reprinted in Rosenberg, *Marcos and Martial Law*, 225–41.

106. William C. Hamilton, "United States Policy in the Period Leading to the Declaration of Martial Law and Its Immediate Aftermath," in Lande, *Rebuilding a Nation*, 514.

107. U.S. Congress, Senate Committee on Foreign Relations, Subcommittee on United States Security Agreements and Commitments Abroad, *United States Security Agreements and Commitments Abroad: The Republic of the Philippines* (September-October 1968), 60–61, 67–68, 161–62, 244–45, reprinted in Schirmer and Shalom, 144–48.

108. "The Philippines Tries One-Man Democracy," Intelligence Note, Bureau of Intelligence and Research, 1 November 1972, in Bonner, 130–31.

109. Klitgaard, "Martial Law in the Philippines," Rand Corporation, quoted in Bonner, 118.

110. Senate, *Korea and the Philippines*, 1–2, 4, 31–33, 37, 41, 45–46 reprinted in Schirmer and Shalom, 166–69.

111. Quoted in Bonner, 234.

112. James Nach, "Communist Movements in the Philippines: Background, Present Status, and Outlook," Cable, Manila 15403, 9 June 1984, quoted in Bonner, 356.

113. U.S. Congress, Senate Select Committee on Intelligence, *The Philippines: A Situation Report*, Staff Report, Committee Print (1 November 1985), 1, 4, 5, 7, 8 reprinted in Schirmer and Shalom, 315–16.

114. U.S. Embassy Report, Manila 9795, 7 July 1969, quoted in Bonner, 65.

115. *U.S. Department of State Bulletin*, 25 August 1969, 141–46, quoted in Buss, 103.

116. Hamilton, 514.

117. Buss, 197.

118. Bonner, 194, 116; Lee T. Stull, "Moments of Truth in Philippine-American Relations: The Carter Years," in Lande, *Rebuilding a Nation*, 522.

119. U.S. Department of State, Cable 14,186, 18 June 1977, quoted in Bonner, 196.

120. U.S. Department of State, Cable 42,011, 17 February 1978, quoted in Bonner, 232, 233.

121. Bonner, 230, 241, 242, 244, 240; Stull, 522.

122. Bonner, 287.

123. Bonner, 200.

124. Lewis M. Simons, "U.S. to Skirt Rights Issue Aid to Friends," *Washington Post*, 11 September 1977, A23, quoted in Claude, "Human Rights," 233.

125. Bonner, 298, 299; Karnow, *In Our Image*, 401; see table 5-2.

126. "Bush Pledges U.S. Support for the Philippines," *New York Times*, 1 July 1981, A13.

127. Bonner, 345.

128. Freedom of Information Act release, quoted in Bonner, 351, 352; see also Wurfel, 35–36. Opposition leader and former Senator Jose Diokno, however, perceived the cancellation as an indication of Marcos's waning support in Washington. See Jose W. Diokno, "The Present Crisis," in May and Nemenzo, 2.

129. "Criticism of Marcos is Unfair, Bush Says," *Chicago Tribune*, 7 October 1983, quoted in Bonner, 353.

130. U.S. National Security Council Study Directive, 1984, in *Philippine News*, 3–9 April 1985, reprinted in Schirmer and Shalom, 322–27.

131. Bonner, 363; John F. Maisto, "United States-Philippine Relations in the 1980s," in Lande, *Rebuilding a Nation*, 533.

132. Bonner, 357; Stanley Karnow, "Reagan and the Philippines: Setting Marcos Adrift," *New York Times Magazine*, 19 March 1989.

133. Paul Wolfowitz, "Challenges in the Pacific," Honolulu Symposium, National Defense University, 22 February 1985, quoted in Bonner, 367.

134. House Subcommittee on Asian and Pacific Affairs, 12 March 1985, quoted in Bonner, 367.

135. "Marcos, Under U.S. Pressure," *Congressional Quarterly*, 9 November 1985.

136. Overholt, 102.

137. U.S. Congress, House Concurrent Resolution 773; Senate Concurrent Resolution 157 and 190, 94th Cong., 2d sess., *Congressional Record* 122, pt. 28 (September 1976), 1469, 1254, 1255; see also U.S. Congress, House, "Legislation Objecting to Proposed Arms Sales to Government of the Philippines," 94th Cong., 2d sess., *Congressional Record* 122, pt. 125, 32751–52.

138. U.S. Congress, Senate, "Recent Human Rights Legislation and Its Implementation, "95th Cong., 1st sess., *Congressional Record* 123, pt. 30 (7 December 1977), 38673.

139. U.S. Congress, House Committee on Foreign Affairs, Subcommittee on International Organizations, *Human Rights and U.S. Foreign Policy*, 96th Cong., 1st sess., 2 May, 10 May, 21 June, 12 July, 2 August 1979, 323.

140. "House Batters Carter's Foreign Aid Program," *Congressional Quarterly Weekly Report*, 25 June 1977, 1283.

141. U.S. Congress, Senate, "Recent Human Rights Legislation," 38673.

142. "Philippine Resolution," *Congressional Quarterly Weekly Report*, 8 October 1983, 2110.

143. "Marcos, Under U.S. Pressure," *Congressional Quarterly*, 9 November 1985; "Budget Cuts Leave Mark on Foreign Arms Aid," *Congressional Quarterly Weekly Report*, 21 December 1985, 2689.

144. "Marcos, Under U.S. Pressure," *Congressional Quarterly*, 9 November 1985.

145. "S960 Foreign Assistance Authorization, Fiscal 1986," *Congressional Quarterly Weekly Report*, 18 May 1985, 953.

146. "Conferees Loosen Strings, Agree on Foreign Aid," *Congressional Quarterly Weekly Report*, 27 June 1985, 1475–1477.

147. Quoted in Bonner, 381.

148. *Christian Science Monitor*, 18 February 1986, quoted in Schirmer and Shalom, 277.

149. Overholt, 102; Schirmer and Shalom, 278.

150. Quoted in Rosenberg, "The Changing Structure of Philippine Government," in Lande, *Rebuilding a Nation*, 344.

151. Karnow, "Reagan and the Philippines," 50; Overholt, 101.

152. Claude, "Philippines," 292.

153. Bernard Gwertzman, "U.S. Tries to Limit Manila Confusion on Reagan Stance," *New York Times*, 13 February 1986, A1.

154. Bernard Weinraub, "President to Send American Envoy to Seek Views of Filipinos,' *New York Times*, 12 February 1986, sec. 1, 1.

155. Leslie Gelb, "President Faults Marcos for Fraud But Announces No U.S. Response," *New York Times*, 16 February 1986, A1.

156. Bernard Gwertzman, "White House Signals Its Support for Two Military Men in Philippines," *New York Times*, 23 February 1986.

157. Lande "Introduction" 42; Karnow, "Reagan and the Philippines," 58.

158. "Part of White House Statement," *New York Times*, 24 February 1986, sec. 1, 5.

159. Quoted in Karnow, "Reagan and the Philippines," 59.

160. "White House Statement," *New York Times*, 24 February 1986, sec. 1, 14.

161. Seth Mydans, "Aquino Says She's Alarmed by the Reagan Comments," *New York Times*, 13 February 1986, sec. 1, 12.

162. Karnow, "Reagan and the Philippines," 59; Lande, "Introduction," 42.

163. Bonner, 344, 352–53.

164. "Transcript of Interview with President on a Range of Issues," *New York Times*, 12 February 1985, A10.

165. *Far Eastern Economic Review*, 6 March 1986, quoted in Schirmer and Shalom, 336.

166. Bonner, 368; Karnow, *In Our Image*, 413.

167. Bernard Gwertzman, "Two Key Senators Fault President on Philippines," *New York Times*, 13 February 1986, A10.

168. Karnow, "Reagan and the Philippines," 54.

169. Bonner, 425.

170. Quoted in Guy J. Pauker, "President Corazon Aquino: A Political and Personal Assessment," in Lande, *Rebuilding a Nation*, 309.

171. Pauker, 309.

172. Emmanuel M. Pelaez, "The Philippines and the United States," in Lande, 53.

173. Pelaez, 53.

174. Pauker, 311.

175. Pelaez, 52.

176. Ronald Reagan, interview with Morton Kondracke, *New Republic*, quoted in Bonner, 360.

177. Karnow, "Reagan and the Philippines," 59.

178. Karnow, "Reagan and the Philippines," 58.

179. Bonner, 441.

180. " 'Disappearances' of Filipinos Goes On Even Under Aquino," *New York Times*, 14 November 1988, A11.

181. Pelaez, 53, 54.

182. Raul Manglapus, quoted in Eduardo Lachica, "Debt Issue Snags Talks on the Bases by U.S., Manila," *Wall Street Journal*, 13 October 1988, A19.

183. "Interim Philippines Accord," *National Journal*, 22 October 1988, 2688.

184. Quoted in Seth Mydans, "Philippine Critics Assail U.S. Accord," *New York Times*, 19 October 1988, A5.

185. Philip Shenon, "Philippines Moving to Bar U.S. Bases," *New York Times*, 12 September 1991, A9; "Aquino Extending U.S. Stay at Bases," *New York Times*, 16 September 1991, A1; Sheila Teffet, "Vote in Senate on U.S. Bases Irks Filipino Military," *Christian Science Monitor*, 25 September 1991, 4; Eric Schmitt, "U.S. Studying Philippines' Base Plan," *New York Times*, 4 October 1991, A9; "Dollars Are Leaving Philippines, Too," *New York Times*, 29 December 1991, A6; Eric Schmitt, "U.S. Exit from Manila: Making of a Hasty Retreat," *New York Times*, 5 January 1992, sec. 1, 12.

186. Sheila Coronel, "With Hope and Tears, U.S. Closes Philippine Base," *New York Times*, 25 November 1992, sec. 1, 3.

187. Philip Shenon, "U.S. and Philippines Agree to Continued Military Cooperation," *New York Times*, 7 November 1992, sec. 1, 2.

188. "Marcos, Under Pressure," *Congressional Quarterly*, 9 November 1985.

189. Larry A. Niksch, "Philippines: U.S. Foreign Assistance Facts," CRS Issue Briefs (Washington, D.C.: Congressional Research Service, Updated 25 September 1990), 5.

190. Diosado Macapagal, quoted in, U.S. Congress, *Human Rights and U.S. Foreign Policy*, 286.

191. Diosado Macapagal, interview with Raymond Bonner, Manila, 22 November 1985, in Bonner, 244.

192. "Panel Plans to Alter Formula for Philippine Aid," *Congressional Quarterly Weekly Report*, 25 February 1984, 448.

193. Seth Mydans, "Aquino Says She's Alarmed by the Reagan Comments," *New York Times*, 13 February 1986, A12.

194. Wigberto Tanada, quoted in Mydans.

195. U.S. Congress, House Committee on Foreign Affairs, Subcommittee on Human Rights and International Organizations, *U.S. Human Rights Policy*, 99th Cong., 2d sess., 19 and 26 February 1986, 21.

196. Claude, "Human Rights," 247.

197. Maria Karagianis, "Marcos Foe Endures; He Says 'Carter Gave Us New Hope,' " *Boston Globe*, 28 December 1980, quoted in Bonner, 288.

198. Philip Shenon, "Philippines Moving to Bar U.S. Bases," *New York Times*, 12 September 1991, A9.

Chapter 6

1. U.S. Congress, House Committee on International Relations, Subcommittee on International Organizations, *Human Rights and U.S. Foreign Policy*, 96th Cong., 1st sess., 2 May 1979, 44.

2. U.S. Agency for International Development, Bureau for Program and Policy Coordination, Office of Planning and Budget, *U.S. Overseas Loans and Grants and Assistance from International Organizations*, 1970 Report.

3. Review of *Congressional Record* 1971–1979; Congress, House, "Other Voices [Representative Fortney H. Stark]," 94th Cong., 1st sess., *Congressional Record* 121, pt. 4, (14 March 1975), 5183.

4. U.S. Congress, House Committee on International Relations, Subcommittee on International Organizations, *Human Rights in Iran*, 94th Cong., 2d sess., 3 August and 8 September 1976; U.S. Congress, House Committee on International Relations, Subcommittee on International Organizations, *Human Rights in Iran*, 95th Cong., 1st sess., 26 October 1977.

5. *Congressional Quarterly Weekly Report*, 16 October 1976, 3023.

6. "The Carter Administration and Latin America, Africa and Asia: State Department Reports," in Judith F. Buncher, ed., *Human Rights and American Diplomacy: 1975–1977* (New York: Facts on File, 1977), 176; "Congress Must Decide on Aid to Nations: Iran Charged with Human Rights Abuses," *Congressional Quarterly Weekly Report*, 15 January 1977, 80; U.S. Congress, Senate Subcommittee on Foreign Assistance, Staff Report, "Recent Human Rights Legislation and its Implementation," 95th Cong., 1st sess., *Congressional Record* 123, pt. 30 (7 December 1977), 38673.

7. The author has reviewed all volumes of the *Congressional Record* from 1971 to 1979.

8. Richard W. Cottam, "American Arms Sales and Human Rights: The Case of Iran," in Peter G. Brown and Douglas MacLean, eds., *Human Rights and U.S. Foreign Policy: Principles and Applications* (Lexington, Mass.: D. C. Heath, 1979), 281–301.

9. U.S. Congress, "Recent Human Rights Legislation," 38672.

10. Somoza also increased purchases of arms from other sources, including Israel, France, and Spain.

11. U.S. Congress, Senate, Statement by Senator Kennedy, 95th Cong., 2d sess., *Congressional Record* 124, pt. 25, (5 October 1978), 33984.

12. U.S. House, Senate, "U.S. Policy Toward Nicaragua," Letter to Senator Kennedy from Douglas J. Bennet Jr., Assistant Secretary for Congressional Relations, 22 September 1978, 95th Cong., 2d sess., *Congressional Record* 124, pt. 25 (5 October 1978), 33984–85.

13. At a June 1991 OAS meeting, diplomats noted that "the final blow that persuaded Anastasio Somoza Debayle that he had to give up power in Nicaragua was a vote of condemnation by the OAS," as quoted in Nathaniel C. Nash, "Latin Nations Get a Firmer Grip on Their Destiny," *New York Times*, 9 June 1991, sec. 4, 2.

14. For more recent examples, see Elaine Sciolino, "Slanting of Intelligence Emerges as Major Issue for CIA Nominee," *New York Times*, 19 September 1991, A11; Patrick E. Tyler, "CIA Analysts Said Iran Assessments Were Warped to Back Arms Sales," *New York Times*, 2 October 1991, A19; Michael Wines, "Battle Over World View," *New York Times*, 3 October 1991, A1; Elaine Sciolino, "Director Admits C.I.A. Fell Short in Predicting the Soviet Collapse," *New York Times*, 2 May 1992, A6.

15. Quoted in Henry A. Byroade, Assistant Secretary for Near Eastern, South Asian and African Affairs, "The Present Situation: A Statement Made Before the Middle East Conference," 12 December 1953, Washington, D.C., reprinted in Yonah Alexander and Allan Nanes, eds., *The United States and Iran* (Frederick, Md.: University Publications of America, 1980), 262.

16. Thomas L. Friedman, "Us vs. Them Is No Longer Enough," *New York Times*, 22 July 1990, sec. 4, 2.

17. Jimmy Carter, *Keeping Faith: Memoirs of a President* (New York: Bantam Books, 1982), 151.

18. As is indicated in Chapter 2, a moderate opposition is defined as a group that professes a pro-Western orientation and an adherence to representative government.

19. Shultz, "Human Rights and the Moral Dimension," 15; see too, Carl Gershman, "The United States and the World Democratic Revolution," *Washington Quarterly* 12, no. 1 (Winter 1989), 131.

20. Miroslav Nincic, *United States Foreign Policy: Choices and Tradeoffs* (Washington, D.C.: Congressional Quarterly Press, 1988), 19.

21. Nincic, 386.

22. George P. Shultz, "Human Rights and the Moral Dimension of U.S. Foreign Policy," *Department of State Bulletin* 84, no. 2085 (April 1984), 18.

23. *The Report of the President's National Bipartisan Commission on Central America* (New York: Macmillan, [1974]), 64.

24. The German Social Democratic Party and Christian Democratic Party have extensively and successfully pursued such activities in the developing world through the Friedrich-Ebert Stiftung and Konrad Adenauer Foundation, respectively.

25. For a discussion of strategies the United States might use in promoting democratization abroad see Larry Diamond, "Beyond Authoritarianism and Totalitarianism: Strategies for Democratization," *Washington Quarterly* 12, no. 1 (Winter 1989), 131.

26. *Report of the President's National Bipartisan Commission on Central America,* 5, 16; see also, Gershman, 132–33.

27. Marcos commented on the division between the Congress and the executive branch in the making of U.S. foreign policy in August 1985 (see Chapter 5). In the fall of 1978, Somoza told a U.S. emissary,

> My record with the United States politicians has been so good that when they tried to halt the military aid to Nicaragua, the Congress, voted to keep me in the aid bill. Finally they were withholding all of these credits in the IDB and the World Bank and AID and I talked to my friends in the Congress. Then they went to see Mr. Christopher, and they told Mr. Christopher that the treatment of Nicaragua on the basis of human rights was not just. . . .
>
> Even Jim Wright from Texas had to intervene and notify Christopher that if he didn't allocate the money he was going to lobby to wreck the foreign aid bill.

Quoted in Anastasio Somoza, *Nicaragua Betrayed* (Boston: Western Islands Publishers, 1980), 321.

28. Mariam Houk, "In Cambodia, U.N. Begins Its Most Ambitious Peacekeeping Role Ever," *Christian Science Monitor,* 18 October 1991; Alan Riding, "Cambodia Treaty to Be Signed Soon," *New York Times,* 20 October 1991, A1.

29. United Nations Development Programme, *Human Development Report 1991* (New York: Oxford University Press, 1991).

30. Paul Lewis, "U.N. Stops Short of Haiti Resolution," *New York Times,* 4 October 1991, A8.

31. Paul Lewis, "U.N. Index on Freedom Enrages Third World," *New York Times,* 23 June 1991, A11.

32. Paul Lewis, "Faction in U.N. Panel Blocks a Rights Group," *New York Times,* 3 February 1991, A11.

33. Quoted in Anthony J. Blinken, "Jacques of All Trades," *New York Times Magazine,* 13 October 1991, 37.

34. Steven Greenhouse, "Aid Donors Insist on Kenya Reforms," *New York Times,* 17 November 1991, A1.

35. Jane Perlez, "Kenya Leader Explains Reversal to Party," *New York Times,* 4 December 1991, A17.

36. Alan Riding, "Responding to Rights Issue, West Suspends Aid to Malawi," *New York Times,* 14 May 1992, A15; see also the World Bank, *Governance and Development* (Washington, D.C.: The International Bank for Reconstruction and Development, 1992).

37. Dankart A. Rustow, "Democracy: A Global Revolution," in *Foreign Affairs* 69, no. 4 (Fall 1990), 75–91; Gladys Ganley, "Power to the People via Personal Electronic Media," in *Washington Quarterly* 14, no. 2 (Spring 1991), 5–22; Brad Roberts, "Democracy and World Order," *Fletcher Forum of World Affairs,* vol. 15, no. 2 (Summer 1991), 9–25; Gershman; Richard P. Claude and Burns H. Weston, eds., *Human Rights in the World Community: Issues and Action* (Philadelphia: University of Pennsylvania Press, 1989), pp. 11–12; Youssef Ibrahim, "TV Is Beamed at the Arabs: The Arabs Beam Back," *New York Times,* 4 March 1992, A4; Chris Hedges, "Turkey is to Broadcast to 6 Ex-Soviet Lands," *New York Times,* 12 April 1992, sec. 1, 12; Philip Shenon, "Mobile Phones Primed, Affluent Thais Join Fray," *New York Times,* 20 May 1992, A10.

38. Graham Allison, *Essence of Decision: Explaining the Cuban Crisis* (Glenview, Ill.: Scott, Foresman and Company, 1971); Henry A. Kissinger, "Domestic Structure and Foreign Policy," in Henry A. Kissinger, *American Foreign Policy,* expanded ed. (New York: Norton, 1974), 11–50.; Morton H. Halperin, *Bureaucratic Politics and Foreign Policy (Washington, D.C.: The Brookings Institution, 1974).*

39. Robert Jervis, *Perception and Misperception in International Relations* (Princeton, N.J.: Princeton University Press, 1976); Ole R. Holsti, "The Belief System and National Images: A Case Study," in James N. Rosenau, ed., *International Politics and Foreign Policy: A Reader in Research and Theory,* revised (New York: Free Press, 1969), 543–550; Richard C. Snyder, H.W. Bruck and Burtin Sapin, "The Decision-Making Approach to the Study of International Politics," in Rosenau, 199–206; Marving Zonis, *Majestic Failure: The Fall of the Shah* (Chicago: University of Chicago Press, 1991), 166–167, 233.

40. Richard W. Cottam, *Iran and the United States: A Cold War Case Study* (Pittsburgh, Pa.: University of Pittsburgh Press, 1988); Zbigniew Brzezinski, *Power and Principle: Memoirs of the National Security Adviser, 1977–1981* (New York: Farrar, Straus, Giroux, 1983), 361.

41. Steven J. Brams, *Rational Politics: Decisions, Games and Strategy* (Washington, D.C.: Congressional Quarterly, 1985); Thomas C. Schelling, *The Strategy of Conflict,* (New York: Oxford University Press, 1963); Allison.

42. Shultz, "Human Rights and the Moral Dimension," 15–17.

43. Nincic, 23.

44. Quoted in Walter Laqueur, "The Issue of Human Rights," *Commentary* 63, no. 5 (May 1977), 33.

45. Zeev Maoz and Nasrin Abdolali, "Regime Types and International Conflict, 1816–1976," *Journal of Conflict Resolution* 33, no. 1 (March 1989), 3–35; see also Michael Doyle, "An International Community," in Graham Allison and Gregory F. Treverton, eds., *Rethinking America's Security: Beyond the Cold War to New World Order* (New York: Norton, 1992), 307–36.

46. U.S. Congress, 11.

47. Shultz, Human Rights and the Moral Dimension, 17.

48. *Report of the President's National Bipartisan Commission on Central America*, 44–45.

49. *Report of the President's National Bipartisan Commission on Central America*, 14, 15–16.

50. Jane Perlez, "Somalia Self-Destructs and the World Looks On," *New York Times*, 29 December 1991, sec. 4, 4.

51. Charles Krauthammer, "Universal Dominion: Toward a Unipolar World," *The National Interest*, no. 18 (Winter 1989), 46–49; Richard Feinberg and Peter Hakim, "Isolationists Talk Is Dangerous," *Christian Science Monitor*, 27 November 1991, 18; George Melloan, " 'Bring the Boys Home' At What Price?" *Wall Street Journal*, 29 September 1991, A15; Philip Shenon, "There's a New World Order in Asia; The U.S. Will Have to Catch Up," *New York Times*, 10 November 1991, sec. 4, 1; Ted Galen Carpenter, "The New World Disorder," *Foreign Policy*, no. 84 (Fall 1991), 24–39; Charles Krauthammer, "The Unipolar Moment," *Foreign Affairs (America and the World 1990–1991)* 70, no. 4 (Fall 1991), 1–20; William G. Hyland, "The Case for Pragmatism," *Foreign Affairs (America and the World 1991–1992)* 71, no. 1 (1992), 38–52.

52. Alan Tonelson, "A Manifesto for Democrats," *The National Interest*, no. 16 (Summer 1989), 36–48.

53. Carpenter; Pat J. Buchanan, "America First—and Second and Third," *The National Interest*, no. 19 (Spring 1990), 77–82; Jeane J. Kirkpatrick, "A Normal Country in a Normal Time," *The National Interest*, no. 21 (Fall 1990), 40–44; David C. Hendrickson, "The End of American History: American Security, the National Purpose and the New World Order," in Allison and Treverton, 386–406.

54. Nathan Tarcov, "If This Long War Is Over," *The National Interest*, no. 18 (Winter 1989), pp. 50–53; Thomas L. Friedman, "Baker Spells Out U.S. Approach: Alliances and 'Democratic Peace,' " *New York Times*, 22 April 1992, A6.

55. Burton Yale Pines, "A Primer for Conservatives," *The National Interest*, no. 23 (Spring 1991), 61–68; Irving Kristol, "Defining Our National Interest," *The National Interest*, no. 21 (Fall 1990), 16–25; Hyland, "The Case for Pragmatism"; James Schlesinger, "New Instabilities, New Priorities," *Foreign Policy*, no. 85 (Winter 1991–92), 3–24; Brzezinski, "Selective Global Commitment."

56. Buchanan.

57. Pines; Kristol.

58. Kirkpatrick, "A Normal Country."

SELECTED BIBLIOGRAPHY

Books, Articles, Reports, Pamphlets

Abueva, Jose Veloso. "Ideology and Practice in the 'New Society.' " In *Marcos and Martial Law in the Philippines*, ed. David A. Rosenberg, 36–57. Ithaca, N.Y.: Cornell University Press, 1989.

Alexander, Yonah, and Allan Nanes, ed. *The United States and Iran: A Documentary History*. Frederick, Md.: University Publications of America, prepared in association with World Power Studies Program, Center for Strategic and International Studies, Georgetown University, 1980.

Allison, Graham. *Essence of Decision: Explaining the Cuban Missile Crisis*. Glenview, Ill.: Scott, Foresman and Company, 1971.

American Association for the International Commission of Jurists. *Human Rights and U.S. Foreign Policy: The First Decade 1973–1983*. New York: American Association for the International Commission of Jurists, 1984.

Amnesty International. *The Republic of Nicaragua: An Amnesty International Report Including the Findings of a Mission to Nicaragua 10–15 May 1976*. London: Amnesty International Publications, 1977.

Annals of the American Academy of Political and Social Science 4, no. 3 (September 1977): 60–63.

Bain, David Howard. "The Man Who Made the Yanquis Go Home." *American Heritage* 36, no. 5 (August–September 1985): 50–61. In *Nicaragua and the United States, The Reference Shelf* 59, no. 2, ed. Andrew C. Kimmens, 16–35. New York: The H. W. Wilson Company, 1987.

Bakhtiar, Shapur. "The Americans Played a Disgusting Role." *MERIP Reports*, no. 104 (March–April 1982):11.

Baldwin, David A., ed. *Economic Statecraft*. Princeton, N.J.: Princeton University Press, 1985.

Barnds, William J. "Political and Security Relations." In *Crisis in the Philippines: The Marcos Era and Beyond,* ed. John Bresnan, 228–258. Princeton, N.J.: Princeton University Press, 1986.

Bashiriyeh, Hossein. *The State and Revolution in Iran, 1962–1982.* London: Croom Helm, 1984.

Bello, Walden, and Severina Rivera. "The Logistics of Repression." In *The Philippine Reader: A History of Colonialism, Dictatorship and Resistance,* ed. Daniel B. Schirmer and Stephen Rosskamm Shalom, 249–253. Boston: South End Press, 1987.

Bendana, Alejandro. "The Foreign Policy of the Nicaraguan Revolution." In *Nicaragua in Revolution,* ed. Thomas W. Walker, 319–328. New York: Praeger Publishers, 1982.

Bermann, Karl. *Under the Big Stick: Nicaragua and the United States Since 1848.* Boston: South End Press, 1986.

Bill, James A. *The Eagle and the Lion: The Tragedy of American-Iranian Relations.* New Haven, Conn: Yale University Press, 1988.

Binnendijk, Hans, ed. *Authoritarian Regimes in Transition.* Washington, D.C.: Department of State, Foreign Service Institute/Center for the Study of Foreign Affairs, June 1987.

Black, George. *Triumph of the People: The Sandinista Revolution in Nicaragua.* London: Zed Press, 1981.

Blinken, Anthony J. "Jacques of All Trades." *New York Times Magazine,* 13 October 1991.

Bonner, Raymond. *Waltzing with a Dictator: The Marcoses and the Making of American Foreign Policy.* New York: Times Books, 1987.

Booth, John A. *The End and the Beginning: The Nicaraguan Revolution.* Boulder, Colo.: Westview Press, 1982.

Borge, Tomas. "Presentation Made to the Inter-American Human Rights Commission," 10 October 1980. In *Sandinistas Speak,* ed. Tomas Borge, Carlos Fonseca, Daniel Ortega, Humberto Ortega, and Jaime Wheelock, 85–104. New York: Pathfinder Press, 1982.

Bowen, Alva M., Jr. "The Philippine-American Defense Partnership." In *Rebuilding a Nation: Philippine Challenges and American Policy,* ed. Carl H. Lande, 449–489. Washington, D.C.: Washington Institute Press, 1987.

Brams, Steven J. *Rational Politics: Decisions, Games and Strategy.* Washington, D.C.: Congressional Quarterly Press, 1985.

Brzezinski, Zbigniew. *Power and Principle: Memoirs of the National Security Adviser 1977–1981.* New York: Farrar, Straus, Giroux, 1983.

————. "Selective Global Commitment." *Foreign Affairs* 70, no. 4 (Fall 1991): 1–20.

Buchanan, Pat J. "America First—and Second and Third." *The National Interest*, no. 19 (Spring 1990): 77–82.

Buncher, Judith F., ed. *Human Rights and American Diplomacy: 1975–1977*. New York: Facts on File, Inc., 1977.

Bundy, William P. "Dictatorships and American Foreign Policy." *Foreign Affairs* 54, no. 1 (October 1975): 51–60.

————. "Who Lost Patagonia? Foreign Policy in the 1980 Campaign" *Foreign Policy* 50, no. 1 (Fall 1979): 1–27.

Burns, E. Bradford. *At War in Nicaragua: The Reagan Doctrine and the Politics of Nostalgia*. New York: Harper and Row Publishers, 1987.

Buss, Claude A. *The United States and the Philippines: Background for Policy*. Washington, D.C.: American Enterprise Institute for Public Policy Research, 1977.

Carr, E. H. *The Twenty-Years Crisis, 1919–1939*. New York: Harper and Row Publishers, 1964.

Carpenter, Ted Gale. "The New World Disorder." *Foreign Policy* 70, no. 84 (Fall 1991): 24–39.

Carter, Jimmy. "Power and Humane Purpose." Address given by the President at University of Notre Dame, 22 May 1977. In *Mortality and Foreign Policy: A Symposium on President Carter's Stance*, ed. Ernest Lefever, 3–10. Washington, D.C.: Ethics and Public Policy Center of Georgetown University, 1977.

————. *Keeping Faith: Memoirs of a President*. New York: Bantam Books, 1982.

Chavarria, Ricardo E. "The Nicaraguan Insurrection: An Appraisal of Its Originality." In *Nicaragua in Revolution*, ed. Thomas W. Walker, 25–40. New York: Praeger Publishers, 1982.

Christian, Shirley. *Nicaragua: Revolution in the Family*. New York: Random House, 1985.

Claude, Richard Pierre. "Human Rights in the Philippines and U.S. Responsibility." In *Human Rights and U.S. Foreign Policy: Principles and Applications*, ed. Peter G. Brown and Douglas MacLean, 229–253. Lexington, Mass.: D. C. Heath and Company, 1979.

————. "The Philippines." In *International Handbook of Human Rights*, ed. Jack Donnelly and Rhoda E. Howard, 279–300. Westport, Conn.: Greenwood Press, 1987.

————. and Burns H. Weston, ed. *Human Rights in the World Community: Issues and Action.* Philadelphia: University of Pennsylvania Press, 1989.

Cochrane, James D. "U.S. Policy Toward Recognition of Governments and Promotion of Democracy in Latin America Since 1963." *Journal of Latin American Studies* 4, no. 2 (1972): 275–291.

Cohen, Stephen B. "Conditioning U.S. Security Assistance on Human Rights Practices." *American Journal of International Law* 76 (1982): 246–279.

Cottam, Richard W. "American Arms Sales and Human Rights: The Case of Iran." In *Human Rights and United States Foreign Policy: Principles and Applications,* ed. Peter G. Brown and Douglas MacLean, 281–301. Lexington, Mass.: D. C. Heath and Company, 1979.

————. "Goodbye to America's Shah." *Foreign Policy,* no. 34 (Spring 1979): 3–14.

————. *Nationalism in Iran,* updated. Pittsburgh: University of Pittsburgh Press, 1979.

————. "American Policy and the Iranian Crisis." *Iranian Studies* 12, nos. 1–4 (1980): 279–305.

————. *Iran and the United States: A Cold War Case Study.* Pittsburgh, Pa.: University of Pittsburgh Press, 1988.

Crabb, Cecil V., Jr., *Policy-Makers and Critics: Conflicting Theories of American Foreign Policy.* New York: Praeger Publishers, 1976.

Crowe, William J., Jr., and Alan D. Romberg. "Rethinking Security in the Pacific." *Foreign Affairs* 70, no. 2 (Spring 1991): 123–140.

Cruz, Arturo Sequeira. "The Origins of Sandinista Foreign Policy." In *Central America: Anatomy of Conflict,* ed. Robert S. Leiken, 95–109. New York: Pergamon Press, in cooperation with Carnegie Endowment for International Peace, 1984.

Daftari, Hedayat Matin. "Mossadeq's Legacy Today." Interview in *MERIP Reports,* no. 113 (March–April 1983): 24.

de Guzman, Raul P. "The Evolution of Filipino Political Institutions: Prospects for Normalization in the Philippines." In *The U.S. and the Philippines: A Challenge to a Special Relationship,* ed. A. James Gregor, 17–31. Washington, D.C.: The Heritage Foundation, 1983.

Del Carmen, Rolando V. "Constitutionality and Judicial Politics." In *Marcos and Martial Law in the Philippines,* ed. David A. Rosenberg, 85–112. Ithaca, N.Y.: Cornell University Press, 1989.

D'Escoto, Miguel Brockman. Interview with Thomas H. Stahel. *America,* no 16 (1986): 318–323. In *Nicaragua and the United States, The Ref-*

erence Shelf 59, no. 2, ed. Andrew C. Kimmens, 132–143. New York: The H. W. Wilson Company, 1987.

de Villiers, Gerard. *The Imperial Shah: An Informal Biography.* Boston: Little, Brown and Company, 1976.

Diamond, Larry. "Beyond Authoritarianism and Totalitarianism: Strategies for Democratization." *Washington Quarterly* 12, no. 1 (Winter 1989): 127–139.

———, Juan Linz, and Seymour Martin Lipset. *Democracy in Developing Countries: Asia* 3. Boulder, Colo.: Lynne Reinner Publishers, 1989.

Dickey, Christopher. "Nicaraguan Aid to Rebels Called 'Peanuts.' " In *The Nicaraguan Reader: Documents of a Revolution Under Fire,* ed. Peter Rosset and John Vandermeer, 40–43. New York: Grove Press, Inc. 1983.

Diederich, Bernard. *Somoza and the Legacy of U.S. Involvement in Central America.* New York: E. P. Dutton, 1981.

Diokno, Jose W. "The Present Crisis." In *The Philippines After Marcos,* ed. R. J. May and Francisco Nemenzo, 1–6. New York: St. Martin's Press, 1985.

Dodson, Michael, and T. S. Montgomery. "The Churches in the Nicaraguan Revolution." In *Nicaragua in Revolution,* ed. Thomas W. Walker, 161–180. New York: Praeger Publishers, 1982.

Doyle, Michael W. "An International Liberal Community." In *Rethinking America's Security: Beyond the Cold War to New World Order,* ed. Graham Allison and Gregory F. Treverton, 307–336. New York: W. W. Norton and Company, 1992.

Emerson, Rupert. "The Fate of Human Rights in the Third World." *World Politics* 26 (January 1975): 201–226.

Fagen, Richard R. "The Carter Administration and Latin America: Business as Usual?" *Foreign Affairs (America and the World 1978)* 57, no. 3 (1979): 652–669.

———. "Dateline Nicaragua: The End of the Affair." *Foreign Policy,* no. 36 (Fall 1979):178–191.

Falk, Richard A. "Khomeini's Promise." *Foreign Policy,* no. 34 (Spring 1979): 28–34.

———. *Human Rights and State Society.* New York: Holmes and Meier Publishers, 1981.

Farer, Tom J. "United States Foreign Policy and the Protection of Human Rights: Observations and Proposals." *Virginia Journal of International Law* 14 (Summer 1974): 623–651.

―――. "On a Collision Course: The American Campaign for Human Rights and the Anti-Radical Bias in the Third World." In *Human Rights and American Foreign Policy,* ed. D. Kommers and G. Loescher, 263–270. Notre Dame, Ind.: University of Notre Dame Press, 1979.

―――. "Manage the Revolution." *Foreign Policy,* no. 52 (Fall 1983): 96–117.

Feinberg, Richard E. "Central America: No Easy Answers." *Foreign Affairs* 59, no. 5 (Summer 1981): 1121–1146.

―――. *The Intemperate Zone: The Third World Challenge to U.S. Foreign Policy.* New York: W. W. Norton and Company, 1983.

Fish, Howard M., "Security Assistance in Perspective." In *Human Rights and U.S. Foreign Policy: Principles and Applications,* ed. Peter G. Brown and Douglas MacLean, 215–228. Lexington, Mass.: Lexington Books, D. C. Heath and Company, 1979.

Fonseca, Carlos Amador. "Nicaragua: Zero Hour." In *Sandinistas Speak,* ed. Tomas Borge, Carlos Fonseca, Daniel Ortega, Humberto Ortega, and Jaime Wheelock, 23–42. New York: Pathfinder Press, 1982.

Forsythe, David P. "Human Rights in a Post-Cold War World." *Fletcher Forum of World Affairs* 15, no. 2 (Summer 1991): 55–69.

Fraser, Donald M. "Human Rights and U.S. Foreign Policy: Some Basic Questions Regarding Principles and Practice." *International Studies Quarterly* 23, no. 2 (June 1979): 174–185.

―――, and John P. Salzberg. "Foreign Policy and Effective Strategies for Human Rights." *Universal Human Rights* 1, no. 1 (January–March 1979): 11-18.

Frente Sandinista de Liberacion Nacional (FSLN). "The Historic Program of the FSLN." In *Sandinistas Speak,* ed. Tomas Borge, Carlos Fonseca, Daniel Ortega, Humberto Ortega, and Jaime Wheelock, 13–22. New York: Pathfinder Press, 1982.

Gaddis, John Lewis. "Toward the Post-Cold War World." *Foreign Affairs* 70, no. 2 (Spring 1991): 102–122.

Ganley, Gladys. "Power to the People via Personal Electronic Media." *Washington Quarterly* 14, no. 2 (Spring 1991): 5–22.

George, Alexander. "Case Studies and Theory Development: The Method of Structured, Focused Comparison." In *Diplomacy: New Approaches in History, Theory, and Policy,* ed. Paul Gorden Lauren, 43–68. New York: The Free Press, 1979.

Gershman, Carl. "The U.S. and the World Democratic Revolution." *Washington Quarterly* 12, no. 1 (Winter 1989): 127–139.

Gordon, Bernard. "The Asian-Pacific Rim: Success at a Price." *Foreign Affairs (America and the World 1990/1991)* 70, no. 1 (1991): 142–159.

Green, Jerrold D. "Psuedoparticipation and Countermobilization: Roots of the Iranian Revolution." *Iranian Studies* 13, nos. 1–4 (1980): 31–54.

Gregor, A. James. "Some Policy Considerations." In *The U.S. and The Philippines: A Challenge to a Special Relationship,* ed. James A. Gregor, 67–84. Washington, D.C.: The Heritage Foundation, 1983.

———. *Crisis in the Philippines: A Threat to U.S. Interest.* Washington, D.C.: Ethics and Public Policy Center, 1984.

Gutman, Roy. *Banana Diplomacy: The Making of American Policy in Nicaragua, 1981–1987.* New York: Simon and Schuster, 1988.

Halliday, Fred. *Iran: Dictatorship and Development.* New York: Penguin Books, 1979.

Halperin, Morton H. *Bureaucratic Politics and Foreign Policy.* Washington, D.C.: The Brookings Institution, 1974.

Hamilton, William C. "United States Policy in the Period Leading to the Declaration of Martial Law and Its Immediate Aftermath." In *Rebuilding a Nation: Philippine Challenges and American Policy,* ed. Carl H. Lande, 505–516. Washington, D.C.: Washington Institute Press, 1987.

Harkin, Tom. "Human Rights and Foreign Aid: Forging an Unbreakable Link." In *Human Rights and U.S. Foreign Policy: Principles and Applications,* ed. Peter G. Brown and Douglas MacLean, 15–26. Lexington, Mass.: Lexington Books, D. C. Heath and Company, 1979.

Hegel, G. W. F. *Philosophy of Right.* Trans. by T. M. Knox. Oxford: Clarendon Press, 1942.

Hendrickson, David C. "The End of American History: American Security, the National Purpose, and the New World Order." in *Rethinking America's Security: Beyond the Cold War to New World Order,* eds. Graham Allison and Gregory F. Treverton, 386–406. New York: W. W. Norton and Company, 1992.

Herz, John. *Political Realism and Political Idealism.* Chicago: University of Chicago Press, 1951.

———. "Political Realism Revisited and 'Response in a Colloquium.' " *International Studies Quarterly* 25, no. 2 (June 1981): 182–197; 201–203.

Hill, Hal, and Sisira Jayasuriya. "The Economy." In *The Philippines After Marcos,* ed. R. J. May and Francisco Nemenzo, 132–146. New York: St. Martin's Press, 1985.

Hobbes, Thomas. *The Leviathan.* Ed. Richard Tuck. New York: Cambridge University Press, 1991.

Holsti, Ole R. "The Belief System and National Images: A Case Study.": In *International Politics and Foreign Policy: A Reader in Research Theory,* ed. James N. Rosenau, 543–550. New York: The Free Press, 1969.

"Human Rights and American Foreign Policy: A Symposium," *Commentary* 72, no. 5 (November 1981): 25–63.

Huntington, Samuel P. "Human Rights and American Power." *Commentary* 72, no. 3 (September 1981): 37–43.

———. "American Ideals Versus American Interests." *Political Science Quarterly* 97, no. 1 (Spring 1982). Reprinted in *American Foreign Policy: Theoretical Essays,* ed. G. John Ikenberry, 223–258. Glenview, Ill.: Scott, Foresman and Company, 1989.

Huyser, Robert E. *Mission to Teheran.* New York: Harper and Row Publishers, 1986.

Hyland, William G. "America's New Course." *Foreign Affairs* 69, no. 2 (Spring 1990): 1–12.

———. "The Case for Pragmatism." *Foreign Affairs (America and the World 1991–1992)* 71, no. 1 (1992): 38–52.

"Interim Philippines Accord." *National Journal,* 22 October 1988, p. 2688.

Jervis, Robert. *Perception and Misperception in International Relations.* Princeton, N.J.: Princeton University Press, 1976.

Johansen, Robert C. *The National Interest and the Human Interest.* Princeton, N.J.: Princeton University Press, 1980.

Kaimowitz, David, and Joseph R. Thome. "Nicaragua's Agrarian Reform: The First Year (1979–1980)." In *Nicaragua in Revolution,* ed. Thomas W. Walker, 223–240. New York: Praeger Publishers, 1982.

Karnow, Stanley. *In Our Image: America's Empire in the Philippines.* New York: Random House, 1989.

———. "Reagan and the Philippines: Setting Marcos Adrift." *New York Times Magazine,* 19 March 1989.

———. "Cory Aquino's Downhill Slide." *New York Times Magazine,* 19 August 1990.

Kazemi, Farhad. *Poverty and Revolution in Iran: The Migrant Poor, Urban Marginality and Politics.* New York: New York University Press, 1980.

Keddie, Nikkie, R. *Roots of Revolution: An Interpretive History of Modern Iran.* New Haven, Conn.: Yale University Press, 1981.

————. "The Iranian Revolution in Comparative Perspective." *American Historical Review* 88, (1983): 579–598.

Kennan, George ["X"]. "The Sources of Soviet Conduct." *Foreign Affairs* 25 (July 1947). Reprinted in *American Diplomacy: 1900–1950*, George Kennan, 102–120. New York: New American Library, 1952.

Keohane, Robert O. "Realism, Neorealism, and the Study of World Politics." In *Neorealism and Its Critics*, ed. Robert O. Keohane, 1–26. New York: Columbia University Press, 1986.

————. "Theory of World Politics: Structural Realism and Beyond." In *Neorealism and Its Critics*, ed. Robert O. Keohane, 158–203. New York: Columbia University Press, 1986.

———— and Joseph S. Nye. *Power and Interdependence: World Politics in Transition*. Boston: Little, Brown and Company, 1977.

Kerkvliet, Benedict J. "Peasants and Agricultural Workers: Implications for United States Policy." In *Rebuilding a Nation: Philippine Challenges and American Policy*, ed. Carl H. Lande, 205–218. Washington, D.C.: Washington Institute Press, 1987.

————. "Land Reform: Emancipation or Counterinsurgency?" In *Marcos and Martial Law in the Philippines*, ed. David A. Rosenberg, 113–144. Ithaca, N.Y.: Cornell University Press, 1989.

Khomeini, Ruhallah. *Islam and Revolution*. Translated by Hamid Algar. Berkeley, Calif.: Mizan Press, 1981.

Kirkpatrick, Jeane J. "U.S. Security and Latin America." *Commentary* 71, no. 1 (January 1981): 29–40.

————. In "Human Rights and American Foreign Policy: A Symposium." *Commentary* 72, no. 5 (November 1981): 42–45.

————. "Dictatorship and Double Standards." *Commentary*, November 1979. Reprinted in *Human Rights and U.S. Human Rights Policy: Theoretical Approaches and Some Perspectives on Latin America*, ed. Howard Wiarda, 5–29. Washington, D.C.: American Enterprise Institute for Public Policy Research, 1982.

————. "Human Rights and Foreign Policy," In *Human Rights and American Foreign Policy*, ed. Fred E. Bauman, 1–11. Gambier, Ohio: Public Affairs Conference Center, Kenyon College, 1982.

————. "A Normal Country in a Normal Time." *The National Interest*, no. 21 (Fall 1990): 40–44.

———— and Allan Gerson. "The Reagan Doctrine, Human Rights, and International Law." In *Right v. Might: International Law and the Use of Force,* ed. Louis Henkin, Stanley Hoffman, Jeane J. Kirkpatrick, William D. Rogers, and David J. Scheffer, 19–35. New York: Council on Foreign Relations Press, 1989.

Kissinger, Henry. *Nuclear Weapons and Foreign Policy.* New York: Harper and Row, 1957.

———. *The Necessity for Choice.* New York: Harper and Row, 1961.

———. *A World Restored—Europe After Napoleon: The Politics of Conservatism in a Revolutionary Age.* New York: Grosset and Dunlap, 1964.

———. *American Foreign Policy,* expanded ed. New York: W. W. Norton, 1974.

———. "Mortality and Power." In *Mortality and Foreign Policy: A Symposium on President Carter's Stance,* ed. Ernest W. Lefever, 59–66. Washington, D.C.: Ethics and Public Policy Center for Georgetown University, 1977.

Klare, Michael T. *American Arms Supermarket.* Austin: University of Texas Press, 1984.

Krauthammer, Charles. "Universal Dominion: Toward a Unipolar World." *The National Interest,* no. 18 (Winter 1989): 46–49.

———. "The Unipolar Moment." *Foreign Affairs (America and the World 1990/91)* 70, no. 1 (1991): 23–33.

Kristol, Irving. "Defining Our National Interest." *The National Interest,* no. 21 (Fall 1990): 16–25.

Labrie, Roger; John G. Hutchins, and Edwin W. Peura. *U.S. Arms Sales Policy: Background and Issues.* Washington, D.C.: American Enterprise Institute, 1982.

LaFeber, Walter. "The Burdens of the Past." In *Central America: Anatomy of a Conflict,* ed. Robert S. Leiken, 49–68. New York: Pergamon Press, in cooperation with Carnegie Endowment for International Peace, 1984.

———. *Inevitable Revolutions: The United States in Central America,* expanded ed. New York: W. W. Norton and Company, 1984.

Lake, Anthony. *Somoza Falling.* Boston: Houghton Mifflin Company, 1989.

Landau, Saul. "The Way of the Sandinistas." *The Progressive,* August 1986, 21–25. In *Nicaragua and the United States, The Reference Shelf* 59, no. 2. ed. Andrew C. Kimmens, 141–154. New York: The H. W. Wilson Company, 1987.

Lande, Carl H. "Philippine Prospects After Martial Law." *Foreign Affairs* 59, no. 5 (Summer 1981), 1147–1168.

———. "The Political Crisis." In *Crisis in the Philippines: The Marcos Era and Beyond,* ed. John Bresnan, 114–144. Princeton, N.J.: Princeton University Press, 1986.

———. "Introduction: Retrospect and Prospect." In *Rebuilding a Nation: Philippine Challenges and American Policy,* ed. Carl H. Lande, 7–44. Washington, D.C.: Washington Institute Press, 1987.

———, ed. *Rebuilding a Nation: Philippine Challenges and American Policy.* Washinton, D.C.: Washington Institute Press, 1987.

Laqueur, Walter. "The Issue of Human Rights." *Commentary* 63, no. 5 (May 1977): 29–35.

Ledeen, Michael, and William Lewis. *Debacle: The American Failure in Iran.* New York: Alfred A. Knopf, 1981.

Lefever, Ernest W. "Limits of the Human Rights Standard." In *Mortality and Foreign Policy: A Symposium on President Carter's Stance,* ed. Ernest W. Lefever, 72–74. Washington, D.C.: Ethics and Public Policy Center for Georgetown University, 1977.

———. "The Trivialization of Human Rights." *Policy Review,* Winter 1978, 11–34.

Leiken, Robert S., ed. *Central America: Anatomy of a Conflict.* New York: Pergamon Press, in cooperation with the Carnegie Endowment for International Peace, 1984.

LeoGrande, William M. "The United States and the Nicaraguan Revolution." In *Nicaragua in Revolution,* ed. Thomas W. Walker, 63–77. New York: Praeger Publishers, 1982.

———. "The United States and Nicaragua." In *Nicaragua: The First Five Years,* ed. Thomas W. Walker, 425–446. New York: Praeger Publishers, 1985.

———. and Carla Ann Robins. "Oligarchs and Officers: The Crisis in El Salvador." *Foreign Affairs* 58 (Summer 1980): 1084–1103.

———, Morris Blachman, Douglas C. Bennet, and Kenneth Sharpe. "The Failure of the Hegemonic Strategic Vision." In *Confronting Revolution: Security Through Diplomacy in Central America,* ed. Morris J. Blachman, William M. LeoGrande, and Kenneth Sharpe, 329–350. New York:Pantheon Books, 1986.

Lijphart, Arend. "The Comparative Method and Methodological Developments." In *Comparative Political Systems,* ed. Louis J. Cantori, 58–79. Boston: Holbrook Press, 1974.

Lim, Robyn. "Foreign Policy." In *The Philippines After Marcos,* ed. R. J. May and Francisco Nemenzo, 207–224. New York: St. Martin's Press, 1985.

Machiavelli, Niccolo. *The Prince.* ed. Quentin Skinner and Russel Price. New York: Cambridge University Press, 1988.

Maisto, John F. "United States-Philippine Relations in the 1980s." In *Rebuilding A Nation: Philippine Challenges and American Policy,* ed. Carl H. Lande, 529–538. Washington, D.C.: Washington Institute Press, 1987.

Malley, Nadia. "Relations with Western Europe and the Socialist International." In *Nicaragua: The First Five Years,* ed. Thomas W. Walker, 485–498. New York: Praeger Publishers, 1985.

Maoz, Zeev, and Nasrin Abdolali. "Regimes Types and International Conflict, 1816–1976." *The Journal of Conflict Resolution* 33, no. 1 (March 1989): 3–35.

McAfee, Kathy. "The Philippines: A Harvest of Anger." In *The Philippines Reader: A History of Colonialism, Neocolonialism, Dictatorship and Resistance,* ed. Daniel B. Schirmer and Stephen Rosskamm Shalom, 292–301. Boston: South End Press, 1987.

McConnel, Jeff M. "Counterrevolution in Nicaragua: The U.S. Connection." In *The Nicaraguan Reader: Documents of a Revolution Under Fire,* ed. Peter Rosset and John Vandermeer, 175–189. New York: Grove Press, 1983.

Meinecke, Friedrich. *Machiavellism: The Doctrine of Raison D'Etat and its Place in Modern History.* Boulder, Colo.: Westview Press, 1984.

Molineu, Harold. *U.S. Policy Toward Latin America: From Regionalism to Globalism.* Boulder, Colo.: Westview Press, 1986.

Momayezi, N. "Economic Correlates of Political Violence: The Case of Iran." *Middle East Journal* 40 (1986)L 68–81.

Moore, John Norton. *The Secret War in Central America: Sandinista Assault on World Order.* Frederick, Md.: University Publications of America, Inc., 1987.

Morgenthau, Hans. *In Defense of the National Interest.* New York: Alfred A. Knopf, 1951.

———. "Another 'Great Debate'; The National Interest of the United States." In *American Political Science Review* 67 (December 1952): 961–998.

———. *Politics Among Nations: The Struggle for Power and Peace.* 4th ed. New York: Alfred A. Knopf, 1967.

Mower, Glenn A., Jr. *The United States, the United Nations and Human Rights: The Eleanor Roosevelt and Jimmy Carter Eras.* Westport, Conn.: Greenwood Press, 1979.

Moynihan, Daniel Patrick. "The Politics of Human Rights." *Commentary* 64, no. 2 (August 1977): 19–26.

Muravchik, Joshua. *The Uncertain Crusade: Jimmy Carter and the Dilemmas of Human Rights Policy.* Boston: Hamilton Press, 1986.

Nelson, Joan, M. *Aid, Influence and Foreign Policy.* New York: Macmillan Company, 1968.

Newsom, David D. "The Diplomacy of Human Rights: A Diplomat's View." In *The Diplomacy of Human Rights*, ed. David D. Newsom, 3–12. Lanham, Md.: University Press of America for the Institute for the Study of Diplomacy, Georgetown University, 1986.

Nichols, John Spicer. "The Nicaraguan Media: Revolution and Beyond." In *The Nicaraguan Reader: Documents of a Revolution Under Fire*, ed. Peter Rosset and John Vandermeer, 72–79. New York: Grove Press, 1983.

Niebuhr, Reinhold. *Moral Man and Immoral Society.* New York: Charles Scribner's and Sons, 1932.

———. *Christianity and Power Politics.* New York: Charles Scribner's and Sons, 1940.

———. *Christian Realism and Political Problems.* New York: Charles Scribner's and Sons, 1953.

Niksch, Larry A. "Philippines: U.S. Foreign Assistance Facts." *CRS Issue Briefs.* Washington, D.C.: Congressional Research Service, updated 25 September 1990.

Nincic, Miroslav. *United States Foreign Policy: Choices and Tradeoffs.* Washington, D.C.: Congressional Quarterly Press, 1988.

———, and Peter Wallensteen. "Economic Coercion and Foreign Policy." In *Dilemmas of Economic Coercion: Sanctions in World Politics*, ed. Miroslav Nincic and Peter Wallensteen, 1–15. New York: Praeger Publishers, 1983.

O'Brien, Conor Cruise. "The Protomartyr." In *Nicaragua and the United States, The Reference Shelf* 59, no. 2, ed. Andrew C. Kimmens, 12–16. New York: The W. H. Wilson Company, 1987.

O'Donnell, Guillermo, Philippe C. Schmitter, and Lawrence Whitehead. *Transitions from Authoritarian Rule: Prospects for Democracy.* Baltimore: The John Hopkins University Press, 1986.

Ortega, Daniel Saavedra. "Statement to the United Nations Security Council," 25 March 1982, *Security Council Official Records, Thirty-Seventh Year*, 2,335th Meeting, S/Provisional Verbatim 2335.

Ortega, Humberto. "Nicaragua—The Strategy of Victory." In *Sandinistas Speak,* ed. Tomas Borge, Carlos Fonseca, Daniel Ortega, Humberto Ortega, and Jaime Wheelock, 53–84. New York: Pathfinder Press, 1982.

Overholt, William H. "Pressures and Policies: Prospects for Cory Aquino's Philippines." In *Rebuilding a Nation: Philippine Challenges and American Policy,* ed. Carl H. Lande, 89–110. Washington, D.C.: Washington Institute Press, 1987.

Parsa, Misagh. *Social Origins of the Iranian Revolution.* New Brunswick, N.J.: Rutgers University Press, 1989.

Pastor, Robert. *Condemned to Repetition. The United States and Nicaragua.* Princeton: Princeton University Press, 1987.

Pauker, Guy J. "President Corazon Aquino: A Political and Personal Assessment." In *Rebuilding a Nation: Philippine Challenges and American Policy,* ed. Carl H. Lande, 291–312. Washington, D.C.: Washington Institute Press, 1987.

Pelaez, Emmanuel M. "The Philippines and the United States." In *Rebuilding a Nation: Philippine Challenges and American Policy,* ed. Carl H. Lande, 45–56. Washington, D.C.: Washington Institute Press, 1987.

Pines, Burton Yale. "A Primer for Conservatives." *The National Interest,* no. 23 (Spring 1991): 61–68.

Pipes, Daniel and Adam Garfinkle, eds. *Friendly Tyrants: An American Dilemma.* New York: St. Martin's Press, 1991.

Ramazani, R. K. *The United States and Iran: The Patterns of Influence.* New York: Praeger Publishers, 1982.

"Report of the National Committee of the Restoration of Liberties in the Philippines." In *Marcos and Martial Law in the Philippines,* ed. David A. Rosenberg, 253–285. Ithaca: Cornell University Press, 1989.

Report of the President's National Bipartisan Commission on Central America. New York: Macmillan Publishing Company, n.d. [1984].

Roberts, Brad. "Democracy and World Order." *Fletcher Forum of World Affairs* 15, no. 2 (Summer 1991): 9–25.

Rosenberg, David A. "The Changing Structure of Philippine Government from Marcos to Aquino." In *Rebuilding a Nation: Philippine Challenges and American Policy,* ed. Carl H. Lande, 329–350. Washington, D.C.: Washington Institute Press, 1987.

———. "Liberty Versus Loyalty: The Transformation of the Philippine News Media Under Martial Law." In *Marcos and Martial Law in the Philippines,* ed. David A. Rosenberg, 153–176. Ithaca, N.Y.: Cornell University Press, 1989.

———, ed. *Marcos and Martial Law in the Philippines.* Ithaca, N.Y.: Cornell University Press, 1989.

Rothenberg, Morris. "The Soviets and Central America." In *Central America: Anatomy of Conflict,* ed. Robert S. Leiken, 131–149. New York: Pergamon Press, in cooperation with the Carnegie Endowment for International Peace, 1984.

Rubin, Barry. "America's Relations with the Islamic Republic of Iran." *Iranian Studies 13, nos. 1–4 (1980): 307–326.*

———. *Paved with Good Intentions: The American Experience and Iran.* New York: Oxford University Press, 1980.

———. "Reagan Administration Policymaking and Central America." In *Central America: Anatomy of Conflict,* ed. Robert S. Leiken, 299–318. New York: Pergamon Press, in cooperation with Carnegie Endowment for International Peace, 1984.

Rustow, Dankwart A. "Democracy: A Global Revolution." *Foreign Affairs* 69, no. 4 (Fall 1990): 75–91.

Saikal, Amin. *The Rise and Fall of the Shah.* Princeton, N.J.: Princeton University Press, 1980.

Schelling, Thomas C. *The Strategy of Conflict.* (New York: Oxford University Press, 1963.

Schirmer, Daniel B. and Stephen Rosskamm Shalom, ed. *The Philippines Reader: A History of Colonialism, Neocolonialism, Dictatorship and Resistance.* Boston: South End Press, 1987.

Schlesinger, Arthur, Jr. "Human Rights and the American Tradition." *Foreign Affairs* 57, no. 3 (1977): 503–526.

Schlesinger, James. "New Instabilities, New Priorities." *Foreign Affairs* no. 85 (Winter 1991–92): 3–24.

Schoultz, Lars. "U.S. Economic Aid as an Instrument of Foreign Policy: The Case of Human Rights in Latin America." In *International Human Rights: Contemporary Issues,* ed. Jack L. Nelson and Vera M. Green, 317–342. Stanfordville, N.Y.: Human Rights Publishers Groups, 1980.

———. *Human Rights and United States Policy Toward Latin America.* Princeton, N.J.: Princeton University Press, 1981.

Schroeder, Richard C. "Roots of Current Antagonism." *Editorial Research Reports* 1, no. 8 (1986): 154–159. In *Nicaragua and the United States, The Reference Shelf* 59, no. 1, ed. Andrew C. Kimmens, 6–12. New York: The H. W. Wilson Company, 1987.

Schulz, Ann Tibbitts. *Buying Security: Iran Under the Monarchy.* Boulder, Colo.: Westview Press, 1989.

Schwab, Theodore, and Harold Sims. "Relations with the Communist States." In *Nicaragua: The First Five Years,* ed. Thomas W. Walker, 447–466. New York: Praeger Publishers, 1985.

Serra, Luis. "The Sandinist Mass Organization." In *Nicaragua in Revolution,* ed. Thomas W. Walker, 95–113. New York: Praeger Publishers, 1982.

Shultz, George P. "Human Rights and the Moral Dimension of U.S. Foreign Policy. "Address given by the Secretary of State at the 86th Annual Washington Day Banquet of the Creve Coeur Club of Illinois, Peoria, Illinois, 22 February 1984. *Department of State Bulletin* 84, no. 2085 (April 1984).

———. "Nicaragua and the Future of Central America." Address before the Veterans of Foreign Wars, 15 March 1986, Washington, D.C. *Department of State Bulletin* 86 (May 1986): 37–40. In *Nicaragua and the United States, The Reference Shelf,* 59, no. 2, ed. Andrew C. Kimmens, 61–69. New York: The W. H. Wilson Company, 1987.

Sick, Gary. *All Fall Down: America's Tragic Encounter with Iran.* New York: Random House, 1985.

Smith, Joseph Michael. *Realist Thought from Weber to Kissinger.* Baton Rouge: Louisiana State University Press, 1986.

Snyder, Richard C. H. W. Bruck, and Burtin Sapin. "The Decision-Making Approach to the Study of International Relations." In *International Politics and Foreign Policy: A Reader in Research and Theory,* ed. James N. Rosenau, 199–206. New York: The Free Press, 1969.

Solarz, Stephen J. "A New Era: An Auspicious Begining." In *Rebuilding a Nation: Philippine Challenges and American Policy,* ed. Carl H. Lande, 57–68. Washington, D.C.: Washington Institute Press, 1987.

Somoza, Anastasio. Interview on MacNeil-Lehrer Report, 19 September 1978, WETA/PBS Network.

———. *Nicaragua Betrayed.* As told to Jack Cox. Boston: Western Islands Publishers, 1980.

"A Statement of the Civil Liberties Union of the Philippines on the State of the Nation After Three Years of Martial Law." In *Marcos and Martial Law in the Philippines,* ed. David A. Rosenberg, 286–297. Ithaca, N.Y.: Cornell University Press, 1989.

Stauffer, Robert B. "The Political Economy of Refeudalization." In *Marcos and Martial Law in the Philippines*, ed. David A. Rosenberg, 180–218. Ithaca, N.Y.: Cornell University Press, 1989.

Stempel, J. *Inside the Iranian Revolution*. Bloomington: Indiana University Press, 1981.

Stobaugh, Robert B. "The Evolution of Iranian Oil Policy, 1925–1975." In *Iran Under the Pahlavis*, ed. George Lenczowski, 210–252. Stanford, Calif.: Hoover Institution Press, 1978.

Stull, Lee T. "Moments of Truth in Philippine-American Relations: The Carter Years." In *Rebuilding a Nation: Philippine Challenges and American Policy*, ed. Carl H. Lande, 517–528. Washington, D.C.: Washington Institute Press, 1987.

Sussman, Gerald, David O'Connor, and Charles W. Lindsey. "The Philippines, 1984: The Political Economy of a Dying Dictatorship." In *The Philippines Reader: A History of Colonialism, Neocolonialism, Dictatorship and Resistance*, ed. Daniel B. Schirmer and Stephen Rosskamm Shalom, 284–289. Boston: South End Press, 1987.

Tarcov, Nathan. "If This Long War Is Over." *The National Interest*, no. 18 (Winter 1989): 50–53.

Tarr, Cedric W., Jr. "Human Rights and Arms Transfer Policy." In *Global Human Rights: Public Policies, Comparative Measures and NGO Strategies*, eds. Ved P. Nanda, Scaritt R. James, George W. Shepherd, Jr., 59–76. Boulder, Colo.: Westview Press, 1981.

Tehranian, Majid. "Communications and Revolution in Iran: The Passing of a Paradigm." *Iranian Studies* 13, nos. 1–4 (1980): 5–30.

Tonelson, Alan. "Human Rights: The Bias We Need." *Foreign Policy*, Winter 1982–83: 52–74.

———. "A Manifesto for Democrats." *The National Interest*, no. 16 (Summer 1989): 36–48.

Tucker, Robert W. "The American Outlook." In *Consensus at the Crossroads: Dialogues in American Foreign Policy*, ed. H. Bliss and G. M. Johnson, 14–43. New York: Dodd, Mead and Company, 1972.

———. "The Purposes of American Power." *Foreign Affairs*, Winter 1980–81: 241–74.

Uhlig, Mark. "Opposing Ortega." *New York Times Magazine*, 11 February 1990.

United Nations. "Vienna Declaration and Program of Action" adopted by the World Conference on Human Rights, 25 June 1993. A/Conf. 157/23, 12 July 1993.

United Nations Development Programme. *Human Development Report 1991*. New York: Oxford University Press, 1991.

Vaky, Viron. "Reagan's Central American Policy: An Isthmus Restored." In *Central America: Anatomy of Conflict*, ed. Robert S. Leiken, 233–258. New York: Pergamon Press, in cooperation with Carnegie Endowment for International Peace, 1984.

————. "Testimony in Congress, House Subcommittee on Inter-American Affairs and the Foreign Affairs Committee." In *Central America: Anatomy of a Conflict*, ed. Robert S. Leiken, 1–20. New York: Pergamon Press, in cooperation with the Carnegie Endowment for International Peace, 1984.

Vance, Cyrus. "Secretary Vance Gives Overview of Foreign Assistance Program." *Department of State Bulletin* 77, no. 1970 (28 March 1977).

————. "Human Rights and Foreign Policy." Address given by the Secretary of State at Law Day Ceremonies, University of Georgia Law School, Athens, Georgia, 30 April 1977. *Department of State Bulletin* 76, no. 1978 (23 May 1977).

————. *Hard Choices: Critical Years in American Foreign Policy*. New York: Simon and Schuster, 1983.

————. "The Human Rights Imperative." *Foreign Policy*, no. 63 (Summer 1986): 3–19.

Vanden, Harry E. "The Ideology of the Insurrection." In *Nicaragua in Revolution*, ed. Thomas W. Walker, 41–62. New York: Praeger Publishers, 1982.

Villegas, Bernardo. "The Economic Crisis." In *Crisis in the Philippines: The Marcos Era and Beyond*, ed. John Bresnan, 145–175. Princeton, N.J.: Princeton University Press, 1986.

Vogelgesang, Sandra. "Diplomacy of Human Rights." *International Studies Quarterly* 72, no. 2 (June 1979): 216–245.

————. *American Dream/Global Nightmare*. New York: W. W. Norton and Company, 1980.

————. "What Price Principle? U.S. Policy on Human Rights." In *Human Rights and American Foreign Policy*, ed. Fred E. Baumann, 13–37. Gambier, Ohio: Public Affairs Conference Center, Kenyon College, 1982.

Walker, Thomas W. *Nicaragua: The Land of Sandino*. 2nd ed. Boulder, Colo.: Westview Press, 1986.

————, ed. *Nicaragua: The First Five Years*. New York: Praeger Publishers, 1985.

————, ed. *Nicaragua in Revolution*. New York: Praeger Publishers, 1982.

Waltz, Kenneth N. "Anarchic Orders and Balances of Power." In *Neorealism and Its Critics*, ed. Robert O. Keohane, 98–130. New York: Columbia University Press, 1986.

————. "Political Structures." In *Neorealism and Its Critics*, ed. Robert O. Keohane, 70–97. New York: Columbia University Press, 1986.

————. "Reductionist and Systemic Theories." In *Neorealism and Its Critics*, ed. Robert O. Keohane, 47–69. New York: Columbia University Press, 1986.

Weber, Max. "Politics as a Vocation." In *From Max Weber: Essays in Sociology*, ed. H. H. Gerth and C. Wright Mills, New York: Oxford University Press, 1958.

Weber, Henri. "The Struggle for Power." In *The Nicaraguan Reader: Documents of a Revolution Under Fire*, ed. Peter Rosset and John Vandermeer, 151–166. New York: Grove Press, 1983.

Wipfler, William L. "Human Rights and U.S. Foreign Assistance: The Latin American Connection." In *Human Rights and U.S. Foreign Policy: Principles and Applications*, eds. Peter G. Brown and Douglas MacLean, 183–196. Lexington, Mass.: Lexington Books, D. C. Heath and Company, 1979.

World Bank. *Governance and Development*. Washington, D.C.: International Bank for Reconstruction and Development, 1992.

————. *World Development Report 1979*. New York: Oxford University Press, 1979.

————. *World Development Report 1982*. New York: Oxford University Press, 1982.

————. *World Development Report 1990*. New York: Oxford University Press, 1990.

Wurfel, David. "The Succession Struggle." In *The Philippines After Marcos*, ed. R. J. May and Francisco Nemenzo, 17–44. New York: St. Martin's Press, 1985.

Youngblood, Robert L. "Church and State in the Philippines: Some Implications for United States Policy." In *Rebuilding a Nation: Philippine Challenges and American Policy*, ed. Carl H. Lande, 351–368. Washington, D.C.: Washington Institute Press, 1987.

————. "Church Opposition to Martial Law in the Philippines." In *The Philippines Reader: A History of Colonialism, Neocolonialsm, Dictatorship and Resistance*, ed. Daniel B. Schirmer and Stephen Rosskamm Shalom, 211–218. Boston: South End Press, 1987.

————. *Marcos Against the Church: Economic Development and Political Repression in the Philippines.* Ithaca, N.Y.: Cornell University Press, 1991.

Zabih, Sepehr. *Iran's Revolutionary Upheaval: An Interpretive Essay.* San Francisco: Alchemy Press, 1979.

————. *The Iranian Military in Revolution and War.* New York: Routledge Press, 1988.

Zonis, Marvin. *Majestic Failure: The Fall of the Shah.* Chicago: The University of Chicago Press, 1991.

Newspapers and Journals

Christian Science Monitor. 23, 25, 27 September, 18 October, 4, 6, 13, 14, 20, 26, 27 November 1991.

Congressional Quarterly Weekly Report. 16 October 1976; 15 January, 25 July 1977; 8 March 1980; 6 October 1983; 25 February 1984; 18 May, 27 June, 9 November, 21 December 1985; 16 October 1986.

The New Republic. 2 December 1991.

New York Times. 28 July 1974; 30 October 1977; 17 December 1978; 18 June 1979; 1 July 1981; 28 April, 5, 8 October 1983; 12 February 1985; 12, 13, 16, 23, 24 February 1986; 24 January, 11 September, 19 October, 14 November 1988; 19 March 1989; 11 February, 22 July, 19 August, 23 September 1990; 15 March, 12, 28 May, 2, 9, 23 June, 1 July, 11, 12, 16, 19, 20, 22, 25, 29 September, 2, 3, 4, 5, 13, 20, 25 October, 6, 8, 10, 11, 17, 18, 21, 27 November, 4, 5, 8, 19, 22, 29 December 1991; 5 January, 6, 13, 17 February, 4, 5, 29 March, 10, 12, 22 April, 3, 10, 14, 20, 21, 29 May, 4, 7, 29 June, 1 July, 7, 25 November, 27 December 1992; 3, 23, April 1993.

Wall Street Journal. 13 October 1988; 20, 23, 29 September, 18 October, 5, 15, 19, 22, 27 November 1991.

Washington Post. 25 October 1977; 9 July 78; 28 August, 19 September, 12 November 1991.

U.S. Government Documents

Agency for International Development, Bureau for Program and Policy Coordination, Office of Planning and Budgeting, *U.S. Overseas Loans and Grants and Assistance from International Organizations.*

Statistical Annex I to the Annual Development Coordination Committee Submitted to Congress. Reports, 1968 to 1987. Microform.

Congressional Record. 4 June 1974; 14 March, 22 April, 12 June 1975; September 1976; 7 December 1977; 4, 5 October 1978.

Development Issues: U.S. Actions Affecting the Development of Low-Income Countries. Annual Report of the Chairman of the Development Coordination Committee Transmitted to the Congress. Reports, 1979 to 1983.

Foreign Military Sales, Foreign Military Construction Sales and Military Assistance Facts. December 1976; December 1978; December 1979; December 1980; September 1981, 30 September 1983; 30 September 1984; 30 September 1985; 30 September 1986; 30 September 1987. (Washington, D.C.: Data Management Division, Comptroller, Defense Security Assistance Agency).

International Finance: The National Advisory Council on International Monetary and Financial Policies Annual Report to the President and the Congress. (Washington, D.C.: U.S. Government Printing Office, FY 1978 to 1985).

U.S. Congress. House. Committee on International Relations, Subcommittee on International Oranizations. *Human Rights in Indonesia and the Philippines.* 94th Cong., 1st and 2d sess., 18 December 1975 and 3 May 1976.

U.S. Congress, House. Committee on International Relations, Subcommittee on International Organizations. *Human Rights in Iran.* 94th Cong., 2d sess., 3 August and 8 September 1976.

U.S. Congress. House. Committee on International Relations, Subcommittee on International Organizations. *Human Rights in Iran.* 95th Cong., 1st sess., 26 October 1977.

U.S. Congress. House. Committee on International Relations, Subcommittee on International Organizations. *Human Rights Conditions in Selected Countries and the U.S. Response.* 95th Cong., 2d sess., 25 July 1978.

U.S. Congress. House. Committee on International Relations, Subcommittee on International Organizations. *Human Rights and U.S. Foreign Policy.* 96th Cong., 1st sess., 2 and 10 May, 21 June, 12 July, and 2 August 1979.

U.S. Congress. House. Committee on International Relations, Subcommittee on Inter-American Affairs. *Central America at the Crossroads.* 96th Cong., 1st sess., 11–12 September 1979.

U.S. Congress. House. Committee on International Relations, Subcommittee on Human Rights and International Organizations. *U.S. Human Rights Policy.* 99th Cong., 2d sess., 19 and 26 Febraury 1986.

U.S. Congress. House. Committee on International Relations, Subcommittee on Human Rights and International Organizations. *Status of U.S. Human Rights Policy, 1987.* 100th Cong., 1st sess., 2 and 19 February 1987.

Unpublished Material

Senator Jesse Helms, Washington, D.C., to Ronald Roskens, Administrator, U.S. Agency for International Development, Washington, D.C., letters dated 27 May 1992 and 22 June 1992.

United Nations Center for Transnational Corporation, Policy Analysis and Research Division, Data Base, n.d., unpublished.

U.S. Department of Commerce, Bureau of Economic Analysis, Balance of Payments Division, Government Grants and Capital Branch, unpublished data, letter dated 7 November 1990.

INDEX

Aquino, Benigno: assassination, 167, 169, 243n.44; evaluation of Carter's human rights policy, 185; opposition to martial law, 150; relations with Reagan administration, 169; U.S. request for release, 169; U.S. House of Representatives resolution, regarding assassination, 172; U.S. reaction to assassination, 176

Aquino, Corazon, 24; in 1986 elections 152, 174; and U.S. bases (1984), 163

Alliance for Progress, 17, 79

Arias Plan. See Esquipulas II

Authoritarianism: defined, 213n.1

Bakhtiar, Shapur, 41, 42–43, 61; on Carter human rights policy, 74

Bani Sadr, Abol Hassan, 45–46, 47, 76

Bazargan, Mehdi, 39; 43, 46; 47, 62, 63, 76

Bravo, Cardinal Obando y. See Nicaragua, Catholic Church opposition

Broad Opposition Front (FAO), 85, 87, 88, 92, 111; and FSLN, support of, 116; as potential opposition alternative, 129

Brzezinski, Zbigniew: and Iran, 47, 60, 73, 226n.138; and Nicaragua, 112

Bush, George, W., 170

Carter, Jimmy administration, 4; human rights defined: 14–16; human rights policy, 26; human rights policy and economic sanctions, 28–29, 34; human rights and military assistance, 34–35, and Iran, 57, 59–66, 67, 69; and Nicaragua, 97, 107–21, 125–30, 131–32, 137,

189. See also United States and Iran (prerevolution); United States and Islamic Republic of Iran

Central Intelligence Agency (CIA), 26; in Iran 43, 47, 49, 67, 69; in Nicaragua, 94, 101, 106, 113, 114, 116, 120, 121, 122, 128; in the Philippines, 161, 173

Chamorro, Pedro Joaquin, 83, 107; assassination of, 84

Chamorro, Violeta Barrios de, 93, 133, 137, 138

Christopher, Warren: and U.S. economic sanctions, 28; analysis of Iran revolution, 10; and Nicaragua, 117

Complex interdependence, 19, 217n.46

Contadora negotiations, 124, 206

Contras, 94, 124, 132

COSEP. See Superior Council of Private Enterprise

Cottam, Richard, 224n.103

Diplomacy, use of, 25–27. See also United States and Iran; United States and Nicaragua; United States and the Philippines

Economic assistance, use of, 29–30; in Iran, 53, 187; in Nicaragua,99–100, 110, 114, 118, 119–20, 212, 122, 237n.213; in the Philippines, 156, 168, 170, 177

Economic sanctions, use of, 27–31, 34, 187; in Nicaragua, 112, 113 , 123

Eisenhower, Dwight D: and Iran, 50, 57; and Nicaragua, 106

279

Enrile, Juan Ponce: anti-Marcos revolt, 153, 175; association with RAM, 151
Esquipulas II (Arias Plan), 125, 133, 206
Export-Import Bank, 27; and U.S. human rights policy, 28; and Iran 53; and Nicaragua, 123

FAO. *See* Broad Opposition Front
Farer, Tom J., 5, 12
Fedayeen Khalq, 40
Feinberg, Richard 5, 10–11
Ford, Gerald, and the Philippines, 168
Freedom Movement (Iran), 39, 43, 45, 46, 62
Frente Sandinista de Liberacion Nacional (FSLN)-(prerevolution) 79, 84, 87, 129; composition of, 91–92, 109, 114, 138, 193; and COSEP, support of, 116; and FAO support of, 116; and Farabundo Marti National Liberation Front (FMLN), 119, 120–121, 135; "final offensive," 88; Group of Twelve, 84, 85, 87, 92, 109; history, 90–91; and Latin America, support of 86, 88, 89, 133; attack on National Palace, (August 1978), 86, 92, 129; formation of provisional government, 89, 230n.59; raid, December 1974, 83, 92; and United States, relations with, 117; and United States, view of, 91; 109, 115, 137, 138
Frente Sandinista de Liberacion Nacional (FSLN) (postrevolution): and Contadora negotiations, 124; and Farabundo Marti National Liberation Front, 124; and United States, relations with, 120; and United State, view of, 123. *See also* Nicaragua (post-revolution); Esquipulas II

Gastil, Raymond, 15
Grenada, 124

Habib, Philip, 175
Helms, Jesse, 239n.260
Human Rights: defined, 14; and Carter administration 14–16, 17–18, 33, 66, 195, 239n.264; and economic development, 15–16, 206; and Ford administration, 17, 33, 58–59; and Johnson administration, 5, 66; and Kennedy administration, 40, 57, 66; and morality, 210, 212; and Nixon administration, 17, 33, 37; and Reagan administration, 18; and realpolitik, 209–10, 212; as cause of revolution in Iran, 74, as cause of revolution in Nicaragua, 138; Third World view of, 15. *See also* Iran (prerevolution), civil and political restrictions; Nicaragua (prerevolution), civil and political restrictions and abuses; Nicaragua (postrevolution), civil rights; Philippines (prerevolution), civil and political restrictions and abuses; human rights, justification; Philippines (postrevolution), civil and political rights
Huntington, Samuel P., 4, 7.
Huyser, Robert, mission to Iran, 61–62, 69

INDE. *See* Nicaraguan Development Institute
Inter-American Commission on Human Rights (IAHCR), 85, 87, 94, 112 International Bank for Reconstruction and Development. *See* World Bank
International Financial Institutions (IFIs), 30–31, 207; and human rights, 207–8; and Nicaragua, 189; and the Philippines, 190
International Monetary Fund (IMF), 30; and Nicaragua, 112; and South Africa, 31
Iran (prerevolution): anti-Americanism, 56–57, 73, 76; clerical opposition 40, 44–45, 193; civil and political restrictions, 37–38, 67–68; civil and political reforms (1976–1979), 40–42; civil, political, and economic reforms, (1960–1963), 40; economic conditions, 38–39, 74; human rights abuse as cause for revolution, 74; military, disintegration of, 43, 70; moderate opposition, 39–40, 66, 72, 193; moderate opposition, view of United States, 74–75, 224n.103; and Nixon "twin pillar" policy, 50, 52, 223n.72; Rastakhiz Party, 38, 41; SAVAK, 37, 38, 42, 69; White Revolution,

39, 40, 58, 193. *See also* Shapur Bakhtiar; Mehdi Bazargan; Fedayeen Khalq; Freedom Movement; Huyser, Robert, mission to Iran; Mohammed Mossadeq; Mujhadeen Khalq; National Front; Tudeh Party, United States and Iran (prerevolution)

Iran, Islamic Republic: clerics, role of, 46; Komitehs, 45; moderate opposition, role of, 46; Revolutionary Council, 45; postrevolutionary governments, 45–46; relations with United States, 45; 46–47, 75, 76, 196; U.S. embassy takeover, 47, 64. *See also* Mehdi Bazargan, Ruhollah Khomeini, Ibrahim Yazdi

Johnson, Lyndon B.: and Iran, 40, 57; and Nicaragua, 106

Kazemi, Farhad, 221n.22
Kennedy, John F.: and Iran, 40, 57, 66; and Nicaragua, 106
Keohane, Robert, 217n.46
Khomeini, Ruhollah 44, 46, 70, 75–76; and anti-Americanism, 44–45, 48–49; death of son, 41; demands on the Shah, 41; and moderate opposition, 45; meeting with National Front, 42; return to Iran, 43. *See also* United States and Iran, religious opposition, relations with
Kirkpatrick, Jeane J., 4, 6, 7, 213n.1
Kissinger, Henry A., 4, 71; and U.S. human rights policy, 6, 17; and U.S. interests in Iran, 50, 53, 56; and Nixon Doctrine, 50; and *Report of the President's National Bipartisan Commission on Central America*, 204–5, 206, 210; and U.S. security assistance, 33

Laxalt, Paul, 174, 175
Lefever, Ernest, 4, 6
Lugar, Richard, 174, 175

Macapagal, Diosdado: CIA, support of, 161; opposition to martial law, 150

Manglapus, Raul, 180; CIA, support of, 161; and U.S. bases (1984), 163
Maoz, Zeev, 210
Military assistance, use of, 31–35; 218n.27; in Iran, 51–53, 187; in Nicaragua, 100–5, 189; in the Philippines, 153–58, 160, 173
Military assistance sanctions: in Nicaragua, 107–8, 113, 135; in the Philippines, 173, 190
Moderate opposition, defined, 25; forms of assistance, to, 203–5, in Iran, 39–40, 66, 67, 72, 74–75, 193; in Nicaragua, 82–87, 111, 113, 116, 117, 129, 134, 135; in the Philippines, 149–50, 151, 62, 169, 174, 176–77, 185 194
Modified structural research program, 217n.46
Mondale, Walter, 162, 169
Moro National Front, 144, 149
Mossadeq, Mohammed, 36–37, 53; and U.S.-British coup, 48
Mujhadeen Khalq, 40

National Committee for Free Elections (NAMFREL), 152, 191; U.S. support of, 177
National Front, 36, 39, 41, 46; 62; alliance with Ayatollah Khomeini 42
National interest: defined, 3–4.
Neoconservative School: critique of, 7–9, 199–201; framework of analysis, 5–7; and realpolitik, 4; Iranian case, applicability of, 70–73; Nicaraguan case, applicability of, 133–35; Philippine case, applicability of, 182–84
Neorealist School: critique of, 13–14, 201–3; framework of analysis, 9–13; and realpolitik, 5; differentiated from structural realism, 214n.8; Iranian case, applicability of, 73–76; Nicaraguan case, applicability of, 135–39; Philippine case, applicability of, 184–86
New People's Army (NPA), 144, 170; and Catholic Church, 151; composition and sectors of support, 149, 150, 166, 167, 182
Nicaraguan Development Institute (INDE), 83, 84, 85; demands on Somoza, 129

Nincic, Miroslav, 16, 204
Nicaragua (prerevolution): Catholic Church opposition, 83, 85, 89–90, 108, 111; civil and political restrictions and abuses, 79–80, 83, 86, 108–9, 114; civil and political reforms, 83–84, 85, 87, 88; Democratic Liberation Union (UDEL) 83, 129; economic conditions, 80–82; economic conditions as cause of revolution 138; economic corruption, 82; human rights abuse as cause of revolution, 138; and IMF, 112; and Latin American pressure for change, 110, 111, 112, 114, 115, 128, 133, 189–90, 230n.46; National Guard 4, 80, 85, 86–87, 89, 100, 108, 114, 128; National Liberal Party (PLN), 79, 87; Nicaraguan Democratic Movement (MDN), 85, 93; OAS-mediated negotiations, 87–88, 112, 113; moderate opposition, activities and composition, 82–87, 134; moderate opposition, demands of, 84, 128, 129, 193; moderate opposition, view of United States, 101, 109, 111, 136–37; National Patriotic Front (FPN), 88, 92; and OPIC, 123; political system, corruption of, 78–79, 99; United People's Movement (MPU), 88, 92. See also Chamorro, Pedro Joaquin; COSEP; FAO; FSLN; INDE; Inter-American Commission on Human Rights; OAS; Pastora, Eden; Robelo, Alfonso
Nicaragua (post-revolution): civil rights, 94; relations with communist bloc, 95–96; and Contadora negotiations, 124, 206; Directorate, 93; and Export-Import Bank, 123; foreign economic relations 94, 96; Government of National Reconciliation, composition of, 93; and IFI loans, 189; and Inter-American Development Bank, 123; role of non-Sandinista groups 93; relations with United States, 124, 196; and World Bank, 123. See also Frente Sandinista de Liberacion Nacional (postrevolution)
Nixon, Richard M.: and U.S. human rights policy, 17; and Iran, 50, 52, 57–58, 223n.72; and Nicaragua, 106; and the Philippines, 168

Organization of American States (OAS), 13, 87, 112, 115, 206, 230n.46; condemnation of Somoza, 252n.13; Nicaragua resolution, 116. See also Inter-American Commission on Human Rights; Nicaragua (prerevolution), OAS-mediated negotiations
Ortega, Daniel, 122, 123, 124, 129
Overseas Private Investment Corporation (OPIC), 27; and U.S. human rights foreign policy, 28; and Nicaragua, 123

Pastor, Robert, 17–18, 110, 120, 128
Pastora, Eden: meeting with Torrijos and Perez, 86; meeting with U.S. officials, 117
Pezzullo, Laurence, 116, 117, 118, 121
Philippines (prerevolution), 195; anti-Americanism in, 159, 161–64; Catholic Church opposition, 151–53, 174, 194, 244n.60; civil and political restrictions and abuse, 145–46; economic conditions, 144, 147–49, 150, 166, 167; human rights abuse, justification of, 146–47; and IFI loans, 190; left-of-center opposition, composition of, 149; martial law, justification of, 144, 147, 164, 181; martial law restrictions, 144; New Developmental Diplomacy, 160; New Society Program, 144, 147, 150; military opposition, 151, 174, 177; moderate opposition, composition of, 149–50, 194; moderate opposition, demands, 150, 166, 181–82; moderate opposition, view of the United States, 162, 163–64, 184–85, 248n.128; "people power" revolution, 175; political system, 141, 240n.2; political system, corruption of, 145, 166; revolution defined, 24, 140; snap elections, 152, 174, 191, and World Bank. See also New People's Army; Aquino, Benigno; National Committee for Free Elections
Philippines (postrevolution): civil and political rights, 179; and communist movement, 25; economic conditions, 179; and U.S. military bases, 180, 181; and the United States, relations with, 179–80, 196

Ramos, Fidel V., 24; and anti-Marcos revolt, 153, 175; association with RAM, 151; U.S. basing privileges, 181
Reagan, Ronald: and Nicaragua, 94, 120, 121–25, 132–33, 137; and the Philippines, 169–78, 182, 191. *See also* United States and Nicaragua (postrevolution); United States and the Philippines (prerevolution); United States and the Philippines (postrevolution)
Reform the Armed Forces Movement (RAM), 151, 174; U.S. support of, 177
Robelo, Alfonso, 85, 88, 93, 129
Roosevelt, Franklin D., and Nicaragua, 105
Rubin, Barry, 223n.72

Sandinistas. *See Frente Sandinista de Liberacion Nacional* (FSLN)
Sharif-Emami, Jafar, 41, 44
Shultz, George: and human rights and U.S. foreign policy, 18, 209–10; and Nicaragua, 132
Sick, Gary, 71
Sin, Cardinal Jaimie. *See* Philippines, Catholic Church opposition
Solaun, Mauricio, 109, 111, 113, 125–26, 127, 189
Structural realism, 214n.8, 217n.46
Sullivan, William, 60, 61, 62, 63, 68
Superior Council of Private Enterprise (COSEP), 83, 84; demands on Somoza, 129; and FSLN, support of, 116; in postrevolution Nicaragua, 94; reaction to Chamorro assassination, 85; U.S. assistance to, 120

Tonelson, Alan, 5, 10–11
Totalitarianism, defined, 213n.1
Truman, Harry S.: and Nicaragua, 106; Truman Doctrine 17
Tucker, Robert W., 4, 6, 11
Tudeh party, 39, 48

United States and Iran, (prerevolution) 195; American civilian presence, 56–57; arms sales, 52–53, 59, 188; business interests and trade, 53, 56; Carter administration, 57, 59–63, 65–66, 188; and Congress, 188; economic assistance, 53–55; 187; Eisenhower administration, 50, 57; history, pre-WWII, 47–48; Johnson administration, 40, 57; Kennedy administration, 40, 57, 66; military assistance, 51–53, 187; moderate opposition, relations with, 67, 74–75, 224n.103; Nixon administration, 50, 52, 57–58, 223n.72; religious opposition, relations with, 60, 62–63, 64, 65, 67, 74–75; Soviet warnings against intervention, 71–72; W.W.II, relations during, 48. *See also* CIA, in Iran; Huyser, Robert, mission to Iran; Mossadeq, Mohammed
United States and the Islamic Republic of Iran, 45, 46–47 64, 75, 76, 196–97; arms sales, 63 Carter administration, 63–65, 67, 69; and Congress, 63; Iran-Iraq conflict, 64
United States and Nicaragua (prerevolution), 195; Anastasio Somoza Garcia (1932), support of, 99; arms sales, 189; business interests, in, 100; Carter administration, 107–18, 189; and Congress, 108, 253n.27; economic relations, 99–100, 102–3; 110, 114; economic sanctions, 112, 113; Eisenhower administration, 106; and FSLN, relations with, 129; history, 97–98, 105–7, 233n.111; Johnson administration, 106; Kennedy administration, 106; military assistance, 100–5, 189; military assistance sanctions, 107–8, 113, 135; moderate opposition, relations with, 111, 113, 116, 117, 129, 135; multilateral development bank loans, 189, 190; Nixon administration, 106; Roosevelt, Franklin D. administration, 105; Truman administration, 106
United States and Nicaragua (postrevolution) 135, 137, 197; Carter administration, 97, 118–21, 125–30, 131–32, 137; Chamorro regime, relations with, 239n.260; and Congress, 119; covert activity in, 121, 122; economic relations, 118, 119–20, 121, 122, 237n.213; economic sanctions, 123; Enders negoti-

ations, 121–22, 132; negotiations, 1982, 123; Reagan administration, 94, 120, 121–125, 132–33, 137. *See also* CIA, in Nicaragua; Contras
United States and the Philippines (prerevolution), 165, 166: and anti-Marcos rebellion, support for, 175; and Benigno Aquino assassination, 176; arms sales, 154; business interests, in, 156–57, 245n.80; Carter administration, 154, 168–69, 183; and Congress, 157, 172–73, 182, 190; economic assistance, 158–59; 168, 170; economic agreements, 141, 142; and Ford administration, 168; history, 140–42; military agreements, 141, 142–43; military assistance, 153–56, 160, 173; military assistance, criticism of, 154, 156; military assistance sanctions, 173, 190; U.S. military bases, 142, 143, 160–61, 164, 178, 180, 181; moderate opposition, relations with, 162, 169; 176–77, 185; Nixon administration, 168; Reagan administration, 169–76, 178, 182, 191

United States and the Philippines (postrevolution), 197; and Congress, 177; economic assistance, 177; Reagan administration, 176–78
U.S. Congress and U.S. human rights policy, 17, 24, 28, 58; and Iran, 63, 188; and Nicaragua, 108, 119, 253n.27; in the Philippines, 158, 172–73, 190

Vance, Cyrus R., 59, 60, 61, 63; and human rights foreign policy, 14, 18; and Nicaragua, 117
Ver, Fabian, 151
Vienna Declaration and Program of Action (1993), 15
Vogelgesang, Sandra, 11, 15–16

Waltz, Kenneth, 214n.8
World Bank 30; and Nicaragua, 123; and the Philippines, 168

Yazdi, Ibrahim, 45, 47, 60, 62, 63, 64